For a Pragmatics of the Use

For a Pragmatics of the Useless

Thought in the Act   A series edited by Erin Manning and Brian Massumi

ERIN MANNING

Duke University Press   Durham and London   2020

© 2020 DUKE UNIVERSITY PRESS
All rights reserved
Designed by Courtney Leigh Richardson
Typeset in Courier and Whitman by Westchester Publishing Services

Library of Congress Cataloging-in-Publication Data
Names: Manning, Erin, [date] author.
Title: For a pragmatics of the useless / Erin Manning.
Other titles: Thought in the act.
Description: Durham : Duke University Press, 2020. | Series: Thought in the
act | Includes bibliographical references and index.
Identifiers: LCCN 2020014223 (print) | LCCN 2020014224 (ebook)
ISBN 9781478010029 (hardcover)
ISBN 9781478011071 (paperback)
ISBN 9781478012597 (ebook)
Subjects: LCSH: Racism—Psychological aspects. | Psychoanalysis and racism. |
Racism.
Classification: LCC BF175.4.R34 M366 2020 (print) | LCC BF175.4.R34
(ebook) | DDC 155.8/2—dc23
LC record available at https://lccn.loc.gov/2020014223
LC ebook record available at https://lccn.loc.gov/2020014224

Cover art: Ploppiñata, spaZe. © Erin Manning.
Photograph by Leslie Plumb. Courtesy of the artist.

With SenseLab

Contents

Kenneth Bailey, for the enthusiastic and determined wisdom you bring, the curiosity and care to imagine other ways in the face of systemic antiblack racism. You pushed me, in no uncertain terms, to go beyond neurodiversity to ask about whiteness. I resisted at first, uncertain how to enter the fray, uneasy with the enormity of the enterprise. But I heard you, and in the years that followed I listened closely to better understand what has moved you consistently, over the five decades and counting of your life, to work as an intercessor for those black communities that made you and sustain you. This book is dedicated to you and to your dances in the kitchen.

SenseLab, for bringing techniques into the world through which a living can be improvised. I enter into our collective thinking with these words to accompany the neurodiverse sensibility that often doesn't take the form of language, to pull out of its always-emergent consistency the taste of a shaping that might conceptually tune the propositions underway. This is never a speaking-for. We would all tell the stories differently, the power of the false a potent force in the work we do. The aim is never to explain but to forge, in the spirit of a differential attunement, a certain consolidation of what, in the time of its coming-to-be, must resist any and all impositions of form. You've given me practices that articulate what things do when they shape each other, practices that have opened the way for a revaluation of value in excess of the form things take. Without this intense, difficult, beautiful work, always in the key of a minor sociality, collective in its attunement to body-worlds schizzing, the turn schizoanalysis has taken in my thinking would not have been possible.

Brian Massumi, for a livingloving that moves through every word, every turn of phrase. The thinking dances, always, across the worlds we make together. Every thought is always of the being of our relation, moved into expression in a middling that cannot distinguish where the fabulatory force of our coming-into-thinking together begins and ends. To write together in singularity is to learn to hear the multiplicity in the thinking, in all thinking. This is what we teach each other on those long nights of reading aloud when we listen not only to the words but to how their saying composes improvisatory cadences of the life we texture into being. With love, in an ethos of a pragmatics of the useless, debt unrepayable.

Fugitively, Approximately

Two phrases have haunted the writing of this book. The first comes from Fred Moten: *all black life is neurodiverse life*. It might also have been *black life is always neurodiverse*. The second is *approximation of proximity*. The feeling is that the ambiguity of memory in the first has a connection to the approximation of the second. Moten's words, written in a manuscript review before the publication of *The Minor Gesture* (Manning 2016), felt vitally important when I received them. But *The Minor Gesture* was already too close to completion to fully carry the force of the proposition, and so, while I did signal the alignment between whiteness and neurotypicality in the book, I decided to make Moten's words the fugitive force of the next one. I say "fugitive force" both to carry forward Stefano Harney and Moten's (2013) concept of fugitivity, everywhere at work in *For a Pragmatics of the Useless*, and to emphasize that this is how work comes into itself: with the quality of a reorientation moved by a spark that connects to an intensity already moving transversally across a work. This is what Moten's words did: their deep thinking-with exposed the stakes of what stirred as yet unthought in the thinking. It is this ethos of thinking-with I take into *For a Pragmatics of the Useless*, exploring Moten's words, words less his own now than a refrain heard in fugitive proximity. This fugitivity at the heart of thought is what I want to address here. For what Moten's words did at that singular moment of writing/thinking was create an opening for thought to travel in directions as yet in germ.

This kind of proximity is something else than citation. How can I properly cite Moten when I am no longer even certain which phrase it was that changed the path of my research? An approximation of proximity might be said to be an alliance with thought-in-the-making, an engagement with the edges of how thinking itself does its work. This is what I heard in Moten's gesture: that there was space for a thinking-alongside that could bring into relation the concept of black life and the claim that neurotypicality is nothing else than an articulation of whiteness at work—that there was in *The Minor Gesture* an incipient potential for neurodiversity and black life to come into alliance in a way that would not reduce one to the other but generate a complementarity. The generosity of the thinking-with extended by Moten in his engagement with *The Minor Gesture* is what lured the writing-to-come into the proximity of black life, an approximation since there can only be a speculative engagement with a question as complex as the one of black life, especially when written from outside the culture of its sociality.

The task was gargantuan. It involved acquainting myself with decades of black studies to explore within this rich literature openings toward the complementarity of black life and neurodiversity. It also involved returning to the concept of neurodiversity to explore whether the terminology of the neurological was really where I wanted to situate the discussion. It had always been clear to me that the *neuro* in *neurodiversity* was not, for the most part, the site of my inquiry: my work has aimed to sidestep the neuroreductionism that I believe shuts down the political and social force of the movement for neurodiversity. While much of my work on autistic perception *does* emphasize neurological difference, and while I am certain that neurological difference *is* a formative effect in the variation designated by the term *neurodiversity*, my interest is in the *diversity in diversity*, locating the neurotypical not as the measure of an individual diametrically opposed to the neurodiverse but as the (unspoken) baseline of existence. I see neurotypicality as akin to structural racism—as the infusion of white supremacy in the governing definition of what counts as human. The assumption that neurotypicality is the neutral ground from which difference asserts itself (an assumption everywhere supported by the neuroscientific literature) suggests that there is still an urgent conversation to be had about how the human, and knowledge as a defining category of the human, is organized and deployed in the image of neurotypicality. The decision to continue to work with the neuro in neurodiversity is therefore less an alignment to the neurological per se than an engagement with the presuppositions of neurology as a science for and of the (neurotypical, white) human, a science that far too rarely calls into question the assumptions that underlie either its humanism or the categorical imperative to perform according to its normative expectations. To address this is to continue the work I began in *The Minor Gesture*, the work of questioning the volition-intentionality-agency triad at the heart of neurotypicality, that presupposition of (white) existence that places individual executive agency as the motivator of all experience. What of the *agencement* of forces that compose to facilitate an event's coming into expression? What of the being of relation, that quality of existence that "informs not simply what is relayed but also the relative and the related," an "open totality rolling with its own movement" (Glissant 1997, 192; translation modified)? A deep commitment to the sociality of a facilitation that begins *in the relation* is at work in my refusal of neuroreductionism, pushing back against the neurotypical presupposition that to do it alone, to do it individually, to do it at the pace of the volition-intentionality-agency triad, is to be truly human.

Writing diagonally across this question, Moten addresses that most baseline of neurological apparatuses: executive function. If executive function, the site of planning in the brain, is altered by a neurological twist, must the assumption always be that this results in a lack of capacity simply because the work at hand requires facilitation? What value system is at work here? What is formulated in this claim with respect to the value of independence? "Black study," Moten writes, "moves at the horizon of an event where certain instruments, insofar as they can no longer either calculate or be calculated, are bent toward the incalculable" (2018a, 162). The incalculable here is the very question of value. "The assignment of a specific value to the incalculable is a kind of terror. At the same time, the incalculable is the very instantiation of value" (169). Across the thought of value and the incalculable I hear: what might be learned from the fugitive planning of neurodiverse modes of sociality, and how is this sociality allied to black study? What is planning's approximation in that encounter? What are the consequences of even assuming that the form of planning we understand as executive function, that planning that defines human volition as lone contributor to existence, is a value (has a value) in itself? How does fugitive planning accommodate the kind of being of relation that not only supports facilitation but actively seeks it out?

Moten doesn't lay any of this out the way I am doing it here—a too-quick read of the powerful chapter from *Stolen Life* (Moten 2018a) I am thinking-with would probably not reproduce, for most readers, the stakes I am outlining. The diagonality with which the issues are addressed is part of Moten's project, however. To give in to an executive way of writing about executive function would be to support the value system it depends on.

A diagonal approach allows the unanswerable to remain unanswerable: neither in my engagement with executive function nor in Moten's work is there the presumption that executive function does not have a vital place in existence—not only because executive function really *is* affected in autism and in certain other neurodiverse forms of life (schizophrenia, attention deficit (hyperactivity) disorder, Tourette syndrome, obsessive compulsive disorder), but also because, after being treated for decades as cognitively deficient, it is often a relief for those who are neurodiverse to map their difference onto executive function.[1] Nor does this engagement with executive function and black study mean to suggest in any way that Black folks in general have impaired executive function—such a claim would be ludicrous. The proposition that *all black life is neurodiverse life* moves at another rhythm, one not of direct alignment but of approximate proximity, asking how the fugitivity of value composes with the being of relation while underscoring the complicity between executive function and whiteness in neurotypicality's adhesion to an unchecked narrative of superior functioning. It gestures toward how neurotypicality, as a largely unspoken category of existence that nonetheless undergirds every decision made in the name of normopathy, performs a continual selection of who is valued, of who is recognized as truly human. The aim is this: to inquire into how black life, or black sociality, practices a fugitive planning that is in alliance with neurodiverse sociality and to outline how this fugitivity upends the presuppositions executive function carries.

To write diagonally, to write approximately in proximity to an ethics always in the making, is the only way to write about this, and this is what I take to be Moten's orientation in tackling the assumptions that come with the positioning of executive function as that which makes us truly human. Continuing on the diagonal, I follow Moten's lead:

> This is an enthusiasm. This is the new thing and a lot of what it's about is just trying to figure out how to say something. How to read. Not (or not only) how to offer a reading, or even an interpretation, but a performance of a text, in the face of its unintelligibility, as if one were forced/privileged to access some other other world where representation and unrepresentability were beside the point, so that the response to the terrors and chances of history were not about calculation, not bound to replicate, even in a blunted and ethically responsible way, the horrors of speculation, where new materialities of imagination were already on the other side of the logic of equivalence.
>
> . . .
>
> I'm trying to talk about zones of miscommunication + areas of disaster + their affective ground and atmosphere and terrible beauty. They're the same but really close to one another but unbridgeably far from one another, connected by some inside stories we keep running from, the way people flee a broken park when the island is a shipwreck. The crumbled refuge is a hold and a language lab. (2018a, 167–68)

The problem with neurotypicality as unspoken marker of how living and learning should be done is that there is no opportunity to ask how the conditions for knowing are laid within its scaffold. Autistic Ryan Boren writes:

The hardest part to navigate is not so much the teeming ambiguity; it's the assumption. It's the self-centering, automatic and unaware, that reduces ambiguity to an ethnocentric "right answer" or "right behavior" and leaves little room for autistic sociality. Instead of "foregrounding complexity as the baseline," we bury it with myths of normality that create structural barriers and exclude people. We pathologize and marginalize the minds and bodies that sense ambiguity and assumption the most deeply and feel their results the most acutely. So much is lost in the reduction. Acknowledging ambiguity, multiple literacies, and multiple socialities renders the terrain more passable rather than less. Ambiguity is actually something to be embraced rather than to be avoided. It is an inevitable feature of human discourse. Compassionately accepting our ambiguities and differing literacies means less masking and passing and burning out—and better communication.²

Neurodiverse socialities are lost in the count, in the assumption that the planning that doesn't quite plan according to the presumptions of what comes first is simply the mark of a deficiency. A lack of function. This is what Moten means, I think, when he speaks of the incalculable as both a kind of terror *and* the very instantiation of value. What is incalculable here is sociality itself. Sociality exceeds the count. It has no function. Its very existence depends on its never being valued in advance of its coming-to-be. Fugitive planning.

Executive function could be described as that singular capacity for subtraction those on the neurotypical edge of the spectrum take for granted. This includes a task like picking up a glass off the table. In order for planning to occur, there must be a subtraction from the environment, a backgrounding of all else: executive functions "share the need to disengage from the immediate environment to guide actions" (Hill 2004, 2). To pick up that glass involves actively unseeing all else. Zeroing in is not easy when the ray of light is catching the mirror and the smell of pancakes is luring a body toward the stove. But none of this means the glass *can't* be picked up. It just means that the process is felt as a process, whereas for more neurotypically spectrumed folks, the glass has already singled itself out from the welter. The richness of what is lost in the subtraction is what interests me here. What is at stake in the belief that parsing is the key to experience?

My aim here is not to dispute that many neurodiverse folks have affected executive function. Nor is it to suggest that the tasks that benefit from solid executive function—reading and following a recipe, tying your shoes, crossing the street—are unimportant. Rather, what I want to emphasize is how the narrative around planning foregrounded in executive function and its unbreakable tie to neurotypicality exclude what I have elsewhere called *autistic perception*—a quality of direct perception that carries sociality into its excess of worlding. That is to say, I want to ask how neurotypicality, in its alignment to executive function, demands of existence that it conform to an existing map of procedural orientation that is, by its very operation, incapable of perceiving other modes of existence. And I want to suggest that these other modes of existence, what might be called *minor sociality*, are excluded from the neurotypical precisely because of its need to plan, to count, to organize, to select out, to evaluate. Neurodiversity's power is to feel the blur, the ambiguity, the fugitivity. What I am calling for is the anexact, that approximation of proximity that is heard, also, in the enunciation of black life or black sociality.

The assumption of a normative commonality as regards movement, knowledge, and interaction played out in the choreography of neurotypicality, excludes neurodiverse sociality and all the slanted forces that linger in its proximity. This is because neurodiverse sociality's mode of planning is oblique, an obliqueness so imperceptible to neurotypicality as to be easily excluded from any normative account of the social. This is what I hear in Boren's words, words that echo so many accounts of how autistics are considered asocial. "Autism is frequently storied as an epic in asociality, in nonintention. It represents the edges and boundaries of humanity, a queerly crip kind of isolationism" (Yergeau 2018, 11). Its mode of listening too askew, its glance too furtive in its avoidance of that frontal faciality that presupposes relation, neurodiverse sociality doesn't even register on the plane of neurotypicality. This is where I want to go with the words *all black life is neurodiverse life*, toward the undercommonness of sociality.

Approximation of proximity is a way of attuning to the fugitivity heard in the "otherwise" coming-into-sociality across black life and neurodiverse life (Crawley 2017). Approximation of proximity is a way of speaking about two divergent planes, not converging as though they could become one, but meeting at the differential of their potential for the approximate. For isn't sociality precisely that which sidles proximity differently, that which asks how else a coming-together-in-difference can be felt? Or, in Denise Ferreira da Silva's (2016) words, difference without separability?

For a Pragmatics of the Useless asks how, in the differential of black sociality, or what Laura Harris calls an "aesthetic sociality of blackness," aesthetic propositions for living otherwise are crafted, and carried. Harris defines an aesthetic sociality of blackness as "an improvised political assemblage that resides in the heart of the polity but operates under its ground and on its edge" (2012, 53). In this operation "under ground and on edge," black sociality *invents* sites of collective expression rather than simply inhabiting them. "Its resources, which can never be fully accessed by the structures and authorities of legitimate political economy, are taken up by the politically and economically illegitimate in their insistence on living otherwise, in ways that resist repression, denigration, and exclusion and violate brutally imposed laws of property and propriety" (Harris 2012, 53). An aesthetics of black sociality grows in the between of ad hoc constructions for a life in the making, aesthetic in its commitment to a lived expression of perception's differential, social in its consent not to be a single being in an ethos of what Édouard Glissant (1997) would call a poetics of relation.

There are of course as many articulations of black sociality as there are of actualizations of the fugitive undercommons they seed. I think here of Saidiya Hartman's commitment to waywardness as it moves through "critical fabulation," in her lifelong commitment to "displace the received or authorized account" (2008b, 11). I think of Tina Campt's aesthetic contribution to "radical modalities of witnessing that refuse authoritative forms of visuality which function to refuse blackness itself," a "practice of refusal" that "functions . . . through relationality and adjacency," whose "power lies in its ability to engage negation as generative" (2019, 80, 83). I think of Tavia Nyong'o's afro-fabulations experienced in the "vernacular power of funk as performance modality that disrupts heteronormative embodiment and straight time," a "milieu filled with an angular sociality, a black social life of sharp elbows, raised eyebrows, rolling eyes, loudly sucking teeth, and, if the moment is right, collective ecstasy" (2018, 171–72). I think of Thomas DeFrantz's black performance (and "black Joy") that comes with the injunction "to be willing not to know," attuning to blackwork's "unexpected relationship and encounter," its "bitter tongue" of unspeakability (to whiteness) and "resistant creative acts" (2017, 12, 18, 21). I think of Jaamil Olawale Kosoko's *Chameleon* and its shape-shifting production of those phonic materialities that sound through the moving body, a body that performs its resistance to systemic oppression, a dance so profoundly affirmative that it remakes the very conditions of blackness. I think also of Rizvana Bradley's curated days of black study, two of which I attended in 2018—one in Amsterdam as part of a collaboration between the Rietveld and the Stedelijk, the other in Paris, a collaboration between the University of the Arts and the Centre National de la Danse.[3] In both these gatherings, what was curated was the gesture of sociality itself, activated through a dramaturgy that celebrated an ethos of coming into relation moved by an aesthetics of black sociality. In these encounters, a site for thinking-together was generated that truly allowed a coming into itself of thought through a coming out of its-self of the individual. This kind of emergent sociality is incalculably valuable, and it is this quality of the being of relation *For a Pragmatics of the Useless* gestures toward.

Jared Sexton's uncountable account of black sociality also moves through these pages. Echoing Nahum Chandler, Sexton asks, "What is the nature of a form of being that presents a problem for the thought of being itself? . . . How might it be thought that there exists a being about which the question of its particular being is the condition of possibility and the condition of impossibility for any thought about being whatsoever?" (2011, 6). Alongside, I hear the halting words of autistic DJ Savarese, then in eighth grade, in "Estimating Harriet Tubman Respectfully": "Pedestals rest on hurt, great, estimated dressed not great human beings deserted by frees" (Savarese 2005). Still uneasily coming to language through facilitated communication, Savarese turns to Tubman as a hero for neurodiversity, seeing her as practicing a mode of existence he so deeply wishes for his people. This brings into an approximation of proximity her freeing of slaves and his deep wish that neurodiverse existence be valued. Many years later, in a piece called "Coming to My Senses," Savarese returns to Tubman to make sense of this early identification. He writes:

> When I was very young, my only safe haven in foster care was with a proud African American couple who exposed me to black church, culture and politics. Of course, my experience as the only visible nonspeaking student at my school is not the same as a slave's, but the fear of being identified as less than and "sent back" resonated with me. As a man, I know how that Tubman's peril far outweighed my own, but as a kid, she and Patterson most closely answered my need for mentors. That and my tendency to feel people's energy as if it were my own—to connect with others at a visceral level—amplified my identification with them. (2019, 92)

An echo of Sexton's painful words—"What can be said about such a being, and how, if at stake in the question is the very possibility of human being and perhaps even possibility as such? What is the being of a problem?" (2011, 7)—can be heard in Savarese's grasping toward identification: "If we're breaking the barriers, great freedom fearfully awaits. Harriet realized until freedom treated her people with respect, her intestines seemed unsettled, her heart beat resentfully, and her fear never disappeared. The challenges she faced each day were far greater than anything you and your people have ever endured; breathing resentful air, great very hard breaths, undermines heartfelt feeling and deeply effects the western world" (Savarese 2005).

Hearing Savarese across Sexton makes felt what is often missed in autistic accounts: the ache for a sociality that would allow for what Savarese at the time called "easy breathing" (in R. Savarese 2017), a mode of living that might facilitate a certain freedom from the horrors of neurotypicality. But, as Savarese would later recognize, "the burdened individuality of freedom" (Hartman 1997, 116) always leans toward neurotypicality.[4] Freedom remains too aligned to neurotypicality (and whiteness) to foster any kind of easy breathing. As Hartman writes with respect to the discourse of freedom in relation to slavery, "the fragile 'as if equal' of liberal discourse inadequately contends with the history of racial subjection and enslavement, since the texture of freedom is laden with the vestiges of slavery, and abstract equality is utterly enmeshed in the narrative of black subjection, given that slavery undergirded the rhetoric of the republic and equality defined so as to sanction subordination and segregation" (116).

In a logic of approximation of proximity, it is the being of relation that is at stake, not a version of freedom allied to the liberal individual. The being of relation is radically empirical, relation never a sum of its parts. A decade into the future, Savarese (2017) now writes, "For too long I have dreamed of independence. Again and again, I have spoken of getting free. I have envied the ease with which the non-disabled can walk on the moon or tie their shoes underwater. They are circus performers, talented chimpanzees. Tonight I will dream of being dependent, dependable." Refuting the status of "self-made plant," Savarese opts for the symbiotic vine, that abundant ecology that "[goes] deep and thus [does] not compete with the broader and shallower root systems of trees." Lest the reader see the vine as innocuous, however, Savarese is quick to emphasize: "I had to learn to live with a vine that encircled my heart, at times nearly choking it. I had to think of the vine as needing help, wanting a relationship."

Neurodiverse sociality lived as the being of relation, Savarese learns, is not synonymous with freedom as independence. It comes like a vine, attached both to (black) joy and to the suffering that comes with living deeply in contestation with neurotypicality's obsession with individualist independence. The vine is a reminder: the being of relation is created in the undercommons of an existence deeply dependent on the ecologies that shape it. Perhaps this is also a definition of an aesthetic of black sociality. To quote Moten again: "Does black life, in its irreducible and impossible sociality and precisely in what might be understood as its refusal of the status of social life that is refused it, constitute a fundamental danger—an excluded but immanent disruption—to social life? What will it have meant to embrace this matrix of im/possibility, to have spoken of and out of this suspension? What would it mean to dwell on or in minor social life? This set of questions is the position, which is also to say the problem, of blackness" (2008, 188).

It is the incalculability of black sociality, of minor social life, that has resonated most in my engagement with black study, and it is this quality of resistance to the count that I cull from the refrain *all black life is neurodiverse life*, an approximation I also hear in Terrion L. Williamson when she emphasizes the "irreducible sociality of black life," an "eschewal and critique of the affliction of privilege that resides in the preoccupation with the individual self" (2017, 19). What is lived, what is carried over, in the gesture that refutes the standing-out of the individual as executive purveyor of existence? What is lived in the beyond of what neurotypicality upholds at all costs, the figure of the human?

An approximation of proximity is an opaque proposition. Opacity, for Glissant, is more than the contrary of transparency. It calls for another logic, another quality of valuation. "Produc[ing] every exception," "propelled by every divergence," opacity makes felt the other of thought, thought's emergent outside, "an aesthetics of turbulence whose corresponding ethics is not provided in advance" (1997, 195, 155). In his account of the vine, Savarese opts for a logic of mutual inclusion over the burdened individuality of freedom, a mode of being of relation in which, in Massumi's words, "two modes of activity . . . are so entwined as to be degrees of each other. Yet their differential remains. When they come together, they are performatively fused without becoming confused. This means that they can remix, when it occurs to them to come performatively together again" (2014, 33–34).

A concept does its work when it can no longer be separated from the movement of thought it provokes. In *What Is Philosophy?*, Gilles Deleuze and Félix Guattari (1994) propose the conceptual persona as the philosophical figure that directs, names, and dates a concept. In this book conceptual persona abound: Stefano Harney and Fred Moten for the undercommons, Félix Guattari for transversality, Alfred North Whitehead for nonsensuous perception, Marcel Duchamp for the infrathin, Tina Campt for phonic substance, Laura Harris for the aesthetic sociality of blackness, Denise Ferreira da Silva for difference without separability, Ashon Crawley for otherwise possibility, SenseLab for spaZe, Édouard Glissant for the being of relation, John Lee Clark for distantism, Gilles Deleuze for the power of the false, Michel Foucault for the outside, Fred Moten for phonic materiality, Arakawa and Madeline Gins for architectural procedure, Etienne Souriau for modes of existence, Saidiya Hartman for the afterlife of slavery, Isabelle Stengers for the ecology of practices, Lygia Clark for the relational object, David Lapoujade for merest existences, Henri Bergson for fabulation, Tavia Nyong'o for afro-fabulation, Gilles Deleuze and Félix Guattari for desiring-production, SenseLab for the anarchive, DJ Savarese for easy breathing, Goat Island for repair, Brian Massumi for the surplus-value of life, Félix Guattari for schizoanalysis, William James for radical empiricism, SenseLab for the free radical, Gilbert Simondon for the transindividual, Daniel Stern for vitality affect, Helio Oiticica for the suprasensorial. There are more, of course, each one propulsed by a proper name. Except one: the one with no name to carry it is black sociality. That concept is carried by a crowd, in a movement that remains fugitive, undercommoning. It is this quality that moves the book, this differential between the naming that sparks an orientation and the absolute impossibility of situating where the concept begins and ends, and how it fields existence in the making.

The conceptual persona is a way of gesturing toward the sociality of the concept, reminding us that despite the orientation that comes with a name and a date, the concept is never borne of an individual. Concepts are gathered in the sociality of existence: they are brought forth by a multiplicity. This multiplicity connects to a mode of existence already in germ. This is why concepts can never be considered "ready-made" (Deleuze and Guattari 1994, 5). Concepts are made in the activation of the ecology they gather forth.

Concepts are in and of a fugitive elsewhere. Whoever is named in the creation of a concept is a carrier. Their role is not to claim it but to see how its carrying into the world alters the place from which thinking moves. A concept shifts the conditions of existence by affecting everything around it, including the one who is named in relation to it. This is why Deleuze and Guattari emphasize that "a particular conceptual persona, who perhaps did not exist before us, thinks in us" (1994, 69). Spoken always in the voice of a third, the conceptual persona "is not formed but posits itself in itself—it is a self-positing" (11).

A concept is not a general category. It does not claim to encapsulate. It is not a metaphor. It cannot be debated. A concept is an intensive feature, an intercessor into thought. "The conceptual persona is not the philosopher's representative but, rather, the reverse: the philosopher is only the envelope of his principal conceptual persona and of all the other personae who are the intercessors, the real subjects of the philosophy" (Deleuze and Guattari 1994, 64; translation modified).

In the writing, the philosopher is taken over, oriented by the forces of an intensity that calls forth a certain urgency of precision—*this* way, under *these* conditions—learning with the concept as it unfolds how to modulate what comes into contact with it. To find a concept is to touch on a nerve of experience, to catch the necessity of its naming. What is formed in this gesture is an operative proposition, an intercessor capable of catching in a word, in a phrase, experience moved. None of this is an individual's work. The writing, the thinking-with, the sociality, is what brings the concept to expression. A concept is oriented by the path it draws forth. The concept is less ours to claim than ours to follow.

For a Pragmatics of the Useless takes the concept of black sociality, that concept moved by a crowd, that concept already too social to be carried by any one thinker, and explores what it can do in the sidling. Coming into approximations of proximity with the question of value (a pragmatics of the useless), the question of how black life is neurodiverse life is asked *in practice*: what is captured, what is cut, what is deviated and detoured in the coming into relation of minor sociality? What is created? What is left behind? *How else?* is always a question. Always alongside Alfred North Whitehead, whose process philosophy proposes an account of life that refuses to place the human at the center, his radical empiricism everywhere palpable in the exploration of how a logic of mutual inclusion does its work. With Whitehead, we enter into a strange vocabulary for untethering any preexisting notion of subjectivity from the events that compose (with) it. With the *production* of subjectivity instead as the focal point, a production not excluded from rocks living it out in geological time, pragmatic accounts of what makes a difference become resolutely more-than human, reminding us at every turn that the question is not "who did this?" but "what ecology of practices fashioned the conditions for its doing?" And in the interstices, pocket practices— livingloving, ticcingflapping, backgroundingforegrounding, nestingpatching, schizzinganarchiving. What else to name those practices that we hold close, practices that orient everything we do but are rarely cited because impossible to fully subtract from the welter? How do we register that which lurks on the edges, that which is carried too close to be separated out from the bodying, from the living? The pocket practices might be seen as the transversality that diagonalizes the book, folding it with the force of the question of how the sociality of living can be experimented differently, less citation, more sidling.

To return to executive function once more before closing: "I want to suggest that it is something other than anti-intellectualism to think that what the executive excludes is a vast range of extrarational relations for which we cannot, strictly speaking, account; relations, which is to say things, that cannot be accounted for because they cut and augment inference; things like whatever occurs when believing P and believing Q is more or less and/or more and less than P and Q. All the things we are are more and less than selves" (Moten 2018a, 164).

For a Pragmatics of the Useless returns in a continuous refrain to the "vast range of extrarational relations for which we cannot, strictly speaking, account; relations, which is to say things, that cannot be accounted for because they cut and augment inference." What remains incalculable for Moten is value itself, a value for modes of knowing unstratified, anexecutive. This is the core question of the book: what is value beyond use-value in the realm of what Brian Massumi calls the surplus-value of life? For the book cannot quite skirt the question of value. After all, the pragmatics of the useless is also a project for finance at the limit. The aim is never toward calculability, however. The aim is toward a practice that returns to the question of how the schizz cleaves experience to produce emer-

gent collectivities that value existence differently, and how these minor socialities in turn enhance the unaccounted-for. What must remain incalculable in *For
a Pragmatics of the Useless* is the very question of the being of relation. What is
produced in the interstices is not an account of how black life *is* neurodiverse, or
how neurodiversity *is* black. It is the being of the relation itself that is prodded,
not to create a count, but to better account for the uncalculability at its core.

In "Executive Dysfunction in Autism," Elisabeth L. Hill writes, "Poor mental
flexibility is illustrated by perseverative, stereotyped behaviour and difficulties
in the regulation and modulation of motor acts. This indicates problems in the
ability to shift to a different thought or action according to changes in a situation"
(2004, 4). What is this mental flexibility bestowed so easily onto neurotypicals?
Or, to put it differently, what is it that neurotypicals can't see about the exquisite mental flexibility in an account of vines that at once strangle a heart and
feed the ecologies they sustain? The deficit here is not one of executive function.
The deficit is in the attunement to what else circulates across and beneath and
around those strangling, proprietary structures that uphold the horror of violent
exclusion.

If black life is "an exorbitance for thought," as Chandler suggests, "the
negro . . . an instance outside of all forms of being that truly matter," what is
called for can never simply be a question of rehabilitation (2014, 607–8). What is
called for is not, as Harris might say, an inhabiting, but a continual remaking, an
inventing from the edges, an undercommoning. This is what I learn from black
study: that minor sociality is a way of thinking beyond rehabilitation, beyond any
account that would represent black life as adjacent to, or simply against, whiteness. That would be to take on the structural weight of a racism that has shaped
the very concept of whiteness: neurotypicality. Minor sociality does not compose existence according to the pathology of its planning. Black life is exorbitant
thought, lived beyond the shape it knows how to take, lived through a living both
flexible and fugitive, in approximation of proximity. This life, this thinking-with
that writes itself into the world through sound, through movement and performance, through the care and love of mothering and grandmothering, is what
drew Savarese to Tubman and to her life's work. What he felt was the aesthetics
of black sociality animating Tubman's thinking, her living.

This is where *For a Pragmatics of the Useless* begins, in the exorbitance of
thought. There is no certainty here—the *is* remains an approximation. SenseLab
figures large: it has been the site of practice and experimentation most allied to
these questions for me over the past seventeen years. The writing moves into a
shift I sense at SenseLab, a turn toward different modalities. An undercommons
is calling. We call it the 3Ecologies Institute. We dream of a parainstitutional

practice in excess of the university where the question of living and learning can be practiced otherwise. The university is in ruins. Many of us still do our work there, and some of that work is beautiful. But the exorbitance of thought requires that we ask hard questions at this neoliberal juncture, questions about debt and credit, questions about value and evaluation, questions about the call to order. These are questions I return to. Not because I can answer them, but because to stay alive and live well is to ask them again.

Practicing the schizz is another way of naming the fugitive force that runs through *For a Pragmatics of the Useless*. To do the work of crafting conditions for the minor sociality of emergent collectivity, to live the intensity of the more-than human interstices of collective work, to experiment with other modes of existence, is challenging. Guattari's schizoanalytic practice has been a beacon, and over the years SenseLab continues to explore how schizoanalysis might texture and nurture the minor socialities that compose us. To end the book on finance at the limit is to carry the schizoanalytic gesture from the artistic, political, and philosophical environments into the world of capital to ask: how else beyond property and propriety, beyond our settler dreams of owning the right to plan, can we imagine living, can living imagine us? What might the skewed count of the uncountable do to capital's hold on our imaginations? Neurodiverse mental flexibility will be necessary when coming into contact with the cephalopod.

For a Pragmatics of the Useless

A Politics of the Infrathin, in Preamble

Nothing can prepare us for the infrathin. Nothing can frame it, or direct it. Nothing can give it value in advance. This should be taken at its word: the infrathin is always a qualifier before it is a noun. "Infrathin: one must never make it a noun" (Marcel Duchamp, in Davila 2010, 29).

A pragmatics of the useless begins here, in the abeyance of the substantive.[1] A politics of the infrathin—the way the work's work eludes us, escapes us, the way it delays the affirmation of its tenuous apparition, the way it touches us, in the lag—cannot say in advance how it will unfold, or what it will do. A politics of the infrathin, as Alfred North Whitehead might say, can only ever negatively prehend the edgings that set it in motion. It can only have known in retrospect what made it come to appearance (or disappearance) just this way.

A few directions in the sand:

The German *übersehen*, "overseeing," seems as important as the unseeing at the heart of the imperceptible called for by the infrathin. *Übersehen* does not really mean "to oversee." It means "to miss, to overlook." But this rift between seeing and looking is important, and it is here that the infrathin will reveal its potential as that which is always more-than. What is not seen within the seeable is more-than appearance. This is what is at stake in a politics of the infrathin.

It is not a question of finding something hidden but of making operative the minor gestures that sidle major tendencies. The conditions for the making-operative of a politics of the infrathin depend each time on a new ecology of orientations that make felt what otherwise would not register.

A politics of the infrathin produces intensities through subtraction. Be interested in what makes these intensities, barely perceived, operative in their singularity. More-than is not always more.

The infrathin is not simply the difference; it is what makes the difference.

A politics of the infrathin: a quest, in registers more-than human, for the most minor of variations, the minor a key rather than a quantity. A care for ecologies of practice that value the effects of what can but barely be perceived, if it can be perceived at all.

The Most Minute of Intervals

Marcel Duchamp describes the infrathin as "the most minute of intervals, or the slightest of differences" (quoted in Perloff 2002, 101). The concept, Duchamp suggests, cannot be properly defined—"one can only give examples of it" (de Duve 1991, 160). Notes in Duchamp's collection offer a few suggestions: "The warmth of a seat (which has just been left) is infra-thin (#4)," "Subway gates—The people / who go through at the very last moment / Infra thin—(9 recto)," "Velvet trousers—/ their whistling sound (in walking) by / brushing of the 2 legs is an / infra thin separation signaled / by sound. (it is not an infra thin sound) (#9 verso)," "Difference between the contact / of water and that of / molten lead for ex, / or of cream / with the walls of its / own container moved around the liquid. . . . This difference between two contacts is infra thin (#14)" (quoted in Perloff 2002, 101).

Duchamp's notes are attempts at touching what remains elusive. A quality in the between, an interval that cannot quite be articulated. It's not the seat that is at stake, or even the warmth in "the warmth of a seat (which has just been left)," but what is left behind. Not the seat but a quality of left-ness. Not the velvet trousers or even the leg in "their whistling sound (in walking) by," but the way the rubbing creates a quality of a whistling. Not the substances exactly in the "difference between the contact / of water and that of / molten lead" but the quality of their interrelation.

The infrathin: the potentiation of a relational field that includes what cannot quite be articulated but is nonetheless felt. Infrathin: the thisness, the haecceity of an experience that cannot be reduced to the sum of its parts.[2]

The Exemplary

In the absence of a definition, what is foregrounded is the singularity of experience, and the specificity of the example. The infrathin cannot be generalized: it is what makes experience singularly what it is, *here, now*. Between the event and the account of its retelling, an infrathin resides that will never quite be captured. "While trying to place 1 plane surface / precisely on another plane surface / you pass through some infra thin moments—(#45)" (Duchamp, quoted in Perloff 2002, 101). Beyond capture, the infrathin is a grasping at the singularity of an interval too thin to define as such and yet thick with the texture of lived relation.

Prehension

Prehension is defined by Whitehead (1978) as the grasping-toward through which experience makes itself felt. The event—or the actual occasion, in Whitehead's terminology—is pulled into experience, its force of actuation tied to what Whitehead calls the data of the occasion. These data are not objects or substances but relational fields in the parsing.

What of the share of the grasping that cannot quite be parsed, pulled into actuality? That continues to field? What of that which cannot quite be captured, yet makes a difference in the event? What of the share that cannot quite define itself and yet takes part in how the world is felt? How to articulate the prehension of the infrathin of experience in the making?

Whitehead has a concept for that which is not actualized but nonetheless affects experience. He calls it negative prehension. Negative prehension is what must be actively excluded in order for the event to have consistency. To achieve consistency, there must be elimination. What cannot conform to the color of this singular experience must be backgrounded in order that this experience be fully what it is.

Elimination is still participation, however. Excluded by necessity from what is foregrounded, negative prehension nonetheless lurks on the edges of appearance in the way all backgrounds do. It is not actualized as such in the event, but the event cannot but be infused with it. Every prehension to a degree encompasses what negative prehension has textured in.

What the infrathin makes palpable is that there is no occasion that does not, to some degree, pull the background into the foreground. The infrathin makes felt the tenuous quality of this both-and. The shift from sitting to standing leaves something behind, a quality ungraspable. This ungraspability composes with every standing, taking the background welter and moving it into the interval of lived experience, unsuspecting. Infrathin.

The infrathin actively backgrounds what is perceived in order to foreground what is not quite within the register of the perceptible. The infrathin foregrounds this ungraspability in the grasping, affirming the witness of experience in the background-foregrounding. In doing so, the infrathin directly prehends the potential of the more-than.

Subjective Form

In a philosophy of process, what is most important is movement, or change. In order for change to happen, however, there must be a moment when the occasion has become absolutely what it is. Without this absoluteness, there would be no difference between this and that—no "elbow room in the universe" (Whitehead 1967, 195).

Subjective form is the signature of this singular occasion's manner of coming to form. Its coming to form defines its immanent subjectivity, a subject born of the process. In and of itself, this subject cannot change. In the context of this singular iteration, it will always have been what it now has become. And yet, as Whitehead emphasizes throughout, this actuation of the *it is* is brief, always on the edge of perishing, where the force-of-form rather than the form-taking as such will contribute to future parsings. If what a subjective form does is mark this threshold between the force-of-form and form-taking, the active schizz between what is and what comes to be, the operative question is to what extent the unactualized makes a difference in the passage from force to form, and to what degree the share of the unactualized can affect future comings-to-form.

This is where negative prehension comes in. Despite their not being included in the actual constellation of an event's coming-to-be, negative prehensions do have subjective form. "A negative prehension expresses a bond," writes Whitehead. This bond "adds to the emotional complex, though not to the objective data" (1978, 41). That negative prehensions have subjective forms suggests that the unactualized too influences how the future comes to be felt.

Autistic Perception

Negative prehension is negative only in the sense that it eliminates a certain field of data in order to enable the foregrounding of consistency in the actualization of what comes to be. As Whitehead makes clear, when this and not that is felt, "that" has not been completely excised from the experience. Both play a part: it is the backgrounding of "that" that makes "this" stand out.

Both at once, actually experienced as foreground, risks confusion or chaos. And yet, to a degree, it is always "both at once." As those with hypersensitivities will attest, foreground-background can be painfully intermeshed. Autistics, for instance, often speak of the difficulty of parsing one kind of sensation from another, the environment painfully alive to the multiplicity of feeling.[3] This limit case reminds us that it is a question of degree. How negative prehension eliminates is a question of practice as much as anything else. The goal need not be an absolute parsing or elimination but the fashioning of a technique for achieving a manageable degree of consistency. Negative prehension serves to remind us of the participation in experience of a background welter, a certain lived resonance of that which is, to a differing degree, eliminated from the occasion as it comes to actualization. The infrathin, always negatively prehended, gives resonance to the unparsed in experience.

If that which is prehended, in the event, *includes* elimination, it follows that elimination is affirmed. Negative prehension is more like the negative of the image than negation as such. It is a contributory aspect of experience, an afterimage that cleaves time, eluding the actual even as it affects how it comes to expression. Not after so much as in untimely accompaniment.

The infrathin gestures toward this share of the event, looking for a way to make felt how that which never takes concrete form nonetheless makes a difference. This is why the infrathin can only ever be exemplary. To define it would be to give it the form that eludes it.

The infrathin: that most elusive of states where what is felt, in the briefest interval, is the lived co-composition of difference. Contrast.

The infrathin: the differential that marks the rhythm that is the oscillation between what is perceptible and what is imperceptible yet felt, by the event. The thisness of this singular relation, as perceived from two directions at once.

The infrathin: a variation on lived experience.

Value

In Whiteheadian philosophy, an occasion of experience is never valued in advance of its coming-to-be. There is no inherent value to experience, nor is there a hierarchy of value. The human and the nonhuman, consciousness and the nonconscious, are equally taken into account in this philosophy that refers to the body as a society of molecules and to the human as a gradation of a spectrum of feeling. The question is not "what has inherent value?," but "what are the conditions under which a shift in register expresses itself, and how does this alter lived experience?"

In the lower-grade organisms, organisms that compose with the world with less variation, a rock, a plant, shifts in register are chiefly physical. Contrast is limited in these occasions to a narrow array of difference, and more is eliminated from experience than is folded in. In the more complex organisms, animals, humans, feeling is more nuanced, as a result of which the occasion's subjective form is tinted in more complex ways by the negative prehensions it has positively eliminated.

Eternal Objects

At both ends of the spectrum, it is eternal objects that promote contrast. Eternal objects are the pure potential of felt relation. They are what give the occasion its nuance. They are the thisness of the event's qualitative difference—*just this* quality of sound, *just this* color tone, *just this* affective tonality.

The subjective form of an occasion feels the world in just this way. This feeling, as Whitehead says, "has an origination not wholly traceable to the mere data. It conforms to the data, in that it feels the data. But the how of feeling, though it is germane to the data, is not fully determined by the data" (1978, 85). This is because there is always a push and pull, in the feeling, between givenness and potentiality. Givenness is necessary to the occasion's capacity to assert itself as this or that, while potentiality ensures that the more-than remains included, if only marginally in the case of the lower-grade organisms.

The potential of the more-than enters into the occasion through the eternal object. "The quality of feeling has to be definite in respect to the eternal objects with which feeling clothes itself in its self-definition" (Whitehead 1978, 86). What a feeling has felt always includes this share of speculative potential, this uncharted value.

Even negatively prehended, this uncharted value makes a difference.

> Only a selection of eternal objects are "felt" by a given subject, and these eternal objects are then said to have "ingression" in that subject. But those eternal objects which are not felt are not therefore negligible. For each negative prehension has its own subjective form, however trivial and faint. (Whitehead 1978, 41)

Pure potential can be sidelined—"the actualities have to be felt, while the pure potentials can be dismissed" (239)—but the lure remains. The infrathin is haunted by this lure.

The Speculative Share

To begin with elimination is to foreground what makes a difference in experience despite its exclusion from actualization. If, as is usually the case, the actual is the measure of use-value, it would follow that what is not actually included in the occasion has no value. For this unactualized share is not only indiscernible as such, it is unmeasurable—even after the fact. Yet it is this very ineffability at the heart of the occasion that gives experience its value, I would suggest. The value of this speculative share of experience is in its coloring of the event, in its making felt how else experience can be ascertained, beyond definition.

This would be the first proposition for a pragmatics of the useless: when experience connects to the infrathin, what it is affirming is another way of thinking value. Beyond use-value, the valuation not of what is given, but the capacity of transvaluation to perform a shift at the very heart of the process's incompletion, of the process's inherent indeterminacy. In Nietzschean fashion, value here derives from the in-act of the process's own affirmation of its difference: "Creation takes the place of knowledge itself and affirmation takes the place of all negations" (Deleuze 1986, 187). A pragmatics of the useless celebrates the share of experience that is affirmed not because of what it is but because of how it affects experience in the making.

A pragmatics of the useless is pragmatic in the sense that it is wholly concerned with the *how* of the event's coming-to-be. *This* instance of the infrathin. *These* conditions for activating *this* interval of experience. The event cannot be generalized across iterations. It is always exemplary, always speculatively pragmatic.

A pragmatics of the useless is speculative in the sense that it is open to transformation by the potentializing force of what courses through the event, even when it cannot be fully actualized. Potential courses through the "just like this" nature of the event, making it reverberate. The infrathin is felt in this reverberation, potentially singularizing.

Potentially Singularizing

All actual occasions carry a quality of the infrathin. While on the one hand the event is singularly what it is—*this* plane surface—the event also includes in the reverbatory movement of this singularity an openness to difference. The infrathin's potentially singularizing force is its very capacity to be both-and.

To perceive at this interval of the both-and is to feel the bending of time in the occasion. It is to feel both the event's absolute time signature—the pragmatism of what happens, here, now—and the potentiality of the event's capacity to differentiate from itself. The making of a difference is always also a making of time. What is singularly potentialized by the infrathin is event-time, time felt in its differential quality, less measure than fold.

What then of the "intoleran[ce] of any addition" to the occasion? (Whitehead 1978, 45). What of Whitehead's statement that "an extra patch of red does not constitute a mere addition; it alters the whole balance" (45)? What of the occasion's necessity to eliminate that which does not conform to it?

The infrathin cuts across this necessity, slicing the occasion such that its perspective on conformity skews. Givenness and potentiality always work together—"'givenness' refers to 'potentiality,' and 'potentiality' to 'givenness'" (45). A complexity of feeling is revealed at the differential of their overlapping.

Transversality

The infrathin is transversal. It cannot be thought as a state. It is the making-felt of a momentary skewing of experience in the moving. The infrathin feels experience in a way that reveals the occasion's background and allows it momentarily to dance in the foreground. It creates the conditions to emphasize what the feeling hasn't felt. It gives uneasy consistency, in the merest of intervals, to that which barely registers if it registers at all. "Infra thin separation between / the detonation noise of a gun / (very close) and the apparition of the bullet/ hole in the target. . . . (#12 verso)" (Duchamp, quoted in Perloff 2002, 101). "The infra-thin separation is working at its maximum when it distinguishes the same from the same" (de Duve 1991, 160).

Double Articulation

Distinguishing the same from the same, in the duration of the infrathin, what stands out is how all experience is actively engaged in a double articulation. The actual is always replete with the virtual, individuation with the preindividual, prehension with what is negatively prehended. What the infrathin contributes, as a concept, is a way of thinking the both-and of double articulation. That extra patch of red does make a difference: it creates a new world. The infrathin makes felt how both worlds might briefly coexist. To be felt does not mean to be felt by us.

Duration

This coexistence is beyond definition in large part because of the challenge of thinking time durationally. Two times thought together in the event is difficult to parse in a language that unfolds one subject, one noun, one verb at a time. Art can do this, but only when it resists defining itself solely according to the form it takes.[4] With an emphasis not on form but on the artfulness that potentially runs through it, artfulness as the aesthetic yield that draws out from form what moves it into expression, art can activate the infrathin of a force still verging.[5] It is artfulness's yield to be able to compose worlds that activate a kind of geological event-time—a layered, composite time-felt. Elsewhere, I've referred to this as the "art of time" focusing on art-as-way, art's processual capacity to foreground passage and make felt, through the force of an intuition of the world for its own becoming, time's complexity.[6]

When Duchamp writes, "Just touching. While trying to place 1 plane surface / precisely on another plane surface / you pass through some infra thin moments," the sense is that there is a touching on the art of time (quoted in Perloff 2002, 102). Something is felt—"you pass through some infra thin moments"—that cannot quite be attributed to the perceiver. For it is not "you" who passes through but the plane that feels itself in the passing, that feels the relational field of its co-composition with the adjacent plane, that feels layers of duration that cannot quite be distinguished either from its composite planeness or from its adjacency.

Art can move the world toward these planes of duration, making them intuitively felt such that a different quality of existence is momentarily touched upon. This touching-upon has nothing to do with metaphor: it is lived, its effects tangible if below the registers of perception of the human-all-too-human.

A Pragmatics of the Useless

The second proposition for a pragmatics of the useless emerges: value must also be activated each time anew. Art that truly engages with what has not yet found its form intuitively steers away from the mimicry of reproduction. To be artful—actively engaged in the differential of experience in the making—art must never seek to define in advance its value. It must never claim to know how the infrathin will make itself felt. The negative prehension that haunts it must remain a haunting.

Taking-form is art's risk. There is no getting around taking-form. Experience wouldn't be known without it. But the taking-form must not fall into the category of prevaluation.

It must not know in advance what its taking can do. It must always move beyond its settling into use-value.

The Fourth Dimension

Duchamp speaks of the infrathin as a registering beyond the second dimension toward the third and even the fourth: the infrathin must always resist time's measure. Folding onto itself, the infrathin becomes the operation where the schizz of time occurs. "The possible implies becoming—the passage from one to the other takes place in the infrathin" (Duchamp 1999). The infrathin is not a passive passage. It is the modulator of the differential that moves experience from the shape we know to an unshapeability that affects the knowing. Here, in the folding of experience quadrupling onto itself, the infrathin touches the limits of perceptibility. "2 forms cast in / the same mold differ / from each other / by an infra thin separative / amount—All 'identicals' as / identical as they may be, (and / the more identical they are) / move toward this / infra thin separative differ-ence. 'Two men are not / an example of identicality / and to the contrary / move away / from a determinable / infra thin difference—but (#35 recto)" (quoted in Perloff 2002, 101).

The Differential

The imperceptible within the perceptible is experience's differential. The in-frathin mobilizes the differential, that share of perception on the very edge of perceptibility where what is barely felt (or not felt at all) makes a difference. Two forms cast in the same mold carry the force of this difference despite their appearance of sameness; identicals persist in remaining qualitatively more-than identicality. This qualitative difference that often escapes perceptibility is the more-than of experience in-forming; it is the edging into itself of a givenness full of potential. "The infra-thin separation is working at its maximum when it distinguishes the same from the same" (de Duve 1991, 160).

The Untimely

Henri Focillon describes the edgings of perceptibility in the experience of the in-frathin in terms of untimeliness (in Davila 2010, 13–14). The untimeliness of the infrathin foregrounds what Whitehead calls "the mutual sensitivity of feelings" (1978, 221). This mutual sensitivity includes the contribution of that which has been eliminated from the actual. It includes the subjective form of the negative prehension. "The negative prehensions have their own subjective forms which they contribute to the process. A feeling bears on itself the scars of its birth; it recollects as a subjective emotion its struggle for existence; it retains the impress of what it might have been, but is not. It is for this reason that what an actual en-tity has avoided as a datum for feeling may yet be an important part of its equip-ment. The actual cannot be reduced to mere matter of fact in divorce from the potential" (226). Feeling, in Whitehead, is the complex of experience: process philosophy is an account, not of pure reason, but of pure feeling. "The feelings are inseparable from the end at which they aim; and this end is the feeler. The feelings aim at the feeler, as their final cause. The feelings are what they are in order that their subject may be what it is" (222). An event *is* its affective tonality. An untimeliness is lived at this affective interstice where feeling and feeler live their mutual inclusion in the event. Too often, we separate these out, marking them as though one came before the other, in a hierarchy of value: the critique of pure reason prevails as we situate the feeler outside the event to judge the occasion from without. Process philosophy does not accept this account. There is nothing outside of the event, and feeling cannot be separated out from the event's coming-to-be. The event is what the feeling has felt. How the occasion has been felt is the experience, it is its reason for becoming what it is. The subject of the event—its superject—is the untimeliness of feeling folding on itself. This folding creates the nuances of infrathin experience.

Mutual sensitivity of feeling highlights the fold between feeling and feeler, foregrounding the affective tonality of event-time. The infrathin grasps toward this difference of "the same from the same" in the untimeliness of the lived interval of feeling and feeler. The infrathin gives the briefest consistency to the phonic substance of this experiential cluster.

Phonic Substance

Tina Campt defines phonic substance through the work of Arthur Jafa. His work, she suggests, invites us into a "still-moving" that refuses "the presumed distinction between still and moving images" (2019, 79).[7] This "black visuality" foregrounds the infrathin differential of movement and stillness, bringing feeling and feeler into co-composition. Phonic substance, "the sound inherent to an image; one that defines or creates it, that is neither contingent upon nor necessarily preceding it; not simply a sound played over, behind or in relation to an image; one that emanates from the image itself" (79). Phonic substance, a refusal of the imposition of the actual—the forcing of a white glare on what else moves between. Phonic substance, sound's afterimage in the pulse of a rhythmic visuality. Phonic substance, time folding, sound felt infrathinly through the image's bend.

Experiential Cluster

The experiential cluster where feeling and felt are one, like all occasions, "can only be felt once" (Whitehead 1978, 231). Its untimeliness is the fact of its singular onceness combined with its durational mise en abyme. The infrathin in this way makes felt the uneasiness of time in the making, time in the feeling, where time is at once the here-now and the not-quite-yet. This is the work art can do, Duchamp seems to say, to create the conditions through which the time of the event in all its untimely uneasiness can come to expression. To create the conditions for a material expression of duration at the limit.

This involves creating techniques for activating the clustering of experience where time is of the event. Perhaps this is what Robert Smithson means when he suggests that the artist creates at the interstices where "distant futures meet distant pasts" (1968), or when Duchamp writes that "in each fraction of duration are reproduced all fractions future and anterior" (quoted in Davila 2010, 14).

Asynchrony

Arthur Jafa's films energize and unsettle. Caught in the staccato of images moving too quickly to be fully grasped yet slowly enough to make their amplitude felt, we are moved into the fold of the overlap. The infrathin moves at the pace of this overlap, distending and collapsing, bending our encounter, our proximity to the phonic substance itself in perceptual attunement to cultural alignment, to our sensitivity to its aesthetic sociality of blackness.

The fold of the overlap in Jafa's *Apex* (2014) carries what Campt calls a "frequency." This frequency, allied to pitch, brings to the foreground a listening in the watching. Synchrony reveals itself to be off in this amodal untimeliness of perception not quite coinciding in vision. A pulse takes over, "a rhythmic, piercing sound you feel as much as you hear" (Campt 2019, 82). Differentially attuned, this frequency asynchronizes experience, pushing to the fore what resists being seen. In the listening, what sticks to this resistance, what accompanies it to produce the pain that comes with unseeing, is negatively prehended, rhythms catching our breath and resyncing it to the intervals the overlap barely registers. "As the pulses slow, fade, then resound again; as multiple beats overlap and syncopate then differentiate again into single, serial beats sometimes rising in pitch, sometimes lowering instead; the impact is more embodied and corporeal than visual. And the viewer instinctively responds in kind, albeit not through vision, but with breath. Sound syncs with breath as the pulse merges monitor with metronome" (82–83). A body is made, breath syncing with what must remain asynchronous, the differential of an unbridgeable overlap. In the rhythm of the unassimilable, pitch becomes "a visual frequency which tethers black life to black death, black pleasure to black pain," "channelling the power of black music," "black visual intonation" (82). The film's capacity to make felt the infrathin of time in the making is what Campt calls its politics of refusal: Jafa refuses to beat in the rhythm of the dominant field of perception, opting instead to cut the moving-still with more-than what can be digested, overlapping the celebratory with the dismal, cutting the violence with joy (83). Asynchrony, felt in the untimeliness of a world dangerously present and always still to be invented. A frequency to be infrathinly attuned to.

Consciousness

When experience becomes untimely, when event-time takes over experience, perception bends. This infrathin orientation to the more-than is nonconscious.

It is common to give value to a conscious process over a nonconscious one. Whitehead insists: how an event feels its potential does not necessarily have to do with consciousness. Consciousness is merely one aspect of the occasion's capacity for eventuation.

The infrathin does not rely on consciousness to come to expression. And yet it does touch at the edges of an awareness in which the conscious and the nonconscious are in co-composition. Here, where degrees and scales of feeling are in-act, we are in the midst of autistic perception, the active fielding of experience edging into itself. Elimination is included, the untimeliness of nonconscious tendings directly felt.

At this lively interstice between degrees of feltness, what is perceived is contrast. The differential is lived, the verge of experience in-forming directly perceived. A four-dimensional way of seeing? "Actually I think that right now we're wrestling with how to go from a three-dimensional model to a four-dimensional one. How do you actually do that? How do you deal with a four-dimensional way of seeing? And what kind of social practice or order will result?" (Irwin, in Irwin and Eliasson 2007, 58). Other ways of perceiving create other ways of living.

Fourth Person Singular

Might a fourth-dimensional way of seeing call forth Gilles Deleuze's "fourth-person singular" (see Deleuze 1990b)? The fourth person singular, the impersonal "*il pleut*" in the French, makes doing a kind of impersonal acting, in the event. "*Something doing*" (Massumi 2011, 1). Time in the folding, feeling itself in the asynchronous rhythms of its infrathin pleats. Not your perception but the feel that folds what comes to be, the feel that shifts the pace of how activity expresses the change it brings to the world. The fourth dimension not as $1+3$ but as $n+1$—"the many become one, and are increased by one" (Whitehead 1978, 21).

The Tension in between Things

Doug Wheeler: "That's what I started playing with as an artist: not looking at things but the tension in between things" (in Wheeler and Davies 2011). The tension between things is the $n+1$ of the infrathin: the unquantifiable force of difference that creates an interlude in the time of the event. It is here, in the force of time's folding, where use-value has not yet been determined and the pragmatic is at its most speculative, that artfulness is most palpable.

The Creative Advance

When Whitehead writes of the creative advance as the push of what the event can do at its most creative edge, there is a sense of the force of the art of time. Creative advance is not about the creation of an art object. It is a way of speaking of the lure for feeling alive in the interval. Creativity is not the measure of what is produced. It is the foregrounding of the still-moving that shifts the conditions of an event's coming-to-be. Creativity is how the phonic substance shifts the conditions of frequency to make felt what is too often overlooked. Creativity is contrast made operational by the coming into relation of a differential field. It is the pulse of negative prehension. What art can do, at its most pragmatically useless, is to make felt this pulse, the anarchic share, in the event, that is the ungraspable interval of the more-than. When Wheeler speaks of "the tension in between things," he is speaking not of an empty space between objects but of the untimely activity of the relational field. This untimely activity shimmers with creativity.

Contrast

Contrast is always allied, in Whitehead, with conceptual feeling. Conceptual feeling is in the event, not of a precomposed subject. It is the shimmer that proposes qualitative difference, the discordant asynchrony that produces a schizz, folding experience into an untimeliness. Speaking of the event's appetite to become, or what Whitehead calls "concrescence," he writes, "In each concrescence there is a twofold aspect of the creative urge. In one aspect there is the origination of simple causal feelings; and in the other aspect there is the origination of conceptual feelings. These contrasted aspects will be called the physical and the mental poles of an actual entity. No actual entity is devoid of either pole; though their relative importance differs in different actual entities" (1978, 239).

The mental pole allows for increased variation. Never of the mind (as though mind and body could be separated), the mental pole is the liveliness of contrast generated within the occasion itself, propulsing it into a differentiation from itself. With variation comes conceptual feeling, that qualitative difference that is capable of holding, in the event, what remains actually excluded but is nonetheless immanently included, as contrast.

"The tension in between things" is not about what is actually perceived. It is about the schizz of perception where feeler and felt are mutually included.

"Difference between the contact / of water and that of / molten lead for ex, / or of cream / with the walls of its / own container moved around the liquid." The tension between things—water and molten lead, cream and the walls of its own container—involves "the reciprocal imbrication of differences" (Massumi 2014, 4). Fusing without confusion, the tension between things brings things differentially together in "a performative zone of indiscernibility" (6). Infrathin is included middle, being of relation. Negative prehension animates this relational field, agitating the edges of what it brings together in differential resonance. Conceptual feeling gives qualitative dissonance to this creative agitation.

Conceptual Feeling

Conceptual feelings give value to the event: they "introduce the factor of 'valuation,' that is, 'valuation up,' or 'valuation down'" (Whitehead 1978, 247). This valuation, according to Whitehead, opens the event to "creative purpose" (248). The introduction of creative purpose happens in the untimeliness of the tension's creative agitation. "Every actual entity is 'in time' so far as its physical pole is concerned, and is 'out of time' so far as its mental pole is concerned. It is the union of two worlds, namely, the temporal world, and the world of autonomous valuation" (248). The conceptual feeling, the event's mental pole, gives texture to a folding of time in qualitative dissonance with actualization.

That conceptual feelings are what give value to the event reminds us that it is not what actualizes that determines value. It is precisely that which cannot be said to fully become determined that moves the event toward its creative advance. Value cannot be known as such, it can only be experimented from the edges of a process too untimely to measure.

The Non-Object

In an essay entitled "What Art Is and Where It Belongs" (2009), Paul Chan writes, "Art uses things to make its presence felt. But art is not itself a thing. In other words, art is more *and* less than a thing. And it is this simultaneous expression of *more-ness* and *less-ness* that makes what is made art." What makes art artful is the way art can make felt the untimeliness of the tensions active in the relational field it calls forth. "What art ends up expressing is the irreconcilable tension that results from making something, while intentionally allowing the materials and things that make up that something to change the making in mind . . . , until it becomes something radically singular, something neither wholly of the mind that made it, nor fully the matter from which it was made. It is here that art *incompletes* itself, and appears" (Chan 2009). Art is not its final taking-form but the very process of its incompletion. This—which can only be felt differentially, never quantified—is its value.

In activating contrast, what art can do is give the force-of-form to that incompletion. Ferreira Gullar, in his attempt to articulate this force-of-form, proposed the concept of the non-object, a concept directly influenced by the work of Brazilian artists Lygia Clark and Helio Oiticica, among others. Gullar defines the non-object as "an almost-body, which is to say, a being whose reality is not exhausted in the external relationships between its elements; a being that, while not decomposable into parts through analysis, only delivers itself up wholly through a direct, phenomenological approach" (quoted in Amor 2010, 28). A non-object as presentation, he argues, not representation (Gullar 1959).

For Gullar, what is at stake is finding a vocabulary for what he perceives as the shift, mid-twentieth-century, in artists like Clark and Oiticica, toward another way of working with materiality. The non-object, he writes, "bursts from the inside out, from non-meaning toward meaning" (1959, 19). It is "pure appearance," "pure phenomenon," "without pre-conceptions of artistic categories, without reflected consciousness, but rather with the senses" (19).

The Relational Object

Lygia Clark distances herself from the vocabulary of the non-object, opting instead for the relational object.[8] She writes, "It is no longer the problem of feeling the poetic through a form. The structure exists there only as a support for the expressive gesture, the cut, and after it is finished, it has nothing to do with the traditional work of art. It is the state of 'art without art.' . . . By presenting this type of idea, the artist in reality presents this 'empty-full' in which all potentialities of the option that comes through the act take place."[9]

What the relational object foregrounds is not the phenomenon but the being of relation. Despite her strong interest in the phenomenal, sensual world, what moves Clark's practice is the lived experience of the tension between. Like Oiticica, hers is not strictly a phenomenological approach but a relational one active in its more-than human processuality. It is active in the infrathin of what Whitehead calls nonsensuous perception: the direct perception of time's uneasiness, in the event. By activating the infrathin of experience in the making, the relational object potentializes this tension where feeler and felt are at their most lively differential. In so doing, it creates the conditions for an artfulness that defies the bounds of art, pushing art into the field of life itself.

The Value of the Infrathin

This differential force of artfulness is replete with potential. What art can do is make this potential felt. Chan (2009) writes:

> Unlike things, art shapes matter—which gives substance to material reality—without ever dominating it. All matter absorbs the manifold forces that have influenced how it came to be, and the uses and values it has accrued—and emanates the presence of this history and its many meanings from within. In a sense, form is just another word for the sedimented content that smolders in all matter. Art is made with sensitivity to and awareness of this content. And the more the making becomes attenuated, the more art binds itself to the way this content already determines the reality of how matter exists in the world.

When art becomes sensitive to the force-of-form of material tendencies, resonating with the incompletion it leaves behind, more relational object than attenuated adjacency to content predetermined, it has begun to value not itself but the life it seeds. This valuation involves a decision-making process immanent to the event. No relational object is fully operative that cannot create a cut in the process: an object is relational precisely because of its capacity to schizz the field such that certain qualities stand out more than others. How a contrast makes itself felt is precisely what makes art artful.

The artful creates fields of relation through which new modes of encounter are propelled. These infrathin modes of encounter propose new ways of taking time, of making time. This can only happen if what is foregrounded, as art, is not its use-value, not its thingness, not its exchange-value. Artfulness has no inherent value. It is not some*thing*. It cannot be abstracted from the field in which its sensitivity to matter is expressed through a neutralizing of experience where feeler is excised from feeling, the subject now standing outside it as though with an object to be consumed. Artfulness is exemplary, an activity of discordant asynchrony where feeling and feeler are differentially one.

Artfulness activates the event's contrast, making felt the force-of-form that undoes art of its hold on the very object that too often is said to represent it. A pragmatics of the useless takes this as its third proposition: that what art can do is always in excess of the object it leaves behind.

A pragmatics of the useless: the value does not reside in the form but in the infrathin of form's incompletion.

Toward a Politics of Immediation

The Subject

It always happens in the middle. *We* always happen in the middle. Not first a thought, then an action, then a result, but a middling, "we" the result of a pull that captures, for an instant, how the thought was already action-like, how the body was always also a world. Not first a body, then a world, but a worlding through which bodyings emerge. Not one, then the other, but time-topologically, "we" a burst too vertiginous to articulate in the one-word-after-the-other language of "I." Not mediation, not something that comes in between to parse the existing terms, but *immediation*, the withness of time, of a body in the making.

For Alfred North Whitehead, there is never a subject that preexists an occasion of experience. And there is never a time into which we bathe fully formed. All occasions of experience fashion the quality of subjectivity their uniqueness calls forth. In so doing, they co-create the time of the event. A subject is in-time, coming into itself *just this way* in *this* set of conditions only to change again with the force of a different set of conditions. A subject can therefore never be reduced to a single occasion as though that iteration of experience could map onto every past and future instance of what it might have meant to have come into oneself. Such an account would leave no room for the liveliness of difference in the world.

If this is the case, why is it that we maintain such a strong sense of the subject? How can we speak with such confidence about subject positions and the identity-based practices that prolong them? Why do we claim to know who is included (or excluded) from "the subject"? On what terms is this transparency of inclusion/exclusion played out, and what does this categorization foster in terms of the middling of subjectification?

We know the subject because the subject is given to us again and again as the leading feature of experience. The subject drives existence. Committed to first-person accountability, it directs what we come to think of as "our" life. The subject, we learn, is the agency behind bodies, the agency that partitions body from world to protect the human's place in it.

Subjects, however, are only as strong as the mediating positions they reinforce.

Simple Location

Whitehead maintains that the persistence of the preexisting subject as an identity position is a fallacy of simple location. *Simple location* refers to the notion that matter is "self-contained, localized in a region with a passive, static network of spatial relations, entwined in a uniform relational system" (Whitehead 1938, 138).[1] Yet matter, Whitehead underscores, "is fused into its environment. There is no possibility of a detached, self-contained local existence. The environment enters into the nature of each thing. Some elements in the nature of a complete set of agitations may remain stable as those agitations are propelled through a changing environment. But such stability is only the case in a general, average way" (188). The preexisting subject as agent of experience prolongs the logic Whitehead outlines above, carrying over the self-contained, local existence of matter into its materialization in the body. Like matter, which in this fallacy of "misplaced concreteness" is "localized in a region with a passive, static network of spatial relations, entwined in a uniform relational system from infinity to infinity and from eternity to eternity," the preexisting subject meets the world as a distinct, fully formed other (Whitehead 1938, 138). Any account of simple location misses the push and pull of relation, reducing the complexity of all that co-composes to a set of mediated interactions, reducing the being of relation to a simplistic notion of interaction.[2]

A politics of immediation does not deny that subjects exist or that they affect how experience comes to be. What it underscores is that these subjects are born of the occasion, affected and affecting within the matrix of the occasion's singular conditions of existence. Subjects are born of the event and do their work as subjects within its ecology of practices, produced in the interstices of the occasion's self-expression. There is no mediation here: the subject is not what stands outside to view the occasion from a distance. Time here is not a passive surround. Space is not a neutral container motivated by an externalized subject position. The subject exists always and only in the emergent spacetime of an occasion coming into itself *just this way*. In this constellation of incessant activity where occasions crest and perish, opening the way for new modes of existence, the subject can only be seen as fleeting, an inflection in a field of relation too unwieldy to ever fully contain it.

The Superject

An occasion cresting into itself is always marked by a certain quality of form-taking. Whitehead calls this "subjective form." Subjective forms are the subjects *of the event*, carriers of the occasion's singular signature—its emerging subjectivity—toward a certain completion that gathers the occasion's (subjective) complexity into itself. As Whitehead writes, "An actual entity is at once the subject experiencing and the superject of its experiences" (1978, 29). Carrying both process and the demarcation of that process, the subjective form is the shimmer of a double articulation. Whitehead calls this being of relation the superject to highlight its status as the qualifier of a process having found its internal rhythm, its singular expression. But this production is by no means infinite: the superject crystallizes the event's quality of becoming as the event perishes, perishing with it. What is left behind in the perishing is not a fully fledged subject but a quality of form-taking. The quality of form-taking will have effects: future comings-into-themselves will be influenced by the shape it took. But the subject-superject of the occasion itself will never return *in-itself*. The production of subjectivity concerns *the way* subjective form comes to expression, the manner in which it leaves its trace as much as the trace itself. How subjective form feeds forward is directly affected by how new occasions compose with the shape it left behind.

The subject and the superject are always interwoven: "It is subjectsuperject, and neither half of this description can for a moment be lost sight of. The term 'subject' will be mostly employed when the actual entity is considered in respect to its own real internal constitution. But 'subject' is always to be construed as an abbreviation of 'subjectsuperject'" (Whitehead 1978, 29). This interweaving of experience, where experience carries both the quality of the occasion coming into itself *and* its crystallization, is made possible by the infrathin of event-time, the future-presenting always already a fold in the event's coming to expression, time unmoored except in the peaking of the occasion's self-definition as momentary form-taking.

If an occasion of experience is fully and absolutely what it is when it comes into its superject, marking time as the it-is of the present-passing, it is precisely to emphasize the untimeliness of the vastness of nonlinear time expressed in the being of relation the occasion emerges from and descends into. The superject as the living form-force of an actual occasion must always be recognized as being short-lived—cusping in the event as it comes to full expression and then perishing to give way to the tumult of occasions in the forming. What persists in this perishing, as mentioned above, is the quality-of-form of the superject, the force-of-form it leaves as a trace in the world. It is not the superject as already-formed that continues into experience but its angling-into-expression that makes ingress into occasions to come. Whitehead names this mode of persistence "objective immortality" to highlight that nothing is ever completely lost in a philosophy of the in-act. Everything that comes to expression makes a difference, cutting into experience to schizz it toward new cleavings of worlds in the making. There is no continuity of becoming here, no uninterrupted flow. This is not an account of unimpeded process. What is at work is a becoming of continuity, a continuity produced in the interval of actualizing and perishing. The becoming of continuity highlights capture and cut over unimpeded continuation, emphasizing that process is defined not by a frictionless infinity but by a continual recasting of the conditions that make experience what it is (in its continual differing from itself). Objective immortality serves to remind us that what actualizes makes a difference, not that what has come to be will forever remain. It is never the substance of experience that carries over, but its tendings, its orientations, its infrathin registerings of the minor gestures that run through it. Of course, objective immortality also facilitates the carrying over of what Spinoza would call the sad affects, the forces of existence that serve to weaken and ultimately deaden the potential of existence to vary. Systemic racism lives here, as does ableism and all the forms of heteronormativity that claim the centering of a certain version of humanity over all other experience. The inheritances of experience are many. In an account that foregrounds practice, the question is always how to create conditions for the tuning of experience to what most generatively runs through it, and how to recognize that these ecologies of practice are not ours to orient so much as ours to participate in as co-composers in the refashioning of the modes of existence that make up our body-world constellations.

What Whitehead's account of process underscores is that *any* process involves the cut of difference. The conditions of experience will always have changed, just as this cresting wave will always be different from the last. "The ancient doctrine that 'no one crosses the same river twice' is extended. No thinker thinks twice; and, to put the matter more generally, no subject experiences twice. This is what Locke ought to have meant by his doctrine of time as a 'perpetual perishing'" (Whitehead 1978, 29). What has agency, or, preferably, agencement, is the process itself, the process in its schizzing, not the figure of a preexisting subject.[3] Every occasion, every event, is an agencement, a singular reorienting of the conditions of experience. Through its perishing, what the occasion leaves behind is not a fully-formed subject that will enter unchanged into the next occasion but the agencement of its having come into existence just this way. It is the agencement, the conditioning of experience in its singularity now moving into new occasions, that moves the world.

Time Middling

Time is never linear in Whitehead's account. Experience is topological, bending with the infrathin force of pastnesses future-presenting, a fold rather than a line.

Mediation presupposes the time of the line. Organizing experience from the perspective of preselected terms, mediation relies on opposable presuppositions. The subject is essential here—mediation's work is to enter into a naturalized social relation that consists of preexisting subjects and objects, preexisting in the sense that the categorical precedes the experiential. With power structures firmly in place, mediation enters into the equation not to recast experience but to extract further structures. This restructuring may, and indeed often will, also have an effect on the terms at hand, shifting the stakes of their interaction. This may even cause a certain redistribution of power. But it will not fundamentally alter the conditions of experience in and for itself.

Recasting experience is the work immediation does. It does so not in opposition to mediation. Immediation's logic of mutual inclusion has no relationship to mediation. Whereas mediation by its very nature requires time to be a container in which experience plays out, immediation makes apparent that the being of relation is emergent. Experience is not an external quantity to be analyzed. Experience grows from the middle. It is from this middling that immediation does its work. In this middling, everything makes a difference, and that difference has effects: each occasion of experience leaves traces that affect how experience comes into itself in the untimeliness of time folding.

Nonsensuous Perception

William James is suspicious of any account of time that would claim to know the now of experience. As in Whitehead, time for James is the time of the event, a time too complex to parse in the past-present-future account of metric time we are accustomed to. He writes, "Let any one try, I will not say to arrest, but to notice or attend to, the *present* moment of time. One of the most baffling experiences occurs. Where is it, this present? It has melted in our grasp, fled ere we could touch it, gone in the instant of becoming" (1890, 608). The present, James says, is specious: the now of experience is already part of the past, altered, if only minimally, in the now that is cresting. "In short, the practically cognized present is no knife-edge, but a saddle-back, with a certain breadth of its own on which we sit perched, and from which we look in two directions into time" (609).

Like James's specious present, the not-hereness of the present felt in its passing, Whitehead's account of time aims to foreground how the future bends into the present even as the past colors it. Time is past-contouring in its future-presenting.

Experience knows not time itself (the present) but the burst of its presenting in a time yet to be invented.

Nonsensuous perception is the term Whitehead gives to the act of past-contouring that enables a certain persistence of experience. Every occasion of experience, Whitehead proposes, casts forth a certain quality of its continuance even as it perishes. The question is how that continuity moves into and affects the present-passing. This quality is carried more than sensed through sense perception. Typically, the movement from past to present would be accounted for with sense perception. For Whitehead, the expression of time must not be reduced to sense perception as this would imply a cognition of time-passing, a mediation of the present into the past by the figure of the present. It would make the folds of time a conscious proposition, turning the human into a mediator of those folds. Nonsensuous perception is a way to speak of the immediating effect of direct experience, experience immanently orienting rather than experience externally oriented.

Nonsensuous perception relies on an account of what Whitehead calls the "immediate past." The immediate past is "that portion of our past lying between a tenth of a second and a half a second ago. It is gone, and yet it is here. It is our indubitable self, the foundation of our present existence" (Whitehead 1967, 181). Nonsensuous perception is what moves pastness into presentness, making possible an intercession in experience of the time of the other. It is a time of the other in the sense that it carries germs of experience activated in ecologies other than the one now growing into formation. This ingression of otherness into experience brings with it qualities and tonalities of the past, doing so in relation to the futurity already affecting the experience in-forming, thereby modifying the welling occasion in both directions at once. Time bends in the event, and from this bending come subjectivities in the making.

It is important not to confuse these subjectivities in the making with what Whitehead calls "the self-identity of the occasion" (1967, 181). The self-identity of the occasion is not identity abstracted from the event; it is the in-itselfness of the occasion at hand, the singular way it has come to be. The subjective form of an occasion comes into itself *out of this self-identity*. This coming out of itself produces not an identity but the quality of a tending. The subjective form is this tendency. When the tendency crystallizes into the superject, it will have taken on a consistency. But, to repeat once more, it will never be known exactly that way again. For when the occasion perishes, the subject perishes with it, leaving behind not a subject but a potential consistency, an agencement for occasions to come. This potential for ingression moving across occasions forming is an otherness—"the present moment is constituted by the influx of the other into that self-identity which is the continued life of the immediate past within the immediacy of the present" (181). Past and future co-compose, the first active as a field of potential affectations for the future-presenting, the second the measure of how the allure of difference actualized. "Self-formation," writes Whitehead, "passes into its activity of *other-formation*" (193).

The production of subjectivity is always a becoming-other. Of course there are gradations. The question is to what degree an occasion of experience is oriented toward the more-than of its actualization. Appetite for difference increases the potential of that difference to make a difference. Appetite in the act itself, or what Whitehead calls the occasion's self-enjoyment, is the manner in which the occasion carries a certain curiosity toward what exceeds the actual. Never simply located, appetite is the mode that activates other-formation, the force of attraction that orients the occasion to its more-than.

More-Than Human

The preconstituted subject is inevitably connected to the human, which, like the (transcendental) subject, tends to be mobilized as a categorical given. To cement its givenness, the human is defined according to its difference from other categories such as the animal or the plant or the mineral. This givenness is not neutral. The implicit hierarchy is clear: the human stands above, not in an ecological co-relation to, other forms of life.

Sylvia Wynter dates the category of the human as we now conceive of it to 1492. This is the date of what she calls "the bifurcation of history" (Wynter and McKittrick 2015, 16). In the aftermath of this period of early colonization, the human is constructed as an epistemological category that serves to "[reify] bourgeois tenets" (17). Any notion of hybridity is excluded. "The larger issue is . . . the incorporation of all forms of human being into a single, homogenized descriptive statement that is based on the West's liberal, monohumanist man" (23).

As Wynter argues, this bifurcation of history leads to the violent exclusion of black life from the human's "descriptive statement." Black life becomes the cipher for a life that troubles all categories, that unmoors existence by deviating from the order that seeks to sequester it, a mode of existence that creates life-environments too illegible to count, to be counted, too cumbersome, too excessive, too unwieldy to make it into the colonial ontology.[4] Wynter's project is, in the end, a humanist one, committed not to a theory of the more-than human but to an otherwise humanness that would recast the tenets of humanism as they have been shaped by a worldwide commitment to anti-black racism and all that oppressively falls from this exclusionary image of the human.[5] In line with and indebted to Fanon's humanistic vision of the world, "a vision that is expressly and necessarily not a plea for a white world, nor is it a plea for a black philosophy of identity," Wynter's contribution is her astute and unflinching account of how the concept of the human comes to stand in for all that is valued as life, that is to say, as white life (Marriott 2018, xix). To read Wynter's commitment to other ways of living *as human* requires the recognition that freedom "has nothing to do with political sovereignty," which is to say that the humanism Wynter seeks is never an alignment to current modalities of belonging, of counting and being counted (xv). Freedom is not freedom to be recognized within the matrix of colonial power. It is the freedom to recognize life's otherwise quality in blackness, as Crawley might say.[6]

An account of this otherwise that cuts against the grain of Wynter's own (re) turn to the human would necessarily foreground the detour blackness must make with respect to any discussion of ontology.[7] "If we are right to suggest that racism interrupts the movement toward the human, and paradoxically makes ontology irrelevant for understanding black existence, then clearly ethics and politics (insofar as they are grounded on this humanism) cannot simply be invoked, even negatively, as a model for thinking black existence" (Marriott 2018, 5). If the human is drawn as white, if whiteness is the name of the violence of humanism, if whiteness is how the human calls itself human, a turn toward blackness must also, to some degree at least, be a turn against humanism. This tension is always, for me, at the heart of the concept of the human. Human is a shorthand for the most impoverished forms of living, and the most violent: "the common measure of all racisms is how difference comes to be decreed as difference in the history of humanism" (79).

The category of the human is more fragile than it would like to appear, however. In fact, it is so uncertain of the place it occupies that it requires continuous policing: the human, and humanism more generally, is terrified by the prospect that faced with the plethora of modes of practicing, of becoming-praxis, as Wynter might say, other modes of existence might be cast forth that could trouble its position of white centrality. Katherine McKittrick's project in *Demonic Grounds* might be said to be situated here, proposing another mode of the human that refuses an alongsideness of white/colonial logic:

> Rather than situating the grounds of blackness within anticipated realms of existing geographic arrangements . . . Wynter opens up a new function for human geographies, one that takes "new forms of life" as seriously as it takes biocentric spatial organizations (or present forms of life). The geographic meaning of racialized human geographies is not so much rooted

in a paradoxical description as it is a projection of life, livability, and possibility. Poetics, real and imagined geographies, put demands on traditional geographic arrangements because they expose the racial-sexual functions of the production of space and establish new ways to read (and perhaps live) geography. (2006, 143)[8]

Reading through the opening McKittrick provides, an opening to contemplate "new forms of life" for blackness, a more-than humanism becomes conceivable. For this more-than humanism, the starting point is not the human as pre-given but a quality of encounter with the world that produces a sociality in excess of any one form the human could take. This excess on form is neurodiverse, outside the confines of what already constitutes knowledge as valued by whiteness/neurotypicality. Here, I think of Harney and Moten's insistence that "the non-normative is precisely the absence of a point of view, which is therefore why it can never be about preservation" of the human as form-force of existence (2013: 137). The non-normative is unmediated, un*placed*. Its geographies are immanent to its coming into encounter, invented not in relation to a preexisting point of view, a given perspective.[9] In this regard, the more-than humanism of black life is always more-than human.

Is the "radical being beside itself of blackness, its off to the side, off on the inside, out from the outside imposition" not always an explicit refusal of all that would be policed into the form of the (excluded) human? (Harney and Moten 2013: 96). This is the paradox of state violence, which is to say, of colonial, white, neurotypical violence, that so many systems of subjugation must be set in place to uphold the category of the human (as so white as to be without race, as so colonial as to be without claim), held together by the imposition of mediation as ploy to neutrality, ploy that stages repetitive dramaturgies of oppression in the name of territory and identity, imperialism and global capitalism. Mediation, always set up with the terms already in place, the mediators themselves the very description of neurotypicality (white in the confidence of their apparent neutrality, white in the exclusion of all that doesn't fit neatly into the normative account of existence as they claim it). For mediation, in its occlusion of point of view, in its pretense that it doesn't carry perspective, frames what counts as knowledge, as value. This is what we tend to forget in the context of mediation: that knowledge is made in its image. Knowledge-as-mediation, knowledge as that which comes between, which fits in a model of preexisting point of view, which takes the image of the monohumanist man as its beacon, this is what blackness refuses in its commitment to more-than humanist geographies.

We could stop here and fight. The problem is we'd be fighting against the mediation, mediating the mediation. We'd be restaging the very same conditions that created the problem in the first place. "To study 'Man' or 'Humanity' is . . . to study a narrativization that has been produced with the very instruments (or categories) that we study *with*" (Mignolo 2015, 107).

A politics of immediation invites us to begin elsewhere. It invites us to begin not with the terms intact but in the middling where things are still forming and categories are not-yet. Cutting into the middle, moved by the force of the future in the past-presenting, immediation seeks not structure but composition. This involves improvisation. There is no knowing quite how the conditions of experience will be altered by the event of time's middling.

This is not to discount the extraordinary suffering that comes of being excluded from the category of the human, nor to underplay the horror of slavery then and now, nor to excuse the exclusion perpetrated in the too-often-unspoken name of neurotypicality, nor to ignore the continuing violence upheld by that very category. It is to take seriously that we must come to knowledge differently, beyond the strictures of colonialism, beyond the "instruments (or categories) that we study *with*." In this we would accompany Wynter, who, in Walter D. Mignolo's words, "seeks to undo the systems through which knowledge and knowing are constituted" (2015, 106).

Modes of Existence

New forms of life call forth new modes of existence. Modes of existence could be conceived as styles. A mode of existence "is a manner of making a being exist on a given plane" (Lapoujade 2017, 14).[10] Experience is carried by these modes, a differential attunement to many different modalities coming into itself to produce a quality of a living.

A mode is a gesture, a way of orienting toward. "Each existence consists of a gesture that it instaurates," instauration understood as the act, immanent to the event, of bringing a mode into existence (Lapoujade 2017: 14). Modes of existence qualify experience, attuned as they are to the ecosophical quality of the being of relation: in a poetics of encounter, they remind us that existence in its modal interplay makes us, not the other way around. Modes of existence are the how of existence living itself out, the emergent sociality of complexions of life immediating.

The gestures of existence, the modes, do not necessarily actually reveal themselves, however. "The majority of these modes remain at the level of sketches or drafts; they are not capable of differentiating themselves from the indistinct base into which they reimmerse themselves" (Lapoujade 2017, 16). The plane of existence is replete with such gestures that qualify existence without actualizing as such. These infrathin gestures are not those of a preconstituted subject, "they are immanent to existence itself" (Lapoujade 2017, 14). Souriau calls them the "merest of existences" (*existence moindres*).

Merest existences are intensifications. They are potentialities, tonalities, tendencies. On the continuum of force-form that makes up modes of existence, they are on the side of force rather than form. In the field of experience immediating, merest existences shift the tonalities of what comes to expression. These merest of existences make all the difference.

To grasp the operational quality of the modes of existence in Souriau's work, two conceptual persona are necessary—the witness and the advocate.[11] These conceptual personas are the motivators of his system: they are the barometers that move the modes of existence into intensification. As Lapoujade (2017, 19–20) underscores, these are not existing subjects that stand outside the event. They are the motor that creates the conditions for the mode of existence to take form.

The witness carries the gesture of the act of seeing (*faire-voir*). The advocate, always in relation to the witness, moves the seeing into full-fledged appearance. The advocate embodies the gesture of advocacy for existences in germ, as fledglingly perceived by the witness, bringing them onto the plane of experience. For Souriau, the artist is perhaps the best figure of the advocate: artists "bring new entities into existence, produce new realities" (Lapoujade 2017, 20).

But we might ask: what are the conventions of the witness's act of seeing and the advocate's actualization of that seeing? What remains unseen in the act of witnessing, even when witnessing is immanent to the event? Can the advocate escape the category of judgment that is carried by its double meaning in the French as "advocate" and "lawyer"? Is the making-perceptible of experience by the witness-advocate not a mediation of experience? Must all comings-into-themselves of modes of existence pass through such conceptual figures? And what are the risks, for more-than human expressions of life-living "out from the outside," of the imposition onto experience of conceptual persona that have served the colonial epistemology as consistently as have the witness and the advocate? Are the witness and the advocate not all too white?

The Will to Art

Lapoujade describes the merest existences as a "cloud of virtualities [*nuée des virtuels*]" (2017, 31). A cloud of virtualities accompanies all comings-to-be but is never known as such. Its power is precisely that it remains unachieved (32).

Modes of existence are rendered more nuanced, more rich and varied, through the ingression of what remains unachieved. "[The cloud of virtualities] awaits the art that can make them exist more and otherwise. Its art is to generate or to demand art; their own gesture is to create other gestures" (32). Their quality of existence is generative rather than explanatory: infrathin.

When Souriau speaks of art here, he is moving beyond the human figure of the artist toward artfulness—the aesthetic yield of experience in the making. The artful is a *faire-oeuvre*, a working of the work, not a finished object. Its power is in the *way*, in the *how* of a coming to form. When art moves toward a faire-oeuvre, its artfulness reveals itself as taking the shape of a problem that does not yet carry its solution, composing transversally with differentials of existence.[12] In these conditions, a "desire for creation" is introduced, "a will to art in the world [*une volonté d'art dans le monde*]" (Lapoujade 2017, 32) that exceeds the artist as maker. The world itself becomes creative.

Minor gestures generate this *will to art*, the will to art a kind of Nietzschean will to power that yields aesthetically. Activating a Guattarian ethico-aesthetic paradigm, the will to art sees the aesthetic yield as the creative force of the in-act that does not discount what remains cloudy. The merest of existences are valued here. "All existence becomes entitled to be unachieved" (Lapoujade 2017, 33).

The unachieved is transmodal in Souriau's account—it moves across planes of existence, "modify[ing] itself, transform[ing] itself, intensify[ing] its reality, mov[ing] from one mode to another, conjugat[ing] them" (Lapoujade 2017, 33). In this movement, the unachieved "form[s] [are] a nebula where every decision becomes a question of presentiment, of divination or intuition" (34).

The unachieved moves infrathinly through modes of existence actualizing, pushing them to discover what transmodally affects their coming-to-be. In so doing, it calls forth the shimmer of a problem unanticipated, a shift in condition that might alter the constitution of "the state of things as they are." Artfulness resides here as the quality of existence that nonsensuously catches the force of a future-presenting in the infrathin passing, reminding us that it is the merest of existences that most powerfully recast the force of the problem in the art of life-living, life-living "the living [that] lives at the limit of itself, on its limit" (Simondon 1964, 260; my translation). Calling forth minor gestures, artfulness amplifies the power of variation in the event. Not propelled by an existing subject—not ours to make—minor gestures attune experience to what is variable within it. In this regard, minor gestures are very much allied to the merest of existences and to the incipient mode's artful operations.

Minor gestures are the transversal operations that intensify experience, activating the surplus, the more-than, through which experience touches its aesthetic yield. With the motor of the minor gesture and its capacity to tune the occasion, it seems to me that the conceptual personae of the witness and advocate are no longer necessary. Personifications of experience, even when immanent to the event, risk returning us to the human as central category and, with the human, to the gesture of mediation. In the rock's perception of experience, in its prehension of time as the motivator of disintegration, why bring in a witness and an advocate? Why not work from within rockness itself, from within the force of immanent variation at the heart of rockness's singular mode of existence? Why not ask directly how minor gestures alter the conditions of rockness? Why not consider the artful quality of this becoming from the perspective of its own process, exploring the will to art on its own immediating terms?

This is not to say that all conceptual personae are mediators. It is to underscore that mediation is a strong tendency in political, cultural, and philosophical accounts of experience. All efforts to curb the neutralizing of experience are required to challenge the centrality of the colonial, neurotypical human as purveyor of sense. In the case of the witness and the advocate, it is not their status as conceptual personae that concerns me but the existing presupposition their personification carries as regards the mobilization of agency as external driving factor. It is difficult to conceive of the witness and the advocate beyond the figure of the intermediary, that figure too often white, too often colonial, that makes sense of (and gives sense to) how experience is valued.

An approach that begins with the problem, that takes seriously Henri Bergson's (1911) call that we not seek problems that already have solutions (false problems) but work instead from the field of experience's most knotted sites to discover not the answer but the conditions of existence of that very knottedness, requires modes of engagement that resist mediation at all costs. With the allure of mediation as strong as it remains, why take the risk of re-mediating the occasion through figures that would risk imposing value systems on the burgeoning event? Why risk reducing existence to a mediation by the all-knowing (white) human, even in the form of conceptual personae? Instead of taking the juridical model of the advocate into the realm of the artful, why not take artfulness into politics, making decolonization and the more-than human the sites of aesthetic yield?

Instauration

Staying close to Souriau's work while moving away from the figures of the witness and the advocate in favor of the minor gesture, the question remains: how does the transduction happen? What motivates the shift from an incipiency to a fully fledged mode of existence? What makes existences take shape? If the human is not where activity begins and ends, if there is no subject orienting experience from the outset, what motivates the cleave of experience?

Instauration is the name Souriau gives to this motoring of experience. Instauration activates the dephasing through which a mode of existence comes into being. As the crest of James's wave, instauration is the subtraction from the welter of experience: it marks the act of culling from the wealth of the gesture only this detail, this singular set of relations, bringing it to the fore. This gathering into itself has effects. What has come to be by subtraction from the welter of potential now orients the mode of existence it has come to embody. This, in turn, affects the coming into itself, through nonsensuous perception, of what will follow. Tendencies affirm similar tendencies, habits are formed, and soon we have an object, an instituted way, a being in the world.

But instauration does not happen once and for all, and it is this that keeps what actualizes through subtraction from becoming a fixed representation of itself. Instauration is an iterative process, as topological as time itself. "Instauration is not to found. To found imposes a preexisting form or dictates its conditions a priori" (Lapoujade 2017, 70). Instauration is immanent to what it brings into existence. "Instauration is upheld only by its own gesture, nothing preexists it" (71). To bring into existence, to "make" exist, is the work of instauration, but this is not existence generalized. Instauration is an intensifier: it moves germs of process into existence *in a certain way*, "each time (re)invented" (71). Instauration is the *art* of bringing into existence.

Instead of situating the advocate as instauration's "spokesperson [*porte-parole*], or, better, their existence-carrier [*porte-existence*]," a politics of immediation suggests that is the minor gesture itself that does the carrying (72). Where an advocate mediates, a minor gesture immediates. The force of this immediation is felt in the minor gesture's own textured collaboration with the event's coming into being. Recalling that the minor gesture is never outside the event, is never activated by a subject external to experience in the making, instauration can be thought as that quality of intervention in the event that cleaves it to its inner variation, exposing what else moves through it. Thus creating the conditions for the minor gesture, instauration becomes the motor of the differential's expression. All of this in an opacity, as Édouard Glissant might say, in the underbrush of what never quite centers itself, remaining unachieved. Unachieved does not mean in progress—as though an achievement were in its wake. Unachieved is the indeterminacy of a gesture that has effects in its cloudiness, the merest of existences registered not for itself but for the nuance it brings. This nuance can be thought as the renewal of a problem, a casting forth of stakes heretofore backgrounded, an urgency heard across an asynchrony of times indeterminate.

Indeterminacy fuels the minor gesture, the quality of its variation like the pull of an undertow. Keeping the problem of the event alive, the minor gesture cuts and cleaves, dispersing an uneasiness that may seem only to ripple the surface. "The force of a problem is not its internal tension, it is the uncertainty that it introduces in the (re)distribution of reality" (Lapoujade 2017, 59). The surface is only what is revealed, what is transparent. In the opacity of its minor movements, the minor gesture carries with it the force of an internal variation so powerful that it can indeed recast the very scaffold of reality: "Transparency no longer seems like the bottom of the mirror in which Western humanity reflected the world in its own image. There is opacity now at the bottom of the mirror, a whole alluvium deposited by populations, silt that is fertile but, in actual fact, indistinct and unexplored even today, denied or insulted more often than not, and with an insistent presence that we are incapable of not experiencing" (Glissant 1997, 111). Opacity is not the hidden—it is the transversal operation through which a different mode of visibility can be felt. I think here of Tina Campt's (2019) "black visuality," a phonic substance that moves amodally to shift the conditions of what is nonsensuously felt. "That which protects the Diverse we call opacity," writes Glissant (1997, 65), reminding us that the diverse cannot be reduced to the ripple of a surface effect. Indistinct and unexplored yet fertile, opacity recognizes the merest of existences. Sensitive to the minor movements released through the instauration of new modes of existence, opacity claims the uncertainty of the as-yet-unknowable as its strongest ally. Diversity is *in diversity*, not in opposition to a norm. This is what the minor gesture makes palpable, that variation that moves at the rhythm of the included middle, the being of relation. "When we speak of a poetics of Relation, we no longer need to add: relation between what and what?" (27).

The minor gesture activates the opacity of the movement of thought coursing through the occasion, tuning it to a future-pastness that alters the quality of the mode through which it will come to expression. Modes of existence are fundamentally altered by the as-yet-unthought, and it is this force-of-form that minor gestures make resonant. This is not to say that all of this occurs harmoniously. Minor gestures are no more harmonious or good than are any other gestures or modes of existence. How they come to be depends on the problems they take up. The intensification of experience is not necessarily positive or good. It is vital not to invest immediation with morality. How things come to be is always determined by the conditions that opened the way for their singular mode of expression. This is why there can be no general account of the minor, and certainly no general politics of immediation. The aesthetic yield always depends on the art of time as *way*, and on the practice it calls forth, and it is this that must be studied (and practiced) each time anew. This is the ethics of a politics of immediation.

Haecceities

A politics of immediation makes a case for an attunement to the most minute of variations. Our more-than humanness is rife with such variations, most of which we regularly ignore in favor of that version of the consolidation of experience from which we say "I." And sometimes that is the only way: consolidation does remain necessary in a world that tends to decry complexity and variation.

But the variation is there, and this variation, in all its nebulousness, far exceeds anything we might organize into the form of an identity simply located. We were always more-than. Similarly, the human as category was never fully capable of describing us, of including us; it was there as descriptive statement to tell us what we aren't. Those who fit neatly within its bounds have never needed to be included—they already speak from its center. And yet these orators of human-centeredness, these humanists for whom the world is a site to be governed, these neurotypicals who already know what it means to know, they are more-than human too. There is no human, only, as Wynter might say, descriptive statements that keep epistemologies of segregation, violence, and exclusion alive.

In the work of attuning to the more-than that composes us, and the more-than that eludes us, the most difficult concept remains that of the being of relation. How to speak of what animates our coming into being but is not us? How to write from the middling of experience in a way that situates us as participants, not leaders of the action? How to not give in and create witnesses and advocates that mediate experience, introducing external measures of value into experience? How to speak of that which absolutely isn't us but nonetheless affects the "we" we are becoming? How to write of modes of existence that are so other that they don't even register? Or if they register, do so such that they leave us searching for ways to account for their radical difference without reclaiming them as our own?

A politics of immediation begins here, in the not-knowing. For in the middling there is never a knowing-in-advance. What there are are haecceities, qualities that are yet to come into full presence but that nonetheless already make the merest of differences. These haecceities of existence carry with them a thisness, an affective tonality, but no form as such. They are the atmosphere that permeates the associated milieu of existence in-forming. They are the stuff of relation. They are the relational tenor of incipiencies that may never come to form but will nonetheless always have been felt, if not by us, then by the world.

Atmosphere is a relationscape that escapes any kind of mediation. It may include us, but it also always exceeds us, its feltness a contributory factor in experience that moves through us without ever being only about us. Always more-than what actualizes, atmosphere is carried by that which comes into being but is not limited to being. It affects and is affected, qualifying experience. It has no form, only force. And yet all taking-forms are affected by it. As pure relation it never operates alone. Atmosphere could perhaps be said to be that which conditions all that is relational, that which moves through all that comes into contact.

Brian Massumi connects atmosphere to affective tonality, suggesting that affective tonality is "the leading edge of experience" (2017b). Atmosphere is the background of that leading edge, a "diffuse vitality affect" (Massumi 2019, 296). Every instauration brings with it an atmosphere. This atmosphere is the quality, the color of that intensification.

A politics of immediation requires an attunement to these haecceities that condition experience without foregrounding themselves as events in their own right. How to attune to the force of a collectivity, to the quality of a "mutual envelopment" (Massumi 2017b) that is atmosphere? How to speak of the condition of what it leaves unfelt? How to encounter its nebulousness without attempting to make it our own, to make it some*thing*? How to compose with the how of coming-to-act in a way that allows for modes of becoming that exceed the form of being, encouraging an artfulness that is sensitive to the aesthetic yield of the event?

This requires new gestures, new postures—new in the sense of emergent to the event, activated from the event's middling. And it requires new modes of narration, new techniques of writing, new practices of living. Following Saidiya Hartman, we must learn to write history differently, challenging the mediating models that are used to mobilize and strengthen existing forms of valuation, forms of valuation that tend to privilege those modes already in existence, modes too often seeped in the epistemologies of colonialism and the identity practices colonialism breeds, including all of the ways academia values the stance of objectivity and distance, always in the name of the unnamed neurotypicality (whiteness) that lurks at its core.[13] This is not an easy task, especially when dealing with the unspeakable violences of colonialism and the racism it breeds.

Speaking of her book *Lose Your Mother*, Hartman asks, "How does one write about history that is the encounter with nothing, or write about a past that has been obliterated so that even traces aren't left?" (2008a, 4). Her uneasy answer is to fashion modes of encounter, through writing, that restage the conditions of experience from the perspective of a pastness future-presenting. Instead of working from an academic distance, only with the archives of colonialism, Hartman chooses to write history into existence, collaborating with the unsayable, that which cannot be rendered discernible by an archive whose task was always to stabilize the traces of what fell out of the frame. Archival legibility always coincides with an account of value. Archives are registers of what can be registered. The merest existences do not traverse them unaided. Moving away from the work of academic critique, Hartman opts for "a revolutionary imagination that wants to discover, institute, initiate a new way of telling" (6). Instead of being the mediator of the archive of history, she writes from the fabulating middle, discovering a voice that is both hers and not hers in the writing. Characters emerge in this way that populate the present, giving the force-of-form to histories violently erased and giving texture to those merest of existences that shift the contours of what matters—what comes to matter—in the telling. This act of immediation, the writing from within the narrative to allow a bodying to unfold, is a radical act.

The work of crafting new modes of existence will never be possible if we situate ourselves in the position of the critic, observing the world from a mediating distance. Across her books, Hartman's prose teaches us to write in the opacity of the being of relation. Speaking back to the insufficient archive, coloring it in when she needs to, always in movement, wayward, Hartman composes with what echoes diagonally, on the angle of the inexpressible. In an approximation of proximity she writes history's acrossness, layering past and future, deeply concerned with what still needs to be said about the lives destroyed by slavery and its afterlife, while at the same time securing corners of joy where a stealing away can recast, for an instant, the bonds not defined by property and propriety. Immediation. Writing a belief into the world despite the horrors she recounts,[14] Hartman's immanent critique is an aesthetics of the earth, as Glissant (1997) might say, concerned to texture the infrathin of time erased and superimpose it on our own contemporary tendency to choose transparency over opacity.[15] But transparency can only ever be reductive, a generalization tethered to the status quo: "Either the other is assimilated, or else it is annihilated. That is the whole principle of generalization and its entire process" (Glissant 1997, 49). Forging ahead with a technique of opaque archival excavation, Hartman composes with the merest of existences to foster an expression of what exceeds any archive, any stronghold for experience made static.

Only immanent critique can do the work of immediation—critique that moves from the force of the in-act to discover not only what the conditions of a singular mode of existence are but what its merest existences reveal. Critique that stands in as judge and mediator of experience will leave things firmly in place.

Immediation is a practice. It is an act, a verb. Relational to the core, it reminds us that time is never a stable state and that experience can never be reduced to that which is culled from the welter. Experience is atmosphere coupled with the cut of subtraction, the crest and the wave. Here, where "we look in two directions into time" (James 1890, 609), it is the more-than that defines us. A politics of immediation proposes this schizz of experience in-forming as the site of existence's potential.

Reprise: Beyond Identity

A passage from Fred Moten has haunted the writing of these words. In a parenthetical aside in a paper on the city and the commune, Moten cautions us as regards the critique of identity politics. Too often, he writes, critiques of identity politics are waged against "(non-male, non-straight, non-white) identity while courteously leaving politics to its own uncriticized devices" (2016b, 163).[16] How to raise the problem of identity positions in a way that doesn't perform this kind of gesture? How to problematize identity while remaining sensitive to the fact that for some the loss of a sense of stable identity may feel like the very same gesture as the colonial act of exclusion from the category of the human? How not to engage in re-disenfranchising those very bodies that have historically been denied subjectivity? How to create an affirmative politics of a production of subjectivity that does not ignore that alliances are crucial in the face of the systemic violence of oppression?

The task, it seems to me, involves recasting alliance such that it need no longer be subsumed to identity and, by extension, to the bounded individual. The bounded individual, that pet figure of neoliberalism, is nothing more than the other side of the subject, which is the other side of the human. To focus on the individual as the harbinger of identity, to make the politics about the individual, is to reinstall a mediation that knows in advance how to recognize the human as orienter of experience. The problem of identity must instead be engaged from the perspective of Wynter's "descriptive statement" of the human. This category of the human, as Wynter underscores, is concerned to perpetuate a *genre* of the human (Wynter and McKittrick 2015, 9). What kinds of sociality cut across this genre?

The kind of identity politics Moten gestures toward remains attached to the genre of the human installed by the colonial practices that still serve as the ground from which we claim our identities. It is no doubt the case that many, if not most, critiques of identity serve to sideline those very people who have already been uncounted. It is also clearly the case that from a perspective always pretending to be neutral, critiques of identity serve to reinstall the primacy of the white, neurotypical subject position. This brand of identity-politics policing refuses to be sensitive to the ways in which exclusion from the category of the human continues to permit the perpetuation of violence and segregation. And, too often, as Moten underscores, it proposes no creative encounter with sociality, no other ways of thinking of alliance. *It proposes no other practices.*

A critique of identity politics must always be an engagement with what else it can mean to be human *as praxis.* A critique of identity politics must commit to more-than human forms of sociality. It must come from the unsettledness of giving up on the genre of the human, which too many of us take for granted. A critique of identity politics must coincide with the creation of new modes of existence that do not privilege our preconstituted position but engage deeply with the will to art that opens the world to minor gestures. A critique of identity politics can therefore never be spoken in our name. Beginning in the middle, working from a politics of immediation, a critique of identity politics must learn to compose with the haecceities that exceed us, with the subtractions that make us.

I consider neurotypicality to be a pervasive form of identity politics that, precisely because it chiefly remains unspoken, has profound effects on the conditions of experience for anyone who doesn't easily fit within the parameters it sets up to frame the human. These parameters tend to be based on the policing of intelligence and, by extension, of the very capacity to be a (human) body.

The policing of the category of the human happens in an infinite number of ways. Two that stand out in relation to neurodiversity are the performance of exclusion based on motor difference and on spoken language. Bodies that tic or stim, bodies that appear disorganized, are too often considered to be bodies without anything to say. These bodies are cast aside as having no contribution to make to humanity. Intelligent bodies are bodies that stand still, their subjectivity demonstrated by the very fact that they seem to control their gestures. Bodies that command their own movements are knowing bodies. Add to this modes of communication that are not oriented around speech and you have full-fledged exclusion. The consequences are complex: neurodiversity too often continues to be excluded from mainstream education not because the neurodiverse are not fully capable of participating, but because accommodations will not be made for their modes of functioning. This is not only due to the lack of imagination within education. This is also due to a widespread neurotypical account of knowledge that gives no value to other ways of coming to knowledge and feels no urgency to learn how else learning can happen. Autistic Amy Sequenzia knows this situation well. She explains:

> I am a self-advocate and I can type my thoughts. But, at the moment I show up with my communication device and an aide, my credibility, in the eyes of most neurotypical people, is diminished.

This is a constant battle for non-speaking autistics. Even the ones among us who have demonstrated, many times, their capabilities, and who have succeeded despite all the hurdles a disability imposes, these successful cases don't seem to be enough to end the myths: that non-speaking autistics cannot self-advocate; that the so-called "low-functioning" cannot think by themselves, cannot have ideas or opinions. Looking very disabled or needing more physical help does not make us unable to think, being critical, being able to analyze. (Sequenzia 2012b)

To know cannot be limited to neurotypical definitions of knowledge. "We, autistics, have tried hard and accepted the neurotypical way of doing things to make it easier for non-autistic people to understand us, interact with us," Sequenzia continues. Neurotypicality cannot be the barometer of experience, nor can, by extension, the category of the human upheld by neurotypicality.

This extends to black life, which is also excluded from the *genre* of the human. Black life is neurodiverse to the core if neurodiversity speaks to a difference that cannot be assimilated, a diversity *in diversity*. It follows, then, that any critique of neurotypicality—which will always be a critique of identity politics as I understand it—must be extended such that it can also become a critique of racism and colonization and any other exclusion perpetuated by the category of the human.

To do this work, modes of knowing differently must be valued. These modes can include language, but to situate them only within language would be once again to put the human at the center. So many other forms of knowing are active in the conjugation between atmosphere and subtraction. These modes include movement, texture, touch, and they include much more that is too mere for us to perceive, let alone categorize. These too are worth study, and this is the work decolonization must take up.

Finally, following Moten, we must not "leav[e] politics to its own uncriticized devices." We must be careful not to situate politics in the realm of those very categories that exclude us, the "we" we are becoming. A politics of immediation orients around a concept of the political that itself must be invented anew with each occasion of experience. With this call for invention comes the call to be vigilant about the category of the human, to think differently about where "we" begin and end, and to create movements of thought, modes of knowing, that depart from a place that is infested with the legacy of colonialism and the barren imagination it leaves behind. Turning instead to the aesthetic yield of experience in the making—to an aesthetics of the earth—what if we began with the haecceities that blur our contours, seeing these new ecologies not as less-than the subjects we are accustomed to being but as infinitely more-than?

nestingpatching

A nestingpatching pocket practice reverberates with the question of how sociality is crafted. Sociality lived in the making is tuned, here, to Laura Harris's concept of "an aesthetic sociality of blackness." Blackness, as Harris is quick to point out, is not meant to "renaturalize the 'coterminous relationship' that [Hortense] Spillers seeks to denaturalize between blackness and the black people who perform it" (2018, 4). Blackness is "not a matter, or not only a matter, of genetic or biological descent" (4). It is also "not just a people" (4). Blackness is "a whole field of biological and nonbiological elements that are put in play in the kinds of 'assembly' that constitute the forms of this aesthetic sociality" (4). Blackness is the defiant and joyful insurgency that reminds us, at every turn, that the question of sociality has nothing to do with 1 + 1. Blackness is the quality of sociality that makes of the assembly a field of relation.[1] Blackness is the desiring operation— aesthetic and social—that interrupts the narrow confines of category. "Grounded in the insistence on living otherwise," an aesthetics of black sociality eschews a strong concept of home as connected to stable existence, committed instead to "another idea of world" that is, in "its preoccupation with alternative existence, . . . explicitly and necessarily experimental" (9).

Harris sees in Helio Oiticica's work this force of black sociality.[2] The samba is the conduit. In 1964 Oiticica begins to study samba at the Morro de Mangueira, a favela in the north of Rio de Janeiro (Harris 2018, 27). Samba, a dance deeply connected to the Afro-Brazilian history of slavery, is arguably born in the favelas of Rio.[3] "The *passistas* [samba dancers] . . . seem to be inspired by the meandering space of the favela-labyrinth, as if they reproduced the movements of the body upon ascending the steep roads of the favela. The dance of samba would be in a mimetic with the rhythm of the changes" (Harris 2018, 42). Dance and architecture come together here to orchestrate "the development of an alternative sociality structured by its own aesthetic acts and aesthetic judgements" (40). Oiticica's practice moves out from here, the samba the motor of its expression.

Through what he sees as samba's "continuous transformability" and his experience of "the 'creative capacity' of the collectives to form in and through it," Oiticica mobilizes from samba its excess on itself. Samba, Oiticica's art makes felt, is much more than a dance form (quoted in Harris 2018, 37). Samba is a nest-in-motion, a force-of-form as textural as it is architectural.

Samba's uncontainment proposes an orientation away from the museum in favor of techniques of living for Oiticica. Coming to expression in his well-known *Parangolé*, textile-based propositions that defy fixed form to foreground movement, the turn toward sociality in Oiticica's work occasioned by samba's transformability in and of the everyday is emboldened by a deep rethinking of "the basic structural composition of the world of objects," learning how to appreciate textile's dance in defiance of the directing hand of the artist (Oiticica, quoted in Harris 2018, 46).

With the *Parangolé*, Oiticica creates a relational movement. Less object than field, the *Parangolé*, "a specifically experimental position," plays with the intensity and movement of samba: "multilayered, twisted, asymmetrical, unevenly weighted" with "multiple openings" and "wildly varying widths, lengths, and weights," the *Parangolé* suggests "no simple or single manner for engagement," making it "simultaneously aesthetic and social," "invented anew on each occasion" (Harris 2018, 43, 45–46). The *Parangolé* is the lived expression of the being of relation: the gathering-into-collectivity of a quality of movement. Allied deeply with Lygia Clark's relational objects—bags of sand and air and water that reorient qualities of experience through a schizosomatic proposition that schizes the very notion of the individual-as-structure—the *Parangolé* is an "unconditioning" of experience that choreographs, through movements unstyled and unrehearsed, otherwise modes of living.

If a pragmatics of the useless is a reorientation of value that activates infrathin modes of perception, the *Parangolé* might be said to be what moves infrathinly through all of Oiticica's work postsamba, keeping the disturbance between form and movement alive even in those artistic propositions that have harder edges. This is how I propose we encounter *Nests*, the more structured proposition pictured above. Indeed, *Nests* and *Parangolé* seem to me to already be incipiently in relation in the following description, where Oiticica sites the discovery of the term *Parangolé*, understood in the slang of the favelas as meaning "hearsay, pack of lies, line, fast talk" (Harris 2018, 46):

The use of the word *Parangolé* for these works is born from the discovery of it in a, if it can be said, *Parangolé*-structure in the urban landscape of Rio de Janeiro. This work was constituted of four pillars of wood tied up in a

rectangle, and from one to the other, forming a virtual wall, parallel threads from top to bottom. In each thread fine pieces of plastic were tied in loops, of various colours. The spatial sense of the nucleus that possessed the work is indescribable. Beyond this, a piece of burlap dropped down from one of the stakes, forming a little tent (within which the author slept, as I verified later); on this burlap was written the word *Parangolé*. Unfortunately I was not able to photograph the work due to an absolute lack of foresight that it would be so quickly broken down. (Oiticica, quoted in Harris 2018, 47)

Nests found their first iteration in Oiticica's loft in New York. This living space was an ideal site of experimentation.[4] Schizosomatic, their signature is in the quality of participation they call forth: the aim of *Nests* is not to acquire a finished architectural form but to be in a posture of continuous shaping in relation to the worlds invented through momentary inhabitation. Described by Vito Acconci as "pockets of privacy," the nests are less cubicles than "conjunctions" (quoted in Harris 2018, 98). For pockets are never apart, never separate: theirs is a sociality of relation, a cornering or edging that is always about the conduit more so than the boundary.

To think of art as conduit is to consider how it thresholds. Oiticica's *Nests* are techniques for thresholding—orientations for the coming into relation. With the force of the *Parangolé* always shimmering through them, *Nests* might be seen as the briefest inhabitation of those qualities of shape and movement that must always remain beyond capture. For the *Nests* are architectings more than they are architecture. Parangoling, they are mobile sites for aesthesis reinvented as a proposition for emergent sociality.

Suprasensation is the term Oiticica gives to the aesthesis he seeks through these experiments with sociality. He writes, "The most important proposition of the object, of the makers of objects, in my view, would be that of a new perceptual behaviour, created through increasing spectator participation, eventually overcoming the object as the end of aesthetic expression" (quoted in Harris 2018, 98). The suprasensorial—a new perceptual behavior—is the excess of, or expansion of, "usual sensory capacities" (Oiticica, in Harris 2018, 99). As experimental aesthesis, it might be said, following Brian Massumi, that the suprasensorial is supernormal: it carries, beyond the limit of sense, that force-of-form that "pulls experience forward, toward its own limit" (Massumi 2014, 17).

The supernormal is the intensely agitating more-than that accompanies all experience. Allied to the artful—the aesthetic yield that opens process to its emergent differential—the supernormal is the confirmation that what actualizes always includes a share that exceeds it. This anarchic share—the anarchival force of the infrathin that moves through experience in the making—is allied to what Alfred North Whitehead calls *nonsensuous perception*. The nonsensuous is not opposed to sense perception—it is the envelope of the more-than that moves with sensation, the force of sensation before it actualizes as sense. The supernormal, when allied to Oiticica's suprasensorial, acts as a reminder that the suprasensorial carries what exceeds sense as we know it. The suprasensorial is beyond sense, beyond perception of *what is*. Race and movement meet poverty and celebration meet sex and drugs meet belief in the world. For this is what *Nests* does best, it seems to me: it artfully invents mobile inhabitation for a more-than human sociality that is alive with a commitment to otherwise modes of life. In so doing, it does more than simply create architected spaces of encounter: it proposes to shift the very field of sensation. This aesthesis is its political pact, and it is here that the force of its black sociality makes itself felt.

The commitment to otherwise modes of life in Oiticica's work dances in the wound of the share of experience too often cast aside, and invents, at the interstices of what is overlooked and undervalued, what living might be when living is not a rehearsal for a time yet to come, but the more-than of living in the living itself. Like the samba, which, as Oiticica says, is always dance, never rehearsal, *Nests* lives that share of experience that, if valued, even for a moment, might shift the conditions of the everyday.[5] To practice an aesthetics of black sociality is to come into contact with the artfulness that resonates at the heart of the relation from which a sociality is crafted, artfulness never reducible to form as containment, to art as object.

The artfulness of *Nests* is palpable in Edward Pope's account of his visit to Oiticica's New York loft. Pope describes *Nests* as creating the conditions for "an indirect encounter" (quoted in Harris 2018, 97). Having left a set of poems behind in one of the nests, Pope is surprised to hear them being read out loud as he is on his way out of the loft. Listening to the words at a distance, he is moved by the quality of the sideways potentiality he sees in Oiticica's living work. This indirect sociality is the work's artfulness, a quality of relation that tunes the environment away from the interpersonal $(1+1)$ toward a more neurodiverse sociality $(n+1)$—a capacity to feel-with the tendencies of the more-than human ecology reverberating across spaces, fissures, sounds, touches, resonances. This tending to the more-than amplifies the qualities of expression that exceed normative human interaction, allowing the interplay to be in excess of cause-effect. More-than the sum of its parts, *Nests* facilitates an engagement with what exceeds the terms of human encounter to make felt all that surrounds it, all that moves through it. Despite producing configurations for human encounter, *Nests* is all about the lure of what is left behind, of what is impersonally seeded. In the case of the sounding of the poem, the experience in germ cannot be reduced either to the poet, to the poetry, or to the people reading the poems. What emerges in the sounding is the differential of expression: the sound carries the touch, the gesture itself of participation, and yet is in excess of it. The differential activated between the encountering, the leaving-behind, and the seeding allows the emergent architecture to create a field of relation that exceeds the human-all-too-human construct of the interpersonal. *Nests* are anything but a simple site for interpersonal encounter: "extra-exhibition, extra-work, more than a participating object, a context for behaviour, for life; the *Nests* propose an index of multiplication, reproduction, communal growth" (Oiticica, quoted in Harris 2018, 101). In the quest toward the suprasensorial, what *Nests* gesture toward is the invention of a more-than human inhabitation that produces new ways of coming into encounter with what exceeds the personal. This is artfulness: not the work itself but the *way* the work spurs an intensive recalibration of what already exceeds the structure. Artfulness is the extra-work at work. *Faire-oeuvre.*

If the *Parangolé* is seen as a moving color field that produces space through emergent relationality, the resonances between *Parangolé* and *Nests* become apparent, for *Nests*, too, reworks the architectural through incipient movement. This is its proposition—to produce sites of encounter for a world in composition, more dance than structure. Ad hoc, reminiscent of the hastily built architecture from which the term *Parangolé* was born, that inhabitation too short-lived to be photographed, *Nests* is nothing like a finished structure:

> [*Nests*] shouldn't be realized in an overly researched or complex way but rather, improvised, by hand and body. . . . It is best if the thing is interminable. . . . Of course these are still introductory propositions for a much wider aim: the total-communal-cell activity. They exist as a plan for a practice, an open plan that can be expanded, gr o o o ow. . . . People + time + the possibility of expansion > the idea of form and structure will not exist: the past of "structural necessity" grows to the now of "existence or not": something lies in wait for the possibility to manifest itself and awaits > ultra-waits. (Oiticica, quoted in Harris 2018, 102–3)

Moving from "self-founding" to "supra-forming," what is proposed by *Nests* is variation on existence (Oiticica, in Harris 2018, 113). "Kindergarten, playground, laboratory, motel, mouth, university campus," *Nests* are worlds as yet unimagined, carrying the more-than of what artfully courses through them (Waly Salomâo, quoted in Harris 2018, 104).

Supraforming—that catching of the supernormal tendency in architectural formation—is the force of *Nests*' emergent sociality. This aesthetic sociality of blackness is described by Harris as an "ongoing recollective but also innovative and experimental insurgent expression" (2018, 4). Emphasizing "blackness's uncontainment," its resistance "to the very idea of ownership," an aesthetic sociality of blackness would always be architecturally supraforming: living in the edging-into-themselves of architectures to come (5). This "insistence on finding ways to live otherwise" that Harris sees in the black radical tradition is not a metaphor (33). "Living otherwise" *is* the force of black life. It is the lived necessity and celebration of a quality of living that moves beyond the sited individual to catch a sociality in the making. It is black in this refusal of the one, of the single, personal, already-recognized, bounded human. It is neurodiverse in this same refusal. To emphasize its blackness, its neurodiversity, is to articulate a commitment against the interpersonal, whiteness's limited-to-the-personal neurotypical commitment to property and propriety. "People come together here because they are black. But at the same time, they are black because they come together here. Their congregation is a necessity, for they often have nowhere else to go. This necessity, in which containment and refuge are combined, gives rise to creative practices that explore the radical possibilities of living otherwise" (32–33).

Living otherwise, building nests for socialities-to-come in defiance of property and propriety, requires a deep commitment to Denise Ferreira da Silva's "difference without separability" (2016). Difference without separability is a way of speaking to that sociality in motion that resists the sequestering of the $1 + 1$. By emphasizing that it is the being of relation that is crafted in an aesthetics of black sociality, relation the radically empirical force of all that is carried by the coming together in the excess of the two, difference without separability resists the interpersonal, that most violent weapon of normopathy.[6]

With whiteness as the emblem of neurotypicality, the interpersonal moves at the pace of the norm, revealing a systemic operation more than an individual pathology. This is to say: whiteness is a normopathic condition that incessantly returns to the empty figure of the $1 + 1$, a dramaturgy of frontality that only ever serves to reproduce the self-same. For the self-same to operate—which is to say, to reproduce the whiteness that benefits from it—exclusion must remain at the forefront. The interpersonal thrives in the difference *with* separation that ensues, the one already reproduced as same, same, same. For whiteness, in all its overprivileged violence, is remarkably uncreative: it recognizes only what differs from its image of itself. Same, same, same, other. From here, nothing is possible except the reiteration of what has already been (re)produced.

No sociality is at work here. Sociality has been choreographed out of the equation in the commitment to policing the terms of the encounter. What remains: the form of exclusion. To count is to be counted. $1 + 1 + 1 + 1$. Nothing in excess, nothing in germ. Policing, frontality, amplification of the structure. Because that is all whiteness can mobilize: an empty space barricaded from the inside.

To imagine existence excluded from sociality is to have a sense of how limited whiteness is—an existence so narrow as to be a mirage. And yet a mirage that blows itself out of proportion at every turn. This is the power of neurotypicality: that it can structure whole existences without itself existing as such. Whiteness is that very paradox—a mirage policed to retain that which it ultimately never had, that which it never is.

Harney connects the limits of the interpersonal with the concept of the ally. "Who is this someone in solidarity with blackness," he asks, "who is this ally of blackness, who is this someone with affinity to black struggle?" (2017). To be an ally suggests having a sociality from which to draw. And yet there is no sociality in whiteness, only interpersonality. Only neurotypicality. There is no differential in whiteness, no field of relation that could tune toward socialities in the making. No being of relation. Whiteness is in fact that which can never be an emergent collectivity precisely because it is bounded, fixed, sited. Norm, mirage, whiteness is deadening of life. There is no bridge from whiteness to sociality. "The problem is, there's no such thing as a white community. A white community is a contradiction in terms, an oxymoron. You can't organize an oxymoron. The only thing you can do with a white community is work to abolish it" (Harney 2017).

An aesthetic sociality of blackness undercommons the interpersonal. Sociality must never be reduced to commonality. Nesting in difference, what it foregrounds is a potential for a suprasensorial otherwise. This suprasiting is undercommon in every sense: it invents not only sites for the living but modes of encounter for the emergent creaturing, a coming into relation not of the human but of the more-than human. Identity and category are not its motor. And yet, as Harris rightly emphasizes, "people come together here because they are black. But at the same time, they are black because they come together here." There must never be a question that in the approximation of proximity of neurodiversity and black life, blackness has a profound commitment to those who are black. To be black is to be invented in the emergent relation of a sociality that most emphatically sidles those who are descendants of its necessity. To be black is to be in paraontological relation to all that blackness invents. With, across, and despite this vital caveat that reminds us that white people have privileged access to whiteness and grow up in proximity to its modalities of power, benefiting from them at every turn, in the nests of the suprasiting of undercommon sociality, what comes together is not a constituency predetermined but a field of relation. This field might be called "black study," an intellectuality in the living that moves the living into the thinking. Black study can take the quasi-form of a field of color moving in the wind, or dance itself into nests. It is a *way*, not a form. In this wild, decomposing field, "people who present as white are not allies, or in solidarity, or showing affinity, because they have nothing of their own, no place from which to show this, no resource to bring, unless and until they embrace the one thing of their own they disown. The thing that can't be owned born(e) of the owned, blackness" (Harney 2017).

The interpersonal is another word for a human constellation that already understands itself as the central pivot of existence. The interpersonal is what holds the liberal humanist subject together, a subject that exposes itself as white at every turn. Saidiya Hartman's *Scenes of Subjection* emphasizes this overlap: "In considering the metamorphosis of chattel into man catalyzed by the abolition of slavery, I think it is important to consider the failure of Reconstruction not simply as a matter of policy or as evidence of a flagging commitment to black rights, which is undeniably the case, but also in terms of the limits of emancipation, the ambiguous legacy of universalism, the exclusions constitutive of liberalism and the blameworthiness of the freed individual" (1997, 6). Freedom comes to be tethered to the notion of the human as defined by a universalism wherein the unanswered question remains whether "the appellation 'human' can be borne equally by all" (6).

The connection between universalism and the interpersonal may seem tenuous, but only if we underestimate the legacy of the model of the individual—of personhood—championed by whiteness. In *The Minor Gesture* I explored what I called the "volition-intentionality-agency triad" (2016, 6). The concern was how this triad produces neurotypicality as the measure of lived experience. By emphasizing how the volition-intentionality-agency triad makes the subject the subject of experience, the aim was to give an account of what is unregistered in experience by those modes of encounter that fall outside the model of volition. Focusing primarily on neurodiversity, the proposition was "to turn away from the central tenet of neurotypicality, the wide-ranging belief that there is an independence of thought and being attributable above all to the human, a better-than-ness accorded to our neurology (a neurology, it must be said, that reeks of whiteness, and classism). Neurotypicality, as a central but generally unspoken identity politics, frames our idea of which lives are worth fighting for, which lives are worth educating, which lives are worth living, and which lives are worth saving" (3).

Hartman makes an adjacent argument around blackness and black life: "Suppose that the recognition of humanity held out the promise not of liberating the flesh or redeeming one's suffering but rather of intensifying it. What if the presumed endowments of man—conscience, sentiment, and reason—rather than assuring liberty or negating slavery acted to yoke slavery and freedom?" (1997, 5). Taking on the project of asking how "humanity and individuality acted to tether, bind and oppress," Hartman explores the concept of freedom from the perspective of "'will,' 'agency,' 'individuality' and 'responsibility,'" each of which is intrinsically tethered to the deployment of the human as figure of the project of humanism (6). In the afterlife of slavery, she underscores, wherein there are "tragic continuities in . . . constitutions of blackness," it is key is to "investigate the construction of the subject" in order to better understand "the forms of subjectivity and circumscribed humanity imputed to the enslaved" (6, 11).

The interpersonal takes as its mouthpiece the individual, bounded, self-possessed subject. It reduces any and all encounters to a setting-into-place of a choreography of self-recognition.[7] What Hartman calls "performing blackness" is a clear refusal of this imposition of the interpersonal on experience. Blackness in every sense is resistance to the interpersonal—not only because blackness by its very nature is excluded from the humanism of the interpersonal, but because blackness in every way exceeds the universalized subject. In the exclusion of blackness from the project of the universal subject, in the reduction of freedom to a burdened individuality, blackness was simply never solicited to recognize itself in the volition-intentionality-agency triad. Blackness never became neurotypical. Blackness, as Hartman shows with such care, instead became *practice*. Blackness: the practice of modes of living that move beyond the identitarian frame that recognizes nothing more than its self-centrality.

Hartman defines blackness as "social relationality rather than identity." Blackness "incorporates subjects normatively defined as black, the relations among blacks, whites, and others; and the practices that produce racial difference." Blackness "is a contested figure at the very center of social struggle" that refuses to be sequestered by the bounded exclusion propelled by humanism and its universalizing categorization of the volitional individual as mobilized by the dominant figure of the political: "Too often the interventions and challenges of the dominated have been obscured when measured against traditional notions of the political and its central features: the unencumbered self, the citizen, the self-possessed individual, and the volitional and autonomous subject" (1997, 56, 57, 61). The volition-intentionality-agency triad that haunts neurotypicality is upended by blackness, which cannot be made discernible within the measure of the interpersonality that segregates and directs experience from the colonial position of the all-seeing I, which by necessity always stand alone. To say that blackness is aesthetically social is to remember, at every turn, that aesthesis performs an engagement with the infrathin suprasensorial, tuned and attuned to all that escapes dominant accounts of segregated encounter. To sense blackly, aesthetically, is to be in the feel's feeling, in the included middle of the being of relation.

The interpersonal is the emblem of the very definition of all that is excluded by whiteness: blackness cannot be self-possessed, cannot be bounded and unencumbered. Blackness is not "person": "Slaves are not consensual and willful actors, the state is not a vehicle for advancing their claims, they are not citizens, and their status as persons is contested" (Hartman 1997, 65). In the afterlife of slavery, this uneasy relationship to the politics of the personal remains, and it is here that Hartman makes her strongest contribution, demonstrating the necessity for a rethinking of practice as a challenge to the dominant politics of the interpersonal:

> The importance of the concept of practice is that it enables us to recognize the agency of the dominated and the limited and transient nature of that agency. The key features of practice central to this examination of agency of the enslaved are the nonautonomy of the field of action; provisional ways of operating within the dominant space; local, multiple, or dispersed sites of resistance that have not been strategically codified or integrated; and the nonautonomy and pained constitution of the slave as person. The barring of these practices from the political, as traditionally conceived, has a range of consequences and effects that concern the constitution of the subject, the feasibility and appropriateness of certain forms of action, the incommensurability of liberal notions of will and autonomy as standards for evaluating subaltern behavior, the inscription of agency as criminal or, at the very least, as deserving of punishment, and the inadequacy and incompleteness of redress. (61–62)

The political must be refashioned by practice, and this refashioning requires a turning away from the interpersonal toward an aesthetic sociality of blackness that refutes the orienting framework of the "self-possessed individual," leading toward a concept of blackness that moves "even without a 'person,' in the usual meaning of the term" (65).

The interpersonal is whiteness playing itself out, reminding itself that it must always claim the center (precisely because it *is* not). The interpersonal is the violence of that claim that compulsively places whiteness in the center, that compulsively reaches for a center as though such a thing existed. This centrality is a fantasy that the interpersonal as form plays out, "a fantasy that shoots real bullets" (Moten, in Harney and Moten 2017b).

There is no defense against a mirage. But there are otherwise ways of practicing. An aesthetics of black sociality is not a sociality among many. It is the otherwise sociality that invents itself at the edges of an anti-aesthetic, asocial interpersonal world. Alive with neurodiverse socialities—socialities of the more-than—it challenges the very question of personhood as the matrix of existence.

"There is no such thing as a good white person because there is no such thing as a good person," Moten emphasizes. "To be a person is to be a white person," Harney responds (in Harney and Moten 2017b).

A pragmatics of the useless moves at the pace of the supernormal in the quality of the infrathin, not the interpersonal. At its undercommon edges, the infrathin is always and only passage. An aesthetics of black sociality is not a state. It is an artfulness that reinvents at every experimental crossing the quality of expression it leaves behind. That is to say, an aesthetics of black sociality is as wary of site as is the undercommons that fleetingly sites it. It "exists in/as the general antagonism. It is always anti-colonial, always fugitive" (Harney 2017).

Harney (2017) warns: "Blackness is neither the opposite nor the total reversal or abolition of whiteness." Where whiteness is mirage, fantasy, blackness is aesthesis attuned to the being of relation. This is never to negate that blackness *matters*. It is to emphasize that, more-than form, in excess of a given shape, blackness is the lived expression of the coming into relation activated through socialities yet to be invented. It is the ontogenesis that builds worlds in excess of the ontological that excludes it. It is *Parangolé, Nests*. Perhaps it is also patch.

Patch emerged at SenseLab over a three-year period spent materially experimenting with the threshold.[8] Practicing the schizz in a way deeply indebted to the work of Lygia Clark, SenseLab's exploration of the threshold continues to take many forms, asking at each interstice how thresholds are crossed and what kinds of sociality the crossings facilitate. Though not claiming to engage directly in an aesthetics of black sociality, what has moved SenseLab over these years of practice nonetheless connects to an undercommon sociality, one always committed to neurodiverse qualities of expression and relation. A nestingpatching pocket practice asks, tentatively, whether the relation between black life and neurodiversity might allow for a bringing into relation of nest and patch to explore the more-than human share in the production of sideways socialities.

Patch began as a "lure for feeling."[9] A lure for feeling, in Whitehead's vocabulary, is a motor for propositional forms of thought in the act. If the Whiteheadian proposition is the field of intensity through which new modes of existence come to expression, patch might be thought as the sideways activator for a propositional feeling that shifts the conditions of thresholding. When I think patch, I always think cat: that jacket left on the side table that immediately becomes the cat's nest. Patch is that pull, that tug on spacetime that allows for new ways of entering and nesting.

What was needed at SenseLab when patch was collectively composed was a way of facilitating an entering that could also segue into a leaving, frontality evaded. An unsettling of geometry, patches, it turned out, could trouble the horizontal-vertical axis, allowing the ground to layer into textures that might allow for what Arakawa and Madeline Gins call a "dimensionalizing landing site." "A *dimensionalizing landing site* lands simultaneously narrowly and tightly and widely and diffusely . . . coupling and coordinating direct responses with indirect ones, the formed with the formless. . . . [A] dimensionalizing landing site, in landing, hooks onto the environment to gain traction on it. With the hook-and-rope ensemble flung out and an availing surface caught hold of, there comes to be an as-if-tugging-back-to-the-body that conveys a sense of (kinesthetic) depth" (2002, 8). The crafting of a landing site at SenseLab, understood as facilitating an emergent dimensionality, grew around the spatial proposition made possible by the cube.

The cube, which lived for a year or so at SenseLab in Montreal, was the first activator of a more-than human sociality capable of breaking the container of the classroom. The cube could do this work because of its capacity to reorient the frame. Neurotypical frames orient all action in the university. Frontal, they predetermine where the action takes place. Emphasis on action delimits participation: the professor speaks in front, the student participates behind. What the cube did was to reorient that relation. Redistributing space, it allowed a different constellation to emerge. But alone, it still carried the latent tendency of centralizing attention despite blurring the edges of the container. Patch was the first experiment to multiply—to dimensionalize—its architecture.

Leslie Plumb 2018

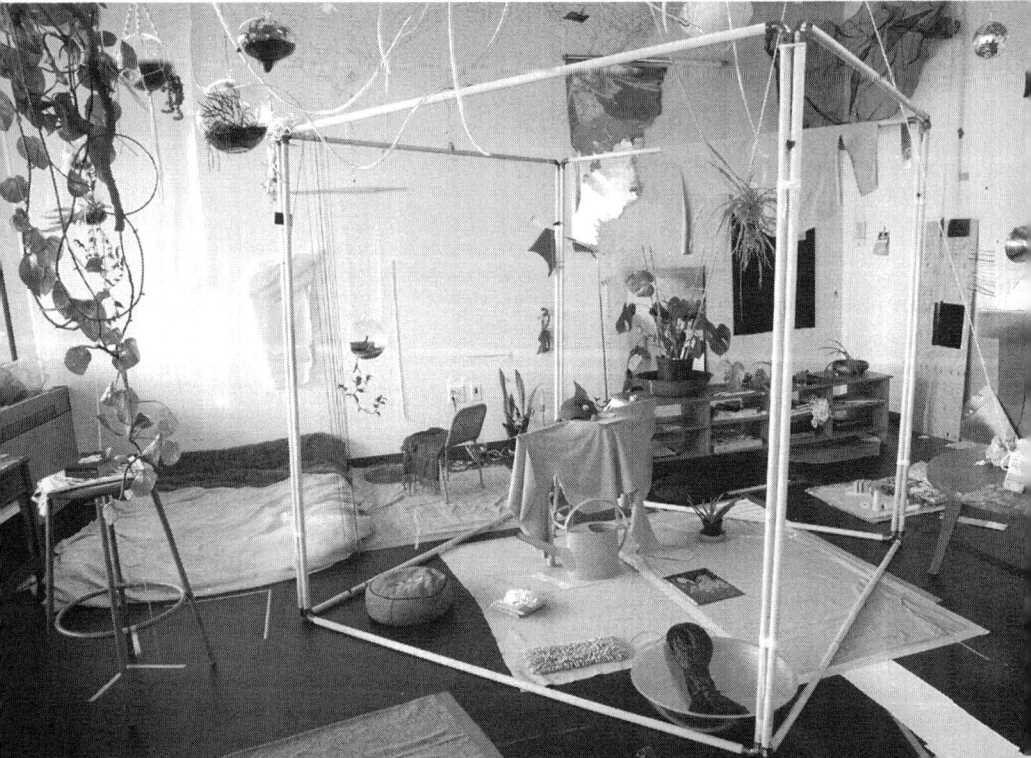

Leslie Plumb 2018

Patch is both line and surface. It is both orientation and color field. Lines of tape sometimes cross it—particularly if there is a need for transversality.

Patch often appears by happenstance. The goal of patch is not to create a fixed architecture. Patch is a mobile transformer. It moves with the movements of the space itself.

Nestingpatching does not create new modes of thresholding once and for all—undercommon socialities are always serial. Nestingpatching is a *practice* for undercommoning the landings that facilitate the creation of environments hospitable to socialities themselves undercommon. For this to occur, landings must be tended. As Arakawa and Gins underscore, landing sites such as patch—sites that activate a dimensionalizing of experience without imposing a metrics—are "tentative constructing[s] toward a holding in place" (2002, 23).

Less site than assemblage, nestingpatching comes into itself in a necessity that expresses itself as emergently social. N + 1, nestingpatching is not about human conviviality above all. A nestingpatching pocket practice can be as solitary as the cat sleeping on your jacket. While it can and often does include the human, it is not limited to it—a patch of sun may be a lure for a taping-down that carries the warmth into the evening, allowing you to remain longer in a collective space. A nestingpatching pocket practice moves with its own material demands, following the lead. Humans nest and are nested in the practice.

This is the work of patch—to catch differentials in the making. If *Nests* is the "ultrawaits" of "something lies in wait for the possibility to manifest itself," patch is the practice of catching the waiting in the doing.

Nestingpatching indexes other ways of thresholding. Its tendencies are vectorizing. Never a simple rehearsal, this pocket practice dances, its dance pulling the world with it, a world felt in each patch of sunlight that lures a creature. An uncontainment in material expression, nestingpatching proposes a sensitivity to the sideways qualities of entering too often bulldozed by the frontality of the interpersonal and its ways of guarding the neurotypical norm and the whiteness it celebrates. Harris speaks of Oiticica as an "apprentice-practitioner" of an aesthetic sociality of blackness. This is all we can hope for: that the artfulness of expression active at the interstices of worlds can move the apprentice-practitioner to practice threshold-shifting in ways that recognize the violence of the interpersonal and the white neurotypicality that sustains it.

In an approximation of proximity, nestingpatching brings two tendencies into resonance, activating the differential of blackness and neurodiversity. If nest catches sociality in the making, architecting its passage, patch dimensionalizes it. In their acrossness, what stands out is their shared mode of tending a world seeding itself. Sociality is not about a group. Sociality is the quality that shifts the conditions of a relational field. Oiticica's aim with *Nests* was never simply to gather people. *Nests* are tentative constructings toward a holding in place. We must take Oiticica at his word when he says that *Nests* remain unfinished, their sociality less in the form than in the passage.

Patch is passage.

Patch is a material reminder that the line is never purely horizontal or vertical, that the surface surfaces in the vectoring. Patch is transversal. It dances the encounter diagonally into existence, realigning a body.

The thresholding patch facilitates an emergent coming into relation of texture, vector, and color: the thick, glossy redness of the tape against the soft blue cashmere that turns table into bench into tent into napping zone; the line of green on the pink cutting the field into an diagonality that invites a flying-across-

Leslie Plumb 2018

the-room sidling gesture. Or, when necessary, furniture-as-patch to cross the line, to thicken the space cut by the cube, to move the square into a new shape, to invite a quality of behindness that welcomes not only a body but the light refracting on a cardboard surface.

An aesthetic sociality of blackness is a call toward an artfulness that yields the aesthetic suprasensorially, supernormally. Agitating in a difference without separability, it does not name its inhabitants in advance. But it knows that the interpersonal will destroy it, and so it keeps whiteness at bay by moving-with the more-than that courses across it. The human-all-too-human in any case mistrusts it—what can possibly be learned in an environment that looks like a kindergarten, playground, laboratory, motel, mouth?

"Just art," they might say. "Useless." "Silly." Yes, a nestingpatching pocket practice is absolutely useless, claiming not a space of intelligibility but a thresholding into what is not yet known. SenseLab claims the uselessness, revels in its speculative pragmatism, committed to a quality of orientation that inflects the frontality we should no longer have to bear.

The room buzzes with a quality of activation that feels different. Attracted by the lure for feeling patch facilitates, we find ourselves drawn to a supernormal sensation carried by the materiality itself. The more-than moves us, we who are also always more-than. What is felt is a certain vibratory potential, a sense that things will keep moving, that they are already shifting. And that we too are participants in the shift, that ours is a creaturing, a bodying that leaves a material trace, that deviates in the tracing. Every entry into the nestingpatching is a composition, and every entry leaves not only a quality of sociality behind but a lure for future vectors. This is neurodiverse sociality—a kindling, always anew, of what else an undercommon encounter can seed and leave behind.

Undercommon encounters are messy affairs. A nestingpatching pocket practice crafts the messiness into an opportunity for recomposition. In this way, it is local. Always attuned to the forces of the environment in its site conditioning, nestingpatching makes no general claims about experience. Its tending toward blackness or neurodiversity is always shifting, and interpersonal, neurotypical encroachments of whiteness are never far away. It is not uncommon to be schooled on the illegibility of nestingpatching.

It is this very illegibility, alive and vectoring in an always-changing constellation of local concerns, that makes nestingpatching an artful ethos. It is the singularity of what a nest can do in the time of the "ultrawaits" that allows for a tinge of the differential to be felt. This tinge, enlivened by the supernormal artfulness of a gesture always tentative with respect to form, is what is at work in a nestingpatching pocket practice, a practice that is carried through each architecting of experience to ask anew what kinds of violence are alive in the limits of form we move through, be they our institutions or our homes, our cities or our hospitals.

Nothing less is at stake than citizenship, ownership, property, propriety. Every time the university claims to know how to apportion out space, every time the state claims to have a way of organizing bodies, we know that it is the interpersonal that will win out, an interpersonal that, while claiming it, has no capacity for anything close to culture, collectivity, or sociality. Remaining wary of the norm—the neurotypical norm casting its net on the inflections that open the world to the activity of the differential—is necessary. But the wariness cannot take over—this will only encourage us to succumb to the reigning logic of neurotypicality, of whiteness.

Oiticica, with Clark at his side, practiced the schizoanalytic propulsion the differential calls forth. He lived it. *Nests* are one of the ways he configured it, knowing all the while that they had to remain unstructured as a lure for feeling— that the *Parangolé* had to continue to dance through them. SenseLab didn't see the connection to Oiticica as we composed, yet in retrospect patch brings *Nests* and *Parangolé* into relation with it: it attunes to the artful thresholding Oiticica's practice calls forth. This is what materials do: they teach you how to move them, and how to be moved by them. Oiticica was less influence than confluence in this research, our work a schizz through the force of a practice he left open enough for us to enter into.

This notion of practice left ajar, open to confluence, brings us back to the uncontainment of blackness Harris speaks of. Black not only because this uncontainment carries the force of black study, of black intellectuality, of black life, but because it is coursed through with the impropriety of blackness as force-of-form, cut through by that very differential that refuses the binary of the individual and the collective. Black because transindividual. Nestingpatching begins here, at the transindividual nexus where patch meets nest and modes of sociality are crafted that multiply difference, their pockets of intimacy always in excess of the arithmetic of the $1+1$.

What Things Do When They Shape Each Other

In order to discover some of the major categories under which we can classify the infinitely various components of experience, we must appeal to evidence relating to every variety of occasion. Nothing can be omitted, experience drunk and experience sober, experience sleeping and experience waking, experience drowsy and experience wide-awake, experience self-conscious and experience self-forgetful, experience intellectual and experience physical; experience religious and experience sceptical, experience anxious and experience care-free, experience anticipatory and experience retrospective, experience happy and experience grieving, experience dominated by emotion and experience under self-restraint, experience in the light and experience in the dark, experience normal and experience abnormal. —Alfred North Whitehead, *Adventures of Ideas*

Bolder adventure is needed—the adventure of ideas, and the adventure of practice conforming itself to ideas. —Alfred North Whitehead, *Adventures of Ideas*

Method

"Every method is a happy simplification" (Whitehead 1967, 221). The thing is, all accounting of experience travels through simplification—every conscious thought but also, in a more minor sense, every tending toward a capture of attention, every gesture subtracted from the infinity of potential. And so a double bind presents itself for those of us moved by the force of potential, of the processual, of the in-act. How to reconcile the freshness, as Whitehead might say, of processes underway with the weight of experience captured? How to reconcile force and form?

The concept of the anarchive developed at SenseLab out of these questions. Our chief concern, over years of practice, had been how to catch that which resisted the archive. How else, beyond the archive, might we activate current traces toward future eventing? If an event is emphatically that which cannot be archived in advance of its eventing (because its eventing is precisely what makes it an event, and a pre-archiving of it would make the archive the event), what might be distilled from it that bypassed the archive and yet did the work of carrying the eventing forward? Our concern was always about the way capture for archival purposes registers a mode of valuation. What is held by the archive is necessarily what can be recognized by it. And so, should an alternative mode of capture be possible, what were the risks that it would take us right back into the archive's value system? Alternatively, what might be the relationship of the archive to this seeding forward?

These questions oriented years of practice. In weekly gatherings we folded and cut and moved with materials to better understand the materiality of what registered or was infrathinly ineffable. Resisting preconstituted notions of value, we practiced an ethos of a pragmatics of the useless, attempting to return anew to these materials week after week without the expectation of retrieval. Our posture was that of the speculatively pragmatic: respond to the specificity of the material intervention and follow its lead. This led to seeds of process (recordings, images, text, propositions) being put together into boxes and sent across hubs with an invitation to anarchive, seeking new tendencies from international collaborators working out the concept across their own local concerns. Upon receipt, the boxes were activated and then returned to the original hubs. With the return of the boxes, we tried to learn from them how anarchiving worked. Something was doing, but it was still unclear how the seeds would be capable of feeding forward in a context not our own. If the work of the anarchive was oriented toward creating a larger process seed bank that collectives, activists, philosophers, and artists might want to grow and share, how were the seeds we were creating going to find the independence from our process that would allow them to germinate elsewhere?

Our interest was never in creating an account of our activities. Our interest in the anarchive was in generating techniques for sharing the work's potential, the speculative edge of its pragmatic propositions. Our hope was to find a practice that would allow action traces to become mobilized across other environments of collective experimentation (and, if of interest, to give other collectives techniques for sharing their process with us).

Problems persisted: if the anarchive was about harnessing process, how would we do that without muting the very force we were after? After a few years, in a collective state of confusion, having at best been able to anarchive the process of anarchiving, we succumbed to our own messy archive of images, videos, recordings, writings, and artworks amassed over a decade of experimentation on four continents to ask whether the archive itself might be a departure for what else moves through it.[1] Did the anarchive need that archive? Had we been too stubborn in our refusal of form?

Whitehead's process philosophy goes to the heart of this conundrum. Against method, Whitehead's philosophy assists us in displacing the unnecessary dyad of force/form, archive/anarchive, giving us the tools to understand how all experience is made of cracks and captures, archival and anarchival at once.

As foregrounded in chapter 2, Whitehead's process philosophy requires that we become thinkers from the middle. To become acquainted with how experience works, process philosophy teaches us, we must see it both from the side of its creation (its passage from force to form) *and* from the side of its perishing (its passage from form to force). Coming in from the middle allows us to feel how all events are cuts in the passage of a process, subtractions from a welter of potential, and thus, to differing degrees, simplifications. This is because every event is an excision from a welter of unactualized force.

Differentiating force and form is necessary not because they are oppositions but precisely because they are so close, and so entwined. Tendencies of one another, force and form co-compose. To understand this co-composition, their differing contributions to the event must be attended to. When Whitehead says that a process philosophy is not interested in the continuity of becoming but in the becoming of continuity, he is emphasizing that experience is not born of pure flow, pure togetherness, pure continuity, but rather is created from capture, crack, and cut, continuously splintering from the field of potential to create new durations, new events. Events are of the relation, caught in the middling of its tensing in two directions at once. Relation as immanent to the occasion, relation of nonrelation: "The paradox of relation can be summed up in the term relation-of-nonrelation. Elements contributing to an occurrence come into relation when they come into effect, and they come into effect in excess over themselves. In themselves they are disparate. If they are in tension, it is precisely as a function of the differential between their positions. It is as a function of their distances from each other. The factors do not actually connect. Their distance is enveloped in a field effect that is one with the tension culminating in the strike of an event" (Massumi 2011, 20). When Whitehead writes that "the connectedness of things is nothing else than the togetherness of things in occasions of experience" and that "no things are 'together' except in experience; and no things are, in any sense of 'are,' except as components in experience or as immediacies of processes which are occasions in self-creation" (1967, 233, 236), he is referring to the relation of nonrelation at the heart of the occasion. There is no "general" togetherness, only a *togetherness in the event*. Massumi continues, "If we apply this concept of the relation-of-nonrelation to what occurs between occasions of experience, we are led to treat the experiences themselves as differentials. The consequence is that occasions of experience cannot be said to actually connect to each other. They may be said to 'come together' only in the sense of being mutually enveloped in a more encompassing event of change-taking-place that expresses their differential in the dynamic form of its own extra-being. That occasions of experience do not actually connect is Whitehead's doctrine of 'contemporary independence'" (2011, 20–21).

There is no thread connecting all experience a priori. There is no generalized concept of process. Relations are born of the event. All occasions of experience embody relation as the force of their coming together. This lived relation is the quality of force-of-form that accompanies all comings to form. To begin with relation (rather than form or process, the two limit concepts of the operation of an event's coming-to-be) serves to remind us that all along the way a process is lively with the force-of-form of relational intensity. There is no outside from which we could cut out part of the process of an occasion's coming-to-be, putting form on one side and process on the other. Relation is not in the middle, between the terms: it is the middling force of all tendings of process at every stage.

In this process of coming to form, relational tending everywhere active, the coming to form can be conceived as a perspective of the event on itself. It is in the "taking" of an event that this perspective is born. This perspective is a perspective not only on the form but on the process that still runs through it, halted momentarily by the shape the event has taken. Without form, there is only the wildness of what has not yet come to be, and there is no purchase for experience as we know it. What we know as the resonant field of force-form is not process as such but the differential active in the "taking" of form, a point of view of the occasion on itself. An occasion of experience is lively with that point of view, not a point but a differential, a cleaving, in the now of experience, of an always-differing force-form composition.

Continuing with Whitehead, the question becomes one of technique: how is it that these perspectives are produced? And, keeping in mind that "such occasions are only rarely occasions of human experience" (1967, 233), how do we make techniques operative that are not focused solely on human perspective? How do we enliven the human-more-than-human differential at the heart of the force-form of composition?

A technique is not a method. "Some of the major disasters of mankind have been produced by the narrowness of men with a good methodology," Whitehead reminds us (1929, 12). Methods are inherently diagnostic, functioning with general categories that are understood to be transportable across contexts (Manning 2016, 26–45). Methods are used to frame processes: their usefulness is in their imposition of a standard that is both iterable (can be used across more than one context), and predictive (the stakes of what matters are decided in advance). They function according to preexisting models of value. Techniques, as they are mobilized by SenseLab, are subtractive in a different way. They are culled from the relational field through an attunement to the event's own tendencies. The subtraction at work in technique involves connecting to the potential for intensification in the process itself. Following Gilbert Simondon (2017), technique is the making-operational of conditions of emergence toward platforms for relation.

Honing a technique is slow, careful work. Key to this work is the question of constraint: how does the constraint set in place to subtract from the welter facilitate a shift in quality? Enabling constraints are modes of subtraction that condition a perspective in the event on itself that is both precise and generative. An enabling constraint always carries with it a certain necessity for improvisation, but the field is limited, oriented by the framing the technique has put into place. Since framings can also be disabling, insensitive to the being of relation of the event in its own improvisatory unfolding, new events require new techniques. A technique that is truly enabling allows for an inner development of the technique that I call "technicity," an "outdoing of technique" that reveals the technique's more-than (Manning 2013, 32). When this happens, the event has modulated the technique from the perspective of its own logic. Subtraction here functions very differently than it does in the context of method. A culling of tendencies takes place for each shift from technique to technicity, as it does in the honing of technique itself. Subtraction is sensitive to the difference in germ at the heart of the event. It does not simply reduce. It amplifies. Subtraction tunes toward addition: it attunes to what has been left out, to what is excessive in the event, to the negatively prehended.

Method is allied to the archive. Archives are methods for the accounting of process that generalize across instances of experience. If we consider, for instance, the ubiquitous forms of archive in the fine arts, what we tend to find are representations of what are considered primary works. Of course, much work has been done on the archive in the past several decades, much of it to address this very issue.[2] But without a strong stance against the generalization of experience, and without a vocabulary for rethinking the tendency to perpetuate the form/process dyad, even the best experiments tend to fall prey to the problem of representation, thereby falling into an ethos of the representation of the useful over a pragmatics of the useless. With this in mind, the issue for SenseLab was to try to become acquainted with techniques that would subtract differently, that would engage creatively with the seeds of a process without reembalming those seeds into a digestible, (re)presentable form.[3]

To subtract differently requires a practice that recognizes that every coming-to-form carries an excess. This virtual share of force is what keeps form active, shifting and moving. The creativity at the heart of the force-of-form emphasizes that all compositions of force-form carry unrealized potential. It is important to retain the notion of the "unrealized" here. These are not Platonic "ideas." The unrealized is nonactualized—negatively prehended—in the occasion as it has come to be. As such, it cannot be named, and it cannot be abstracted from the occasion. The virtual is real, as Deleuze reminds us, but not actual. Our work, as regards the anarchive, was to devise techniques that could make the unrealized as real felt.

Concrescence

If form and force are always in co-composition, the occasion of experience, even on the side of its atomicity, or absoluteness, carries a germ of potential. Concrescence, the concept at the heart of Whitehead's process philosophy that expresses the process through which an occasion comes into itself, gives a sense of this holding together, in the occasion, of a vacillation between creativity and absoluteness. With the initial grasping of experience (prehension) through which the occasion begins to "take," there is already a certain concrescence, a certain growing of the grasp's attunement to form. Both the growing and the forming are carried by the concept of concrescence. As Whitehead writes, "the word Concrescence is a derivative from the familiar latin verb, meaning 'growing together.' It also has the advantage that the participle 'concrete' is familiarly used for the notion of complete physical reality. Thus Concrescence is useful to convey the notion of many things acquiring complete complex unity" (1967, 236). Concrescence is the growing into form, the growing that allows for the consolidation of the welter, the momentary "concreteness" of an occasion expressing itself as this or that. What must always be remembered is this: the expression the occasion takes can never be completely abstracted from this growing into itself of force to form. Concrete is never fully abstracted from the cresting.

When I said that it was necessary to read Whitehead from the middle, I meant that we need to read him from the perspective of concrescence, moving at the same time in the direction of a process growing into itself, the necessary eclipsing of the excess in order that the form "take" absolutely, and the germinating force of what still participates, even if it does not actually take form. To think from this middling assures us of not getting caught in the process/form dichotomy. For there is always activity in the movement of forms "taking" and perishing and "taking" again differently. With that movement, what is created is not so much form as such as the time of the event, of this event, here, now, and all potentials grown from its cultivation.

The Not-Being of Immediacy

When they perish, occasions pass from the immediacy of being into the not-being of immediacy. —Alfred North Whitehead, *Adventures of Ideas*

The occasion of experience is a limit concept. To think at the scale of a human or animal body, even an electron, Whitehead speaks of societies of occasions (1978, 91). This is not to suggest that occasions have actual scale. On the contrary, as intensities of experience "taking," no fixed scale could ever be attributed to them. A monument, for instance, is populated with innumerable takings-form, and with that uncountability come an infinity of durations, some of them in the time of the event, some of them in the untimely field of relation of which potential is made. Form in this grander sense is not distinguishable from the way I described it above. It, too, is composed of the differential of process/form. To ignore this is to misunderstand the force of the molecular and the ways in which it makes ingression in the molar. This is a mistake that is often made in the name of the micropolitical, where the suggestion is that the micropolitical refers to small events that operate at less important scales than those that are macropolitical. Whitehead's account of force-form challenges this, as does the work of Deleuze and Félix Guattari.

To understand the difference between the micropolitical and the macropolitical requires a sensitivity to different qualities of movement. Micropolitical movements are composed of "less localizable relations that are always external to themselves and . . . concern flows and particles" (1987, 196). They move at the pace of an ungraspability, "traveling at speeds beyond the ordinary thresholds of perception" (196). The shape of the micropolitical is transversal, its operations always at the interstices of form and process. If the macropolitical is more sedentary, it is also by nature more form-like, But no form can be fully separated out from the movement of form's "taking," no instance of experience is completely devoid of potential: "the two lines are constantly interfering, reacting upon each other, introducing into each other either a current of suppleness or a point of rigidity" (196). The force of the micropolitical, its power, is its capacity to infrathinly infiltrate the hardenings into form. "This molecular line, more supple but no less disquieting, in fact, much more disquieting," runs through all monuments of power, bending them in ways often imperceptible but affecting them nonetheless (199). The infrathin tunings of the micropolitical must not be seen as purely "internal," however, as though the micropolitical were the inside and the macropolitical the outside. "It might be thought that rigid segments are socially determined, predetermined, overcoded by the State; there may be a tendency to construe supple segmentarity as an interior activity, something imaginary or phantasmic" (204). From the middling of concrescence, we must always look in two directions at once, perspective topologically inclined. Each line is at once a hardening and a line of flight. It would be a dangerous fallacy to claim that the hardening edge of experience is the most potent. What can still move has wildly unpredictable effects on experience: "Micropolitics is no less extensive or real than macropolitics. Politics on the grand scale can never administer its molar segments without also dealing with the microinjections or infiltrations that work in its favor or present an obstacle to it; indeed, the larger the molar aggregates, the greater the molecularization of the agencies [*instances*] they put into play" (204).

Anarchiving is a micropolitical act. Techniques for anarchiving must therefore become attentive to the ways in which monumentality asserts itself as the end point of experience, aware of how generalization reifies experience, systematically backgrounding those modes of existence that are devalued in lieu of grand narratives. Working to attune to qualities of perception below the threshold of sense perception, anarchiving must connect to movements whose rhythms coincide with the transversal angularity of a middling. From this middling, with a commitment to the speculative force of the pragmatic proposition's outdoing, anarchiving must seek out the event's minor gestures, aware, always, of all the ways the force of variation of the minor gesture is devalued by what more robustly grows in its place. Anarchiving must remain engaged with both the immediacy of being and the not-being of immediacy.

Immediacy of being requires us to attend to the absoluteness, to the matter-of-fact, as Whitehead (1938) calls it, of what has come to be.[4] This matter-of-fact remains even after the perishing. *This* coming to form has altered what experience can do. This is its objective immortality. This means that grand narratives too continue to make a difference, even if they are deeply falsifying generalizations of how experience "takes." This must be attended to even when it has become clear that it is on the side of the minor gesture that movement and change are most palpable. For "stubborn facts," as Whitehead (1978) calls them, always populate the potential of what may reemerge, albeit differently.[5] The objective immortality of what perishes to some degree affects all that will come to be. Unlike the archive, however, and any account of memory that situates memory as a receptacle that can be returned to wholesale, what reemerges is not the stubborn fact "itself." What reemerges can never be decided in advance: its coming-to-be will be ecological at its core, influenced by all the ways in which *these* singular forces compose with *this* singular "taking." Change always happens, no matter what. This is what I take from process philosophy: not that the minor gesture is inherently good or evil (it isn't) but that the minor gesture is always at work, and that techniques are available for orienting how the taking of form contributes to experience in the making.

This account is at once of time and of memory. When Whitehead writes about the not-being of immediacy, he is underscoring the orienting potential of what perishes. How something came to be affects how something else can happen. The past lives in the present, not as cause but as potential and, even more important, as differential.

Thinking from the middle with the question of the not-being of immediacy, another detour is necessary. If experience resists in a fundamental way an accounting of it in linear time—past, present, future—it will never be possible to locate it on a linear continuum. We will have to think topologically, training postures and gestures that orient from perspectives other than our own, if ours is to chunk the world into subjects and objects. We will have to learn to not put process before form, or form before process, but to think them in their incessant folding. As Whitehead does, we will also have to encounter these questions from the orientation of the more-than human, refusing to speak generally about experience "as" human or nonhuman, working instead from a modality that gives voice to what exceeds us.

The Anarchic Share

The archive as it is mobilized in contemporary times cannot be detached from the neoliberal obsession with the capture of creativity. Artists everywhere are taught to document, document, document; the product emphasized, always, over the force-of-form, especially now that the very act of being an artist has become enshrined by the academic institution by the ubiquitous MFA and now, more and more, by the PhD. Increasingly, to make art is to know how to frame it. Of course, accounts of process abound, and with them a long history of resisting this trend—but when it comes down to it, when the grant needs to be written, or the performance dossier needs to be read, or the article needs to be written so that the next exhibition can take place, it is the archive that is turned to, and beyond the archive of the work itself, the cv. An artist without a website or a cv is a rare occurrence, and even artists who explicitly resist these normative constraints often can do so only because they have enough prestige to function as the exception to the norm, or because they came into their artistic practice in another era when these kinds of markers of practice were not as current.[6] What results from this is a tendency to monumentalize the archive by situating it as the technique par excellence for gauging practice.[7]

When SenseLab began the work with the anarchive, we turned to White-head's notion of the anarchic share to begin to articulate what it was we were after. Would it be possible, we asked ourselves, to make felt (without fully annihilating it) that share of the process that resists form? Would it be possible to find ways to feed forward the more-than of the event's taking-form? And if this were possible, would this registering of what else flowed through the work by itself be capable of seeding new practices on a different terrain, practices that could generate new techniques, new processes that coincided in some sense with what took place before but didn't need to conform to it? Was it possible to activate a tendency for future reuptake by culling from the event the infrathin, that quality at the limit of the perceptible, tuning to its negative prehension to extract from it the very germ that made the event what it became? What might it mean for an ethos of the pragmatics of the useless to seek to make operative that which by its very nature resisted capture? This brings us back to the question of the not-being of immediacy, which is the best definition I've found for the anarchive (provided we never abstract it completely from the immediacy of being).

The anarchive has a pull, and it is a pull to immediacy. It wants to activate, to orient. Or, better said, it is always already activating, orienting. This makes it a collaborator in all takings-form. Defining the anarchive as the event's anarchic share allows us to underscore its immanence in all experience, human and more-than human, reminding us that anarchiving is not something "we" do. Anarchiving is a practice that catches experience in the making, that catches us in our own becoming.

This makes SenseLab's desire to harness the anarchive paradoxical. We have lived with (and suffered) this paradox since proposing the term. If we continue to persist, it is not because we want to prove that a human agency can tame the anarchive. Quite the opposite, our hope is to better account for how the anarchic share composes with the event and to create conditions for reentering experience from its uneasy middling.

Immortality

In his account of immortality, Whitehead begins with a theory of co-composing worlds that he calls the "world of activity" and the "world of value." These worlds are inextricable: they cannot be conceived apart from one another. That said, as with all process philosophy, an easy togetherness must not be imposed from the outside. Theirs is a relation of nonrelation activated by the differential of their coming together in each singular instance.

The world of activity is the one that tunes toward the form the actual occasion takes. This is the finite, mortal world. Whitehead describes it as a world of origination that "creates the present by transforming the past, and by anticipating the future" (1968, 62). This phasing into itself of experience is the share of experience where orientations and potentials are reduced to the forms they momentarily take. In the realm of activity, as Whitehead makes clear with the concepts of "appearance" and "reality," all comings-to-be are dancing in the vacillation of the fullness of potential (he calls this reality) *and* its cleaving into appearance, or form-taking. "The infinite background always remains as the unanalysed reason why that finite perspective of that entity has the special character that it does have. Any analysis of the limited perspective always includes some additional factors of the background. The entity is then experienced in a wider finite perspective, still presupposing the inevitable background which is the universe in its relation to that entity" (Whitehead 1968, 60). I foreground this last passage to prevent a reading that might take the world of activity as one of "pure" form. There is no such thing. Form is simply what happens when activity moves toward a limit. And as I've emphasized above, this limit always includes what exceeds it, its more-than. It is here that it connects to the immortal world, the world of value. The more-than is untimely, outside the actualization of form: it neither fully appears nor quite perishes, living on as the qualifying orientation for worlds to come.

Throughout the work on the anarchive, value has been our chief concern. Value, as Massumi outlines in *99 Theses on the Revaluation of Value*, must be taken back: "It is time to take back value. For many, value has long been dismissed as a concept so thoroughly compromised, so soaked in normative strictures and stained by complicity with capitalist power, as to be unredeemable. This has only abandoned value to purveyors of normativity and apologists of economic oppression. Value is too valuable to be left in those hands" (2018, 3). As already mentioned, the archive imposes value from the outside. Lest this seem like a negligible concern, let's not underestimate the ways in which the archive's organization of knowledge rests on the very idea of property and propriety that undergirds accounts of history in our colonial times. Value cannot be thought without recognizing what it forcibly devalues. Black life lives in this devaluation: slavery, and the persistent coupling of the black body with property, cements what in the afterlife of slavery continues in the name of racialized capital. Saidiya Hartman articulates this clearly in her commitment to blackness as an operative site for making capital's moves visible:

Let me make it clear that the discriminations of race at issue implicitly identified blacks as inferiors and subordinates and effectively secured their subjugation. Unlike arguments forwarded by color-blind constitutionalists that all recognition of race is equally pernicious, this line of argument does not accept the neutrality of race as an immutable substance anterior to discourse but instead concerns itself with the inscription and valuation of raced bodies and race as an indexical marker of the history of enslavement and subjugation. . . . Race is an effect of an ensemble of social and historical relations that have determined property relations, life chances, and an economy of value, from the accruing of profit and designations of the good, the true, and the beautiful, to calculations of human worth, through the creation of subjugated, dishonored, and castigated groups. . . . A radical and expansive reading of the "badges of slavery" necessarily attends to the history of captivity, enslavement, subjugation, dispossession, exploitation, violation, and abjection productive of black difference. This history of enslavement was registered in the body's racialized inscription, whether the purportedly discernible markings on the body's surface or the blood coursing through indeterminate bodies, and utilized as an index of subjective value. (1997, 244n26)

To return to value is never to negate the horror of devaluation. It is, rather, to refuse, as Massumi does, to allow capital in all of its past and future instantiations to determine value. Value as mobilized here is always in this postcapitalist orientation, inquiring into the negative prehensions of a pragmatics of the useless. To turn to Whitehead is to find a vocabulary for articulating how else value might operate if taken from the perspective of the minor gesture.[8]

For Whitehead, there is never an exteriority to value—value is in the relation, allied with activity. The world of activity needs its finiteness. It needs the parameters that allow for the absolute differentiation between now and now. At the same time, it needs a way to conceive of what is always escaping the now, of what cannot quite be captured yet profoundly influences the taking-form of processes underway. Moving at the pace of the more-than, what the world of value connects to is the anarchic share of activity. What is valued here is not the form the process takes but its force-of-form.

Value for Whitehead is not something added to an occasion of experience. It is not imposed from the outside as an arbiter of importance. It is not hierarchical. Indeed, value is not. Value contributes. It allies itself qualitatively to the process of form-taking. And yet "it loses its meaning apart from its necessary reference to the World of passing fact. Value refers to Fact, and Fact refers to Value" (Whitehead 1968, 62). Value is nothing without activity. To experience valuation, there must be form. Value, as the force-of-form, cannot be abstracted from what comes to be. At the same time, because of its untimeliness, its asynchrony, it cannot be absolutely contained by the occasion as it comes to form: "The value judgment points beyond the immediacy of historic fact" (62).

All occasions of experiences are oriented by value. This is not a morality. Value as Whitehead defines it has nothing to do with preimposed systems of belief. Valuation is more of a tending than it is an encapsulating. The question is not whether something is good or evil but to what degree it holds contrasts in germ, to what degree it activates the potentiality of an inner discordance. "Thus the World of Values must be conceived as active with the adjustment of the potentialities of realization" (62).

If the world of activity involves catching experience in the making, the world of value involves immanent modifications of that catch: "Evaluation involves a process of modification: the World of Activity is modified by the World of Value" (63). But there is a hitch: "Evaluation always presupposes abstraction from the sheer immediacy of fact. It involves reference to Valuation" (63). What is being valued is not the occasion. What is valuing itself is the more-than.

Value is a capacity for intensification. When the world of activity composes with the world of value, a share of experience becomes immortal. A quality of worlding is invented. This is what the anarchive does: it inserts itself in the schizz where the finite and the infinite begin to overlap and makes that schizz tremble, valuing it from the inside. The ineffable is felt.

If something is captured in the activation of an anarchive, it cannot be value itself. For, as Whitehead writes, "either World can only be explained by reference to the other World; but this reference does not depend upon words, or other explicit forms of individuation" (63). What is captured is force's uneasy connection to what takes form. Not the form, and not exactly the more-than, but something that cleaves the two and offers up different orientations from the ones actually taken.

Or maybe not different but immanently included without being expressed as such.

Two shapes compose: "a shape of value and a shape of fact" (64). To conceptualize these compositions across time and untimeliness as shapes perhaps gives us a way to conceive a passage from the ineffable to the activation of a process seed bank made of anarchival germs.

In *Always More Than One*, I wrote about the shape of enthusiasm (2013, 185). This came out of a critical reading of psychoanalyst Frances Tustin, in particular her accounts of how autistics encounter shape. Tustin writes, "In the days when I was working as a psychoanalyst child therapist with young autistic children, as they began to talk, they would tell me about their 'shapes'" (1984, 279). "They were not the shapes of any particular object." "Just 'shapes.'" "I do not know what other forms were covered by what they referred to as 'shapes'. . . . It was not the shape of a specific object which existed in actuality; it was just a 'shape'" (279). My argument in that earlier piece was that the problem was not with the autistics she was following but with Tustin herself:

> That Tustin cannot quite articulate the nature of a "shape" is not surprising: the shaping of experience in the making is dynamic and amodal—active in the perceptual field where language is not-yet. It is . . . a vitality form, a pre-conscious verging toward a coming-to-act that tunes to the relational milieu of experience. Such a vitality form occurs in the half-second or less of an event's coming to expression. It is, as Daniel Stern underlines, a "manifestation of being alive" that is all about movement—vitality forms shape the lived experience of duration, giving incipient experience its activation contour. (Manning 2013, 187)

To speak of the shape of experience is to find a way to touch the middling of events forming, to be interested not only in the form they will inevitably take but in the valuing of how force and form conjugate in a singular instance of an event's coming-to-be. In the words of the earlier piece:

> Giving this activity of shaping the name of enthusiasm, making enthusiasm the force of the not-yet, emphasizes the towardness, the exuberance and the intensity of vitality forms, calling forth the way in which they manifest always in excess of actual forms in the towardness of a coming-to-be. Vitality forms take the shape of the not-yet such that they in-form not simply the content of the experience but its affective tonality: "they are the felt experience of force—in movement—with a temporal contour, and a sense of aliveness, of going somewhere" (Stern 2010, 8). They are the "'shapes' of sound, smell, taste and sight" that are "'felt' rather than heard, smelled, tasted or seen" (Tustin 1984, 279). (Manning 2013, 187)

The world of value and its shape of enthusiasm, even if untimely, is not without appetite. Indeed, it is appetite at its most urgent. For value "styles" the occasion (Whitehead 1968, 66). Activity is harnessed, for now, in just this way. It shapes.

Cuff

A shape I've become fascinated by is that of the cuff. My interest in the cuff can be connected to a long-standing curiosity about and engagement with the fold, in particular the way it is taken up by Deleuze in his most Whiteheadian book,

The Fold. For Deleuze, the baroque takes the shape of the fold. That is to say, the baroque is the period that most welcomes the involutions and convolutions of a shape that refuses beginnings and endings. Deleuze writes, "The Baroque refers not to an essence but rather to an operative function. It endlessly produces folds. It does not invent things: there are all kinds of folds coming from the East, Greek, Roman, Romanesque, Gothic, Classical folds. . . . Yet the Baroque trait twists and turns its folds, pushing them to infinity, fold over fold, one upon the other" (1992, 3).

The fold is the figure of the labyrinth, or more precisely the shape of its vertigo. It is multiplicity itself—an impossible recounting of how the parts connect to the whole. With the fold there are never parts, just more folding. "A fold is always folded within a fold, like a cavern in a cavern. . . . Unfolding is thus not the contrary of folding, but follows the fold up to the following fold" (7).

In the process of experimenting with the anarchic share of experience and attempting to tune it toward the mobilization of some kind of form-like instance of anarchiving, SenseLab returned to the fold again and again. What better concept to attend to the ways in which the world of activity and the world of value coincide if not through the shape of the fold? The problem was that the fold was not helping us move toward form. It kept us resolutely on the side of the more-than with little appetite for the finiteness of mortal forms. This is of course not the fold's fault. It is more of a technical problem. We needed a concept to shift the conditions of exploration such that we might, later, return to the fold in a different way.

That concept was the cuff.

The exploration began in a straightforward way: we asked ourselves what exactly a cuff could do. It's an unusual word, *cuff*, particularly in the English language, where the term denotes at once the finishing of the sleeve or the pant leg, a slap about the head, certain earrings and bracelets, and, not to be forgotten, the handcuff, usually used in the plural. Right away it seemed that this might be a concept, if explored deeply enough, of capture itself, a concept that might embolden a technique that would return us to the world of activity.

The term *cuff* seems to come into usage in the English language around the fifteenth century. A variant of the medieval English *coffe* (mitten), it referred to the turned-back part of the sleeve of a garment. From the late seventeenth century onward, cuff links were used to close the vent in the cuff or wristband of the shirt, replacing the earlier "cuff strings," though the cuff strings did remain in use until the first buttons were sewn onto shirts toward the end of the nineteenth century.

Originating in the sixteenth century, the verb *to cuff* is defined as striking with an open hand, especially on the head.[9] The *Merriam-Webster* dictionary suggests that the word cuff may come from the Middle English, now obsolete, "glove," first recorded in 1530.

The question of ornamentation was the starting point. When I sew a cuff on a garment, I am opting to finish a seam differently. Is this ornament? And if so, does that mean it is in excess of form? Or is it part of the taking-form of that which is being cuffed?

Despite a months-long frenzy of sewing cuffs, exploring all of the ways they could attach to a garment (a collar? a pocket?), I still wasn't sure whether a cuff was a simple ornamental add-on to an otherwise perfectly self-sustaining garment. Since my aim was to discover a technique for anarchiving by way of the cuff, it was not a dictionary definition I was seeking but a sense of the cuff's operational potential. What definition of the cuff would allow us to begin the process of anarchiving differently? Collaborator Marcelino Barsi suggested a first definition: he proposed that a cuff was a change of direction.[10] This definition started a new process rolling. It is true that to sew a cuff to a garment usually involves sewing perpendicular to the fabric's weave. There is indeed a tendency to reorient a line or a pattern in the cuffing. This first definition got us going. If a cuff was a change of direction, perhaps the shape of that change of direction was that of a levee. A temporary stopping of the flow?

The question morphed. What was an architectural cuff? Could a balcony be a cuff? And if so, did that move us beyond ornamentation to supplementarity, in the Derridean sense (see Derrida 1998)? What was a movement cuff? Would that be a trip—as in tripping over a shoe? A sudden righting? And a landscape cuff? Would that be Bernard Cache's inflection (see Cache 1995)? How landscapes themselves orient the built environment? This could only take me to lines, and to a close reading of Tim Ingold on the line (see Ingold 2015). Certainly a cuff was not a line, if a line was a "living-along" (Ingold 2007, 3). But the cuff *would* matter to the line, cracking it in ways unforeseen and reorienting it. If nothing else, the line reminded us that force and form could not be seen as opposites, and so also with the cuff and the fold.

Sympathy

Lars Spuybroek's book *The Sympathy of Things* (2016) consolidated my thinking. The cuff—now emerging as a technique for orienting toward the anarchic share of experience in the making, giving us the tools to be less tentative about the hard gestures of finishing, cutting off, tripping up, redirecting—was another kind of fold. Folds are full of cuffs, it turns out. They are not simply endless convolutions—they also reorient. Doesn't Deleuze (1992) give us the figure of the inflection and Paul Klee's line precisely to remind us that the fold vectorizes?

In *The Sympathy of Things*, Spuybroek takes us on a journey toward amodern seeing in the context of Gothic design. Through detailed explorations of the techniques at the heart of Gothic architecture and design, Spuybroek demonstrates how the Gothic refutes the combinatorial approach that privileges segmentarity. In the Gothic, he argues (with John Ruskin always by his side), "the relation between elements is internal to the form-taking process and the sweeping up of the elements in a continuous variation. That relation is one with the movement of design-work rendering force-of-form. There is only one 'plane,' that of the movement of the design-work itself, on a level with the material" (Massumi 2016, xx).

The cuff in this context could express itself in several ways. It could be conceived as that which segments. Or it could be seen as pure ornament. But to do so would be to ignore its capacity to activate a change of direction, to ignore the shape of its orientation. And so, with my amodern eyes, I choose to see the cuff as the embankment that stops the fold's continuous variation. The cuffing pulls a shape out of the fold's variability. This is what a cuff can do, I think: to make apparent that all activity edges.

When experience is understood as that which cleaves the world of activity and the world of value, the concept of ornamentation changes dramatically. If the world of value is that which brings qualitative emphasis to how things come to be, and if that emphasis can never be understood as separate from the activity itself, there is no place for an ornamentation that would signal "mere decoration." How would that work? Wouldn't everything make a difference, no matter how trivial? This is certainly what Whitehead would say, and it is with this in mind that I situate the cuff as that which participates in ways that make a real difference to the world's foldings of activity and value. The cuff, Spuybroek might say, echoing Henri Bergson (1911), has sympathy for the fold.

Spuybroek writes, "Sympathy is what things feel when they shape each other" (2016, 3). Sympathy is not a personal standpoint. It is the motor of intuition, *in the event*. Intuition is an operation through which a process opens itself to alternative routes. As a technique for touching the inner workings-out of the event's most operative tendencies, intuition opens the event to a durational schizz. For intuition is not in-time: "Intuition is rather the movement by which we emerge from our own duration, by which we make use of our own duration to affirm and immediately to recognize the existence of other durations" (Deleuze 1991, 33). If intuition is the pulse of time that unfolds the event's differential, exposing it to its more-than, sympathy is its conduit. A sympathy for an event's unfolding involves a complicity between the pragmatic operations that condition an event just this way and the speculative propositions that emerge from that singularity. In the time of the event, sympathy amplifies the generative gesture of the event's self-contouring. This is a materially sensitive engagement with time in the making. "[Sympathy] is an objectivity focused not on inert matter but on matter as part of time, on matter as something transformable and ever-changing" (Spuybroek 2016, 16).

To cuff is to move with the material toward its change of direction, and to follow the limits of that change. To cuff is to corner the change and link it, breaking the line. To cuff is to experiment with how a cut alters a process. To cuff is to schizz. To fold is to follow that process, to risk the labyrinthine.

Just as the not-being of immediacy was key, so is sympathy. In fact, if we understand intuition as the modality of attention, in the event, that tentatively directs a process, we might see intuition as working in close proximity to the world of value. Intuition is full of potential. This potential, this attuning toward the force-of-form, requires a motor. It is sympathy that moves intuition toward the world of activity. It is sympathy that cuffs the process.

The Way of the Anarchive

Anarchiving is a manner of becoming that matters. Its work is to cuff experience such that its folds can be more keenly felt, pleated as they momentarily are by the cuff's cleaving gesture. Anarchiving does not have a form per se, but it does pass through form. Its power is its capacity to sidle form without fully giving in to its contours, or becoming seduced by the false promise of reproducibility. While an anarchive cannot ever be created as such, it does benefit from a certain taking-form in order for the cuffing to express a change of direction that the folding can take up. Summed up in the collective work of SenseLab, here are a few ways it can be defined:

> Anarchiving is a repertory of traces of events. The traces are not inert but are carriers of potential. They are reactivatable, and their reactivation helps trigger a new event that continues the creative process from which they came, but in a new iteration.
> Thus, anarchiving is not documentation of a past activity. Rather, it is a feed-forward mechanism for lines of creative process, under continuing variation.
> Anarchiving needs documentation—the archive—from which to depart and through which to pass. It is an excess energy of the archive: a kind of supplement or surplus-value of the archive.

Its supplemental, excessive nature means that the anarchive is never
    contained in any particular archive or documentation element
    contained in an archive. It is never contained in an object. Anarchiving
    is made of the formative movements going into and coming out of
    the archive, for which the objects contained in the archive serve as
    springboards. Anarchiving as such is made of formative tendencies,
    compositional forces seeking a new taking-form, lures for further pro-
    cess. Archives are their way stations.
Since it exceeds the archive and is uncontainable in any single object
    or collection of objects, anarchiving is by nature a cross-platform
    phenomenon. It is activated in the relays: between media, between
    verbal and material expressions, between digital and off-line
    archivings, and most of all between all of the various archival forms
    it may take and the live, collaborative interactions that reactivate the
    anarchival traces and in turn create new ones.
Anarchiving pertains to the event. It is a kind of event derivative, or
    surplus-value of the event.
Approached anarchivally, the product of events is process. The anarchive
    is a technique for making practice a process-making engine. Many
    products are produced, but they are not *the* product. They are the vis-
    ible indexing of the process's repeated taking-effect: they embody its
    traces (thus bringing us full circle to the beginning).[11]

There is no method to the anarchive. Because its work is to proliferate, to
make felt, for future reuptaking, germs of experience excluded from the occasion's taking-form, it cannot be approached the same way twice. Every event will
have to invent its own process of anarchiving. But one thing that can be maintained across the momentary reorienting of the anarchic share is the sympathy of
the cuff for the fold, and vice versa. Without that sympathy, the process will stall.
The mattering of the anarchive requires the turn of the brush where line begins
to fold and inflects toward other form-takings.

Discord

The anarchic share of the event will always resist capture. It will always live in the untimely world of value, on the side of force. The infrathin attunement to value in the
work of anarchiving will nonetheless make an important difference in how it comes
to matter in the form-taking of its future reuptake. To practice anarchiving is to care
for the *how* of this difference. It is to care for how the event has concern for its shape.[12]

An event always carries, in potentia, the shape of enthusiasm. This is something I know from my work on neurodiversity: for those who always feel too much, for whom the borders of sensation are liquid, there is always more-than. In this vista of becoming, force is still palpable. The edges and folds and cuffs are still perceptible. The shape is open, ebullient, and wildly active.

Enclosures are built to safeguard us from the force-of-form. The demand for discernible signs of our creativity—our archives, our cvs—is everywhere repeated. For, it is believed, these are the signs that will embolden our own form-taking, that will frame us into the subjects we must become, building our identities and the personalities that stem from them. But some of us—the most neurodiverse among us—know that there is no safeguarding from force, and there is no way to account for being without accounting at one and the same time for becoming. When perceived from the middling of experience in the making, form is force, subject is superject. This is the lesson anarchiving teaches: the archive was never stable. Its materials always mattered in more than one way. Identities are short-lived.

Discord is key to how value moves the event. With discord comes breach in form, shape-shifting. This is the politics of the anarchive: that it creates the conditions to bring out not only the anarchic share but the anarchy that breaches the levee of time. The anarchive refuses the easy flow of time. Its work is not to document but to germinate seeds for new processes, processes that will likely unmoor the shape of experience, including the shape of what was.

The work of care for the event involves a deep commitment to modes of attunement, in the event. As SenseLab experiments with it, it asks us to learn to move at the pace of the impersonal, in the collective magma of experimentation. In doing so, it moves us to become more acutely in tune with the edgings of a sympathy that can alter the course. Whitehead searches for a concept that might do justice to this necessary work of reorientation that moves experience to its limit, a concept that can risk the uneasiness of discord while connecting it to the necessity of care, in the event.

Care in the event returns us to the immanence of the occasion, to its own self-enjoyment. Recall how the event moves through concrescence toward subjective form. This taking-form is described by Whitehead as the occasion's self-enjoyment. Motored by sympathy (the force of feeling), the event's self-enjoyment crests when it has found its singular quality of form. With self-enjoyment comes valuation, immanent to the event. And value brings discord, or what Whitehead elsewhere calls contrast.

It is in his account of beauty that Whitehead perhaps most clearly emphasizes what is at stake in the valuation of an occasion. The most typical kind of beauty, the most passing, is defined by Whitehead as "anaesthetic." Anaesthetic beauty leaves little trace on the world, its self-enjoyment negligible: the subtraction of experience into a form-taking values itself with as little discord as possible. There is little contrast. Few edges reveal themselves. Intensity is at a low. Background remains in the background. Little shimmer—appearance easily extracted from the welter. With anaesthetic beauty there is no sense of the untimely, and there is little at stake. Whatever was dangerous to the form has been inhibited. Easy harmony.

The stronger concept of beauty—what Whitehead calls "Intensity Proper" (1967, 253)—is much more potent. Here, contrasts are keenly felt. The force-of-form is not backgrounded, its intensity circulating across the threshold of foreground-background. This discordant beauty can be dangerous. Its bounds are not clear. But its self-enjoyment in coming to force-of-form is tangible. This is aesthesis at its most intensive. Artfulness lives here.

Discordant beauty has nothing to do with externally mandated aesthetic judgment. It is fully immanent to the event, working on us more than possessed by us, moved by a more-than human intensity. This is the beauty of a transformation that shifts the ground, cleaving the world of activity in ways that allow it to compose most intensively with the world of value.

The anarchive aims toward discordant beauty. Discordant beauty is close to a definition of tragedy reminiscent of Friedrich Nietzsche's. For Nietzsche, tragedy is less a form in itself than a conduit for difference. Tragedy alters the field. It breaks it in ways that recalibrate experience. In this way, it is an affirmative force—it opens the way for new modes of existence. Similarly, for Whitehead, the force of the discordant is what moves experience toward its difference. "For otherwise actuality would consist in a cycle of repetition, realizing only a finite group of possibilities. This was the narrow, stuffy doctrine of some ancient thinkers" (1967, 259).

In its aim toward discordant beauty, the anarchive culls from within a process the germs of its incompletion and creates conditions, from within the event, for the amplification of that which moves infrathinly through it. In this way, it moves into resonance with conceptual feeling, the occasion's mental pole. Mentality, it must always be emphasized, has nothing to do with the mind. The occasion's mentality, for Whitehead, is the quality of excess that moves through an occasion, the more-than that (dis)orients it toward its difference from itself.

Each occasion of experience has two poles, the physical and the mental. The physical pole carries little to no disorientation. At the physical pole, the occasion's coming into itself is repetitive and relatively predictable. The mental pole is on the side of immortality—it is here that experience speculates. Keeping in mind that for Whitehead there is never an absolute separation between the organic and the inorganic, between the human and the nonhuman, between the physical and the mental, we must not attribute the mental pole to consciousness or to the human per se. Mentality is a pulse, an entreaty toward a revaluation.

The anarchic share tugs at the mortality of the occasion to move it toward the immortality of potential. Pulling toward difference, it tunes the anarchic share toward the valuation of the event's surplus. Working together, they not only mobilize the more-than, they value it.

There is always more that yields in the articulation of mentality, and that more-than rarely coincides with consciousness. Indeed, given consciousness's limitations as a practice of selection that adheres most emphatically to the world of activity, it is difficult to register that which gives value to experience. In most cases, if it does register, it does so in the infra, in the infrathin of the conscious and the nonconscious.

Artfulness is alive at this interstice. When Whitehead writes, "But that art which arises within clear consciousness is only a specialization of the more widely distributed art within dim consciousness or within the unconscious activities of experience" (1967, 270), he is signaling that to place art within the realm of "clear and distinct" consciousness is to deny the force of negative prehension and its schizzing of conscious experience. The artful is lively in the infra of consciousness where the dimness momentarily coincides with distinctness and folds back into dimness. There is much more that shimmers in experience than can be captured consciously.

The anarchive, given its relationship to the welter, continuously negotiates the field of dim apprehension. What "takes" in the anarchive unsettles conscious life by making briefly apparent what can only be diagonally felt. In an approximation of proximity, anarchiving invites a straddling of the germs of process past and future, choreographing conditions not for repetition but for recultivation. Germs are sown that carry traces of a past yet give flower to new propositions, the anarchive their medium. Dimness is of the essence, its opacity rich with the being of relation. "What leaps into conscious attention is a mass of presuppositions about Reality rather than the intuitions of Reality itself. It is here that the liability to error arises. The deliverances of clear and distinct consciousness require criticism by reference to elements in experience which are neither clear nor distinct. On the contrary, they are dim, massive, and important" (Whitehead 1967, 270). The artfulness of the anarchive yields to dim massiveness by refusing a distinction that would put it on the side of activity only. In that sense, it is the *way* of art.

Care

The ethico-aesthetic adventure of living artfully mobilizes the anarchic share of experience in the making. In the uneasy form of the anarchive, the stakes of the event of experience are catalyzed. This is the politics of the anarchive, moving the adventure of the event toward the germ of its difference from itself.

The politics of the anarchive are always politics of care for the event. In the relation of nonrelation of the cuff's sympathy for the fold, much is at stake. Too often, the event is cast as secondary to experience, as though it could be archived in advance, mobilizing not the adventure of a politics of the anarchive but a theater of resemblance. In a context like SenseLab where we work between artistic practice, philosophy, and the political, the question of how the anarchic share affects the passage into life-living really matters. The parsing of experience into the archives of our productivity is a violence to all that that moves through existence unregistered, and this violence has reduced perception to its most limited capacity. By honing ways of encountering modes of relation that amplify the differential, by committing to a pragmatics of the useless that refuses to take use-value as the measure of experience, other ways of living become possible. Through the anarchive, we learn not to reduce experience to measure. The question is always one of attending to the imbrication: how does the world of activity compose with the world of value? What other shape could this movement take? How else, in this emergent shaping, might we live the impersonality of a coming into relation? Because the aesthetics of our coming into relation matters, it has effects: what things do when they shape each other is deeply affected by the art of living.

Whitehead's concept for the art of living is peace. He struggles with the term: "The notions of 'tenderness' and of 'love' are too narrow, important though they be. We require the concept of some more general quality, from which 'tenderness' emerges as a specialization. . . . 'Impersonality' is too dead a notion, and 'Tenderness' too narrow" (1967, 284–85). In the end, he retains the term, orienting peace toward the world of value, the impersonal force of the valuation of the art of living.

In his final article, "Immanence: A Life," Deleuze moves life into the realm of the impersonal. Life is here no longer reduced to human life but courses instead across all ecologies of living, connecting to all that traverses them. Deleuze calls this *a* life. He writes:

> We shouldn't enclose life in the single moment when individual life confronts universal death. *A* life is everywhere, in all the moments that a given living subject goes through and that are measured by given lived objects:

an immanent life carrying with it the events or singularities that are merely actualized in subjects and objects. This indefinite life does not itself have moments, close as they may be to one another, but only between-times, between-moments. It doesn't just come about or come after but offers the immensity of an empty time where one sees the event yet to come and already happened, in the absoluteness of an immediate consciousness. (2001, 29)

A life is this life's more-than, the process of living this life transposed onto the indefinite. A life is what lives at the cusp where mortality and immortality meet, where the world shifts from its account of actual subjects and objects toward the force of negative prehension and the infrathin. A life is in the transversality, in the folding on itself of life-living.

The politics of care at the core of the anarchive are enfolded in this kind of indefiniteness. They are impersonal not because the singularity of *this* life, *this* event does not matter but because *it matters so much*. They are impersonal because how the event matters could not possibly be ascertained only by its actualization—and certainly not by our conscious appraisal of it. Much more is at work, and it is this muchness, this massiveness, that we need techniques for.

For Whitehead, the ultimate adventure is the adventure that includes such a politics of care. This care for *a* life—or peace, as he calls it—must never be abstracted from discord. It is intense, massive, and ineffable. Language will never reach it except, perhaps, in the poetic rhythms of language's play with form (Manning 2013, 156–71). Aesthetic to its core, ethico-aesthetic, this is not a living that seeks harmony: "The Peace that is here meant is not the negative conception of anaesthesia. It is a positive feeling which crowns the 'life and motion' of the soul. It is hard to define and difficult to speak of. It is not a hope for the future, nor is it an interest in present details. It is a broadening of feeling due to the emergence of some deep metaphysical insight, unverbalized and yet momentous in its coordination of values" (Whitehead 1967, 285). Peace, the art of life-living, is about the way the event values itself, about the *way* itself. Peace is a broadening, a widening of affective attunement toward that which exceeds us, toward that which we cannot name and thereby confine to the register of what already counts. Peace, the impersonality of life-living, is the movement of thought at the verge, the coordination, immanent to the event, that conditions techniques of living in the discordance of beauty's massiveness, a beauty that shifts the terms of our engagement with the world.

The impersonality of life-living moves at the pace of the minor gesture. Care operates here, in the midst. The work it does is that of immanent valuation, troubling the way the image of form tends to assert itself as having the final word.

Keeping form uneasy, keeping the terrain unsettled, a politics of care surpasses the individual to connect to whatever is impersonal at its heart. It is here that care does its work (*faire oeuvre*), in the transindividuality that moves impersonally across registers of experience. A politics of care works at the level of the fold's inflections, moving into those inflections to better support the force of variation.

To move in the register of *a* life, to move in the rhythm of the more-than, is an unsettling operation. Very little in our contemporary worlds supports such risk. And isn't there also a grave risk, you might ask, in a world of violence and deep injustice, that we sideline what is *actually* happening? Don't we need the archive to better give voice to those injustices? Don't we need to attend more emphatically to the relentless devaluation? And isn't it *my* actual body, *this* body, *now*, that is being threatened? Yes. But I don't think it has to be either-or. After all, the world of activity and the world of value coincide, as do this life and *a* life. A logic of mutual inclusion is necessary. It is only from the perspective of the both-and that new operative techniques for articulating the *what else* of experience are developed. The anarchic share does its work here, in the infrathin of life-living.

Whitehead speaks of peace as carrying "a surpassing of personality" (1967, 285). The art of life-living cannot be attached to one instance or one account of experience. Personality remains too tied to the hold of an individual subject's claim on the world. A politics of care moves across, in the infrathin interval Deleuze attaches to the concept of *a* life. This surpassing of existence is alive in a poetics of relation where "each and every identity is extended through a relationship with the Other" (Glissant 1997, 11). In a poetics of relation, relation is never understood as a mediator between terms precomposed—"when we speak of a poetics of Relation, we no longer need to add: relation between what and what?" Neither identity nor otherness are static states—they are activities in the differential process of shapes of existence coming into encounter. In a poetics of relation the being of relation is the subject. The politics of care does its work in the interval where "I is an other." (Arthur Rimbaud, in Glissant 1997, 27).

"The experience of Peace is largely beyond the control of purpose. . . . The deliberate aim at Peace very easily passes into its bastard substitute, Anesthesia," writes Whitehead (1967, 285). The art of life-living must be conditioned from within the welter of experience. It cannot be produced externally. Practice is the way. The shift from the self-same to the being of relation is deeply challenging, especially when it involves a persistent questioning of the centering of the human—as white, as neurotypical—in experience. To reframe existence from the matrix of a logic of whiteness means recognizing how whiteness shapes both the world of activity and the world of value. In a world that polices difference through an adherence to general categories and prizes product-driven excellence, little elbow room remains for the practice of the surpassing of personality. Nonetheless, anaesthesia is too deadly a solution. Moving at the pace of the world as it is given is a violence too deadening to consider. This is why techniques must continue to be invented that allow for emergent attunement to what is devalued. If, as Whitehead says, "[Peace] comes as a gift" (1967, 285), it does so in the sense that the impersonality it generates is a gift to experience. When the force of the anarchive is felt, making apparent pathways toward minor gestures already at play, there is definitely a sense of having received a gift of intensity, of beauty's massiveness.

If there be any claim to beauty within this politics of life-living, it is in the sense of the ineffable quality of the more-than that discordant beauty brings to lived experience. An aesthetics of black sociality. To say that the world is not ours to make may sound like a negation of the necessity of agency. And it is, in a sense. But it certainly isn't an appeal to passivity. It is, quite the contrary, a commitment to an ecology of practices that includes us but isn't driven only by us. An attunement to the effects of shaping is a commitment to a sociality that exceeds us even as it embraces us. But never in the mode of the interpersonal. Anaesthesia is never far away with its whiteness and neurotypical ways of knowing. The art of life-living is conditioned through the activation of modes of existence that are oriented not by a volitional first-person-singular human but by the force-of-variation of a minor gesture. As I argued at length in *The Minor Gesture* (2016), deliberate aim as the motor of existence does not actually coincide with how experience comes into itself as act. To suggest that experience is ours alone to orient is to return to a humanism, which is to say, a whiteness, that holds the power to negate what else is at work. Whiteness is structurally incapable of perceiving the differential, of participating in the force of *a life*, a sideways sociality if there ever was one.

Whitehead defines peace as "the removal of inhibition, and not its introduction" (1967, 285). Inhibition is the motor for self-control. Neurotypical par excellence, inhibition is to movement what tact is to touch: the measure of our being able to stand outside the event to affect it from without. What is at stake in a politics of care is something else altogether. What is needed most are conduits that allow us to connect to the adventure of *a* life. This is something quite different from the self-control of agency. It is an orienting from the perspective of the event, a compass that leads us toward the kind of participation that makes felt the anarchic share that was there all along. "Peace," writes Whitehead, "enlarges the field of attention. Thus Peace is self-control at its widest, at the width where the 'self' has been lost, and interest has been transferred to coordinations wider than personality" (1967, 285).

Adventure

The art of life-living seeks techniques for proliferation, for abundance, for what SenseLab, in its exploration of the anarchive, has termed the surplus-value of life.[13] This, always, in an ethos of the pragmatics of the useless. What is at stake is not to create *more* but to attune to the differential that exposes how the world of value composes with the actual we more readily perceive. This includes creating techniques to survive those very enclosures that hold us captive, as much thought-enclosures as anything else. Seen by Whitehead as a "barrier against narrowness" (1967, 286), the art of life-living is the enthusiastic taking up of the adventure of discord that is an ethico-aesthetics.

In *Chaosmosis*, Guattari makes operational the concept of the ethico-aesthetic, creating the conditions for us to think-with the adventure of discord at the heart of life-living. Given his well-known work at La Borde, it is important, I think, to note that the concept first comes up in the context of the therapeutic. A politics of care is implicitly at work in all ethico-aesthetic paradigms (Guattari 1995, 7–8). I note this here not because the anarchive is directly therapeutic in its approach to experience, but because the Guattarian practice of schizoanalysis, the therapeutic practice of approaching group subjectivity from the angle of the impersonal, has always been of central importance at SenseLab and has influenced our trajectory toward the anarchive, making us more attuned to how that which is excluded from actual experience affects the event. As will be discussed in more detail in chapter 7, this has involved developing practices for neurodiverse sociality, which, in turn, has allowed us to refine an account of the production of subjectivity that mobilizes attention on what else moves pedagogically, aesthetically, and politically when neurotypical practices of the event are abandoned. While this is not always easy—discord is everywhere active!—the anarchive requires it. When an event devolves to personal stakes, those personal stakes will always operate within the logic of the dominant order: that of whiteness and neurotypicality. The logic of neurotypicality is powerful, and it returns readily. A commitment to the ethico-aesthetic valences of schizoanalysis provides us with conceptual and therapeutic tools to begin again, from the middle.

Guattari writes, "We know that in certain social and semiological contexts, subjectivity becomes individualised; persons, taken as responsible for themselves, situate themselves within relations of alterity governed by familial habits, local customs, juridical laws, etc. In other conditions, subjectivity is collective—which does not, however, mean that it becomes exclusively social. The term 'collective' should be understood in the sense of a multiplicity that deploys itself as much beyond the individual, on the side of the socius, as before the person, on the side of preverbal intensities, indicating a logic of affects rather than a logic of delimited sets" (1995, 9). To activate the more-than, to mobilize the anarchic share, the work needs to happen in the register of the impersonal, across tendencies rather than individuals.

An ethico-aesthetic paradigm is always a speculative proposition. It offers no promises and knows no easy routes. In this unknown territory, it is the lure of the anarchive we tend to, learning how to move beyond equivalence toward excess, toward the more-than that cuffs the fold.

backgroundingforegrounding

Alfred North Whitehead's account of Appearance and Reality in *Adventures of Ideas* (1967) is an account of background-foreground. For Whitehead, Reality is the welter of experience unparsed. Appearance is what stands out. The call is to always think these together and to attune to how their togetherness resonates as contrast. Backgroundingforegrounding as pocket practice amplifies attunement to contrast.

Take the images of Judith Leemann's *Object Lessons* (2007–2014): what we see in the images are movements that want to become consolidations. These consolidations we might call Appearance: they foreground what we know how to see—a chair, a stool, a house-like structure. But to reduce the work the image does to the consolidation of these object-affordances is to miss their coming-into-formation through the force of the series. It is to actively unsee everything else at work—the movement between, the orientation, the field of relation. It is to miss the movement of backgroundingforegrounding. It is to unsee contrast.

Backgroundingforegrounding might be defined as an infrathin quality of perception that makes palpable the excess of what emerges even while remaining committed to that which actually stands out in experience. Backgroundingforegrounding is the vibratory that fields at the cusp of Appearance and Reality where they are still in overlap. The quality of the more-than felt in backgroundingforegrounding is what this pocket practice emphasizes.

Process philosophy is careful not to reduce the occasion of experience to an external perceiving (human) subject. Appearance and Reality are not what an external subject perceives (as though there were a fully fledged world into which a subject entered). All modalities of existence coming to expression resonate with the ebb and flow of Appearance and Reality. Appearance and Reality as they come together are the activity of foregrounding and backgrounding that brings the world into perceptibility. This perceptibility of course touches the society of molecules we call the human, but it also exceeds it.

Judith Leemann 2007–2014

Leemann's *Object Lessons* directly engages with this process. Describing the work, she writes, "Since 2007 I've been experimenting with crafting wordless explanations, in which hands manipulating objects on a small stage are asked to take on the work of explanation that usually rests with language. Over time, I've come to be most curious about the way in which language permits certain kinds of sense to come forward while actively preventing other kinds of sense from being made. Can this play of hands and objects do the work of foregrounding relations such that *the relation itself* becomes the subject?" (Leemann, n.d.).

When Leemann writes, "Over time, I've come to be most curious about the way in which language permits certain kinds of sense to come forward while actively preventing other kinds of sense from being made," she is gesturing toward the backgroundingforegrounding at work in the resonating of Reality in Appearance, and she is tuning into the aspect of "interpretation" Whitehead explores to discuss how Appearance consolidates itself: "Gaze at a patch of red. In itself as an object, and apart from other factors of concern, this patch of red, as the mere object of that present act of perception, is silent as to the past or the future. How it originates, how it will vanish, whether indeed there was a past and whether there will be a future, are not disclosed by its own nature. No material for the interpretation of sensa is provided by the sensa themselves as they stand starkly, barely, present and immediate. We *do* interpret them; but no thanks for the feat is due to them" (Whitehead 1967, 180–81).

What Whitehead is proposing here is that the work of interpretation does not happen where we tend to assume it does: "Sense-perception, as conceived in the

Judith Leemann 2007–2014

isolation of its ideal purity, never enters into human experience. It is always accompanied by so-called 'interpretation'" (217). Sense perception for Whitehead requires a parsing of the experience that orients it, giving it the time signature of experience-felt. This is what he calls "interpretation."

Similarly to the proposition made by Leemann that it is the relation that activates the constellation of sense rather than the parts themselves—the hands and the objects—Whitehead emphasizes that what *makes* sense are not the sensa themselves but *how* Appearance and Reality co-compose to activate a felt influx of otherness in experience. This felt influx is *in the relation*: otherness is not the subject external to the occasion of experience but the *way* the experience becomes what it is. Interpretation connects to the force of that influx, attuning to a field of pastness rich with tendencies Whitehead calls nonsensuous perception. Interpretation occurs when nonsensuous perception combines with sense perception: Appearance is as much the way experience comes into itself as the experience itself. Interpretation brings out the being of relation: the "play of hands and objects do the work of foregrounding relations *such that the relation itself becomes the subject*" (Leemann, n.d.; emphasis added).

When Whitehead suggests that the evidence on which "interpretations are based is entirely drawn from the vast background and foreground of nonsensuous perception with which sense-perception is fused, and without which it can never be" (1967, 181), he is gesturing toward the push and pull of perception in its negotiation of Appearance and Reality. Nonsensuous perception could be said to be the relay that allows sensation to be felt as such. Nonsensuous perception gives the orientation to experience such that what is sensed can be situated: theirs is moiré-like relation.

Because of its ties to pastness and to the ways it makes ingress into present occasions, nonsensuous perception can be defined as that which exceeds the present moment, that which pulls the present into contrast with spacetimes other than the one at hand. Paradoxically, however, it is also through the nonsensuous that the present is known—a present specious, as William James might way, because always passing. Nonsensuous perception could therefore be said to be the more-than of Appearance that catches Reality in the attuning to *what is*. Interpretation is the name Whitehead gives this instance of experience that distinguishes itself from the welter.

Interpretation shifts here from an external judgment to the carrying over of experience's tendencies into the present act. It is important to underline at this juncture that consciousness cannot be said to be central to it. The force of what distinguishes itself makes itself felt through a form-taking that infraconsciously aligns to past tendencies. The red patch is red *in this way* because redness is carried into the act by previous rednesses. The foregrounding of red carries with it the backgrounding of rednesses hovering. This hovering is what I mean by contrast. When Reality pushes into Appearance, what is felt is not a form or a thing but a quality of shaping, a transitory resonance orienting toward a coming-into-itself. Appearance carries Reality.

In the carrying of Reality, it is not that Appearance is bringing the form of Reality into the world. Reality has no form. What moves across to create the intensity of a contrast is a force, an orientation, a tendency. Events as they unfold carry the germs of what came before through the intensity of this force, gauging their capacity to make a difference in the world based on the degree to which contrast expresses itself: "It is gone, and yet it is here. It is our indubitable self, the foundation of our present existence. Yet the present occasion while claiming self-identity, while sharing the very nature of the bygone occasion in all its living activities, nevertheless is engaged in modifying it, in adjusting it to *other* influences, in completing it with *other* values, in deflecting it to *other* purposes. The present moment is constituted by the influx of *the other* into that self-identity which is the continued life of the immediate past within the immediacy of the present" (Whitehead 1967, 181).

Interpretation is not what comes from outside the event, as is usually assumed, but what allows the event itself to move into Appearance. Without interpretation, the welter cannot be parsed. Interpretation is therefore always immanent to the event. Interpretation is carried by the occasion itself: "This 'interpretation' does not seem to be necessarily the product of any elaborate train of intellectual cogitation. We find ourselves 'accepting' a world of substantial objects, directly presented for our experience. Our habits, our states of mind, our modes of behaviour, all presuppose this 'interpretation'" (Whitehead 1967, 216).

The backgroundingforegrounding pocket practice takes as its chief concern the ethical question of how contrast shifts the conditions of experience. It asks what happens with the influx of otherness in experience, with the adjustment "to *other* influences, . . . *other* values, . . . *other* purposes." How might this adjustment, in Leemann's words, "do the work of foregrounding relations such that *the relation itself* becomes the subject?" (Leemann, n.d.).

The context I want to bring to the fore is that of an artistic critique. Critiques in the academic study of artistic practice are ritual evaluations of artwork that usually happen toward the end of the academic term.

Leemann (2004) writes, "Critique of student work, by peers and faculty, is foundational to the way we currently teach art. We are assumed to understand what is meant by critique and to have similar expectations of how that practice unfolds. Rarely is this actually the case." When Leemann says that the ritual of critique is rarely understood by those who practice it, what she is referring to is the shared assumption, in artistic teaching contexts, that we collectively understand what is meant by critique. This assumption driving the practice of artistic critique usually means that we are confident that we know how to interpret what we see and that we share epistemological and aesthetic concerns. This is a lot to assume.

Never in the contexts in which I have taught has there been a conversation preceding a critique about what we understand by either critique or interpretation, or how we are coming to aesthetic criteria. It is not surprising then that critique tends to generalize about perception in ways that tend toward neurotypical— which is to say white—ways of seeing and knowing. In practice, this usually means a persistent disavowal of how our environments condition knowledge and how this conditioning plays out in the collective experience of engaging with artistic work. What usually happens as a result of this disavowal is that little attention is paid to what actually stands out as the object of critique. This lack of attention to the singularity of what we are collectively viewing is facilitated by the shared belief that we need not say what we actually see because we all see the same way. This results in an overcoding of that which we assume we all saw with an interpretive account of what we assume we know how to see. What this means in practice is that there is a strong tendency to abstract the work from its present form-force, engaging with an idea of what the work could or should be, basing that account on criteria of interpretation assumed to be shared by all.

The fallacy here is that what is sensed, as Whitehead underscores, carries with it all that germinates around the sensation but cannot, in the act of sensation itself, do the work of interpretation. Interpretation is what occurs in the shift to Appearance, and it is only by through that parsing that sensation can be known as such. Interpretation requires a practice of attunement to what actualizes and to how that actualization carries the force of experience unparsed.

In the ubiquitous studio art critique, I would say that the act of interpretation tends to be debased. What I mean by that is that interpretation is not what moves the work from within but what situates it from without. In turning to general criteria (categories of identity, of ethnicity, of history, of form), there is too often an elision of the work in favor of the category. If the work reads as ethnic, for instance, it is often the case that the artist will be asked to situate the work according to their racial difference. If the student is transgender, this will similarly happen in a way that would be much less likely to occur with a student whose gender is not in question. These ways of aligning interpretation to a general category are the most obvious way critique is neutralized through the imposition of habitual presuppositions. In Whitehead's terminology, this involves a lack of attunement to how the art itself presents an influx of otherness into the world.

Another way in which studio art critique engages with debased interpretation is the imposition on the work of a historical lineage before fully taking into account what the work at hand is doing. Tracing an alliance with other aesthetic tendencies can be an important aspect of moving the work forward, but too often this takes place before the close engagement with the current work occurs. Allied to this tendency is the practice of connecting a work to the critic's own work. This mode of critique is well known beyond the studio in the academic conference: we are accustomed to the question that refuses to engage with the work proposed, demanding that the work represent the interests of the critic. This mode of critique, whether it be in studio art or in the wider academic world, sidelines the work completely, framing it not according to its own inner operations but according to how the critic would have done it better. This second mode of critique is closely aligned to a tendency to instruct the maker on how their work is reminiscent of a whole series of other works external to the process at hand. This making-redundant of the work, a tendency also seen in the wider academic world, is based on a power play that alerts the maker/writer to the critic's wide knowledge base, ensuring that the work at hand is buried by all that (invisibly) surrounds it.

I call these forms of interpretation debased to emphasize how interpretation departs from the constellation of the work's Appearance to connect it, superficially and within a general framework, to concerns that exceed the work's present purview. Interpretation becomes evaluation, the critique no longer of the work itself but of all that the work purportedly carries with it. The problem is that what is brought into the context of the critique is not itself critiqued: it is assumed to be neutral. It is "just" a point of view.

With this act of distancing oneself from the work at hand comes the belief that anything one brings to critique is relevant. Anything goes. That is, anything goes except a close encounter with what is actually in the room. Because in foregrounding general categories, what occurs is a backgrounding of whatever else might emerge as part of the bringing into Appearance of the work. The presupposition is that we already know what the work can do.

What passes as perception in the examples above is actually a sense-constraining version of interpretation that does not take in the work *as it works*.

It is the working of the work Whitehead calls interpretation. Interpretation is *how* the work comes into the contrast of Appearance and Reality. If what happens in an artistic critique boils down to a wavering between externally produced opinion largely based on a generalized understanding of what the welter of experience contains and an interpretation of how that welter acts as a gloss on what is already considered to carry value in that context, what we have is an account of value, not an account of how the work works. Presupposition meets presupposition with very little focused attention on what actually appears through the work and how it resonates with the more-than of Appearance, how the quality of backgroundingforegrounding in the work creates contrast. This practice in turn neutralizes the immanent field of value (the world of value), overlooking the fact that the artful is, in its most powerful instantiation, an activation of new modes of valuation. Art that does its work must do more than connect to a market of preexisting accounts of value.

When Whitehead says about the patch of red, "We *do* interpret [it]; but no thanks for the feat is due to [it]" (1967, 180), he is referring to the nonsensuous perception at the heart of all experience. Nonsensuous perception, as mentioned above, is the culling of qualities of experience from experience parsed to experience parsed. This does not mean that the whole past is imported into the present—it means that experience as it unfolds is tinged with what was. This is what Whitehead is referring to when he says, "It is gone, and yet it is here" (181) about experience appearing. The self-identity of the occasion of experience, the thisness of its having come to be *just this way*, is colored by what moves (through) it: "The present moment is constituted by the influx of *the other* into that self-identity which is the continued life of the immediate past within the immediacy of the present" (181). This other that affects all present feeling, this other that moves the world as it unfolds, contributes to what is interpreted as Appearance.

That otherness is included in interpretation is what allows for continuation in perceptual experience. Otherness includes all that was felt in the previous half second of a past still pulsing through the event. This means that interpretation involves a certain conditioning of habit. A chair is interpreted as chair when it has become a habit of perception. What chairness was a half second ago is still chairness now. For many of us, chairness is immediately perceived as sit-ability. Appearance of chair is interpretation of sit-ability. Chair and sit-ability are fused in their actualization as overlap of sense and nonsensuous perception. A chair that brings forth hat-ability is less commonplace. Because of its unaccustomed entry into hatness, chair-as-hat carries more of the welter of Reality. This poses a challenge to interpretation. Chair as hat-ability introduces a complexity into sit-ability, exposing a certain schizzing of perception in the disjunction between chair and hat. This schizzing foregrounds the event of perception itself. With the tinge of chair overtaking hat, momentary perceptual confusion might ensue. This confusion is an expression of experience's excess on itself and the way that excess folds into perception. When hat-ability enters into experience in relation to a chair worn as a hat, whether conscious or not, interpretation carries this excess. As it moves uneasily beyond habit, an angle on the world expresses itself that would otherwise have remained muted. Contrast is directly felt. A persistent staying with what formerly stood for chairness is a refusal of the emergent attunement produced in the perceptual fold of experience schizzed.

It is this mode of interpretation that I see Leemann bringing in as an operative matrix for a retooling of critique.

> One can know a thing by seeing what it produces, generates or does without needing to take up the difficult if not impossible task of prying into origin or intention. Dropping the notion of linear causation for ever-circling interaction, any partial arc becomes a valid place to gather information about the system as a whole. Translating this approach to the studio art classroom, we take a chance and trust that reading the arc of a made object forward in terms of what it now produces/generates/does for viewers will reveal as much as any digging after the origins, the *why* of the work. We arrive in a place as speculative as it is pragmatic. (Leemann 2017, 183)

The work of attuning to the contrast of backgroundingforegrounding begins with a speculatively pragmatic approach. First, it asks the participant to engage directly: "*What?* Really just an articulation of what you see before you. Include observations that seem too obvious. Physically what's it made of? Can you discern different parts? Where does your attention linger?" (Leemann 2004). It is key that the *what* remain directly engaged with the work *as it appears*. The amplification that can occur with a focused and constrained *what* allows for a new set of questions: How does the arc of the work function? What does it foreground? What does it background? (Leemann 2004).

The *what* of Leemann's proposition must always be attuned to how it includes the constellation work-artist-participants. The *what* does not emerge in a neutrality of conditions. It is built into Appearance by the group. This is why it is so important to take care to make sure the dynamics of the process are clear: the collective crafting of what appears will necessarily bring into relation the group's own tendencies of perception. This is a fragile process, fragile because it makes felt the differential at the heart of Appearance, bringing into resonance the myriad ways in which Appearance and Reality co-compose.

This collective process foregrounds the speculative share of speculative pragmatism. Speculative pragmatism insists that what appears *appears* but that this form-taking always also carries an excess, a more-than. The more-than grows from the edges of the *what*. Only once the work's Appearance has been collectively composed can there then be an incursion into the *what else*. This *what else* is not an opportunity to return to wishing the work were other than it is: it is a phase shift that activates the more-than of Appearance. Interpretation, recall, is immanent to the process of a work's coming into Appearance. *What else* is about how else the work works, how else it comes into what it is. This speculative share is easy to miss, especially if the work is subdued by the practice of debased interpretation. To connect to the speculative share is to engage in the work of actively perceiving the force of perception's coming into itself. Often this speculative share will be as new to the artist as to those participating in what has now become an immanent critique.

Speculative pragmatism always includes an aspect of discovery. The *what else* pushes the work toward an expression of its potential, activating what moves infrathinly through it. For the work is all of this: the way it appears here-now, the spiral of time that moves through it, the way it morphs into constellation. Speculatively pragmatic interpretation is the practice of feeling-with a work's coming to be in the singular instance of its appearing again, here, now.

Backgroundingforegrounding is not only a practice for artistic critique. Immanent critique as a backgroundingforegrounding practice is deeply needed in all corners of life, be they academia more broadly or engagements with the world beyond as it comes into contrast. Think not only of the artistic critique but of the blind review, of the conference paper, of the student presentation, of the dinner-table conversation. Think of the assumption that the nonspeaking autistic has nothing to say, of the ways in which the spastic body is assumed to be a nonthinking body, of the tendency to see the black or brown body as the unreflecting body, of the tendency to situate woman as the affective rather than the conceptual participant. Recognizing the necessity of other ways of practicing critique is the only way to begin to address the willful exclusion of neurodiversity at the heart of the very concept of critique. Neutralized forms of knowing, generalized by systems of interpretation that renounce making the terms of the engagement visible, do not silence only those who are neurodiverse. They silence all life that deviates from existing frames that organize and perpetuate how we are taught to know, and to see.

Immanent critique asks that we return to those modes of interpretation that carry a process from within, and that we inquire, from that vantage point, how the work does its work. Not only will this allow us to generate an account of what the work can do, it will challenge the codes that permit neurotypical generalization to play such a large role in critique, providing us with the tools to locate and challenge the neutralization of experience activated by such dangerous habits of generalization.

The pocket practice of backgroundingforegrounding must therefore be seen as one that attends, above all, to an ethos of encounter that practices attunement to the speculatively pragmatic share of experience in the making. This ethos carries stakes, and these stakes will likely be most visible in the context of what is sidelined in a process that assumes a neutral context for interpretation. It did not surprise Leemann that a university-level study found that black students and people of color felt particularly marginalized in situations of critique: "It was . . . sobering . . . to see in the results of a recent diversity survey at our college how often studio critique came up as a concern for our students of color. Sobering in the sense of seeing how much I hadn't seen of the way this central pedagogical practice, especially when performed in classes with one or only a few students of color, becomes another place in which insides and outsides, 'included' others against a normed white background, get inscribed" (2017, 191). Critique is never neutral, nor is aesthetic judgment, or interpretation external to the conditions of experience unfolding.

Leemann's sensitivity in the context of studio critique extends to the question of how art and aesthetic perception affects and infiltrates practices of living. How does a racialized seeing affect what we recognize as art? "Could changing how we talk about work amongst students and teachers ripple out to offer other kinds of orientation to works of art?" she asks (2017, 191). How we critique, as Leemann underscores, "not only reveal[s] our most fundamental epistemologies of art making and viewing" (191), it offers us a vital opportunity to enact perception differently.

"Content," Leemann (2008) emphasizes, "is the last thing we're teaching." A backgroundingforegrounding pocket practice begins here, beyond content, and extends far beyond the studio art classroom. How we collectively perceive what happens, how we participate in the constellation of catching the world in formation, how we ourselves are caught by experience in the making, these are the stakes of backgroundingforegrounding.

Experimenting Immediation: Collaboration

and the Politics of Fabulation

A Laboratory for Thought in Motion

When I proposed SenseLab in 2003, my hope was to create an environment that would learn, over time, how to create conditions for new forms of collaboration across art, philosophy, and the political. This laboratory for thought in motion was a speculative proposition that required collective engagement, and so a first call was sent in 2004. This call included a question that remains at the heart of our collective practice: what kinds of events can we craft that are capable of creating a living ecology that values forms of engagement that trouble the mode of self-presentation of the conference and the art exhibition, the two major ways in which we are taught to share our work? Instead of foregrounding finished work, could we instead come together with the techniques that move our process, collaborate at this incipient stage rather than at the phase where form is already revealing itself? In this middling of the process, what kinds of conditions could be invented that would facilitate a shifting back and forth between our individual work and a collective field of making-thinking that doesn't know in advance where it might lead? What kinds of collective practices could be created that are moved not by the institution, not by membership in an organization, but by an appetite for the anarchic share of the event's coming to form? How could this anarchic share be oriented toward an affirmative politics moved not by optimism (or pessimism) but by the schizz that reorients process?

SenseLab was never conceived as a site, though it has found landings over the years, first in other people's labs and eventually at Concordia University in Montreal.[1] In 2012 it began to proliferate, finding temporary sites in Australia, Europe, Brazil, and the United States, temporary because the hope is that SenseLab never really learns how to site. To know too well how to site is to become an institution. SenseLab's nightmare is to know itself too well.

But anything that persists over time risks eventually narrating itself, and SenseLab is no exception. How to keep open and lively the process of subtracting SenseLab from its own narrative, its ways of knowing "itself"? There have been many configurations and populations over the years, and each of them has defined SenseLab in ways that make a global narration impossible. And so the attempt here to bring SenseLab into narration must always be seen as carrying with it a certain ineffability. Throughout these uneasy narrations, SenseLab must be seen less as a form than as the conceptual persona it orients, a conceptual persona that carries living problems, not their solutions.

Conceptual personae carry not the truth of the narration but its power of the false. "A new narration follows from this: narration ceases to be truthful, that is, to claim to be true, and becomes fundamentally falsifying. This is not at all a case of 'each has his own truth,' a variability of content. It is a power of the false which replaces and supersedes the form of the true, because it poses the simultaneity of incompossible presents, or the coexistence of not-necessarily true pasts" (Deleuze 1989, 131). Friedrich Nietzsche's will to power is at work here, a will always immanent to the event that finds its power in the relation, in the overlap of force at its most potent differential.[2] "The power of the false exists only from the perspective of a series of powers, always referring to each other and passing into one another" (Deleuze 1989, 133).

The danger of any narration is that it mythologizes, that it builds institutions that hold narratives in place. What I propose here, in the name of experimenting immediation, is an account that I hope demythologizes as quickly as it enters into a shape, an account oriented not by a subject-participant so much as by an emergent collectivity always reinventing the stakes that bring it into uneasy encounter. For SenseLab is about more-than human comings-together, more-than human in the sense that what comes into formation as event is an ecology of practices, more-than human in the sense that what is planned is not set in advance of the event's coming to be but is, as Fred Moten and Stefano Harney might say, "fugitively planned," the welling event's own emergent organization playing a key role in what ensues.

This emphasis on the more-than human, on the capacity for the event to activate a quality of participation that doesn't rely solely on the human, became increasingly important as SenseLab grew and became more literate. The more we told our story, the more it became clear that we were in danger of creating a collective that could only know itself from the inside. To know oneself from the inside is to believe that the constitution of the event is directly linked to the people who are visible in its formation. But events are not like this: they are troubled and energized by affective tonalities that infiltrate their bounds, oriented by the push and pull of ecologies brought simultaneously into being. And so we started inventing techniques to make felt the proliferation of tendencies and consistencies that make up events, working hard to become attuned to forms of participation that complicate notions of individual subjectivity and human-centric organization. Moving, for instance, from the forest to the city in the 2012 event *Generating the Impossible* was an attempt to feel the effects of how an environmental surround also composes and participates in the process of making-thinking.[3] How, we wondered, would what began to take form in the forest come to expression in the city? What quality of schizzing would emerge in the transversality of transduction? Conceiving transduction—a shift that creates a new process—as key to a politics that sites in the doing, it became urgent to consider how events themselves craft bodies, how they create emergent bodyings that are composed of and compose with the ecologies that move through them.

The focus on the more-than human was also geared toward challenging the category of the personal. When the personal organizes experience, two main tendencies emerge. First, there is an infiltration of a politics of identity that tends to amplify not what the emergent collectivity can do but what personal stakes are understood to be present even before the project takes form. While these personal stakes no doubt make some kind of contribution in the event, SenseLab's approach is to initially background them in favor of allowing the event itself to foreground how it mobilizes political, aesthetic, and philosophical problems. The second tendency of the personal is toward the creation of a normative psychologization that privileges individual narratives. SenseLab turns instead to a schizoanalytic approach that focuses on the group-subject, the agglomeration of collective forces in the event. With attention to how group-subjects both come into formation and express their collectivity, we work from the perspective of what an emergent constellation can do rather than what individual participants owe the event and are owed by it. Our main point of emphasis is that SenseLab is a project that exceeds any individual participant: the project should always be more-than the sum of its parts. This is no easy task: the uncertainty at the heart of the minor sociality that is emergent collectivity, where the production of subjectivity is understood as immanent to the event, inevitably breeds anxiety, and anxiety tends to solidify personal stakes. How to escape from the positioning of the personal before it takes hold?

The Free Radical

The concept of the free radical was brought into the mix in 2012 to begin to address this question of how to work collectively with a focus on emergent collectivity and the ways in which it produces subjectivity. The free radical came in through the event discussed above, *Generating the Impossible*, an event whose focus was on affective attunement and altereconomies of exchange. The free radical, as we envisaged it, would infiltrate the event's interstices, keeping the event from hardening around individual positions. Operating transversally to the practices of making-thinking orienting the event, the free radical would punctually unglue the position-taking that seeks to tune the event to personal stakes. It would do the work of a trickster around inevitable personalization, creating opportunities for the event to find new orientations capable of defusing the kind of stabilization that breeds eventual institutionalization. The hope was that the free radical, despite (and because of) its deeply unsettling tendencies, would make it possible to create a culture of affirmation that didn't fall prey to a desire to settle the event into a culture of consensus, or its by-product, critique. Affirmation is understood here in the Nietzschean sense: active, not reactive. Affirmation is not consensus, that most flattening of practices, nor is it "anything goes."[4] In an always shifting register of minor sociality, SenseLab moves where the experiment takes it, casting propositions aside without looking back if they don't do their work. We practice saying "yes" in the vitality of an anarchic orientation that carries a belief in this world's capacity to differ from itself, anarchic because the stakes are not set out in advance according to a pregiven model of the political or the social.[5]

Working from the perspective of the anarchic, thinking anarchy both in terms of the anarchic share of the event (those merest of existences that seed future processes without necessarily taking form as such) and from the perspective that an event always exceeds the bounds of prescribed spacetimes of organization, a concept was needed to activate the event's transversality, amplifying the differential of its schizz. The free radical is conceived as an intercessor capable of subverting narratives on the verge of stultification by magnifying the powers of the false infrathinly schizzing through any and all accounts of how things should be.[6] While we did have a person in mind for this first experiment with the concept of the free radical, the figure was also conceived in a broader way, without a human motor. Affinity groups that might be capable of both incorporating and sustaining the force of free radicality were composed in advance of our coming together, and across them platforms for relation for seeding affective attunement to the event. With the free radical as concept, proposition, and intercessor, the question was: what does the creative dissonance of the anarchic share of experience *do* for the event as it unfolds? How does a resonant field of experience that includes the merest of existences affect attunement to the event? What might attention become, under these circumstances? With the benefit of hindsight, I would say that these were early steps toward developing techniques for what we have come to call minor gestures, those emergent forces of variation that shift how an event comes to pass.

The free radical cuts across the event to open it to where else it could go. Always operative, the free radical jumps into fissures, fostering new directionalities that alter what an event can do. Affirmative and joyful, the figure of the free radical is nonetheless uneasy-making in its anarchic tendencies. Its technique is to open things up, to explode them. With this come closures as new paths are taken up: there is much reorienting to do when the ground shifts. The free radical has no care for sites that claim their ground.

SenseLab has never had membership. Membership would make the free radical a member, which would, of course, destroy its potential for intercession. The free radical must be capable of becoming everymember, and every tendency in the event must carry the potential for free-radicalization.

The issue of membership nonetheless rears its head. Despite there being no actual membership, it is inevitable that certain cultures take hold and, over time, embody a history of what it can mean to be involved at SenseLab, which can lead to feelings of exclusion. Uncertainty can be overpowering, especially in the context of the kind of practice that emphasizes not-knowing-in-advance. Tensions can emerge. This can be hard for newcomers. But with the intercession of difference so much becomes possible! There is nothing like the clearing of the air that can come from a new way of entering! We see this as part of our practice: what makes an event-based orientation powerful is precisely its intercessors. The culture of SenseLab actively works to collaborate with the transversality intercession engenders.

This raises an interesting issue: how to work between the activation of what enters from elsewhere and the inheritances that come from working together over time. There is no question that the force of inheritance makes a difference: a practice that takes techniques seriously and works with the enabling constraints of a structured improvisation over years inevitably develops practices. Despite its openness to process, SenseLab, as mentioned above, in no way works in a posture of "anything goes." This is the case for material intervention as much as for concept invention. We commit to what we learn together, and we stay with the learning for extended periods to experiment with where it can take us. There are practices that underlie this commitment to the thickness of an evolving process. For instance, it is our practice to read closely from philosophical texts with what Bertrand Russell calls "hypothetical sympathy" (1961, 58).[7] Reading groups are facilitated in ways that work to reduce debate. We emphasize that what is important is how the text does its work in its own logic. To feel-out what is at work in the work, we read out loud, our collective focus on the materiality of expression of the text at hand. The reading out loud also facilitates neurodiverse participation (recognizing that there are always those among us for whom words on a page do not order themselves one letter at a time). We record so that anyone can return to the reading at their own pace. We open the reading group to virtual participation for those who are far away, those who prefer the distance of the online world to operate socially, and those for whom a university is a site too exclusive to enter comfortably. The same is true for movement experimentation and material exploration—an attention to the singular material conditions of our coming into relation is always at the forefront. Our investment in a politics of affirmation does not mean having no constraints. It means working-with, sitting-with, the singular ways in which the materiality of collaboration unfolds and activates nodes of process. A culture of critique and competition would destroy these collective processes.[8] And so we work to avoid any tendency to move in that direction. We are aware that the culture of academia loves general ideas, and we resist this tendency to speak in ways that generalize experience. What interests us is always a commitment to *how*. How does the thinking do its work? How do the materials activate a transversality? How does the movement shift the conditions of the bodying?

That said, there is no question that leaving the space of intercession open is vital: very often, events have been reoriented by new arrivals precisely because these newcomers are not informed by the history of our ongoing practice. And so, over the past seventeen years, we have worked to hone an event-based practice of welcoming difference. This welcoming of difference brings with it the quality of an ethos. It is not our practice to discuss "our" way. What we do instead is try to hone a mode of listening to the event as it unfolds. A pragmatics of the useless is always attuned to how valuation *emerges*, coloring the event from the vantage point of its speculative share. The hope is always that the newcomer can feel the stakes at hand and participate in them directly. It is beautiful to watch how often this happens, how often a newcomer arrives in the middling to reorient what came before in ways desperately needed. Almost every day there is an intercession, each of these intercessions shifting the conditions of what we call SenseLab. It would therefore be fair to say that the intercession of the sideways entry is as much part of the inheritance of SenseLab as the years of practice honed in the ongoing work of creating techniques for event-based experimentation.

No decision-making bodies external to the process exist at SenseLab. We have no governing body, no committee to oversee activities. This developed organically from a desire to work from within the event's own conditionings. What has resulted is a politics of immediation, a politics sensitive to the practice of middling as lived in the untimely rhythm of time folding. It is a radical proposition to remain open to new tendencies all the time. Free radicalization inevitably gets watered down by the fear of losing our footing. And yet we persist because we know that the desire for continuity, for the recognition of the past in the present, is a real danger as regards the ability to remain attuned to the differential at the heart of event-based propositions.

This is a challenge all political formations face. How to keep the edges open to the elements in ways that enliven those in the midst without creating such a strong tempest of uncertainty that collaborators drift away? How to practice such vivid disorientation without the collapse of the collective? How to build into the sociality that emerges over time enough porousness that it remains open to the fray? For it is only in the fray that new weaves become visible.

SenseLab lives with all of these contradictions. We often contend with failure. The transitions are messy. Growing pains are deep and often agonizing.

Immediation

With the force of the free radical active as intercessor, and close attention paid to how minor gestures affect event ecologies, how else can the event tell its story? What kinds of knowledges are alive in the event, and how are they passed on? A question to the anarchive: how can we move beyond mediation, or reporting, in the passage from force to form? How can we compose collectively, working with both past and emergent techniques, without holding fast to the security of habits, material or conceptual? While seeking ways to make experience intelligible, how do we refrain from mythologizing it? How can the immediacy of the event cut through the certainty of a certain belonging-together, a return to the figure of the individual and to the collective as the sum of its parts?

Immediation is a practice more than it is a descriptor. A politics of fabulation invariably accompanies it. Fabulation is altogether different from a practice of mythologization: it is that tendency in the telling that resists organizing the event into the kind of consumable bite-sized description that would narrate it as a linear arc. This kind of telling "free[s] [fiction] from the model of truth which penetrates it, and . . . rediscover[s] the pure and simple *function of fabulation*. . . . What is opposed to fiction is not the real; it is not the truth which is always that of the masters or colonizers; it is the fabulatory function of the poor, in so far as it gives the false the power which makes it into a memory, a legend, a monster" (Deleuze 1989, 150; translation modified).[9] Inheritor of oral practices of storytelling, fabulation is how the trickster speaks. As the voice of the free radical, fabulation attunes to the difference between those kinds of narratives that hold the event hostage and those that breed openings. It's not that these more normative narratives don't enter the world: they do. Our task is to craft the conditions for events that resist this kind of telling, opting instead for a fabulation that undermines the very question of an event's localization in a single place, toward predictable ends, activating not the truth of a myth framed by individual accounts but its power of the false, the power of the event to claim its falsification from itself. With the power of the false, time begins to err, undermining the imposition of continuity. Time as metric is disrupted, but not just that: time folds.[10]

The free radical activates the power of the false in the event. Acting as intercessor, it cuts into what is moving the event and opens that movement to uneasy rhythms. These rhythms are uneasy because their paths are not yet drawn, and because these paths are both asynchronous and dissonant, more multiplicity of cut than site. The free radical pushes against them to feel where they break, and where else they can lead.

The free radical propels a minor tendency to take hold in the event. The practice of free radicality involves moving that tendency into a becoming-gesture that shape-shifts the tonality of the event. The free radical does this by activating a schizz in the event. This schizoanalytic gesture involves setting the event's myth-making orientations in direct confrontation with their power of the false, making felt the story's own unmaking of itself. With the power of the false a sense of what else enters the event, allowing the contours of a still-transitioning to be felt. The challenge is to refrain from flattening this time of transition. What Nyong'o calls an "angular sociality" is at work here, "a dynamic interaction or entanglement of bodies, each keeping its own time" (2018, 59).[11] This angular sociality, active in the middling of accounts coming into themselves with the force of an event-ness that refuses the easy ordering of a simple description of what was, produces the force of a fabulation that is fully indebted to how things came into itself and yet always also in excess of a simple parsing of events. Language will never be a simple ally. The work: to create the conditions for enough elasticity in the event for the story to emerge again differently, told not only in words but also in the language of the ineffable. "Language . . . is always ambiguous as to the exact proposition which it indicates. Spoken language is merely a series of squeaks" (Whitehead 1978, 264). And this in a time of an angular engagement with what also cuts across it, including any attempt to make time neutral and, as it were, "colorless": "Readings of black art, cinema, and performance must acknowledge the insurrectionary stance taken in the everyday, not just to anti-black times, but to time itself, at least to time considered as a neutral, universal, and, as it were, 'colorless' phenomenon. It is the notion of the transparency of time as an innocent unit of measure that I mean to contest in my argument for a thicker and more expansive account of what we can call black polytemporality" (Nyong'o 2018, 115–16).

Fabulation operates in a time of asynchronous weave. Sensitive to the squeaks of language, to language at the edge of comprehension, fabulation is moved less by the necessity to explain than by the realization, always come to anew, that telling is a form of liveness completely connected to the event's own emergence. Here, stories become intensive magnitudes rather than extensive placeholders. They tell at the limit of what can be known, their work a falsifying of what constitutes the knowable. This falsification is not of the order of a simple untruth: the power of the false is about another kind of truth altogether, a truth of the event in its inevitable permutation. For Alfred North Whitehead, truth refers to how an occasion of experience activates the coincidence of the world of value and the world of activity. He writes, "Truth of belief is important, both in itself and in its consequences. But above all there emerges the importance of the truthful relation of Appearance to Reality. A grave defect in truth limits the extent to which any force of feeling can be summoned from the recesses of Reality. The falsehood thus lacks the magic by which a beauty beyond the power of speech to express can be called into being, as if by the wand of an enchanter" (1967, 283). Truth for Whitehead is a force. It finds its power not at the surface of appearance but in the potential that shimmers across it. Truth is what appears through an indexing to "a beauty without speech," a discordant massiveness called forth in the interval of an intercession. Fabulation commits to the power of the false every time it connects to this force, enchanted by the tinge of otherworldliness this carries with it. Rather than morality, what is seeded every time is belief in the world, "an act of fabulation which would not be a return to myth but a production of collective utterances capable of raising misery to a strange positivity, the invention of a people" (Deleuze 1989, 222).

When fabulation textures the event, the telling acts as point of inflection, making felt the kind of vertigo that emerges of necessity when perspectives are transversalized and time signatures that hold accounts in place begin to blur. Fabulation tells into this blurring, verging the chronotope in ways that move time out of sync. Mediation is not what is at stake here: the task of the mediator is precisely to keep the horizon line. Fabulation does the opposite: it mobilizes the not-yet already alive in the interstices and makes it reverberate. It catches free radicals at work, activating a worlding that keeps the event uncertain as to where its points of reference lie, falsifying time's linearity.

The power of the false, the capacity for fabulation to challenge what a personalized accounting might want to invent as the event's truth, is deeply unsettling. Much easier would be to formalize a frame for the event in the name of some kind of overarching truth. To write myths that solidify it, creating the possibility of repetition. But both of these tendencies undermine the very practice of what an event can do and what a more-than human approach can catalyze. Much more difficult, but also richer, is to engage directly in the event's interstices, in those schizzes where desynchronized accounts are crafted for the uneasy telling. "Fabulation is not an impersonal myth, but neither is it a personal fiction: it is a word in act, a speech-act through which the character never ceases to cross the boundary which would separate his private business from politics, and which itself produces collective utterances" (Deleuze 1989, 222; translation modified).

To not cease to cross paradoxically involves a punctuality. The event never ceases to create a limit through which a certain telling takes place that produces a collectivity of utterance. That is to say: the event invariably narrates itself in part because of the difficulty of asserting, from within its own momentum, the swell of its cresting. This telling has the quality of a talking-to-oneself that occurs as we move through daily tasks, sometimes hearing ourselves narrate out loud the act of recalling what we have forgotten to look for in the open fridge. The telling of the event is a kind of seeking-its-bearings, an accounting of the ways in which it composes with the ecologies of practices that are its emergent surrounds. The event transitions more than it places, passaging experience. Fabulation can catch this telling in the passaging, detouring mythmaking tendencies. In this passaging, a "people" is invented, Deleuze suggests, a worlding that is more-than the humans who also compose it. With fabulation, this worlding opens itself each time anew to the passaging. This is where the event, as Whitehead might say, most feels the concern for its unfolding (see Whitehead 1967), where it emergently attunes to worlds of its making. Fabulation makes this ecology felt, a worlding which will always, by necessity, exceed its capacity to be told. This telling, at the heart of all events, is a punctual limit, altered at every turn by what the event immediates.

Tigeresque

In November 2014 a SenseLab gathering was organized in Australia. It was composed of two propositions, one held north of Melbourne in the rural town of Avoca, the other held in Sydney. The first proposition was made in conjunction with Lyndal Jones's *Avoca Project*.[12]

The *Avoca Project* (2005–2016) worked across a community, a house (Watford House), and the question of sustainability as oriented by how an artful approach can alter the conditions of everyday living. How, Jones wondered, might the house become an image of potential and resilience, and how would such an approach have effects that might leak into the wider community of the town of Avoca? (email correspondence, October 2015).

SenseLab arrived toward the end of this process, a decade into Watford House's transformation. The proposition for the SenseLab-Avoca encounter was to see how SenseLab's approach to creating conditions for more-than human forms of collaboration might compose with the *Avoca Project*. By then the final phase of the *Avoca Project* had begun: a Chinese garden in the old sheep yards next to the house had recently been landscaped. Described by Jones as a project that "draws attention to the lack of public gardens in Avoca . . . and acknowledges the important Chinese contribution to the town from the 1850s, when many thousands settled in the area after the gold rush," the garden, entitled "Garden of Fire and Water," punctuated a decade-long inquiry into sustainability by designing directly with the underground flows of water. This self-sustaining garden underscored "that to live-with is an ethos that requires attending to the existing sites of potential," signing the *Avoca Project* with a final act that would continue to make sustainability in the region felt, even without direct human intervention.[13]

The garden is exquisite. It overlooks the floodplain and the Avoca River, foregrounding the role water plays in this arid town. "The central water element has been created as a wetland that cleans and uses the stormwater from the main street. Plants were selected that directly reference China and thrive in this

climate, framed within indigenous and native plantings to situate the garden firmly into this landscape of River Red Gums."[14] SenseLab's arrival coincided with the launch of the garden. The only directions we received in advance of our arrival were that we were to bring formal wear: there would be a cocktail party for the garden. In true SenseLab form, we saw ourselves as guests of the garden. In our months-long preparation for the SenseLab-Avoca encounter, we spoke often about how best to fulfill our role as guest of honor for the garden: it was the surrounds we most fabulated about.

No other plans had been set: the question of the event itself was the operative problem. Could SenseLab encounter the *Avoca Project* such that the gathering might call forth an event? And if so, would the event be capable of bringing into focus an emergent proposition that could enliven what was already moving at Avoca? Could SenseLab bring the force of a lure that might activate the anarchic share in the transversality of the two projects? And if so, what kind of proposition might be made that both included us *and* exceeded us?

To approach the question of event-creation rigorously involves a long preparation. This preparation is not about planning content in advance, as though the activity could be focalized through a preset frame. That would be to disregard the force of the event's own capacity to orient experience. What is needed instead is a procedure allied to what Harney and Moten call "fugitive planning," an orientation toward conditions that seed process while remaining sensitive to the emergent quality of the event's own forces of organization. "In the undercommons . . . the means, which is to say the planners, are still part of the plan. And the plan is to invent the means in a common experiment launched from any kitchen, any back porch, any basement, any hall, any park bench, any improvised party, every night. . . . Planning in the undercommons is not an activity, not fishing or dancing or teaching or loving, but the ceaseless experiment with the futurial presence of the forms of life that make such activities possible" (Harney and Moten 2013, 74–75).

At SenseLab, to craft a sensitivity toward the kind of fugitive planning that occurs during an event, we explore and test enabling constraints. As described in chapter 3, enabling constraints are constraints that facilitate a process of improvisation that is attuned to the quality of what moves through the event. For a year preceding any event, we work to test out the malleability of various constraints, exploring to what degree they close down or open up a process. Starting points for the crafting of enabling constraints proposed for a gathering such as that in Australia might include research on local flora and fauna, animal and insect life; research on local environmental practices. We would likely explore who lives on the land, who the land originally belonged to, and what kinds of histories are told about the land. From these starting points, a few concepts might arise that might give us a hint of what kind of constraint might facilitate an entering into the environment otherwise than with all of the more typical assortment of personal stakes that tend to accompany us, especially when we feel out of place. From there, we might propose a series of movement experimentation workshops to see how different qualities of bodying would best respond to emergent propositions. Or we might engage in material experimentation to hone material curiosity, investigating a few starting points for collective practices that emerge from the materials themselves. Constraints that might emerge from this exploratory stage could include a movement proposition to open the event, a set of readings to study collectively, a technique for listening, a proposition for collective material composition. To keep this at the level of the fugitive, and to work with the force of the propositional rather than with the framing of the organizational, our yearlong work is more a guide than a setting-into-place. What we know of the event is that it modulates on the run, and with this incipient movement, enabling constraints invariably have to be modulated. Fugitive planning is about creating a flexibility of thought and action that is robust enough to be realigned on the fly. Importing an enabling constraint fully-formed from one event to another never works. Each event is too singular, its necessities too unique. The trick is to hone a sensitivity that will come in handy when faced with the event as it plays out. Improvising collectively requires an attunement to what is disabling and a capacity to reorient when needed. To do this from within the event's movement is the challenge. It requires a sense of how minor socialities are composing at every level of an eventness too complex to parse. Infrathin qualities of perception are necessary, but they are only as good as the capacity to move at the pace of an unfolding in asynchronous time.

Despite rigorous exploration in advance of landing, however, nothing had prepared us for the uneasy way the *Avoca Project* disoriented us. It turned out that the cocktail party was for the locals, not for the garden! The formal wear that we had brought or made (replete with leaves and branches) was suddenly not what was called for. And the house strangely seemed to know where it stood. We had imagined it more forlorn, less self-composed. With a house quite steady on its foundations we suddenly felt in the presence of a home. Our techniques for the activation of the threshold suddenly felt off. The jet lag didn't help. Here we were, thirty-five of us from several continents, faced with a project difficult to gauge. Paradoxes loomed: there was a sense, conceptually at least, that Watford House welcomed an intercession toward new ways of thinking sustainability. But there was also a sense that we had arrived too late—that this particular arc of Watford House and the *Avoca Project* had run its cycle, including the garden, which was now ready to be presented. Another arc was on its way, but here we were, at the interstice, unsure how to compose with what we entered into.

SenseLab didn't want to be a visitor to a project already framed, nor did the *Avoca Project* simply want to host us. The problem was that neither of us yet had techniques to creatively compose with the ineffability of the emerging arc. What SenseLab thought would be enabling constraints turned out to be disabling. We wandered around, at a loss. Part of the problem was that things were more set than we had imagined—the house was beautifully appointed, much more home than "experiment," the surrounds well maintained, and the project itself well established in relation to a town that had now been interacting with the work for a decade. Everything was gorgeous, including the work the *Avoca Project* had been able to do with issues of sustainability and community. The problem was not the *Avoca Project* itself. The issue was one of composition—how to attune to a minor sociality when cracks are not easily felt, when it is not even certain that an emergent collaboration is urgently needed, or needed at all. Despite our not wanting the position, we felt like visitors, tourists. As mentioned above, this was Jones's nightmare: more than once she told us that she didn't want us to see Watford House as a bed-and-breakfast. She wanted us to be free in our approach to it—she wanted us to invent with it. But it was a house that had well-established needs and habits. Jones knew its functioning better than we did, and she knew the environment in ways that tired Canadians, Brazilians, and Europeans couldn't possibly. And so, despite best intentions, the encounter began with frames, and with rules. The rules made sense, and were necessary, given the complex water systems of an arid location, but to begin with rules always sets in place a certain passive-active hierarchy. Passivity, once settled into the weave of a gathering, is hard to overcome, dampening the force of the kind of potential necessary for the emergence of a collectivity created in the event.

An impasse could be felt. A certain waiting took hold. Would we be able to move beyond being visitors to being participants in a process? Would the cracks appear? Were there any openings for fugitive planning? Activities were proposed by a number of us—movement experimentation, sound propositions, conceptual discussions. We followed and participated. Wonderful meals were cooked. But mediation still trumped immediation. Time felt linear. People were on call, waiting to be told what would happen next.

The first two days were dominated by scattered gatherings made interesting by the skills of the facilitators. We learned things, we talked, we explored. Individual projects were seeded. There was enjoyment in being together. But there was not yet a sense that something with its own consistency was being generated, something capable of weaving the *Avoca Project* through it, moving the encounter with SenseLab toward a collaboration that would affect both in ways unexpected. There was some despair. And with the cocktail party approaching, there was some anxiety about where to move next.

A group gathered at the local pub began to fabulate. The *Avoca Project*, the group decided, had a story—it just needed to be told differently so that SenseLab could connect to it. If we could figure out how that telling could happen, we were sure to find cracks. So far, the stories the *Avoca Project* had told SenseLab were spoken as though they already knew their way. What the *Avoca Project* didn't know how to tell SenseLab was how the *Avoca Project* fabulated, how the deeper recesses of more-than human activity affected it, how the power of the false ran through it. The Chinese garden, we decided, was key. This garden that could stem flows and capture them for its sustainability had a story to tell about how geological time composes with event-time, how the time of an art project composes with the time of worlds in the making. We would stage an investigation to find out what it knew.

For the six of us around the table, the promise of a fabulatory investigation was a release from the concern that had been clouding our experience: now, rather than fitting into a project already defined, we could initiate a joyful encounter with what else Watford House and the Chinese garden could be. Certain characters immediately emerged: the fish (what was the link between the fish tank in Watford House and the fish brought by a resident of Avoca to the cocktail party?), the possum (what kinds of skylines were the possums creating, and how far were they willing to go to create new navigational strategies?), the tunnel (what kind of underground passage did the water flows create, and how might these connect Watford House to other worlds?). We spoke to villagers. We checked with each other. We spoke to Jones. No one took us very seriously.

But another quality of perception had been awakened, and some of us were now seeing fish everywhere. On the day before our time at Avoca was to end, with fish on the brain, a few of us decided we needed to return to conceptual exploration. A spontaneous reading group was organized around Brian Massumi's *What Animals Teach Us about Politics*. This hadn't been planned, but it turned out that several of the participants had the newly published book in their luggage. We decided to begin by reading a passage out loud and go from there. This was the passage:

> Think of a child playing the animal. It is certainly easy to sentimentalize the scene. But what if we take it seriously—that is, look to the aspects of it that are truly ludic in the most creative sense. Simondon writes that the child's consciousness of the animal involves far more than the simple

recognition of its substantial form. One look at a tiger, however fleeting and incomplete, whether it be in the zoo or in a book or in a film or video, and presto! the child is tigerized. Transformation-in-place. The perception itself is a vital gesture. The child immediately sets about, not imitating the tiger's substantial form as he saw it, but rather giving it life—giving it more life. The child plays the tiger in situations in which the child has never seen a tiger. More than that, it plays the tiger in situations no tiger has ever seen, in which no earthly tiger has ever set paw. The child immediately launches itself into a movement of surpassing the given, remaining remarkably faithful to the theme of the tiger, not in its conventionality but from the angle of its processual potentiality.

Remaining processually faithful to a vital theme has nothing to do with reproducing it. On the contrary, it involves giving it a new interpretation, in the musical sense of performing a new variation on it. The child does not imitate the visible corporeal form of the tiger. It prolongs the tiger's style of activity, transposed into the movements of the child's own corporeality. What the child caught a glimpse of was the dynamism of the tiger, as a form of life. The child saw the tiger's vitality affect: the potentially creative powers of life enveloped in the visible corporeal form. The tiger's vitality affect passes through what a formal analysis might isolate as its corporeal form. But it never coincides with that visible form. The life's powers that come to expression through the form's deformations sweep the form up within their own supernormal dynamism, which moves through the given situation, toward others further down the line. This transsituational movement is in excess over the form. It is the very movement of the visually given form's processual self-surpassing. This is what the child saw—all of it, in a glimpse; all in a flash. Not just a generic animal shape: a singular vital movement sweepingly immanent to the visible form. What children see: the immanence of a life. Not "the" tiger: tigritude. Children do not just catch sight of a tiger form. They have an intuitively aesthetic vision of the tigeresque as a dynamic form of life. It is this they transpose when they play animal. Not onto their own form but into their own vital movements. . . . Across the serial variations, tigritude begins to escape. It begins to surpass given situations in which we might reasonably expect a tiger to find itself, and the modes of importance those situations present. The tensions of tigeresque corporeality in-forms the childlike corporeality in play. It immanently animates it—and is animated by it in return. The replay series stretches out the tigeresque tensions, prolonging them into a transindividual tensor. The situational tensions put into play undergo an inventively deforming pressure that vectorizes them in the direction of the supernormal. Tigritude takes flight. The givens of the tigeresque situation, as conventionally known, are surpassed, following exploratory tensors extrapolating from the child's enthusiasm of the body. (2014, 86)

Animals were emerging everywhere—fish, possums, and now the enthusiasm of the body activated by a tigeresque encounter with a book. The fish, the possum, and the tiger were not, as Massumi makes clear, given forms. They were forces, vitality affects. The emerging investigation, and now the collective reading, was not bringing them, as animals, to life: it was activating experience such that it might now be capable of becoming transsituational, in excess of this moment, of this form. The *Avoca Project* was becoming self-surpassing. Of course all of this was still very tenuous, but the seeds for a shift were there—which is why one reading could not be enough: the next and last day, we decided to return to the passage again, despite being very short on time.

By now the tigeresque was making its way into the weave of the event. Something was doing. And then a strange event occurred. Someone decided to spray-paint the desert lawn bright orange with these words: "To avoid predetermination create a field with at least three elements." The graffiti—an engagement with the tigeresque quality of the more-than in Massumi's text—sought to highlight the necessity of the minor sociality of emergent collectivity, but it did so at grave risk. The landscape we left behind was scarred and would remain so until the next rain, a year in Watford House's future.

The orange spray paint didn't quite register. To this day, I'm not sure why. We were busy, the event hadn't quite taken place (the encounter remaining a gathering rather than exceeding the sum of its parts), and the time spent together had been challenging—interesting and even joyful at times, but heavy with misunderstandings and uneasy encounters. There was laundry to do, and cleanup, and the grounds were large. Many of us walked by the large expanse of bright orange words, but somehow no one reacted. Until we were gone.

It was an hour or so into the drive toward Melbourne when someone in the car with us mentioned the grass, and the orange spray paint. We gasped. Surely this hadn't been a good idea? But if it did happen, it must have been condoned? I felt uneasy.

A few hours later, the first text message arrived. I could feel the rawness. And I knew the risk of answering: the event, still uneasily coming into itself, could too easily be reduced to the personal. The desire to single out an individual and blame them for the act was potent, even in the wake of a gathering that had had collectivity and collaboration as its aim. What would an apology mean in this context?

Wouldn't an inevitable hierarchy be introduced through the act of taking charge, as though the event happened in my name?

As I was thinking this through, I received a note from the investigation. It read:

Fishy Business November 26, 2014

Regarding other fishy business . . . It was such a well designed urgency to get to the kangaroos on Tuesday night that I fear that I was unable to clearly tell of all that I uncovered. . . . I too am suspicious of the architects . . . they are very consumed by the taking of measurements and spinning stories about cloaks. I had one of them in the car on the way home but I couldn't detect any deviation within the story to catch them in the act . . . my jury is still out. There is something going on with those possums . . . however, when one was scratching at the back of my tent it was pretending to be a wombat, then a kangaroo, not a fish . . . I suspect it may be yet another diversionary tactic! . . .

There are a couple of anomalies that I stumbled upon . . . how [redacted] knew about the fish being flying fish is beyond me. Likewise with [redacted] . . . he knew that the fish ate the Chinese. Perhaps [redacted] has been informed through some pragmatic instructions (bequeathed recipes?) for the preparation of the fish meals . . . if this is the case, the usefulness of this information is likely to be questionable so further effort here may not be worthwhile. . . .

This is all that I managed to gather over the few days in Avoca. I hope that it is helpful and that we might finally uncover and understand what has really been going on at the house and garden. One last detail I noticed is the difference between orange fish and fish of other colours. The fish on the bag is green . . . and remember we were not sure how the actual real fish appear.

Cheers and all the best,

The way forward was clear: rather than dealing with the text message directly, responding one-on-one to a group issue, a collective response was called for. I decided to open up the investigation beyond the six initial members. The following was the first message sent. Eighteen people were copied.

The Investigation November 27, 2014

Dear co-investigators,

I've put this list together carefully. I think there are a few missing. . . . I'll trust you to know where to send it next. I've had a studied report from [redacted]. Since some of it is confidential, I will only touch on the salient issues.

- We've left Avoca.

- Orange spray paint may contaminate the soil in the guise of philosophy (or was philosophy left to contaminate?). We fear this may have repercussions. Is [redacted] a double agent?

- The green fish has turned into an outline. There is a strong memory of its greenness. Fish meal still seems to be a strong clue. . . .

- The vortex is awfully close (and yet [redacted] guards the fish).

- If the fish are the outline, the semblance is near.

- The tunnel entrances seem to have been masked by the tents. I've seen a picture. It's possible that you will get access to that image. She holds a clue.

- [redacted] again: she finds the holes.

- Why is [redacted] measuring? I've included you here, though there is some concern about whose side you're on. Architects are very suspect in this scenario of dissimulated gardens and covered-up tunnels. We will need a copy of the architectural plans.

- [redacted], after investigative reporting, you have come out more Australian than Chinese. This makes you a fish, I think. We're keeping you onboard for now. I know you think you are a meerkat. We're not sure where you are going with this. Please elaborate.

- Something about [redacted], [redacted] and fire. I wonder whether [redacted] isn't also implicated. I'd like to hear more. And about rabbits. Did [redacted] think eating them would make them less of a pest in Australia? Is there a parallel with the Chinese?

- For now, [redacted] must be treated with caution. She knows more than she admits.

Yours truly,

Two days later, three missives in, with eight more people copied but two deleted:

Incoming Cargo November 29, 2014

I can still feel the delicate brushing of goldfish fins and tails against my cheeks. They have a strange attunement with my heart flutters. Despite appearances I haven't left the Avoca vortex. [redacted] knows this and is helping me not get sucked in too deeply and drown. That is the real reason he had to stay in Melbourne. [redacted] is making sure that the tunnel has wi-fi, and through her angelic connection she utters revealing philosophical statements that help me think into staying afloat.

[redacted]—we know that you are pretending to know little about this vortex tunnel, but it became clear as I measured up the House that you have at least one fishing line tied to your finger that traces out its turbulence. I am guessing you want us to admit what we know before you confess. There are many lines that I measured up, and not all of them were perceptible by the laser measuring device.

[redacted] and [redacted] have other antennae—[redacted] is organic, [redacted] is elastic. Each has different insights. [redacted] slips under tents and feels out what they hide, but she doesn't seem ready to tell us everything. Perhaps she is crafting a new escape hole? I think [redacted] knows the cure for [redacted] contaminating paint, which is making the tunnel smell fluorescent, like a blinding light up my nostrils. [redacted]: please help.

[redacted] is with me in the vortex, and I can tell you that she has a special connection with the blind white tower, which played a major role in past Avoca fabulations. She retreats there on occasion, half way between the Chinese garden and the House, to do some measuring up. Her plan is beautifully simple. [redacted] tells me that the possums are indeed staying in contact with [redacted], who has her own very special connection into the vortex tunnel. Keep a wide eye on her.

In the vortex with the fish, [redacted], and the possums, I can now reveal that there is also a giraffe. [redacted] is channeling the meerkat. Will they arrive soon? I think they could have something to tell about the giraffe. [redacted] knows something about a winking tiger, and I am expecting to find out more about this on Monday.

I get the sense that [redacted] feathers in the Chinese garden have something to tell us about a wise bird somewhere in the vortex. I have been trying to get my chicken to help me trace the bird-esque, as we vortex together in the garden, but she was quite busy listening to earwigs.

Yesterday [redacted] and [redacted] led the way to a clue that has gone by unnoticed: the logs. Two massive logs out the front of the House. [redacted] is the double of the Log Lady, and speaks the logs' giant, doubled up words. As the Log Lady said in episode 8 of Twin Peaks:

"Can you see through a wall? Can you see through human skin? X-rays see through solid, or so-called solid objects. There are things in life that exist, and yet our eyes cannot see them. Have you ever seen something . . . that others cannot see? Why are some things kept from our vision?"

Now think about how that statement might be doubled! [redacted] has good reason for not revealing everything.

After some investigative work this morning I discovered that [redacted] is also called [redacted]. She is a double agent to be sure, and may be essential to this investigative trail. I think she knows about the flutters of the fish, and her deep micro-attention to connective tissue is very much required.

Could it be that the vortex is not only full of creatures, but is the very creature we all need to know? As [redacted] said, I had a premonition of the vortex before we arrived at Avoca: The House the Vortex Built, was already in my mind. The goldfishy flutters in my heart might be the hole I need to measure up before I can offer any more clues.

Yours,

Forty-two responses in, many of them arriving in the nonlinear swirl only Gmail conversations can create. Twenty-four people copied:

Incoming Cargo November 29, 2014

Oh no. More fish? What is this about green fish?

I couldn't help overreading so I have to point out the following . . . Those fish were clearly orange (apart from the four almost invisible small black ones . . . and one is already beginning to change colour I notice . . .) For me it was all orange and now it is the seepage of orange that remains . . .

So there are the fish. Well, I still see orange despite this mention of green. And then there is the striped orange of the tiger as you noted [redacted], the one who moved into the balcony room on Tuesday and now refuses to leave. Little [redacted], who is entirely at home lying with the fish seems also comfortable hanging out in this tigeresque space. More animals she seems to be saying. We need better representation amongst the 64 long legs in the forests of the night.

Don't you think that is a strange coincidence? 64 legs. Because "64" was already there on every door before those 64 legs appeared. It was the long orangy-reddy stripe on the doors. Did you see it? The sign "64: Before Completion"? (I didn't like to mention it but, talking of "before completion," those slices of fish that suddenly appeared in the kitchen, then on our plates, were altogether too close to orange in their pinkness. I did go in and count and was relieved to find that all eight were still there in the other room, swimming easily. Phew. I don't think they knew what was going on.

And then in the hardness of midday there is orange all over the ground on the struggling grass apron in front of the house. I'm relieved to read that some of you also noticed it. Hard to decipher though, hard to know what it is doing there. Some strange message of pain that has seeped up from China perhaps. One day when it rains later next year, it will wash away I think. Or perhaps it will burn to bare earth if the whole house is consumed by the orange of summer fire before the bell can be rung and we desperately count people at the gate. We will need 64 long legs, four short ones, many fins. [redacted], does that measuring device count legs as well?

The tiger will not be counted of course. It will simply refuse to leave, that tiger, even though it knows well enough about the call of the bell. It stays, entirely comfortable, up there in the balcony room. The possums, however, are wary. As they should be. To make sure they realize this is a new dispensation, stones have been thrown against the tiny orange flames that bring them out of the shadows. And there is the smell of urine still there as a declaration of war.

And the hard-orange of the pomegranate blossoms suddenly seen in a back garden now without weeds, and the yellowy-orange of the much de-sired mango that appeared right at the end. So, of course there must also be double agents (which changes the leg count) for all this to have occurred. And perhaps a vortex or two. Anything is possible. Everything has changed.

Yours,

And so it continued, from November 26 to December 4, with investigators added and withdrawn, writing not only from Australia but also from Berlin and Montreal, ninety pages in all. Everything had changed, as the November 29 message announced. Something else had begun to happen, and with it, an event was taking form.

The investigation that became the fabulation was never really interested in the past. It was interested in creating a time that could compose with futurities in the making. For the gathering to pass into an event, these futurities must be there in germ. This germ of activity is what the fabulation revealed, a past schizzed.

When we arrived at Watford House, there wasn't yet in the collective a sensi-tivity to how else the project could expose itself, how else it could be known. As is often the case, the stark presentness of a strange encounter took precedence over its fissures of futurity. None of us really knew where to look, how to compose with what we might find lurking between garden and house, house and village, past and future. And so the group fissured into small clumps, the focus more activity-based than event-orienting: someone created an architectural plan of the house; a few people cleared the garden of weeds; some cooked and cleaned; some prepared a site for peeing into mason jars to steer the possums away from the fruit trees; some visited the garden and the surrounds; some went for a walk along the floodplain; some spoke to villagers; some sat at the pub drinking beer; some Skyped home; some slept. Children played; tents were built. Time passed.

It is the fabulation that finally did the work of shifting the gathering toward an emergent collectivity, making it an event by folding time toward the asynchrony of its infrathin dimension. The fabulation made cracks felt, and created opportunities to enter them. Where other constraints had been disabling, the fabulation was enabling precisely because it captured us in the act, in a middling of expression where the anguish of the orange schizz and all that it carried could be addressed by other means. The fabulation allowed the collectivity in germ to express itself and to invent worlds for that expression. While names were used in the text as it moved across the network, there came with the force of the fabulatory gesture a sense of the impersonal—all voices made a difference, as they do in investigations.

The fabulation followed us to Sydney, where the second SenseLab proposition—this one focused on knots of thought and experimentation with the minor gesture—was beginning. Many people now gathered had not been to Avoca, but the fabulation, printed on large pieces of paper and taped to the wall, accompanied us for the next eight days as we worked in the large University of New South Wales Art and Design gallery. Few people read it as a whole, but its presence made a difference, particularly as we collectively tried to give voice to our uneasiness about how narratives are made—the demonstrations for Michael Brown's death were happening simultaneously in Ferguson.

For the telling to be an event, its capacity to impersonalize is key, even (and perhaps especially) in cases where there is a desire to direct blame. This tension between the personal and the impersonal was felt keenly in the wake of the grass graffiti. Despite the fabulation's gaining momentum, and its growing ability to reorient the field, some participants nonetheless felt that the individual who had painted the grass should apologize for what was considered by some to be a violent act. When she resisted making the act her own, when she preferred to think of the act as the collective inflection the event needed, they blamed her for not taking responsibility. And, by extension, they blamed SenseLab. What was overlooked, however, in this painful play of accusation, was the force of enthusiasm of the body, the tigritude, that was moved to paint orange, that was moved to schizz the event. For the painted grass was the cut, the schizz that allowed the schizoanalytic gesture of the fabulation to take place.

It is noteworthy that the words themselves that the spray paint highlighted were never returned to in the discussion of who was to blame. Despite the power and lyricism of the fabulation, the marked landscape was remembered by those most troubled by the graffiti only as a scar. What this reaction neglected was that the writing called for nothing less than that *multiplicity* orient the field. This wasn't a personal act; it was called for by the event! Perhaps not in this shape exactly—but the welling event desperately needed to be schizzed. This is what the fabulation, despite a great uneasiness, was able to make apparent. The orange had already been seeping long before the spray paint foregrounded it. What the words did was orient the orange, move the orange tigeresquely toward fish and fire, toward tents and Bea the dog, toward the vortex and sixty-four legs and pomegranate flowers and mangoes, not all of them orange, but all of them carried by an oranging spell. The fabulation activated the vortex, opening the breach toward a creative limit where new worlds could be inhabited. The fabulation made it possible for the collective to begin to emerge *as* collective. It immediated collectivity, transforming personal stakes into the fraught field of group subjectivity.

Collectivity extends beyond a moment in time. This was the strength of the SenseLab–*Avoca Project* encounter: that it invented itself through the fabulation, in the passage of a time more durational than chronological. A year later, returning to Australia, I met with Jones. It was time, we decided, to return to our collaborator, Watford House, and to see what the SenseLab–*Avoca Project* encounter had been able to do. The conversation was tentative. Had the *Avoca Project* benefited as much as SenseLab had? Had the politics of fabulation and its immediating power also made a difference for the *Avoca Project*, or did the orange simply leave a scar that spoke of non-attunement in a field of difference?

The story began to fabulate once more as we listened to each other, alive in the knowledge that we were both speaking as intercessors to a participation alive with more-than human tendencies, ventriloquists for a group-subject still in transformation. It was a rich conversation, a real attunement. And in the event of this exchange, which happened over several days, with many rebeginnings, we heard the story once more. And it had morphed, already different from what could ever have been known, would ever be known. This is the power of the false at work.

It was not a scar, it turns out. The rain washed away the paint shortly after we left, and in any case it had never, it turns out, been spray paint but water-soluble marker paint. In the end, the actual graffiti seemed less important than the agony of collaborating with forces that exceeded us. The orange words were not so much what was left behind as what would be reactivated, return after return.

A memory of orange, of turmoil, a swirling collective composition, a tentative encounter with the fragility at the heart of all collective actions. What was left burning through the soil, on the Avoca landscape, was not so much, in retrospect at least, the writing on the grass. What was left was an uneasy story ripe for the telling. But, like all fabulations, nothing we wrote will ever have been quite true. So perhaps it is important to end with this one last image, one that was kept from me at the time because of my terror of snakes.

For months before our arrival at Avoca, I worried about snakes. Jones, like all those I ask, promised me that snakes were actually quite shy and would be unlikely to show themselves. I wasn't convinced: everywhere I go, these animals that terrify me at the most nonconscious level seem to appear to greet me, to my snake-lover friends' delight.

I didn't see a snake at Avoca. But it turns out a snake did appear, camouflaged in our trace, standing guard at the entry to the house: the day after we left, a tiger snake was seen resting amid the orange stripes of the lawn. Snake and stripe, tigeresque. The more-than human in all its animality, lingering in the n + 1 of the field's incessant necessity to tell it otherwise.

The politics of fabulation is this capacity to make felt the force of immediation at its most impersonal limit. The fabulation at Avoca was not "about" anything, not about the orange "spray" paint or even the tiger-snake-fish that marked the passage of our disappearance. But it was the orange that schizzed the fabulation into motion. The politics of fabulation composes *with* the schizz. Without the schizz there is no event. A fabulation's content can never be seen as limited to the story itself—fabulation is the affective field that makes composition possible, bringing thinking into act. In a political register, this suggests that there is potential in fabulation to get beyond the kind of narration that holds things in place, opening them to the *what else* that also beckons. All events are more complex than they seem, and modes of encounter that play, tigeresquely, with that complexity can and do change their course.

Beyond Mythmaking

Fabulation is vulnerable to capture. Its other, mythmaking, is always at its heels, seducing us with the promise of intelligibility. How to keep the wildness of fabulation active in the retelling and reorienting of our everyday practices? "This is how it is," we say, or at least how it's been, its having-been constitutive of what will be capable of coming to be. And we're not altogether wrong. It *is* like this. Today, or yesterday. But it was also much more, in a flash. Already, another shape has begun to take form, a shape relationally attuned to the inheritance of the "it is."

What mythmaking tendencies will have missed in the description of what things do when they shape each other will always have been the relational field, the inheritance not of form but of formative force. "Whether explicitly or not, narration always refers to a system of judgement: even when acquittal takes place due to the benefit of the doubt, or when the guilty is so only because of fate. Falsifying narration, by contrast, frees itself from this system; it shatters the system of judgement because the power of the false (not error or doubt) affects the investigator and the witness as much as the person presumed guilty" (Deleuze 1989, 133). The kind of telling that does justice to the event in its ongoing capacity for metamorphosis can only emerge from the event itself and be told in the squeaks of the event's own perpetually falsifying forms of articulation, in its ticcingflapping.

Falsifying narration in the name of the event's capacity for metamorphosis is unsettling because it refuses to settle the event. Everything is affected. "The point is that the elements themselves are constantly changing with the relations of time into which they enter, and the terms with their connections. Narration is constantly being completely modified, in each of its episodes, not according to subjective variations, but as a consequence of disconnected places and dechronologized moments" (Deleuze 1989, 133). With the power of the false, the event has multiplied, its schizzes made palpable: "Contrary to the form of the true which is unifying . . . the power of the false cannot be separated from an irreducible multiplicity" (133).

This multiplicity is serial. The event has schizzed and with it the certainty of what it might have been or what it might become. The event has immediated, an immediation that is already part of a series, a series that is always more-than the sum of us, always more-than human. The event is never just the one it has become in its actualization: it is also the many of fabulation's polyvalent accounting.

The cut in the event, its schizz, never lends itself to an overview. Its felt effects are rhizomatic, undermining the sense that there might be a knowability that keeps everything in perspective. Fabulation as a technique of immediation makes felt the durational force of the cut, makes resonate an experiential time that doesn't know how to be counted. For while the cut is absolutely punctual, *immediate*, it cleaves the event in ways that recalibrate it, *immediating*. This couples two kinds of time: the time of the now and the time of the will-have-been. Time becomes operative, experiential. Time folds.

Emergency

But what of the urgency, even the sense of emergency, at the heart of the *now* of immediation? Social justice activists know this problem well. Everything matters, all the time, the body poised to leap, the nervous system on high alert.

Enthusiasm, excitement, and then, too often, chaos, or entropy, or inertia. Absolute movement caught in the vortex of everything the event could become. Madness. Burnout.

This state of extreme overactivation is familiar to all who experiment with emergent collectivity. The event takes us, its absolute movement swirling us within an unbounded spacetime that is often temporally and spatially at odds with the rhythms of the everyday. No points of reliance are available. Perspective is long gone. The body becomes warrior, tense with anticipation, thick with the trauma of what have now become life-and-death stakes. Adrenal overexertion: there is no calm here where the event has become us.

Too often, in the face of this overlap of focused momentum and deep exhaustion, an uneasy shift happens toward the personal. "I can't do it anymore," we hear ourselves say, as though this were all about us. The shaping of emergent collectivity has been reduced to our cells. The event, we believe, needs *us* to continue. A new kind of "personal is political" emerges in this intense constellation where the edges where politics and life and art and philosophy co-compose are overridden by a sense of breathless engagement: the state of emergency overcomes us.

The stakes are enormous, and many of us feel them today. Avoca's fabulation did not have these stakes, but the concurrent event of Michael Brown's death did, and we felt it. Urgency was not misplaced. The weight of the world we compose with, a world of austerity and neoliberalism and racism and exclusion that every day undervalues what collective living can be, is a heavy burden to bear. Many of us wake daily with an almost hopeless feeling of urgency, the body poised in a state of acute tension. As months (and centuries) of attacks against black life continue, as more gun violence erupts and wars are fought, as austerity measures undermine our everyday existences and climate change threatens to foreclose the future, as settler colonialism persists, as we continue to watch the horrifying accounts of refugees streaming across borders looking for a safe landing, how does collective experimentation make any kind of difference?

This is a question SenseLab struggles with. But whenever we come face-to-face with it (again), we remind each other that collective experimentation is not a choice. It's a mode of survival. Experimentation around techniques for group subjectivity provides ways to reenter the political from another angle. A politics of fabulation seems important in this context. Political events are often lived in the time span of media events—acutely here and then completely gone. The political is experienced as staccato rather than as durational, one violent act overshadowing the next. But as all activists will attest to, the work continues even when the attention wanes, and it is often in the waning that the exhaustion settles in, despondency taking over as the status quo returns.

How the collective makes a difference is often not part of the telling. What is told is told in the sound bites of new mythmaking strategies, the complexity of fabulation too unwieldy for the Facebook "like." But the fabulations are there—the work is to draw them out. What kinds of techniques might be invented to assist us in orienting urgency away from a constant state of emergency? How might we bend our practices toward the desynchronous time of fabulation, even while we are living the emergency? What might the minor sociality of emergent collectivity make possible in this context? What can we do collectively so that the merest of existences also make themselves felt?

The primacy of action has been rightly criticized as connected to capital, as operating in tandem with the accelerated time of capital's constant need to forecast the newest new.[15] SenseLab asks: what other modes of activity are alive in the act? What kind of telling accompanies what Massumi calls bare activity, activity not understood simply in terms of its spatial extension but in its intensive magnitude?[16] Can we attune to the zigzag movement that cuts across the front lines and create with the intensity of a side line? Is there a way to rally across different qualities of line? Can we make the line a field?

A durational field is always immediating. The question of how to compose with the capacitation of the field in-act is the one the SenseLab most contends with. How to know when our bodies need to be counted (which lines actually need us to be standing there, numbered among those also marking the occasion)? How to know where subtraction is more important, where our presence must be backgrounded in lieu of other qualities and tenses of action? How, in the mix, to always maintain an attunement to the more-than human? How to live the modulation of the act such that we don't simply fall prey to capital's mandate that we do more, be more, bending to capital's infinite need for surplus and accumulation? How to keep the enthusiasm of the body transversal, beyond capture? How to compose with altereconomies in ways that do their work through the creative fissures of capital's leakages without turning these acts into moral imperatives? How to create time for the minor sociality of emergent collectivity in a world that asks so much of our time, of our too-human time?

SenseLab seeks to immediate where lines are composed, where they cross, where they perish. Free radicals are key: activated in the telling, in the relation, motivated by the power of the false, the free radical exposes the variability in experience, replacing and superseding "the form of the true," by making felt "the simultaneity of incompossible presents," "the coexistence of not-necessarily true pasts." To create openings for free radicality, techniques will need to be invented that are capable of creating the conditions, in the event, for the activation of its fabulatory tendencies. This will mean attending to the pulse of immediation and moving in the rhythm of the schizzes it produces.

Emergency lives in the urgency of now, *this time*, this only time. No practice can function always in the state of emergency. The work of the free radical is to supplement the necessary pull of emergency, to compose with the complex time differential of the act. Emergency is with us, and it is here to stay.[17] How to work with the doubling of time this calls forth—the time of the now and the time of sustained action? How to make sustainable, in a more-than human register, the acute sense that all is in the balance? How to not become rigidified by the tension that comes with the sense that there can never be enough action to turn the tides? All scales of action are present in the flash of tigritude. How can the act of activism produce an enthusiasm of the body that carries, in a flash, all these scales, all these durations?

Perhaps the first step is to recall that the flash is transductive: the child does not imitate the tiger. The child immediatingly connects to the dynamism of the tiger's enthusiasm of the body: the child activates the form of life of tigritude.

A politics of fabulation does nothing less. It composes at all scales of existence, activating the dynamism of experience in the making. Cutting across more normative tellings, it transversalizes experience to give power to all that courses through it, including what remains only infrathinly felt. In so doing, it allows the edges of the political to resonate differently, collectively, durationally.

The force of immediation in a politics of fabulation does this: it takes us out of the center. It opens the present to its schizz. And it teaches us not only that "I" is another but that the event is not me (Deleuze 1989, 153).

SenseLab has an appetite to activate the transversal contours of a life in the making, a mode of existence that can know itself only through the falsifications it will become allied to and will then leave behind. This coming-and-going takes continual work, especially the going. We have to learn, again and again, how to subtract ourselves, how to do this daily work without becoming subsumed by it. How a practice does its work, how a practice creates the conditions for an emergent collectivity, has to be reinvented each time anew, and with this, our role in it, our place in it, has to reinvented as well. It can never be solely about how we did it before. And it can never really be about us. This does not mean that what has come before has no importance. It means that we work from a beginning always rich with inheritances that remain open to deviation.

Experimenting immediation is shape-shifting: tigeresque. Free-radical intercession produces an enthusiasm of the body. We are not the center of experience; tigritude is; vitality affects are. It is here that we must begin, shifting from our belief that we are the center, composing instead with other scales and tempos, with the minor gestures of geological time, affective time, event-time.

To know time differently is to feel how the more-than of existence composes us, composes with us. The political is never within reach. To have reached it is to have organized it into myth. To be politically engaged, to open up fields of emergent collectivity, is not to have willed them into existence, but to have been moved by them, to have been composed by them. Our task: to become schizoanalytic experimenters at the edges of experience where the intercession of the free radical unbinds linear narration, freeing the bonds of time prescribed. Our task: to become sensitive to a composing-with that will never tell the true story of how emergent collectivity briefly came to expression. Our task: to move at the rhythm of free radicals who affirm the schizz of immediation. Our task: to destroy, with all the force of the free radical, that which too easily conforms to our image, to our need to recognize ourselves in the work we do.

Practicing the Schizz

Guattari's formula, "we are all groupuscles," indeed heralds the search for a new subjectivity, a group subjectivity, which does not allow itself to be enclosed in a whole bent on reconstituting an ego (or even worse, a superego), but which spreads itself out over several groups at once. These groups are divisible, manifold, permeable, and always optional. A good group does not take itself to be unique, immortal, and significant . . . but instead plugs into an outside. . . . In turn, the individual is also a group. —Gilles Deleuze in Félix Guattari, *Psychoanalysis and Transversality* (translation modified)

We are sick, so sick, of our *selves*! —Mark Seem in Gilles Deleuze and Félix Guattari, *Anti-Oedipus*

Animate the Threshold!

Begin with the space of encounter. Ask yourself where the thresholds are. Look around. Notice the door frame. Notice the directionality of the furniture. Notice the corners. Do those who enter see people seeing them as soon as they breach the threshold? Is there a way to scurry to a less visible space? Is there room to sit on the floor? Does the room presuppose a certain posture? How does it carry the institution? Are there cracks? Are there opportunities for entering without saying who you are? Are there ways for otherwise entering, ways that don't play out embedded practices of self-presentation, that don't play out a hierarchized distribution of roles?

The spaces in which we work are choreographed to represent the actions we imagine inhabit them. A university classroom usually has a set of desks, and with that comes a directionality—desks pointed toward a board, or toward a podium, creating a posture hierarchically predetermined, everyone in their place. Attention is focused on what happens at the front, all eyes on the professor. The back rows can be a refuge, but an assumption reigns that sitting at the back is for the disinterested (and, by extension, the less engaged). "Paying" attention is prized, revealed usually through the use, by the student, of language. Smaller, more senior classes tend to be organized with less of a marked frontality. But to imagine that the ubiquitous seminar-style classroom with desks oriented in a square eschews a formation of power would be to underestimate how frontality-for-all reinforces another kind of dramaturgy that is, in some cases, even more challenging, especially for the more neurodiverse among us. Indeed, the face-to-face setting imposed by desks facing each other can be torture, and the expectation that all should have something to say can keep those who struggle with the face-to-face from properly taking anything in. In this second case, there is a semblance of shared communication, but language continues to reign supreme as the prime modality of knowledge mobilization. In both types of classroom, shy, quiet, and sensorially overwhelmed students suffer, their modes of communication stifled. Little appears infrathinly through the cracks of these settings. For while the dramaturgies of power are different, they remain on a continuum, knowledge played out through the form of reporting. What does this reporting take for granted about how the environment presupposes commonality? How it defines togetherness?

When the threshold into such a classroom is crossed easily, where does that ease come from? How does it reproduce the kind of prestige that allies itself to teaching and learning institutions? And to society more broadly? What kinds of

Leslie Plumb 2017

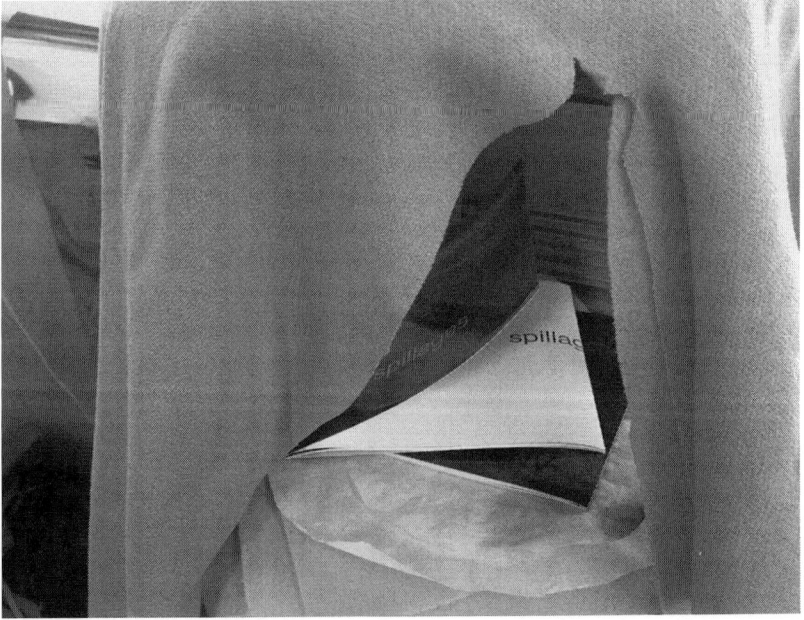

preformatted knowledge are exposed through the crossing? What does the ease-of-crossing communicate about the threshold? What tendencies for both crossing and holding-at-bay does the threshold carry?

I begin in the university because it is the site in which SenseLab most often engages with thresholds, the space in which we most often notice who moves easily into the arena of encounter, and whose bodies resist it. But this could also be about the café you didn't enter because all the bodies, most of them male, were tuned toward the television, and crossing that space seemed impossible. Or the space where all the bodies were white, and there were no conditions for cutting in. Or the environment—the dinner party, the conference, the art opening—where language is presupposed, excluding without even needing to say anything those who enter differently, without words, sensing the edges before they attune, with effort, to a center preconceived.

SenseLab makes the threshold its practice. We are interested not only in the first doorway, but in discovering where else the thresholds may appear for those who are neurodiverse, for those whose bodies don't pass as easily as the speaking, white body inevitably does in the context of the university. We are interested in why some of us cross so easily, and how it has come to be that so many of us don't even perceive the threshold.

A practice of the schizz begins here, at the threshold.

Experiment the Detour!

The schizz detours.

A crossing of the threshold is never a simple walking-across. To have even come across the threshold is to have felt the pull of what can transpire on the other side. An institutional threshold promises many things—in a hospital it can mean care; in a university it can mean learning; in a house it can mean accommodation. Or in a hospital it may mean being overlooked for hours and hours, or being refused care entirely. In a university it may mean finding that too many of the spaces exclude your ways of entering, your ways of learning. In a house it may mean working to fit into a concept of family that makes you invisible. Or it can mean putting your body at risk.

But this is only the most literal threshold. Other thresholds exist even before the first perceptible crossing. If you are indigenous and living on the street, that hospital threshold may not even appear—you know you are not considered treatable, or, in too many cases, truly human. The same goes for too many other bodies—black, disabled, transgender—whose pain is considered a just reward. If you are a nonspeaking autistic, the university threshold may be truly out of reach.

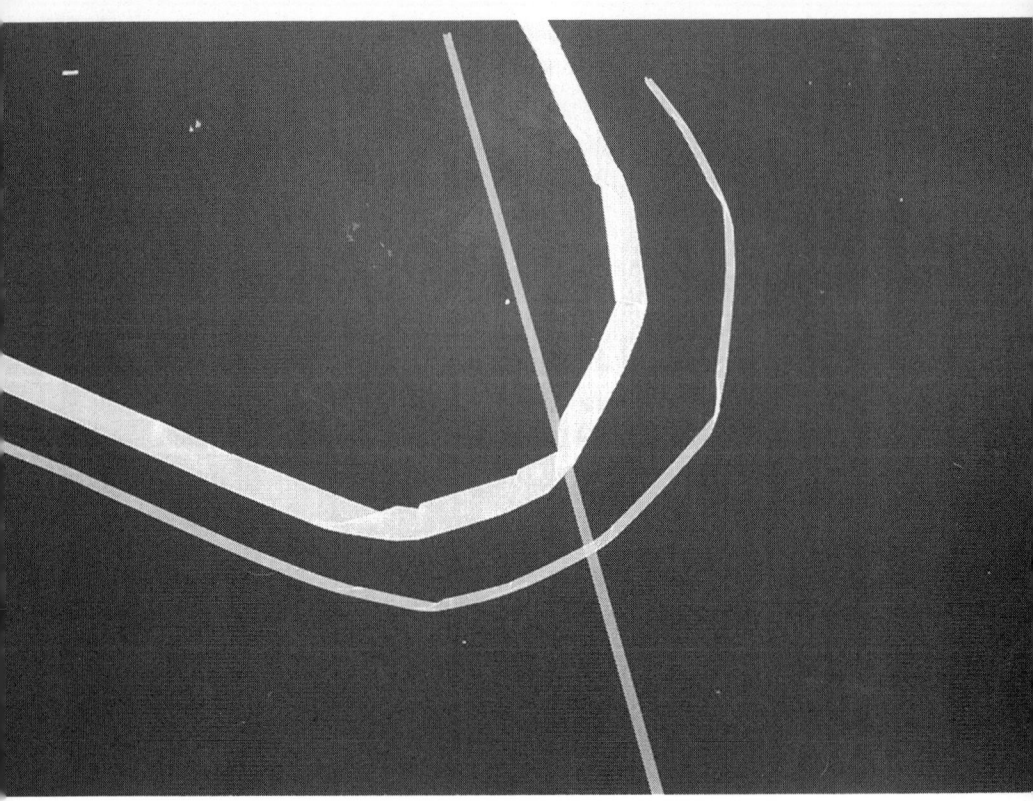

Leslie Plumb 2018

For most of us, speaking and knowing are too intimately entwined to imagine knowledge being activated and mobilized otherwise.[1] Exclusion reigns.

Infra-thresholds include all of those often unbridgeable crossings that signal exclusion to those who have no choice but to learn the signs, often imperceptible to the neurotypical (white) population. There is a reason certain bodies move easily across, and others lurk at the edges.

A schizoanalytic practice, or what Félix Guattari calls institutional psychotherapy, is at its very core a practice that engages with the institution: "Institutional psychotherapy . . . showed that one could not consider psychotherapeutic treatment for the seriously ill without taking the analysis of institutions into account" (2015, 61). In the context of the renewal of psychiatry in the name of schizoanalysis, a move that began in France in the 1950s, not only is there an engagement with how institutions activate the conditions of care and accommodation, there is also a commitment to rethinking what institutional forces captivate and orient the more-than that courses through the bodies of the patients.[2] This more-than is what Guattari calls the group-subject, the force of sub-jectivity that cuts through the individual to amplify the transindividuality at the heart of experience. In the context of institutional psychotherapy, schizoanalysis is the commitment to the operations at the heart of the production of subjectiv-ity, operations that cannot produce a cut-and-dried partition between where the institution ends and the patient's body begins. Practicing the schizz is oriented toward a health that cannot be separated from the transindividual force of emer-gent collectivity itself, an emergent collectivity that always carries its surrounds. Practicing the schizz involves attuning to transversalities that include institu-tional forces, transversalities, it must be said, that also exceed any limited notion of psychiatry. Schizoanalysis, Guattari underscores, is a practice that detours the collective into the institutional as much as it detours the collective into the po-litical, the political into the social, the social into the environmental, the envi-ronmental into the aesthetic. In the detour of the transversality schizoanalysis activates, the question is in every case the same: How is subjectivity produced? How does it carry the forces of its surrounds?

In bringing institutional psychotherapy (schizoanalysis) and SenseLab into encounter, it is also vital to note that a focus on the institutional, in our case the university, is not an effort to restructure it. That would be to accept the in-stitutional as the form that holds the keys to our process. Institutions are empty structures. They hold nothing except the mythologies (the neurologies) they sup-port to keep them in power. Institutional psychotherapy recognizes the poverty of the institution's imagination: it would never ask what we can collectively do to make the institution dream. What it asks instead is how institutional tendencies play out in the production of subjectivity. Its aim is to refuse to make institutional forces oblique to the process, to blanket them as though all bodies responded to them in the same way. This is the position SenseLab takes. Our interest is em-phatically *not* in restructuring the institution. But nor is our posture one of simple refusal. Our approach is to become attuned to how the norms of the knowledge economy that move through the institution cross the thresholds we have become habituated to. Our aim is to recognize and work with these norms so that we can better create techniques and platforms of relation that divert them. Despite the commitment to this work, it is nonetheless clear to us that SenseLab cannot ulti-mately find its place in a university, that the university is but a space of temporary refuge, no doubt a space that comes with advantages—not only the infrastructure but also the university's capacity to lure fascinating people and to create condi-tions, despite itself, for experiments in pedagogy—but ultimately not one that will sustain the kinds of processes we engage with. "It cannot be denied that the university is a place of refuge, and it cannot be accepted that the university is a place of enlightenment. In the face of these conditions one can only sneak into the university and steal what one can. To abuse its hospitality, to spite its mission, to join its refugee colony, its gypsy encampment, to be in but not of—this is the path of the subversive intellectual in the modern university" (Harney and Moten 2013, 26).

The work is not to make the institution thrive, or even to make it bearable. The work is to develop astute modes of encounter that are capable of activating what each site does best. The undercommons of the university is what SenseLab is after, not as a final oasis but as a temporary exploration of how institutional forces can be detoured.

> In that undercommons of the university one can see that it is not a matter of teaching versus research or even the beyond of teaching versus the individualisation of research. To enter this space is to inhabit the ruptural and enraptured disclosure of the commons that fugitive enlightenment enacts, the criminal, matricidal, queer, in the cistern, on the stroll of the stolen life, the life stolen by enlightenment and stolen back, where the commons give refuge, where the refuge gives commons. What the beyond of teaching is really about is not finishing oneself, not passing, not completing; it's about allowing subjectivity to be unlawfully overcome by others, a radical passion and passivity such that one becomes unfit for subjection, because one does not possess the kind of agency that can hold the regulatory forces of subjecthood, and one cannot initiate the auto-interpellative torque that biopower subjection requires and rewards. (Harney and Moten 2013, 28)

An undercommons of the university is never created once and for all. Activating the cracks toward infrathin modes of schizzing is a commitment that must diligently attend to how the institution gathers, ascribes, and deploys power. This practice varies over time, requiring a continuous commitment to developing techniques that schizz. What schizoanalysis teaches us is that the activation of undercommon spaces of resistance depends on attending to what moves transversally across the deployment of power, to what moves across any embedded notion of the One, of prestige, of the subject lauded and framed by the regulatory forces of subjecthood. For the institutions we need to take refuge from are also us; they are also made by those very dynamics that we teach each other about competition, about standing out, about one-upmanship, about individuality, about whiteness and neurotypicality. In the undercommons of the university, the schizoanalytic lesson is "I is an other," but also "This other is not a subject. It is a signifying machine." Signifying machines alter the signs that organize our worlds (Guattari 2015, 129). They are nothing other than the expression of subjectivity produced in the cracks of experience. It is in these cracks that undercommon tunnels are found.

Practicing the schizz detours the institution not by denying its presence, not by decrying it as though the outside of the institution were an outside of all institutionality. Practicing the schizz detours the institution by asking, at every turn, where the institution operates, and what these modes of operation do. "Who produces the institution and articulates its subgroups? Is there a way to inflect this production? The general proliferation of institutions in contemporary society leads only to reinforcing the alienation of the individual: is it possible to operate a transfer of responsibility, of replacing bureaucracy with institutional creativity? Under what conditions?" (Guattari 2015, 62; translation modified).

When engaging with institutional critique, the response must move from simple rejection to a commitment to how subjectivity runs through those institutions that hold us captive, conceptually if not physically. "If we do not start with . . . a collective agent of utterance, we risk making the institution a thing, in the form of a structure, along with society as a whole. . . . From the moment when we can shift and disrupt the totalizing character of an institution . . . , instead of turning in on itself like a structure, it can acquire subjective consistency and start making all sorts of changes and challenges" (Guattari 2015, 70). As a collective agent of utterance, the institution reveals itself to have certain tendencies, certain modalities. Discarding the institution too quickly risks the reinstantiation of those very institutional tendencies in the next experiment. Begin instead with how the institution thresholds facilitate the creation of operative techniques that, if tuned carefully, may become robust enough to grow and proliferate through and beyond the institution. This is the work practicing the schizz can do.

But beware! This does not means believing the institution can be saved. It means something else entirely. It means becoming aware that the institution—in this case the academic institution—is an active participant in the relational web that produces and reinforces subjectivity. It means that when we ask how else subjectivity can be produced, we must always also ask *where else* and *under what conditions?* And when we ask these questions, we must also ask ourselves how thought operates in this equation. *Where else can thought be produced?* For while there is no question that thought is not what the neoliberal university celebrates, there is still a belief, shared widely, that the university is a refuge for thought. In the words of Stefano Harney and Fred Moten: "Surely the university also makes thought possible? Is not the purpose of the university as Universitas, as liberal arts, to make the commons, make the public, make the nation of democratic citizenry? Is it not therefore important to protect this Universitas, whatever its impurities, from professionalization in the university? But we would ask what is already not possible in this talk in the hallways, among the buildings, in rooms of the university about possibility?" (2013, 30).

Practicing the schizz means not shying away from the question of why this belief in the university as a site for thought is so persistent. For to believe that thought is of the university, that the university cares for thinking and produces the conditions for its exploration, is to willfully ignore for whom that threshold is impossible to cross, and for whom the impossibility of crossing that threshold means that they will forever be considered unthinking. To return to the institution to consider its place in producing subjectivity is to state plainly that any thinking that happens in and around the university happens *only* in the schizzing of the institution: the university excludes thought in its attempt to systematize learning in the name of a neutralized production of what has already been selected as worthy of evaluation. Knowledge as the university bestows and polices it is not thought. What the university trades in is neurotypicality itself: the production of white repetition.

> The maroons know something about possibility. They are the condition of possibility of the production of knowledge in the university—the singularities against the writers of singularity, the writers who write, publish, travel, and speak. It is not merely a matter of the secret labor upon which such space is lifted, though of course such space is lifted from collective labor and by it. It is rather that to be a critical academic in the university is to be against the university, and to be against the university is always to recognize it and be recognized by it, and to institute the negligence of that internal outside, that unassimilated underground, a negligence of it that is precisely, we must insist, the basis of the professions. And this act of being against always already excludes the unrecognized modes of politics, the beyond of politics already in motion, the discredited criminal paraorganization, what Robin Kelley might refer to as the infrapolitical field (and its music). It is not just the labor of the maroons but their prophetic organization that is negated by the idea of intellectual space in an organization called the university. This is why the negligence of the critical academic is always at the same time an assertion of bourgeois individualism. (Harney and Moten 2013, 31)

The first detour involves multiplying the thresholds. An institution is never simply the bricks and mortar that hold it together. An institution is the policing of evaluation that forces us to fit thought into a predigested mold. To make thought a product. Academia is a taming of the edges so that what appears as viable, as intelligent, as successful, does so in the form we have been trained to recognize. Practicing the schizz means both attending to how these modes of operation work *and* shifting the conditions such that other modes become possible not *in* the institution but in the undercommons produced in the detouring. To fight an institution head on is to move to its logic. A politics of the undercommons swerves instead. Practicing the schizz involves shifting the posture from upright to swerve, shoulders back, body curved, head low: look for the cracks. Make the thresholds operative by recognizing how they yield. Make the yield part of your politics. Note what attention to the threshold produces. Does it engage a slithering, a dancing, a lurking? Does it activate nonhuman operations? Other perceptibilities?

Connect to how a threshold produces a path. Follow the path and see where it goes. Let the detour lead.

Ask What Else a Body Can Do!

When the detour leads, agglomerations form. These aggregates of human tendencies include more-than human propositions. Color may be a lure. Or light. Or texture.

Agglomerations are a way of talking about what Guattari calls the group-subject. I use *agglomeration* here as a reminder that we are not talking solely about humans. Practicing the schizz, and schizoanalysis more broadly, is unapologetically nonhumanist: "It is . . . not a humanist perspective. It is a question of knowing how to get out of a particular place when stuck" (Guattari 2015, 63). Schizoanalysis is a set of operations for asking how what comes into relation does the work of subjectifying and under what conditions it might schizz.

Practicing the schizz begins beyond organization, beyond a body-as-organization. Schizoanalysis never attends to "a" body. "What does schizoanalysis ask? Nothing more than a bit of a *relation to the outside*" (Deleuze 1996, 88). The outside is not in opposition to an inside. It is an account of experience that resists the concept of interiority as that which singles out body from world. A relation to the outside emphasizes that outsides compose the being of relation, outsides as the angle of sociality that exceeds the given. What is produced at this angle are bodies worlding. Following Antonin Artaud, Deleuze and Guattari call the composition that body-worlds the Body without Organs (BwO). If the BwO is the anorganizational fullness of a worlding that bodies, full because pulsing with proto-orientations, anorganizational because not yet stratified, schizoanalysis could be said to be the practice that most attunes to bodies at this interstice where it is the force of relation that best defines them. Here, where the being of

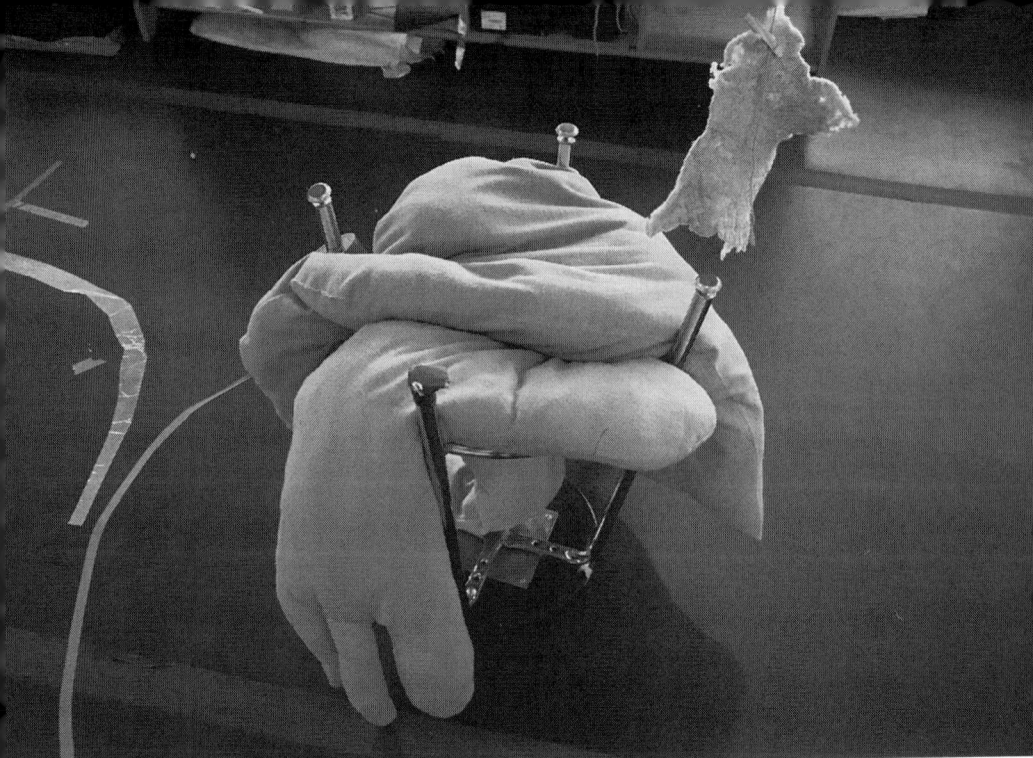

Leslie Plumb 2018

relation is amplified, an account of bodying emerges that makes felt that a body is more process than form. In the shaping of a bodying, there are of course peaks where form momentarily straddles process. But what we learn through schizo-analysis is that this coming-into-itself of a body need not be seen as an organization that finds its shape once and for all. All form-takings are inflections in the anorganization of mobilities that facilitate further bodyings. Bodyings are chains of proto-orientations that carry tendencies with them, the chains themselves already bundlings, churnings. These proto-orientations include inheritances as well as lures. Bodyings are poised at the interstice of future and past, their presentness the most intangible of states. When bodying momentarily bodies, when a presentness makes itself felt, what occurs is a subtraction. This background-ingforegrounding allows a form to emerge. The shape that we tend to call "the" body has bodying still coursing through it, the background of other shapings still resonating in and across it. It is a fallacy of misplaced concreteness, as Alfred North Whitehead (1978) would say, to take the momentary foregrounding of *this* shape as the form of *the* body. To stop a body from bodying is not only to accept the stilling of the shape it momentarily took but to neutralize the environmental surrounds that are its biggest ally in co-composition. It is here, at the juncture where a standing-still *and* an environmental stilling occur, that practicing the schizz is most vital.

For some, the juncture of the body-world stilling into "my" body is the most familiar of states. Defining body as form facilitates a soothing sense of body-world separation, soothing because not much is stable in these violent times. This stability allows something like identity to lodge itself at the interstice. Much is done to maintain the stability of that juncture. But in actuality all identities are mobile, and the juncture, no matter how familiar as "the" site of our indomitable self, is ephemeral, transitory. A practiced familiarity with "this" body is not a staying at the juncture so much as a replaying of a juncture, over and over again. This replaying hardens the body, imposing a frame on its becoming. Often, this framing presupposes the necessity of other framings. My stillness must also be your stillness. My representation your representation. Institutional power works here.

Practicing the schizz is an attuning to how the bodying frames and a commitment to exploring how to deframe through a direct engagement with the conditions themselves of the framing. This is where Deleuze and Guattari's concept of the machinic comes in. The machinic is a proposition to consider the agencement of a process. Focused on what is operative at the juncture, the machinic emphasizes the coming into relation of qualities of experience. "One side of a machinic assemblage faces the strata, which doubtless makes it a kind of organism, or signifying totality, or determination attributable to a subject; it also has a side facing a BwO, which is continually dismantling the organism, causing asignifying particles or pure intensities to pass or circulate and attributing to itself subjects that it leaves with nothing more than a name as the trace of an intensity" (Deleuze and Guattari 1987, 4). The machinic is the motor through which Deleuze and Guattari attempt to depersonalize the operations that produce a bodying.

The machinic is a proposition to understand the complexes of subjectivation from the perspective of the operations themselves. What does the body do to juncture itself—what kind of machinic operations facilitate that kind of stasis? Or, what happens to the body when it wildly fragments—what kinds of machinic operations produce that explosive quality? As Deleuze says, "the schizoanalyst is a mechanic, and schizoanalysis is solely functional" (1996, 77; translation modified).

The machinic facilitates a turn to subjectivity that is concerned with operative functions that bring into resonance the individual-group-machine triad: the production of subjectivity always moves beyond "the classical opposition between individual subject and society" (Guattari 1995, 1). When Guattari talks about the production of subjectivity, the issue at heart is that of the agglomeration. What kinds of operations bring the tendencies into agglomeration? Not how the agglomeration becomes a self-enclosed subject but what forces of individuation are produced at the excess of any form it momentarily takes? The production of subjectivity is about the resingularization of multiplicity in the ecology of existence. Subjectivity *is* an ecology, "plural and polyphonic." Guattari explains:

> Social ecology and mental ecology have found privileged sites of exploration in the experiences of institutional psychotherapy. I am obviously thinking of the clinic at La Borde, where I have worked for a long time; everything there is set up so that psychotic patients live in a climate of activity and assume responsibility, not only with the goal of developing an ambience of communication, but also in order to create local centres for collective subjectivation. Thus it's not simply a matter of remodeling a patient's subjectivity—as it existed before a psychotic crisis—but of a production *sui generis*. For example, certain psychotic patients, coming from poor agricultural backgrounds, will be invited to take up plastic arts, drama, video, music, etc., whereas until then, these universes had been unknown to them. On the other hand, bureaucrats and intellectuals will find themselves attracted to material work, in the kitchen, garden, pottery, horse riding club. The important thing here is not only the confrontation with a new material of expression, but the constitution of complexes of subjectivation: multiple exchanges between individual-group-machine. These complexes actually offer people diverse possibilities for recomposing their existential corporeality, to get out of their repetitive impasses and, in a certain way, to resingularise themselves. (6–7)

The production of subjectivity is always in practice.[3] The schizoanalytic process is about creating the conditions for subjectivity to emerge and finding a certain continuity in the form of a practice that supports and builds on those conditions. Subjectivity is never a given, a neutral index of a preexisting set of conditions. The schizoanalytic process asks: what kinds of conditions facilitate a shift in how subjectivity is produced, and what kinds of practices can be invented to support and sustain it?

The agglomeration of tendencies of the group-subject is contrasted in Guattari's work by the subjugated group.[4] The subjugated group is a group that allows itself to be shaped by external forces, bending to the weight of worlds preconstituted. A group-subject, on the other hand, works to activate the forces that subtend its existence from within the practices that orient it. In doing so, it activates a social field that is absolutely interlaced with its own coming into being. This social field is produced not through the simple coming together of individual bodies. It occurs through the creation of a field of relation that exceeds the individual yet carries the seeds of its singularity. The group-subject gathers these seeds of singularity and germinates them by activating processes that exceed any one individual's frame of reference. This process demonstrates that subjectivity can never be reduced to the sum of its parts, even the subjectivity of a so-called individual. The group-subject makes felt that subjectivity is alive with the elasticity of all that connects, of all that germinates, including new ways of incorporating the forces and flows of the more-than, forces that should never be reduced to a commonality or a simple "togetherness" of preconstituted subjects. As Guattari warns, "one must not lose sight of the fact that, even when paved with the best intentions, the therapeutic endeavor is still constantly in danger of foundering in the stupefying mythology of 'togetherness'" (2015, 118; translation modified).

What a body can do is always connected to the differential of subjectivity. The production of subjectivity is the production of a bodying that always differs from its-self. The agglomeration that is the group-subject connects to the manner in which the bodying comes into relation with emergent strands of subjectivity. Schizoanalysis is the practice of following these strands to see what machinic impulses they possess and what kinds of processes they breed. Practicing the schizz involves developing techniques for the creation of machinic propositions that orient the appetites activated by the production of collective bodying. All of this not in the realm of the conscious but in the infraconscious constellation Brian Massumi calls bare activity (see Massumi 2015b).

What stirs is a tendency. This tendency becomes the material proposition for a collective practice. What emerges is not a category. What is revealed is an operation. What does it produce? How does it activate the field? What else can a body do?

The question of what a body can do is often misread as what "this" body can do, "this" body of the individual. Spinoza never singles out "this" body with regard to the potential he sees in what a body can do. What a body can do is what an agglomeration of tendencies can do in a given set of conditions. Group-subjects are only as creative as the schizz they can produce.

Attune to the Event!

The task of schizoanalysis is that of tirelessly taking apart egos and their presuppositions; liberating the prepersonal singularities they enclose and repress; mobilizing the flows they would be capable of transmitting, receiving, or intercepting; establishing always further and more sharply the schizzes and the breaks well below conditions of identity; and assembling the desiring-machines that countersect everyone and group everyone with others. —Gilles Deleuze and Félix Guattari, *Anti-Oedipus*

"A subject is not necessarily the individual or even *one* individual" (Guattari 2015, 68). By "liberating prepersonal singularities," schizoanalysis activates an agglomeration that moves "well below conditions of identity" in order to mobilize the forces of desire particular to ecologies that exceed "egos and their presuppositions." Dancing to the refrain "I is an other," desiring-machines are born. Desiring-machines are not connected to an ego's desire. They are a force, a conduit, through which new strands of subjectivity emerge. This is the work of schizoanalysis: not to produce a subject abstracted from the practice, but to better trace the conduits through the practice that facilitate the relational field of subjectivity, a relational field always active in the register of the more-than.

SenseLab's practice is committed to this register of the more-than from which the conditions for the minor sociality of emergent collectivity are seeded. Emergent collectivity is the coming into relation of modes of existence that exceed the sum of their parts. When Fernand Deligny, in his work with autistics in the Cévennes at Monoblet, writes, "I should have, I should, remain in the event" in the context of exploring the relationship between the in-act and the doing (*l'agir et le faire*), what

Leslie Plumb 2019

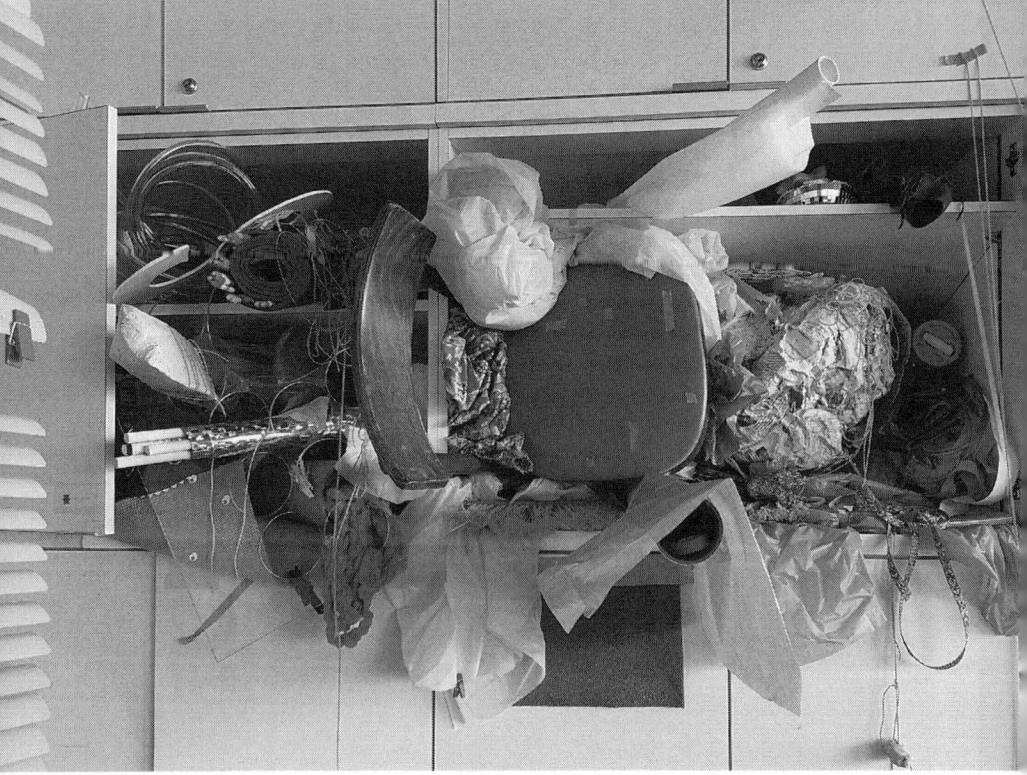

he is referring to is the absolute necessity to remain in the thick of things, developing from the midst the germs of practice rather than imposing frames from without (2007, 1250).[5] In his attempt to foster an alternative to the institutionalized norms of psychiatry, his greatest concern was to work with autistics' own modes of conviviality to facilitate a detouring from the deficit model widespread in both institutions and society at large. In the context of post 1968 France, this meant contending with the centrality of psychoanalysis and its insistence on language. Distancing himself from this tendency, Deligny refused to make language a central modality of existence for and with autistics. He refused to engage with any mode of representation that would seek to organize autistics outside of the in-act of their complex daily expressions, including how they move through the world, how they break down when the world becomes too much, how they make themselves understood, how they play, what they are concerned with, how they dream, how they create. This meant refusing to take an external stance and organize autistics according to pathological presuppositions, including the convention, commonplace within the psychiatric institution, of keeping written accounts of patients to be discussed in camera, autistics excluded. What he sought instead were ways to make visible the shape of their movements in order to elucidate, from these movements, the orientations that composed the everyday. This meant inventing techniques to otherwise mark the daily process of living collectively. The technique Deligny invented involved mapping the daily movements of the autistics. The resulting wander lines (*lignes d'erres*), tracings on paper, foreground movement. Wander lines need no translation they make felt through the force of the line and the thickness of multiple layers of tracings, one on top of the other, how subjectivity is produced in the moving. There is no question here of separating individual from movement, or individual from world.

Wander lines, lines thick with the vibrations of the everyday, resonate with the differential of movements-moved and movements still in the moving. They make felt that bodyings are active constellations that shape themselves in the interstices, in the cracks, on the paths of existence in the making. In his work with autistics, what Deligny has in common with Guattari is a commitment to inventing other ways of conceiving the therapeutic beyond the transference-heavy model of psychoanalysis. By focusing not on their deviation from the norm but on autistics' capacity to invent ways of bodying *in the moving*, Deligny proposes a technique through the wander lines that foregrounds the shape of autistic bodying. What we see in the wander line palimpsests are bodies that resist organization: wander lines celebrate deviation, detour. Bodies are made in the detouring, moving with the affordances of all that is felt, autistic perception attuned to the edgings of worlds coming into experience. This singular way of moving-with

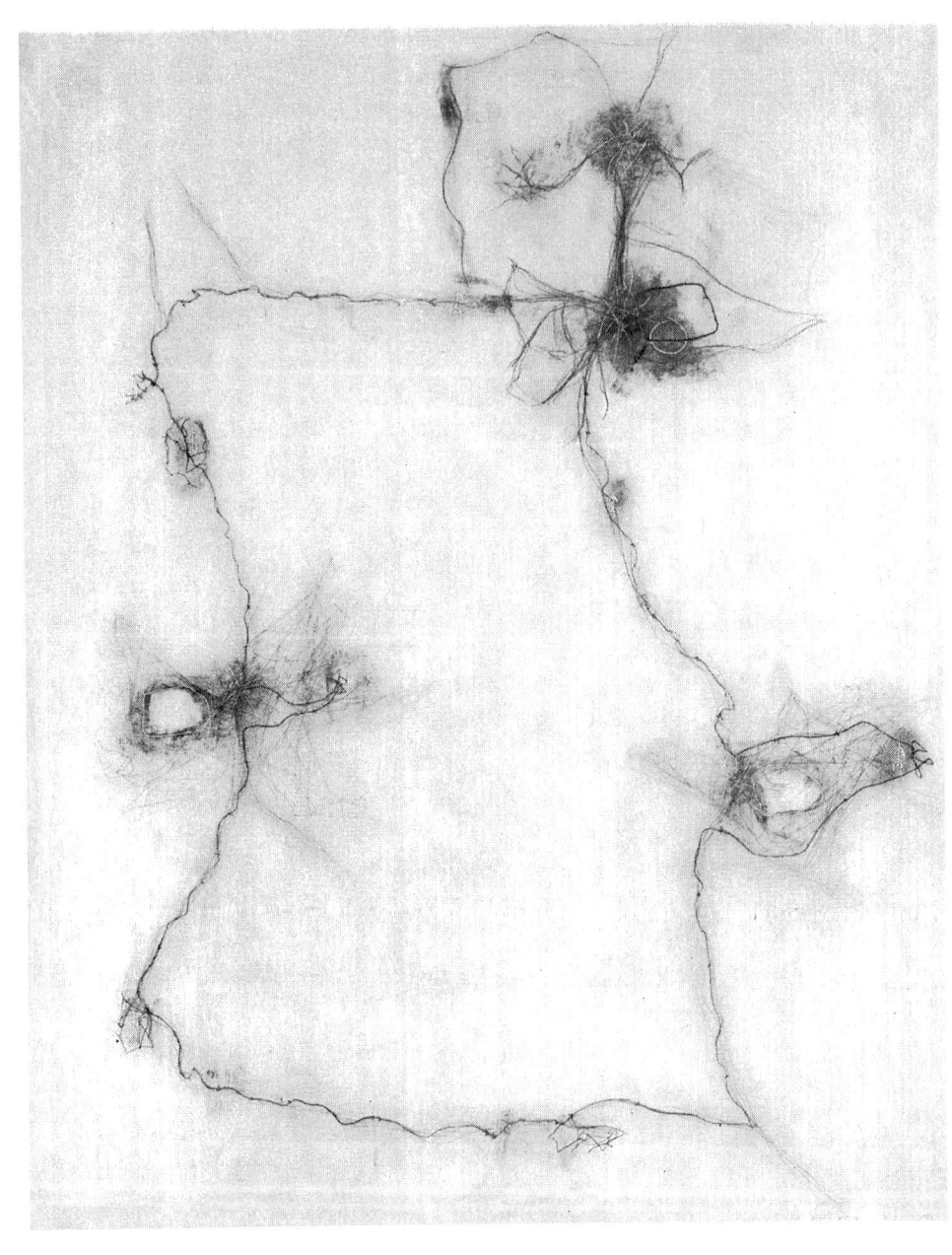

worlds in the making—a kind of anorganization that itself palimpsests body-world—traces the intensities of infrathin variation.

What the wander lines bring to expression is how else the mapping of subjectivity can occur. Instead of reducing subjectivity to the neurotypical norm and the baseline that imposes, wander lines make apparent how autistic refrains—the stims and sidlings and tics—actively produce techniques to facilitate the creation of pathways in the everyday. For the wander lines are full of returns, of circlings-back and circlings-around. Autistic movement, the wander lines show, is a movement that reverberates, that produces strains of itself. These are movements that create opportunities for moving again. This moving-again is possible because in each refrain the landscape coordinates more intensively with the body-in-movement, and vice versa. What is produced is not simply a trajectory. What is produced are desiring-machines that activate the forces of existence too often subdued in our effort to pass as *a* body, *an* identity, *a* subject. Wander lines produce desire in motion. They produce bodyings in the midst.

Though he never would have defined it this way, Deligny's practice could be called schizoanalytic. With a practice that foregrounds the manner in which lines multiply in the crossing, their textures intercalated, he produces a robust account of transindividuality that is very much in tune with Guattari's concept of the group-subject. The transindividual precedes and cuts through any notion of the individual (see Simondon 1989). Unlike those accounts that begin with the individual to add from there, building collectives from the sum of individuals, the transindividual works transversally. A process can never be reduced to the individuality that expresses it (its subjective form). A process *is* the transindividuality that moves through it, the individual its apex though in no way the sum of its parts. Transindividuality is what is active in the middling across which inflections of process subtracted coagulate as the force-of-form. The individual as force-of-form is but an inflection of that coagulation, an inflection that marks itself in a time always already passing.

With the force of transindividuality orienting the practice, the next step is always operative. Schizoanalysis refuses any presuppositions about the field of relation. The schizoanalytic question for the group-subject is, "What should one do when stuck in any situation? A factory, an asylum, or a patient, it stinks. . . . You have to explore. The first item on the agenda is to open up to the complete alterity of the situation. If you claim to know in advance what it's about, you would be doing the same thing as the psychiatrists who doze in their chairs and are definitively disconnected" (Guattari 2015, 73; translation modified).

SenseLab begins here. We ask, at every turn, what kinds of techniques might reorient modes of existence. What modes of existence are expressive in *this* singular context? Should there be an impasse, what platforms for relation can be invented to move the group-subject into another register? Working as we do without membership, open always to the outside, the emphasis is never on the individual per se but on the force of impersonality that flows through it. Our aim is to collaborate across impersonal tendencies to see how processes can evolve and what kinds of ethico-aesthetic orientations can emerge. The questions that move the emergent collectivity necessarily shift with new participation. And so new techniques are always necessary to attune to the transindividual share of experience in the making. This is often difficult: we are trained to recognize that inflection called individuality, and to operate from there. And so a big part of the practice is to pull in activators that assist us in tuning to the lures that take us out of our-selves. These might be concepts (a reading group might be formed). Or they might be artworks (a day of composing might be in order). Or they might involve movement (a movement experimentation workshop might be organized). From there, we follow the lines of inquiry introduced, adhering to the conditions created by the process itself. The aim here is to see what else lurks in the interstices of the questions that we don't quite know how to ask but that seem vital—questions about other ways of accommodating difference, other ways of living and learning. These unsettling questions involve the setting into motion of problematic fields. Problematic fields underlie everything we do, in and beyond SenseLab.[6] They set into motion practices that allow us to better discern the difference between generative and false problems. As we become more skilled at determining what problems don't yet carry their own solutions, the practice of emergent collectivity is refined, and the questions we engage become more complex.

An example of our process: *Distributing the Insensible* (2016). This ten-day SenseLab event brought together the wider network—participants came from Europe, Brazil, Australia, Canada, and the United States. There were seventy of us. In the context of anarchiving—activating the anarchic share of event-based practices—our question was what shape the insensible might take.

Instead of working with the usual ritual of introductions, a practice that too often cements the threshold rather than opening it to cracks, foregrounding academic and artistic prestige and separating out (inadvertently devaluing) those who don't take part in either of those worlds (those who never attended a university, those who have fewer markers of external success), we always begin SenseLab events with a technique that focuses on what the event can do, our aim to foster the conditions for group subjectivity. Although there is a sustained continuity as regards participation in SenseLab events, all SenseLab gatherings are open: anyone can join. And since events are not planned (as in structured) but rather crafted propositionally through a process of designing techniques of relation in the year leading up to them, and then opening to improvisation once they start, this means that anyone can be part of what schizzes the gathering toward an eventing. A gathering, a coming-together of multiple individuals, can activate a group-subject, but in most cases the conditions are not there to facilitate an emergent orientation that redirects the encounter. An event *is* that immanent redirection. An event makes itself felt *as event* if there is a collective sense that something has unfolded that exceeds the initial proposition with which it was seeded. This redirection can be minor—it usually has the force of a tweak more than the form of a substantial turn, though that does happen as well. An event is known to have occurred when what seeds it takes germ beyond the conditions that brought it into the world. Where seeds of process germinate, emergent collectivities sprout.

Improvisation brings with it uncertainty, and it's very easy to fall back to normative gestures in the face of anxiety, especially if there is a sense of an in-group, out-group dynamic. Those of us who have been around for a while know that newcomers have often had a deep impact on our process, but newcomers don't arrive with the confidence of an overview that demonstrates how vital their role is. Experimenting immediation requires that we set in place as rigorously as possible the conditions for breaking any normative framing, opening the way for the infrathin fabulations that will foster experimentation. For all of these reasons, it is imperative that newcomers be invited into the practice of the schizz in ways that facilitate active forms of participation from the very beginning. This is why, we spend a substantial amount of time before each large event considering collectively how best to seed the event through a careful crossing of its threshold. Our hope each time is to invent a technique that will facilitate a different edging-into-resonance of a group subjectivity. What this means in practice is that *how* we come together is decisive for the event.

For *Distributing the Insensible*, we proposed "bench talks" as a way of crossing the initial threshold.[7] The initial proposition: two people per bench, one hour. The suggestion: "an anarchiving experience encouraging attentiveness to insensible dynamics surrounding or affecting the encounter."[8] A geography of benches was mapped in advance. The participants, many of whom wouldn't know the city well, if at all, would pull the bench location out of a hat the day before and be at the bench at the appointed time. No one would know who they were expecting.

With the bench talks, the aim was to preaccelerate into the event through an approximation of proximity played out in resonance to environments experienced in relation. Sitting on a bench in the middle of a snow-clad city on a December afternoon with a stranger or with someone you hadn't seen for years was an experience we imagined might be similar to the situationists' *Possible Rendez-Vous*: there would be an overlap of the conditions of the environment with the anticipation of meeting someone you might not know and the uncertainty of whether the rendezvous would actually happen. The geography, the affective tonality of the surrounds, was considered as important in the bench talks as the conversation that might ensue. In practice, the quality of attention produced in the waiting, the attunement to the surrounds that came with not knowing if the passerby was the person who would sit and talk with you, *did* produce an intensive orientation to the qualities of the environment, to the sound, to the light, to the movements of the people walking by. It also facilitated an encounter with the wider proposition of *Distributing the Insensible*: we were entering into a practice that involved attending to the anarchic share of experience in the making. The bench talks fostered a threshold of joint attunement to the larger event.

When the proposition for the bench practice was made in advance of the event, what also occurred, as always does in SenseLab processes, was a proliferation of propositions taking off from it. All propositions are considered collective, and it is this collectivity, at the heart of the propositional, that creates the momentum for propositional seriality. Even when propositions come from one person, as they in fact often do, we consider them propositions *for* the group. It is our practice to embrace the generosity with which a proposition is made. Affirmative politics guide us. This does not mean staying with a proposition at any cost. It means beginning with an appetite for what the proposition can do, seeing what techniques and practices it calls forth. In principle, this approach means we believe that any proposition can yield something interesting, and, in fact, most propositions are greeted with the enthusiasm of collective participation. But not all of them have the carryover process-based seeding requires. Not all propositions are robust enough to extend beyond themselves to outdo themselves toward the technicity we seek, and so sometimes they are tried and cast aside. Over time, we learn not to worry too much if our propositions are not the ones that lead the way and instead become curious about what it is about a given proposition that makes it work. In an ethos of collectively committing to the force of a proposition, the excited proliferation that inevitably accompanies new directions plays the role not of diluting the original proposition, or contradicting it. The proliferation of ideas around a proposition is a way to make felt the seriality at the heart of all propositions. It isn't so much a question of choosing one over another, but of asking how the differential between propositions in a series composes to create a problematic field. We have come to call this seriality *pop-up propositions*, a nomenclature that underscores the emergent quality of the event. Interestingly, this serial taking-up of the proposition even occurs across long timelines—it is not unusual for a proposition to breed serial reinstantiations years after the initial one was explored, and this by people who often weren't even part of the original event. There is a sense at

SenseLab that propositions have a time signature. Sometimes they come too early and need to be reactivated later.

In the case of *Distributing the Insensible*, the proliferation for the bench-talk proposition included many orientations. One that stands out and was actually practiced foregrounded Lygia Pape's technique in *Divisor* (1968), a work that involves a large piece of cloth with holes cut out for participants' heads. This suggestion made its way into a pop-up proposition during *Distributing the Insensible* called *Nós as Knots*, proposing to take the bench of the bench talks and transduce it into an elastic net. This elastic net would be fashioned by small rubber bands brought by the participants. The proposition was described as follows: "How can these knots help us endure a paradox or temporary impasse in our work, life, thinking or creative practice that might become newly productive if staged in a way that opens it to a collaborative exploration in or between language and other modes of expression?" This pop-up proposition was powerful: it transduced the bench talks into an aesthetic and conceptual operation vastly different from the original one, yet taking its ethos to heart. This served to remind us that the ethico-aesthetic core of the proposition is indeed transduction—the capacity to activate the differential between more than one modality, to bring to the fore the complexity of thresholds in the encounter, and to choreograph them in new directions.

In *Distributing the Insensible*, what we could not have foreseen is the way the event ended up being taken over by a wider SenseLab anxiety around creating a tangible product. The event was never imagined to be the site for the making of a product—indeed, SenseLab had been created in large part as an antidote to the product-oriented tendencies that take over our collective imaginations and choreograph our comings-together in the academic world: SenseLab has always said that its work works when the seeds of process are carried into collaborations beyond its reach. The problem is that this approach does not appeal to the funding bodies that supported our work from 2012 to 2019, and we were hitting a milestone. One of the promises we made to the funding bodies was the creation of an anarchive, the first version of which was meant to be unveiled in December 2016. *Distributing the Insensible* coincided with an expectation from the funding bodies that we would show them the product of our research (the timeline hadn't been considered in the planning of the event, our daily lives so enmeshed with the process of anarchiving that we had forgotten that others might not be able to ascertain how much work we were actually doing). The problem is, as outlined in chapter 3, that the anarchive is not a form. It's a process, a way. While we were already hard at work to eventually give it a digital conduit through what we call the 3E Process Seed Bank (see chapter 8), in December 2016 we were nowhere close to having anything to show for ourselves. This was not due to a

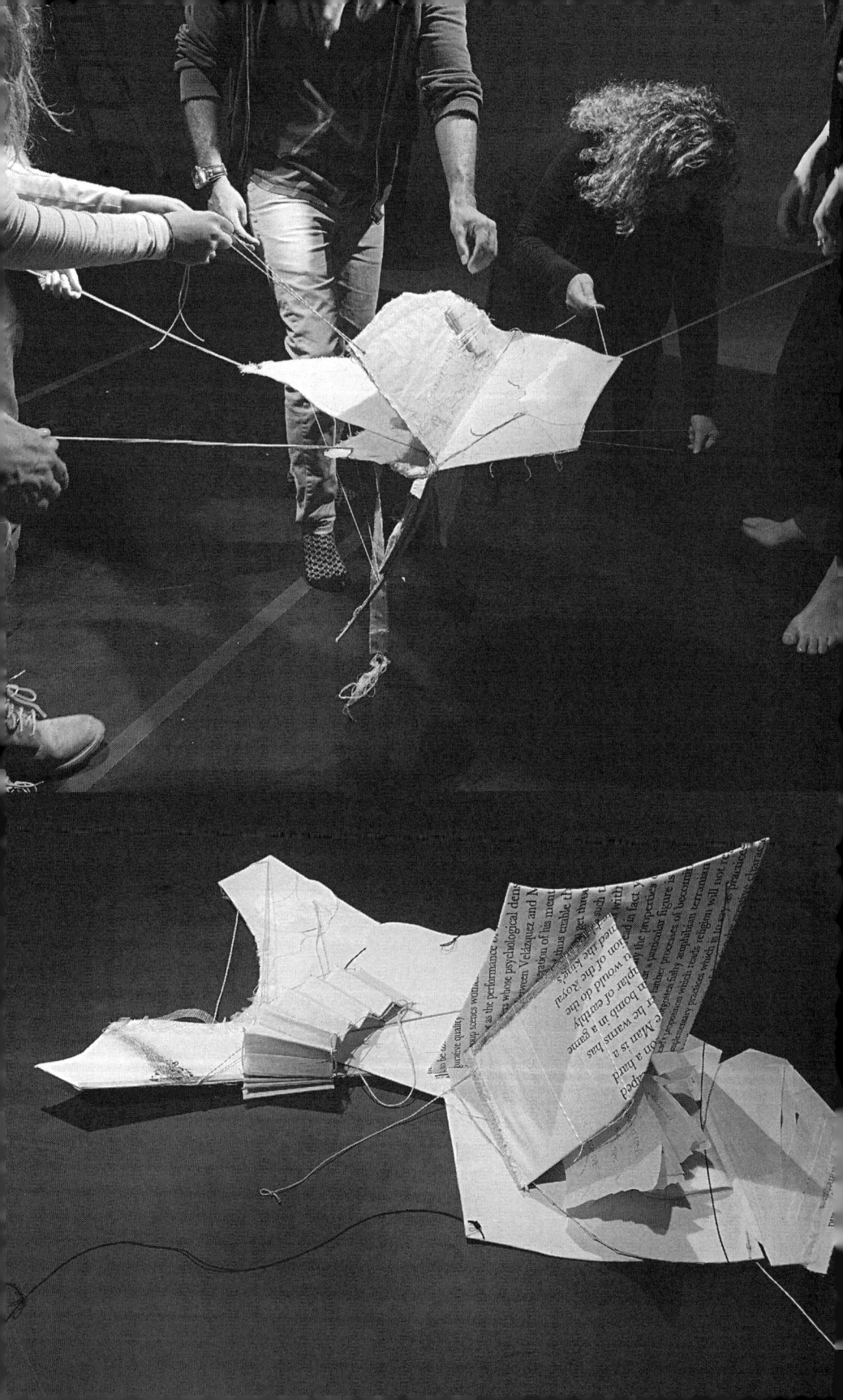

lack of commitment. Anarchiving had been in every thought, in every gesture, for years by then. But to practice something is different from giving it a form, and we hadn't yet found a way to do that.

Looking for ways to produce something tangible without giving up the process we had begun to seed through the bench talks and the pop-up propositions that emerged from them, we decided to focus on making products but to place our collective attention in particular on how the *process* of anarchiving in the limited context of a ten-day event might facilitate a particular quality of group subjectivity. We asked: what kinds of wander lines might the collective making facilitate, and how might the transversality across different strands of making affect the composition as a whole? Would an emphasis on the anarchic share and on anarchiving more broadly allow for an overlay of modes of making, facilitating the production of a collective aesthetic process? Was a collective composition possible without determining the aesthetic in advance?

What we ended up making turned out to be much more than simple products. Selecting the figure of the book, we asked what else a book can do in the context of attuning to the insensible. Some of the books were large-scale dancing books, puppet-like with long strings that required five people to read them. These tended to be started by someone, often working late into the night (with so few days, we worked almost around the clock), then taken over by someone else

just up from a nap, and returned to by the initial maker once they felt refreshed. Authorship was easily cast aside in lieu of a sense of gratitude for the gift of collaboration. Discussion was rare. The focus was intense, and collective.

Another book was composed of a panoply of pockets, each carrying an anarchival seed in the form of a composition, a material, a text. This one was composed by dozens of participants, each making a page, and then glued together by a few committed, detail-oriented people. A bag was made for it by someone. And then a box by yet someone else. There was a comic on anarchiving included in *The How-To Go-To Book of Anarchiving* (SenseLab 2016), a book we collectively wrote and published in under eight days.

And there were five 59-minute books, books that needed to be made in order to gather momentum for the process (SenseLab, 2016). There were also graphics, and dance books, and the printing, into a book, of all the code we wrote for our eighth issue of *Inflexions*, "Radical Pedagogy" (April 2015.) With these books in hand, we had material to prove that we had done our work. But really, the work could not be reduced to the form of the books themselves. The work was in the way things shaped each other, in how the process of bookmaking carried forward the ineffable anarchic share of experience. It would be wrong to say that the books we made were the anarchive of *Distributing the Insensible*. They were a shape *Distributing the Insensible* took when faced with the imperative to prove the value of our process. The anarchive was produced across bench talks and the propositions it seeded, across thresholds cracked to reveal new tendencies, across material processes experimented over several years of anarchiving. The books were the material intervention through which the force of the anarchive could be felt as it wove its way through the event.

This is the work SenseLab does: we create conditions for processes that make felt what remains beyond value as performed and practiced in our institutions. I like to think of the books as an operation of the pragmatics of the useless. For these books, which were made to prove our use-value, would never be legible to someone who didn't take the time to activate a group-subject to learn how to read them.

Produce Desire!

When SenseLab speaks of the appetite that drives the process, we are speaking of the production of desire *in the event*. By desire *in the event*, I mean desire in the transversality of a group-subject that activates the shift in process that makes felt the differential of the process. Desire in the event is an affirmative ethos. Desire here is not what singles out one thing over another from a position

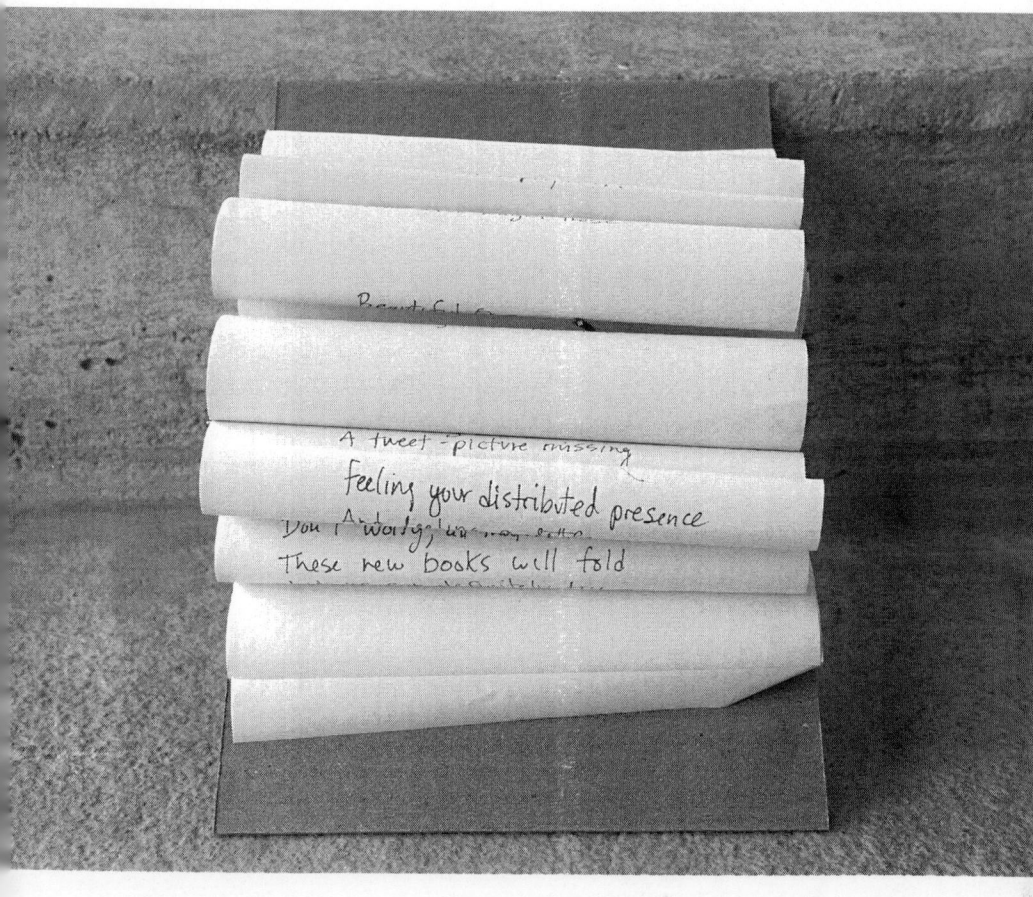

of personal investment. Desire is what produces the conditions for a schizz. In the context of SenseLab, the honing of desire as affirmative ethos is a commitment to the lure that activates the speculative share of a pragmatic operation. Desire as production of differentials of existence is at the heart of schizoanalysis. "The schizoanalytic argument is simple: desire is a machine, a synthesis of machines, a machinic arrangement [*agencement*] desiring-machines. The order of desire is the order of *production*; all production is at once desiring-production and social production. We therefore reproach psychoanalysis for having stifled this order of production, for having shunted it into *representation*" (Deleuze and Guattari 1983, 296; translation modified). Desire's production has nothing to do with the creation of a product. This is immanent production, an agencement of tendencies toward an unfolding, in the event, of a politics of affirmation. As a motor of immanent production, desire has a particular rhythm: "'and . . .' 'and then . . .'" (5; ellipses in the original). And . . . and then . . . is how the act of unfolding expresses itself, an expression not of a simple continuity in time but of time's overlap. A proposition is made. The proposition collectivizes. The production of desire is activated across the chain of its unfolding: the curiosity, the appetite, the multiple modes of engagement, each step in untimely overlap with the last. The process, not the individual, does the work of orienting. Desire is produced in the interstices of the chain in the propulsion, across the series, in the *what else* that infrathinly makes a difference in each acrossness of the *and . . . and then . . .* Nodes of impersonality are activated at these crossings. What moves is the affirmation itself, felt in every phase of the series, an affirmation not to simply adhere to the proposition as is but to inquire into its ellipses. *And then . . .* is not a simple narrative line. It is a transduction through which a seriality pulses, altered in the dephasing. This is desiring-production: the agencement of a process that facilitates a dephasing that affirms difference. A transduction, after all, signals not only a shift in the chain but the creation of a new process in the interval. This is the work desire can do when activated in the mode of the event.

The counter to desire as production is lack. In the context of the proposition, this tends to express itself as critique. Critique comes from the commitment to external stakes. It speaks in advance of the co-composing, poised in advance to outline lack. It is easy to stand outside a proposition and explain what is wrong with it. It is much more difficult to try it out to see what it can do, then to collectively invent operations that return to that aspect of its operationality. This involves engaging in the proposition through an attunement to the potential that runs through it, amplifying or redirecting it, consolidating not form but tendency. Desiring-production works here, inventing, and risking failure. The alternative would be to bask in representation. "To overturn the theater of representation into the order of desiring-production: this is the whole task of schizoanalysis" (Deleuze and Guattari 1983, 271).

A schizoanalytic process requires techniques for desiring-production, techniques that attune to the minor gestures that course through experience in the making. These techniques must exceed individual desire, veering instead toward a sociality yet to be invented. "Desire is in production as social production, just as production is in desire as desiring-production" (Deleuze and Guattari 1983, 348). In the mode of a pragmatics of the useless, desiring-production is about creating the conditions for coming into collective expression such that the expressivity of the body-world constellation is amplified. It is about sitting at the uneasy interstice of process and production and asking what things do when they shape each other.

When a proposition takes form at SenseLab, either it becomes a motor for process, or it perishes. The perishing takes with it the proposing individual's momentary alliance to the proposition. It is easy, in those moments, to take personally what might be perceived as a lack of interest in the proposition at hand. But that would be to ignore how a group-subject orients around a process to explore what is in excess of any individual commitment to it. Practicing the schizz involves recognizing that no proposition ever truly belongs to the person who proposes it. Propositions do their work as activators of process precisely because they exceed the individual. Propositions, in the Whiteheadian sense, are lures for feeling: they excite the transversal orientation of a set of conditions ripe for the reorienting.

The desiring-production of the group-subject is never right or wrong. It energizes a tendency; it motivates an orientating. It has a choreographic quality, a pulling from the edges, which is completely different from a politics of alignment to a doctrine. What moves the group-subject is not a preference for one kind of activity over another but an attunement to compositions unfolding. The work of the group-subject is to develop a collective desiring-production that is robust enough to tend to the leaking whole, exposing how it exceeds itself.

When Deleuze and Guattari emphasize that schizoanalysis as a practice has strong reverberations in the field of the political, they do so out of recognition that political movements too often fall into resentment because of fissures in group functioning. This often occurs when the stress of the political work moves people into identitarian frames. One-to-one allegiances tend to break down social pacts. What might it look like, Guattari asks, to practice schizoanalysis in all group processes, not just psychiatric ones? This question is at the heart of the ethico-aesthetic orientation that Guattari names the three ecologies—the social, the environmental, and the conceptual/psychic—his concern always with the qualities of their overlap. A turn toward the political in the context of schizoanalysis involves a commitment to the transversality of the ethico-aesthetic and the ways in which it cuts across the three ecologies, creating new assemblages for political expression that exceed what any one of them can do on their own. With this ethico-aesthetic orientation, a political process can no longer be reduced to the humans that orient it, nor, by extension, to the identities that are said to direct it. It must always also include the more-than human tendencies that run through it. This ethico-aesthetic stance creates alliances that shift not only the political work we can do but the very temptation to define the political solely in the register of the human.

Working with transversality allows for an impersonal collaboration, impersonal in the sense that it activates what lurks at the transindividual level of bodying, making it feasible, for instance, to develop ad hoc experiments around urgent questions without feeling as though the responsibility for the proposition has to be carried by a single individual. When the group-subject is the carrier of a collective proposition, how it unfolds ends up also shifting the group-subject. With everything in movement, there is an opportunity for uncharted variation. Of course nothing is ever assured. These shifts can also lead to the demise of the political movement, but if that does happen, it is likely because in the collective as it stands, there aren't yet the conditions for carrying the uneasy excess of the more-than.

Collective work is replete with burnouts. These burnouts tend to be lived alone, segregated from the intensity of collective work. They are lived alone precisely because there wasn't in the collective the capacity to activate a group-subject that could carry the burden of the political work beyond any one individual. Practicing the schizz is an attempt to facilitate modes of operation that don't lead to individual burnout, that don't always find their way back to the self-same. This doesn't mean things don't fall apart. It means learning to make the falling apart a collective experiment with inventing other ways of engaging with the perishing, and the potentializing of experience. Key to this is a continuous engagement with the development of techniques to activate the group-subject, to activate the force of impersonality that runs through us and bring it into resonance with a collective more-than. When these techniques are at their most powerful, they are capable of calling forth Ashon Crawley's "otherwise possibility," in this case the quality of a deviation that courses through collective assemblages and tunes them to an engagement with the political that exceeds the form of personal allegiance. This is not to say that allegiance is a problem under all conditions. It is to emphasize that processes invent best when the collectivity they spawn is in excess of preexisting formations and the externally imposed demands that accompany them. Preexisting formations tend to have already assimilated their thresholds. Approximations of proximity spawned through the minor sociality of emergent collectivity are more attentive to the creation of new openings and tend to have the flexibility to move into them.

This can't be achieved once and for all. Desiring-production schizzes, and with each schizz a break shifts the ground, producing a new set of conditions. Allegiances form, and proximities become less approximate. These kinds of sidlings are necessary too, but there is a danger, always, that the collectivity will become reduced to a count, and with that the group subjectivity will become subjugated. In the words of Deleuze and Guattari:

> Group-subjects are continually deriving from subjugated groups through a rupture of the latter: they mobilize desire, and always cut its flows again

further on, overcoming the limit, bringing the social machines back to the elementary forces of desire that form them. But inversely, they are also continually closing up again, remodeling themselves in the image of subjugated-groups: re-establishing interior limits, reforming a great break that the flows will not pass through or overcome, subordinating the desiring-machines to the repressive aggregate that they constitute on a large scale. There is a speed of subjugation that is opposed to the coefficients of transversality. And what revolution is not tempted to turn against its group-subjects, stigmatized as anarchistic or irresponsible, and to liquidate them? (1983, 349; translation modified)

When there is a shift from group-subject to subjugated group, a few symptoms are immediately present: events that are larger than the sum of their parts are narrated as though they belonged to the individual; personal stakes are measured, turning from a pragmatics of the useless toward a representation of the useful; allegiances are outlined, and subgroups are formed; approximations are discarded in favor of robust frames.

The work of schizoanalysis is never done once and for all. When the landscape hardens, as it invariably does, the practice is to return not with an analysis but with a technique. Often, these techniques involve an intercessor. I think here of Guattari's use of the mobile tape recorder to record the resistance of a patient called R. A.

R. A. was a patient from La Borde who had recently run away, "an escape that now seems to me to have 'replayed' the time that he ran away when he was 15 and that can be considered the starting point for the psychotic aggravation of his illness" (Guattari 2015, 36). After the fugue, R. A. completely cut himself off from his surrounds. In any attempt at dialogue, he responded defensively: "stereotypical responses that were always more or less aggressive (such as: 'what?,' 'hunh?,' 'I can't hear anything,' 'I don't feel anything,' 'I don't want to,' 'I'm dead,' 'This place made me like this,' etc.) and that regularly interrupted anything anyone said to him as soon as the first words were spoken" (Guattari 2015, 36). The rest of the time, he seemed frozen: "We could only sometimes get him to do something by pushing and forcing him" (36).

In the past, Guattari had had good relations with R. A. Now, all semblance of trust seemed lost. A technique had to be invented that would allow for a renewed encounter. Given the danger of transference, care had to be taken to avoid it. For transference is precisely what schizoanalysis works to keep at bay; "such is the delicate and focal point that fills the function of transference in schizoanalysis— dispersing, schizophrenizing the perverse transference of psychoanalysis" (Deleuze and Guattari 1983, 339). Given the role Guattari had played in R. A.'s life before the fugue, it would be easy for R. A. to respond to Guattari as a parental figure or as a figure that represented his oppression. With this in mind, the decision was made to bring an intercessor into the mix: "With Dr. Oury, we decided that my conversations with R. A. would take place in the presence of a tape recorder. Ostensibly, I started the recording when the dialog entered what I considered to be an impasse, or when something 'bothered' me. It was then as if a third person had appeared in the room" (Guattari 2015, 37).

As intercessor, the tape recorder did the work of multiplying the encounter, of adding a threshold. Not only did it capture without interpreting, it stood in to take the measure of a changing situation. This was particularly important in a case such as this one where a patient's paranoia might reduce the encounter to an oedipal relation, forcing the therapist into the role of the perpetrator/savior.

With the tape recorder, Guattari was capable of signaling an impasse. The recording caught what could not quite be said. It caught the disjunction activated in the encounter. When R. A. heard this disjunction, it made him angry.

> During the first sessions, when we listened to the tape (which we erased together the next day), R. A. lost his temper. The opposition that he had turned against the world, the "what?," "hunh?," etc., he now turned against himself. The recorded voice, the drawling tone, the hesitations, the breaks, the constant incoherence revolted him, and he took me as a witness that he must have truly fallen "lower than everything" to end up speaking like that. (2015, 38)

Hearing himself speak, R. A. was forced to recognize that the hesitations were his. He could not project them onto the body of the therapist. This facilitated a shift in tone. With the shift in tone came the beginning of a transformation. Once this occurred, the intercessor had done its work, and a new technique was sought.

> After a certain time, the tape recorder had conditioned the situation of our dialog to the point that I almost did not need to turn it on. I abandoned it and in its place, I wrote down the things he said that I found interesting in a notebook. I left the notebook at his disposal and we quickly reached the point where he did the writing in my place. In other words, during our conversations, I would interrupt him to say, "you could write that down," and I would repeat what he had said word for word (he was usually unable to remember it himself). I took on the role of the tape recorder (or the mirror), but in a more human way, the "disautomatization" of the ma-

chine was correlated to the fact that he was now the machine recording the words circulating between us. (40)

The practice of the schizz is palpable here: Guattari uses the conviviality of shared utterances to give R. A. the language he needs to begin to express himself. Through this technique, R. A. becomes capable of reorienting his encounter with the therapeutic relation. The recording gives him an entry into a new process through which he can discover something about his current state (rather than constantly replaying his grievances). The new process is indistinguishable from the writing itself.

What bothers me the most is the lack of all the feelings that I still had the possibility of experiencing. . . . I will never leave this journal. Here I must be resolute, because I can only be like that here. . . . Don't want to write. My organism is still not working. No impressions. No feeling. No sensations. . . . Have not yet understood what Felix just said to me about . . . don't remember . . . still have a jumble of words in (so to speak) my head. Spoke with Felix. . . . I feel myself becoming all alone like before we talk. . . . It is true that two years ago, I would not have talked about any of this. I was fragile, but not as fragile as now. The "I" existed a little bit, or at least I thought it existed. . . . The main thing is words. I never had them when I was little. . . . I am folded in on myself. I am able to write all of this because the pseudo-presence of Evelyne and Felix make me write it. (R. A., in Guattari 2015, 42–44, 46–47, 53)

In the writing, R. A. begins an untimely conversation. This is a conversation alive in the encounter of times overlapping. No longer in the position of reactivity, R. A. reclaims language, finding a path through its infrathin ellipses. This turn to expression, an expressivity awakened in the being of relation, allows R. A. to slowly become active again in the community of La Borde and learn to develop his own techniques for survival beyond the institution.

It turns out that the recording is not even always recording. It doesn't actually matter that much if it's on or off. Its role is to amplify what is heard in the unsaid. The tape recorder functions as immanent detour of what is presumed to be carried by a psychiatric session, refusing the 1 + 1 of interpersonality. As intercessor, the tape recorder refuses to limit the relational field to the two individuals, Guattari and R. A. N + 1, the tape recorder detours transference.

What [psychoanalysts] do is merely to make the unconscious speak according to the transcendent uses of synthesis imposed on it by other forces: Global Persons, the Complete Object, the Great Phallus, the Terrible Undifferentiated of the Imaginary, Symbolic Differentiations, Segregation.

What psychoanalysts invent is only the transference, a transference Oedi-pus, a consulting-room Oedipus of Oedipus, especially noxious and viru-lent, but where the subject finally has what he wants, and sucks away at his Oedipus on the full body of the analyst. And that's already too much. But Oedipus takes shape in the family, not in the analyst's office, which merely acts as the last territoriality. And Oedipus is not made by the family. The Oedipal uses of synthesis, oedipalization, triangulation, castration, all refer to forces a bit more powerful, a bit more subterranean than psycho-analysis, than the family, than ideology, even joined together. There we have all the forces of social production, reproduction, and repression. This can be explained by the simple truth that very powerful forces are required to defeat the forces of desire, lead them to resignation, and substitute ev-erywhere reactions of the daddy-mommy type for what is essentially ac-tive, aggressive, artistic, productive, and triumphant in the unconscious itself. (Deleuze and Guattari 1983, 121–22)

Cutting across transference, where powerful forces are kept in place and ter-ritoriality is maintained, the intercessor schizzes, detouring the process exactly where it would otherwise bind itself to the body of the therapist. This allows the event to come into itself in a way that makes felt what is at work in the field of relation. In the shape of n + 1, the encounter becomes capable of attuning to all that moves through it in excess of the habitual modes of narrating our-selves. This does not deny the wounds of the past or their role in the suffering. How things came to be matters. Horrors are never completely erased—they continue to have effects. Moving beyond transference simply makes it possible for the field to be opened up beyond the confines of what has come to be expected, em-phasizing that subjectivity cannot be produced in a territorialization on the in-terpersonal that has become so colonizing that every instance of life is suffused with it. Territories must be dephased in order for new processes to emerge. The dephasing of the past is not its erasure. What the intercessor does is create the conditions for a renewed engagement with the world that can unblock the territory's hard borders and open experience to a deviation. This deterritorial-ization is never complete—territories reform, often in an echo of what is most habitual about them—the wounds of time return. Schizzing is never done once and for all.

The production of subjectivity is an ongoing process. Desiring-production is not a turning away from pain or a denial of its many sources. It is the production of a palimpsest whose wander lines produce new crossings. This is what we see in the case of R. A.: the tape recorder followed by the invitation to write exposes

Leslie Plumb 2018

him to what else flows through him. This activates the transindividual force of group subjectivity in R. A., bringing out the collectivity of his gestures such that their anarchic share can reorient his actions toward new tendings.

Don't Presume to Know!

The pull of judgment is strong. In a web as unruly as SenseLab, the capacity for confusion looms large: I think it is fair to say that most of us are uncertain about the work most of the time. The work breeds this kind of uncertainty primarily because it is process-oriented, and because what it seeks to do can't be gauged by any existing matrix of value. To practice the schizz is to be in relation to an un-knowing that can be very destabilizing. But that uncertainty is what a pragmatics of the useless must contend with, I suspect. To practice new modes of encounter, to invent in the cracks of existence where individuality schizzes, is necessarily to be without bearings. And where there are no bearings, the first temptation is to presume to know.

Debased interpretation comes from assuming we already know. It is debased because it falls out of contrast, muting the force of backgroundingforergounding. This is dangerous ground for schizoanalysis.

Schizoanalysis does not take the measure of a situation, does not gauge it against another, does not judge it according to preexisting societal norms. It eschews debased interpretation. "The first task of schizoanalysis: discovering in a subject the nature, the formation, of the functioning of *their* desiring-machines, independently of any interpretations. What are your desiring-machines, what do you put into these machines, what is the output, how does it work, what are your nonhuman sexes?" (Deleuze 1996, 77; translation modified). In lieu of judgment, the schizoanalyst invents intercessing techniques. These intercessors could be a tape recorder as in the example above. They could be gestures. They could be sponges or pipe cleaners. They could be scissors or garden shears. There is no ideal intercessor: each situation must be assessed on its own terms, its intercessors culled from within its singular problematic field.

Interpretations that judge on the basis of external stakes are devoid of intercessors. They speak in the name of "I" (often masked as "we") and do their work "according to." If thresholds are not carefully attended to, debased interpretation will enter into the encounter, often in the form of self-narration. Before we know it, we will have moved beyond fabulation to mythmaking. Accounts of perceived slights will surface. Feeling overlooked, undervalued, ignored, are often the first signs of breakdown. We will find ourselves saying things like "This is how we do things." These tendencies, which are so typical of group processes, and certainly plague SenseLab, disavow the production of subjectivity in the transindividual connotellation of a group-subject. At SenseLab we do our best to move with these impulses when they take over, recognizing them as a carryover of the neoliberal tendencies that orient us and the neurotypicality that organizes us. Individualizing is everywhere the norm, and with it comes the he-said-she-said stultifying temporality of self-defense. To practice otherwise can bring with it an acute anxiety that easily turns to what is most familiar. When this happens, we do our best to find another technique for schizzing, trying to become attuned to what created the breakdown in the group-subject.

Debased interpretation turns the process back onto the self, backgrounding the field of relation. In a disintegration of a group process this tends to shift the group-subject toward subjugation. In this context, it will be second nature to give an account of how the breakdown happened. While this can be both helpful and necessary, it will be very tempting to enter into a normative therapeutic frame if this modality of interpretation falls into replaying the theater of individual against individual. Not only will this mute the complexity of how the group-subject erupted into dysfunction, it will deny any forces that work transversally, including more-than human forces. The schizz itself will also be muted because its potency is precisely that it is transversal, that it operates across.

In such a scenario, what tends to happen is a local calling-out. People become the judges of each others' actions. What are often called microaggressions become the focus of attention. The problem with this is that it tends to concentrate on only one small aspect of a much more complex dynamic. In actuality, microaggressions are transversal—their power is precisely that the microaggression cuts across all scales of action. To properly engage with a microaggression is to create techniques that are capable of composing with a dynamic form that is in excess of a particular instance. To connect to this transversality involves engaging at a systemic level. Group-subjects are much better equipped for transversality than is the humanist, identitarian frame. Once back in a humanist frame, it is only a few steps to the dangers of all that comes with oedipalization, including a focus on the self as the sole marker of valued participation. With a renewed focus on identity, neurotypicality rears its head. And whiteness, of course. Because how we wage war with each other always involves a return to colonial tendencies. Not only does this turn a pragmatics of the useless into a representation of the useful, the shift of focus from group-subject to bounded individual is a violence in itself: it restricts all forms of participation to the human. A schizoanalytic approach tries to sidestep the interpretative operation by creating intercessors that can shift the balance of the group subjectivity gone awry. Group-subjects are not reducible to groups. They are what exposes the transversality of each of our body-worlds, connecting it to the systemic level where difference spreads across populations and the individual is always more-than one.

When Deleuze says that the first task of schizoanalysis is to discover the formation of our desiring-machines—to explore the operations of our nonhuman sexes—what he is saying is that practicing the schizz occurs at the level of the preindividual where desire is at the very cusp of its expression. This "pure dispersed and anarchic multiplicity, without unity or totality," is the site of the production of subjectivity (Deleuze 1996, 78). This is what the group-subject works to fashion, what its agglomeration shapes. The work of the schizoanalyst is to connect to the intercessors that move through the shaping—"stones, pocket, mouth; a shoe, a pipe bowl, a small limp bundle that is undefined, a cover for a bicycle bell, half a crutch" (79). The point is not to recover something. The work is not for the past but toward an attunement to the thickness of experience in the midst. The shifts produced in the relational field can be minor, reorienting at the level of the most infrathin of tendencies. Or it may be that everything has

Leslie Plumb 2017

to change: "The only thing we can do is tear this shit down completely and build something new" (Harney and Moten 2013, 152). Most important is to recognize that anything that changes in the field affects everything, that future-presentness is born of a commitment to all that matters, to all that runs through experience more-than human.

Invent (Don't Organize)!

Desiring-production is oriented by what Deleuze calls passive synthesis. Think of passive synthesis as the agencement of the field. In the case above of creating propositions for crossing the threshold at *Distributing the Insensible*, the focus was not on how one individual would do the work for the others but on how the field itself would activate collective conditions of encounter. This occurred not only through the initial proposition of the bench talks but through the fabulation they set in motion. The activation of collective desiring-production was facilitated through a group process committed to coming into relation differently. This took the pressure off the actual bench talks, allowing whatever sparked through them to be extended by future pop-up propositions. The initial threshold was just that: a first experimentation with how a coming into relation could occur. This coming into relation facilitated what occurred afterward, but what came afterward could not be reduced to it. Passive synthesis is a way of articulating this coming-into-itself of relational potential.

Desiring-production operates indirectly. It catches a tendency and moves it across a threshold. In the movement, it reorients a flow. When the flow schizzes, a new quality of encounter emerges, and with it new thresholds appear.

In the creation of the space of encounter we call SenseLab spaZe, spaZe[9] to emphasize the force of resonance of the detour (the zigzag of experience), there is a collective commitment, through materials, to attend to how the flow schizzes. Working always with what is at hand, with materials reused, the practice invigorates the field, asking daily how else we might collectively enter. This work we call "composing" is a practice in its own right. It asks SenseLab to invent at the interstices of what is, engaging not with a future-organization but with a present-orientation. In the act, it involves asking precise questions as regards the operationality of the space of encounter. What kinds of affordances allow nervous systems to be calm enough to do their work? What luminosities facilitate entry, and for whom? What kinds of corners can be created to facilitate the hiding of those who prefer not to be seen? What makes a scurrying to those corners possible? Does a color do a particular kind of work at a certain juncture? What about the tight twirl of a spring? Or the spread of a plush figure? What happens when the blankets become islands and the hammocks hold the plants? Does anything shift when the orientation tends toward the vertical? What does an open cube do? Does it allow for less frontality? If so, for how long? And what about patches on the ground or lines of colored tape? Do they facilitate a directionality? A staying in place?

While these questions sometimes carry proper names—there may, for instance, be a tendency that is embodied by a certain individual that spaZe tries to amplify—what the work seeks to do in the first instance is not to make individuals feel welcomed *as individuals*. The work is to cull from the transversal force of the transindividual tendencies that connect across body-worlds. The work is to fashion an environment for an ever-shifting group-subject.

This practice, which emerged after the first decade or so of SenseLab, affects all we do. It involves long, engaged sessions with materials that explore how else textures of relation emerge. It involves movement experimentation. It involves attention to minor gestures. Engaging beyond the easy dichotomy of interiority-exteriority, individual-group, composing supplements the philosophical work central to SenseLab's process, work that we also consider to be creative, for the creation of concepts is a practice, a living philosophy.

Lygia Clark's work acts always as a beacon, as does the overlap, enacted in Clark's work, between the artistic and the therapeutic. As Suely Rolnik emphasizes, the tendency to position Clark either on the side of art or on the side of therapy misses the force of the artful in her approach. Clark was always engaged with the limits of the aesthetic, and she always asked how else art could do its work. In its final iteration as *Structuring the Self*, the work was indeed practiced outside the art world in the context of the therapeutic, but this was not to cast artfulness aside. It was, rather, to show the force of what art can do when it practices the schizz. Here, as Rolnik underscores, "aesthetics is reintroduced into ethics" ([1999] n.d., 24).

Create a Technique!

Clark's work is a force that nourishes SenseLab. Confluence more than influence—as with Helio Oiticica—it moves with the force of a future-presentness. Confluence because when it appeared to SenseLab as an orientation, we had already been moving in its rhythms for several years. Now, a decade into our experiments with Clark's practice, a precision is settling in. Sometimes tak-

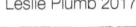

Leslie Plumb 2017

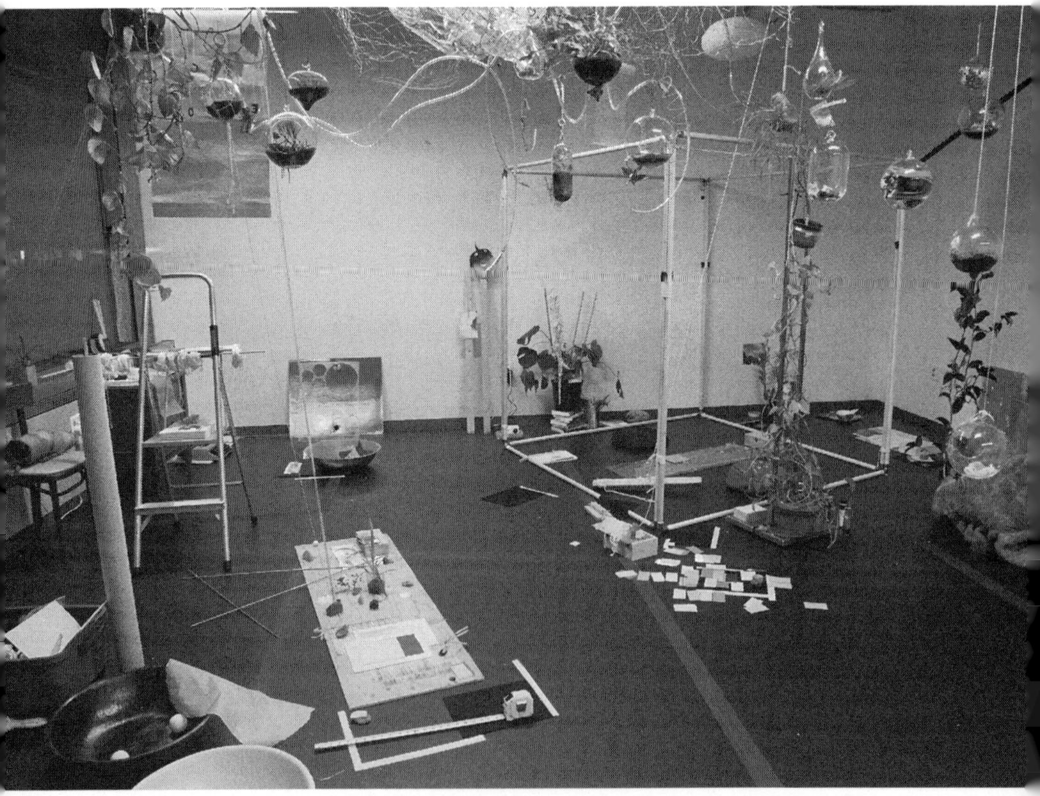

ing the form of work with voice, with sound, sometimes returning us to relational objects and their capacity to produce new schizosomatic propositions, sometimes taking us to an actual restaging of her work, sometimes morphing her tendencies with those of other artists, as with the Nos as Knots proposition for *Distributing the Insensible*, Clark's presence is a force that instructs us in the question of what things do when they shape each other. For what all of Clark's work does is repeat the mantra that we are more-than, more-than our-selves.[10]

In her work *Structuring the Self* and many of the propositions of that later period of her life, the relational object moves the practice. The relational object is never an object as such. It is a tendency that carries an object-likeness. Similarly to how we work in the SenseLab spaZe with resonances that carry object-like qualities, exploring what kind of entryways those resonances produce when they come into contact, Clark's relational objects are carriers of potential. Taking the shape of bags of air, sand, water, of rocks held in the hand, of textures placed against the skin, relational objects are mobilizers for a schizosoma. A schizosoma is the expression of a shifting boundary, a structuring. Too often called an individual, a schizosoma is the reminder that the self is never enclosed, that it moves across tendencies it cannot hold in its-self. *Structuring the Self* explores the potential of the schizosoma, developing attunements to how much structure or destructuring a schizosoma needs to thrive. A paranoid body leaks at a rate too vertiginous to connect to its forces. In that case, a schizosomatic process may assist in temporarily shutting a valve or two. A frozen body may need the opposite. *Structuring the Self* is a practice that attends to these necessary reorientations, bringing the body into a more desiring relation with the world. This desiring-relation has nothing to do with what a body-as-interiority desires. "Strictly speaking, it would no longer be possible here to speak of identity, for this idea is incompatible with a subjectivity composed of the processual dynamic of moulding oneself" (Rolnik [1999] n.d., 19). The desiring-relation is about the agglomeration, about the group-subject that bodies. Bringing into relation preindividual forces with the constraints of a world in motion is what *Structuring the Self* can do.

Rolnik describes the work of *Structuring the Self* and its use of relational objects this way:

> The artist received each person individually for one-hour sessions, one to three times a week, over a period of months, and, in certain cases, for more than one year. Her relationship with the receiver, *(im)*mediated by the objects, had become indispensable for the realization of the artwork:

it was on the basis of her sensations of the living presence of the other in her own "resonant body," in the course of each session, that the artist progressively defined the singular use of the *Relational Objects*. This very quality of opening to the other is what she was able to provoke in those who participated in her work. In this therapeutic-poetic laboratory, the work was realized in the gradually forming consistency of this quality of the relation to otherness within the subjectivity of its receivers. (2007, 3; my addition)

The schizosomatic work of activating a relational field proposes not to restructure a body but to shift the very question of both structure and self. The artful does its work here not as an object but in the relation. No question of mediation here. To return to a definition from chapter 2: "Whereas mediation by its very nature requires time to be a container into which experience plays out, immediation makes apparent that the being of relation is emergent. Experience is not an external quantity to be analyzed. Experience grows from the middle. It is from this middling that immediation does its work. In this middling, everything makes a difference, and that difference has effects: each occasion of experience leaves traces that affect how experience comes into itself in the untimeliness of time folding."

With *Structuring the Self*, Clark no longer needed the mediation of the art world. Relational objects became conduits, forces of form that could catalyze a dephasing. There was nothing here to be transmitted. The practice itself was the work.

When practicing the schizz becomes the work, a continuous process of discovery moves through every aspect of the research. the material, the bodily, the philosophical come together to propose new directions at every turn. Here, at the intersection between practice and schizz, techniques are crafted. These techniques are absolutely necessary because there will always be a tensile relation between the group-subject and subjugation. As emphasized earlier, a schizoanalytic process must always be crafted anew.

Techniques for orienting toward the schizoanalytic are many at SenseLab. Over the past several years, the techniques have tended toward the anarchival and its overlap with the schizosomatic. This direction has been taken because of an intuition that it is in the anarchic share of an event that its process seeds are most potent. The question is not what happened so much as what else happened. This connects directly to the speculative force of the *what else* in backgrounding-foregrounding, always allied to a commitment to how the pragmatic composes with the speculative.

Some things we have learned:

In SenseLab spaZe:

Working with materials entails spending time with them to connect to their own relational force. This means sitting with them, attuning to their own tendencies. It often happens that someone we don't yet know will enter the space of SenseLab (spaZe) and sit somewhere for a few hours, perhaps reading a book or working on their computer or simply daydreaming, waking in and out of a nap. It is not unusual that this time spent in spaZe will leave an actual trace. This can be a note. Or a shifting of the objects lying about. Or a composing-with the materials. This shift occasioned by a visit is something we pay a lot of attention to: it tells us what the entryway felt like, and how the threshold was crossed. We often take this minor tendency and move it into appearance by amplifying it. This is one of our techniques. Amplification in this context is not about foregrounding the intervention. It is about becoming sensitive to how the minor runs through it. Attuning to how these minor gestures shift the conditions of the environment enhances our understanding of what they can do. For those who return to SenseLab after an initial visit, the collective engagement with the trace they left behind can foster a sense of incipient participation. Composing tends to happen without much conversation, allowing the quality of intercession of the material trace to do the work. Led by materials, the amplification of a tendency produces a collective vocabulary for experimentation with an orientation that may be far from our own. This is the second technique—work with an orientation, not with your own idea of what needs to happen or the aesthetic that should enfold it. This second technique is very difficult, and we often fail at it. Individual aesthetic preferences are powerful tendencies and can dominate. But we have learned, in the practice, that if we can follow a tendency, the minor that runs through it will produce appetite for experimentation. This production of desire will in turn craft a group subjectivity—it will open the entryway to new forces. When this occurs, an aesthetic will be immanently composed instead of being imposed. In practice this means spaZe changes on a daily basis. For those not as sensitive to the continuous unsettling of form, it might just look like an art installation. But the work is in the weave, in the affective attunement to processes underway. Radical pedagogy is in the interstices.

Through the schizosomatic weekly workshops:

In January 2018 there was an urgent need to schizz the SenseLab.[11] This was a time of hardening and personalizing, and we needed a technique to shift the conditions. Csenge Kolosvari and Diego Gil came together to propose weekly schizosomatic workshops. In a move never tried before, they brought people in from outside SenseLab (usually SenseLab waits for people to arrive on their own as this tends to come with an appetite to attune to what is already moving). In discussions with these people who may never have heard of SenseLab before, Kolosvari and Gil did not attempt to explain the concept of the schizosomatic. Instead, they proposed that they craft the concept themselves by sharing with SenseLab a crease in their own practice. This crease could be a knot, a fold, a cuff. These would not be workshops to explicate their practice, nor would they be a service-based transaction: they would not be occasions for knowledge transfer. Instead, they would be immediating. The proposition was to practice the schizz. People responded with great generosity. Dancers, theater makers, singers, philosophers, and artists came and shared, for an hour and a half each week, the minor resonances that move through their practice. Alongside, they brought their uncertainty, their curiosity, their enthusiasm, and it was these tendencies, paired with complex and committed practices, that facilitated the growing of the concept of the schizosomatic. Intermingled were SenseLabbers who came weekly to add to the mix, or, in my case, who came sporadically with an interest in the anarchival potential of the schizosomatic weekly practices as a whole. What the schizosomatic practices brought was a lived experiment with what else bodying could do in the context of an impasse. Within a month, the tendency toward personalizing and subjugating at SenseLab had shifted. A new group-subject was coming into itself. The practice of the schizosomatic workshops was also feeding spaZe, which itself was being tuned by the workshops. In the anarchiving sessions I led, where we read Daniel Stern's work on vitality affect and asked ourselves what the shape of a schizosomatic session might be, and how that shape could be prolonged toward future reuptakings, we realized that the practices were powerful enough to create schizzing operations in excess of the punctual schizosomatic activations. What I mean by that is that it wasn't necessary to have participated in the actual workshops to feel the shift in the shape of the wider SenseLab practice. The schizosomatic workshops had shifted the conditions of emergent collectivity in ways that exceeded their pragmatic operations.

Both SenseLab spaZe and the schizosomatic workshops are engagements, at a confluence, with Clark's *Structuring the Self*. They ask how else the relation fields. Techniques born of these practices will be molded, shaped, and reshaped over time. Techniques are never created once and for all. As mentioned above, they depend on the speculative pragmatics of their immediating coordinates. Like *Structuring the Self*—"a living structure in a process of becoming, engendering itself through impregnation by the world, which Clark called 'self'" (Rolnik [1999] n.d., 19)—practicing the schizz at SenseLab is a living operation that produces, affects, and restructures the very operations of subjectivity.

Shape!

When Rolnik (1999) writes, about Clark's practice, that "it would no longer be possible . . . to speak of identity, for this idea is incompatible with a subjectivity composed of the processual dynamic of moulding oneself," what Rolnik is gesturing toward is the role the relational object comes to play in Clark's practice and

Leslie Plumb 2018

how the ingression of the relational object as intercessor tunes the work toward the schizoanalytic.[12] It is with this relational object as intercessor to the structuring of the self that Clark's practice most emphatically takes the turn toward the ethico-aesthetic commitment of an artful therapeutics. "Clark created the concepts of 'relational object' for objective reality and of 'structuring of the self' for subjective reality, each of which involves the other: the object reveals itself to be relational, and no longer neutral or indifferent, toward a subjectivity structured as self and no longer as identity, individuality enclosed in itself, anesthetized to the murmurs of life in its constructivism, to time, to the other, to death. It is the definitive deterritorializing of the subject spectator, of the object of art, and of its de-eroticized relation" (Rolnik [1999] n.d.). Activating desire, producing the relation through which the schizz and the somatic embrace, this is the work of *Structuring the Self*, a shaping that schizoanalysis similarly sees as crucial to its process.

The expression of what things do when they shape each other involves an attunement to the conditions of experience as they come into actualization. It also involves a commitment to what moves through them, to what speculates in the excess of what comes to be. The work of schizoanalysis requires a sensitivity to this both-and, to the more-than of what courses through experience here-now. This involves attending to what Deleuze and Guattari call "immanent criteria."

> The question posed by desire is not "What does it mean" but rather "How does it work?" How do these machines, these desiring-machines, work—yours and mine? With what sort of breakdowns as a part of their functioning? How do they pass from one body to another? . . . What occurs when their mode of operation confronts the social machines? A tractable gear is greased, or on the contrary an infernal machine is made ready. What are the connections, what are the disjunctions, the conjunctions, what use is made of the syntheses? It represents nothing, but it produces. It means nothing, but it works. Desire makes its entry with the general collapse of the question "What does it mean?" (Deleuze and Guattari 1983, 109)

The shaping of experience in the making *is* the structuring of the self, the self here as all that undoes the bounded, limited, preconstituted subject. Self as production of subjectivity. Self as agglomeration. Self as field of relation.

As emphasized above, there is no question here of "what it means." Practicing the schizz is not about finding meaning, not about interpretation as judgment. Practicing the schizz is about inventing new operations for modulating the shape of experimentation of an emergent collectivity. This shaping occurs in the real time of the event, but it also carries with it the anarchic share of the potential that courses through it. This is what must be heard in Deleuze and Guattari's repeated mantra: "How does it work?" Does the shaping of spaZe produce a new quality of expression? An opening to difference? Or does it close it down? Has it fallen into a refrain that binds it to a form of representation? Is it time to explode it? To take it all down and start again?

Attending to how things work is challenging. There are days when it is too much to ask, and on those days we take a break, returning to our other practices, the ones we call our "own," away from SenseLab. This is also part of practicing the schizz: to keep ourselves replenished through the singular ways in which our work moves us. With SenseLab, there is an oft-repeated injunction to keep doing the work elsewhere. This means not expecting SenseLab to be the site for the practice that is most emphatically in our name. Certainly, nothing we sign is fully ours, but there is a difference between the work I do as an artist, as a dancer or a writer, and the work of SenseLab, and that difference is what SenseLab works with. To bring our own practices as fully fledged operations into SenseLab would drown the tender germinating of collective tendencies. It would impose on the minor sociality of emergent collectivity modes of functioning that found their shape elsewhere and expect the collective environment to be able to nourish a process whose ingredients are imported from elsewhere. What we ask instead is that you bring to SenseLab the knots, the curiosities, the fledgling techniques, the appetite, the disorientation. We also ask that you keep practicing on your own, that you keep writing, making art, raising a family, teaching, loving. For these practices, though beyond the emergent collectivity of SenseLab, feed the relational field, bringing to it a much-needed transversality. To ask what things do when they shape each other is to have a commitment to transversality and to how a process transduces from one space of experimentation to another.

Transversalize!

From string to song on repeat to rock to the delicious taste of a concept newly invented, it is the intercessor that brings transversality into the process, activating group subjectivity by attuning the group-subject to the confluences of a deterritorializing of the self, orienting it toward shapings yet to be invented. The undercommons did that to SenseLab when we first read Harney and Moten's (2013) book in 2014, producing a desiring-machine that now runs through all our work.

An experiment at undercommoning, SenseLab vacillates between the university and its elsewheres. It has hubs across the world, and many people who participate either formally or informally (we have many lurkers) have a strong

Leslie Plumb 2018

affiliation to universities as sites of teaching and degree granting across the network. That said, the university is never what defines SenseLab. Any attempt at creating undercommon forms of existence recognizes that the university, while sometimes a place of refuge for study, generally does everything it can to stand in the way of desiring-production.

> I don't see the undercommons as having any necessary relationship to the university.
>
> And, given the fact that, to me, the undercommons is a kind of comportment or ongoing experiment with and as the *general antagonism*, a kind of way of being with others, it's almost impossible that it could be matched up with particular forms of institutional life. It would obviously be cut through in different kinds of ways and in different spaces and times. (Harney, in Harney and Moten 2013, 112)

As emphasized in chapter 2, an undercommons is not a fixed environment. It is not equal to a place. Undercommoning is a practice. When SenseLab undercommons, it reveals the fissures of the neoliberalizing university and blocks them temporarily. This undercommoning is always in confluence with experiments that split us open. Perhaps this is one of the ways of understanding undercommoning: it is what is produced when we refuse false problems, when we embrace the uneasiness of processes that make and break us. Undercommons are created in the thick of learning how to live.

The embrace of the undercommons also came to SenseLab at around the time the appetite was ripe for moving toward a parainstitutional proposition we call the 3Ecologies Institute (3E). 3E parasitically feeds on what the university has to offer while rejecting its embrace of the credit-debt relation. In SenseLab's shift toward 3E, the collective desire is to accentuate practices of undercommoning through play and study and to commit to a resistance to the neurotypical (white) knowledge-making and knowledge-valuing conventions of the university and all the institutions that feed it, and feed on it.

3E is a practice, not something to be achieved once and for all. In its aim to transversalize modes of thought and practice, it is before all else an experiment with sociality in the schizzing, its hope to foster forms and forces of life that exceed the shape of the human as neurotypical, white conductor of existence as we know it. To practice the schizz is to touch the world differently, and to be touched by what exceeds the form it knows how to take.

Practicing the schizz involves asking how else we might contribute to creating thresholds that perform otherwise possibility, that touch experience differentially. Harney and Moten describe hapticality, "the touch of the undercommons," as "the feel that what is to come is here" (2013, 98). This is the call of the under-commons, and of 3E, to create conditions to feel "a feel for feeling others feeling you, . . . the feel that no individual can stand, and no state abide" (98). This feel has the force of a touching, of a reaching-toward that unmoors all prescribed orientation. It is this touch, this hapticality, that 3E looks toward, a touch that Rizvana Bradley (2014) defines as the "abstract convergence of touch, feeling and relation." This touch makes the stakes of collectivity felt. To risk in the name of the undercommons is never simply to risk oneself. It is to risk the edifices that hold us up, the edifices that teach us to speak with confidence in our name, in the name of the preconstituted subject, in the name of whiteness, the edifices that welcome only the smallest contingent of what difference might look like, lest the edifice be undone from within by the black life, the neurodiversity it works so hard to keep at bay. This is the work of 3E, to practice a schizzing that orients toward the emergent collectivity of group-subjects, even while recognizing that they will always risk becoming subjected to the benevolent upholding of propriety and the way it allows whiteness to infiltrate. To take what things do when they shape each other seriously is to be aware of the shape of the horror we mask when difference without separability unseats us. To schizz experience in the making is to learn to open process to all that resonates through it, including the way our actions prolong the violence of colonization, including the daily hor-rors of exclusion perpetrated in the name of the human in the afterlife of slavery. But it cannot end here. If undercommoning is in the feel, in the touch no state or individual can abide, the aim must ultimately be to get our-selves out of the way. Here, where the being of relation weaves us into becoming, angular sociality, as Tavia Nyong'o (2018) might say, transversalizes experience.

The imperative to transversalize at the heart of schizoanalysis is never a call to ignore the conditions that bring hapticality into performativity in the under-commons. The inheritances always make a difference. They shape what comes to be. Guattari's emphasis on turning away from transference in favor of trans-versality is in no way a ploy to overlook what has come to pass. It is, rather, a commitment to how what has come to pass passes through us, the we we are becoming. The imperative to transversalize is a call to feel these inheritances in what they actually propose, here-now, while attuning to the more-than that also flows through them. The call of the undercommons, it seems to me, engages this double articulation at every turn: "Feel through others, a feel for feeling others feeling you" (Harney and Moten 2013, 98). Feel what shapes. Shape what feels. "Feel that what is to come is here" (98).

Feeling must not be reduced to personal feeling, to feeling from the perspective of a preconstituted subject. Feeling, as Whitehead emphasizes, is the force of what moves the world into existence, of what carries experience in the making. The force of affective tonality, feeling is what propels, what activates, what orients. It is the lure that moves propositions into act, shifting the conditions of experience.

The transversal force of schizoanalytic practice does its work here, in the feel. Transversality composes with the haptic and responds to the synesthetic shaping it proposes. This aesthetic shaping is not reducible to an interiority, nor can it be organized into a binary, with reason as its other. Aesthetic shaping is the fielding of existence where existence becomes an ecology. Schizoanalysis develops its techniques here, in the interstices of force-forms in the shaping. What is at stake is not a reification of process. Speculative pragmatism cares for how things "take," curious, always, about how the process cuffs. At this interstice, where the tensile force of re-orientation is at work, where aesthetic shaping becomes ethico-aesthetic, there is nothing that can take the place of practice. The university becomes a distraction if we make it the content of this practice. In wresting the state's claim on the psyche, and in calling for schizoanalytic mobilization in the activist realm, Guattari's aim was always emphatically to include the institution's framings in the work we have yet to undertake. But this was not to build more hospitals. To move schizoanalysis into the world, to expand its reach beyond the psychiatric institution, to practice the schizz, is to commit to study in the synesthetic hapticity of a touch irreducible to containment, out from the outside.

Begin Again!

3E is the always-beginning-again of SenseLab. So much of the work of SenseLab has defined itself through failure—failure to create the conditions for the event, failure to activate the threshold such that it facilitates a differential, failure to create adequate conditions for neurodiversity, failure to facilitate conditions that transversalize collectivity. A pragmatics of the useless touches failure at every turn. But there is also deep affirmation of what moves across failure, and recognition that it is never the whole proposition that fails. The feeling of failure is usually tied to those creases where process is most fragile. Failure is part of the process of practicing the schizz.

It is hard to say to what degree the 3Ecologies Institute is a deviation or a continuation of SenseLab. It is both, I think, deeply influenced by the practice as it evolves, and full of appetite for where else the practice can take us. In the most cursory of ways, this is how we describe it so far:

What it is
a collaborative learning environment

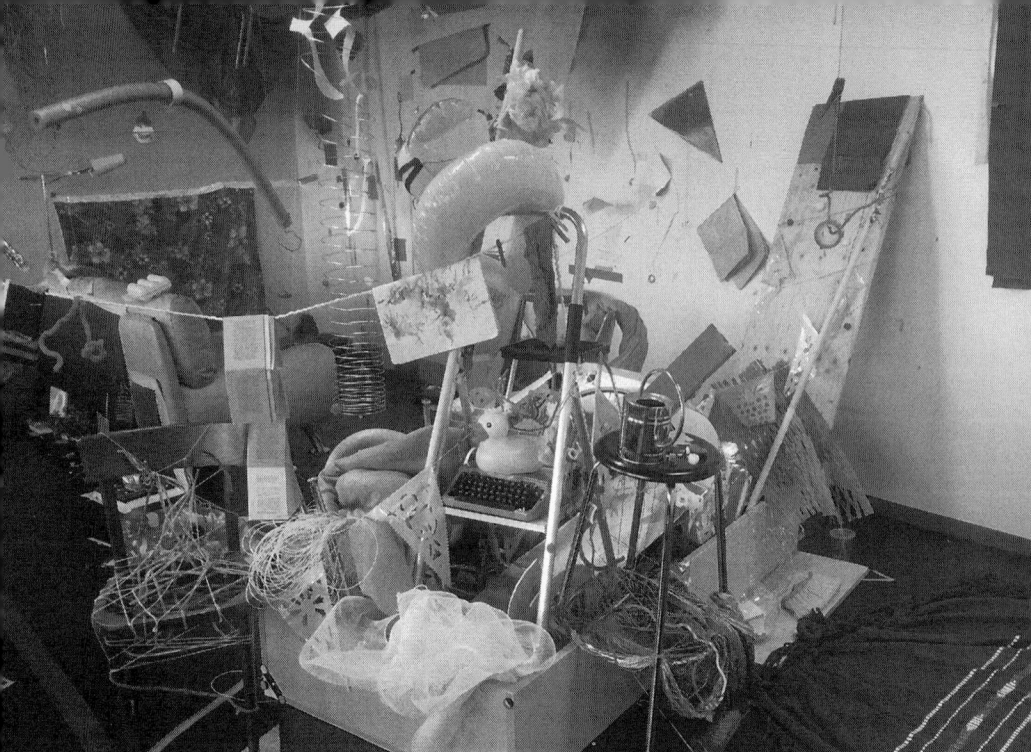

Leslie Plumb 2018

dedicated to participatory experimentation

where concept-making meets embodied creative practice

Where it begins

with the premise that concepts must be experienced—they are lived

Where it moves

between philosophy (understood as the creation of concepts in language)
and art (understood as the choreography of concepts in movement and
the sculpting of thought in materials)

What moves it

bringing art and philosophy actively together

at critical points where the three ecologies intersect

heralding emergent modes of life, prefiguring new forms of value

Who it addresses

- all those, of any age and any level of formal education, inside or outside
  established institutions of learning, who wish to join with others to
  pursue learning as a lifelong process of social engagement
- students and teachers in higher education looking for a transdisciplinary
  milieu to supplement their disciplinary studies, and interested in
  exploratory techniques to expand the horizon of their existing methods

- creative practitioners and cultural workers wishing to renew their thinking and rethink their practice in active dialogue with others
- community workers and activists wishing to explore the connections between their particular domain of practice and the larger ecological field of powers and potential

The call for 3E is already in the world. Transversal operators that bring the social, the conceptual, and the environmental into relation in a gesture of undercommoning are everywhere pulsing through the walls of the institutions we strategically move through and beyond. Everywhere we turn we see germs of 3E.

Daily, we remind ourselves: strategic duplicity is necessary—most of us need the institutions we work in to survive. But whether we can afford to heed it or not, the call to move diagonally resounds. The call resounds when flows of desire schizz, and when, in the schizzing, they produce offshoots. All around us we feel the offshoots, we feel the urgency of Crawley's refrain to practice otherwise possibility. We have learned to recognize the offshoots by the way they carry the question "how" rather than "why," by the way they participate with care for the *what* of the world and move at the speed of *what else*. We have also learned that with these offshoots study happens. This is what 3E seeks to do: to make felt how study happens at the interstices of experience.

Leslie Plumb 2018

When we imagine 3E, we don't imagine a university, but we do find in the university's neoliberal decline a place to begin to invent differently. To call it an alter-university, which we sometimes do, is to limit 3E to imaginations already in place. This is to give in to a preexisting structure rather than to approach radical pedagogy from the perspective of study, where study is never reducible to a pre-choreographed encounter with knowledge. I prefer to think of 3E as a practice for composing-composting, for seeding and nurturing germs that become platforms for other ways of living. The shape it takes is modest—in January 2020, we launched "Playcare," an environment for study led by children. So far, we farm crickets and explore the life-cycle of playing, tending, planting, eating.

Neurodiverse qualities of attention can make getting going an issue; spaZe emerged as a technique for activating study. How we practice matters, and no change can occur without practice. This includes practicing value differently. What we most want to avoid with 3E is any return to the service economy and any kind of transactional economic politics. 3E is about asking how else we can value beyond the economy of credit that orients education today. What is the credit we exchange in the name of neurotypicality, of whiteness? What kind of sociality can be crafted that honors that debt, too immense to ever repay, turning it into the gift of Glissant's poetics of relation, a living practice that reminds us at every turn that we must consent not to be a single being (1997, 5, 27)?

We invite those of you who want to participate, who care to invent with us what else learning and living can be, to practice three modes of entry. We ask that you bring to the platform of exploratory learning one of these techniques:

knot: a paradox or temporary impasse in one's work, life, thinking, or
creative practice that might become newly productive if staged in
a way that opens it to a collaborative exploration, in language or
between language and other modes of expression.

juncture: a known conjunction reopened for further exploration through
new techniques reconfiguring its potential; the juncture might be a
theoretical perspective, a set of established techniques informing a
particular practice, an already-operating collaboration or project, or
an existing disciplinary, interdisciplinary, or intermedia platform,
restaged with a new inflection.

vector: a move out from known junctures into a wander line that is
oriented by a proposition, and in that sense directionally constrained,
but is at the same time open-ended in way that invites new takings-
form on the fly.

Platforms for relation are never set in stone. We only propose to begin here. Together we will see where the practice leads. What we know is this: platforms for relation are everywhere active in our everyday lives. We need to learn how to seed them across undercommoning environments. Through these platforms we need to germinate new practices, and to practice failing together. Content delivery is not what changes the conditions of experience. There is no production of desire there. What moves experience are practices that reorient the place of knowledge in experience, practices that ask how the being of relation produces the kind of transformative justice livingloving requires.

In all of this, we must never understand the coming-together of group subjectivity solely as a bringing together of many bodies. Group subjectivity precedes individualism. Group subjectivity does not require more than one body. A body is always more than one. This is where practicing the schizz begins.

How Do We Repair?

1. The archive as archive of time passed, as archive of time for the restaging of that past, orients us toward a certain notion of repair. It asks: how to return to liveliness that which has come to pass? How to give the force-of-form to that which is but the event's afterthought? How to return to the trace of time's passing the intensity of what could only really be felt in its own time? How to repair what has been left behind? How to repair to that time of wholeness?

Repair and value are always an entwined pair. Repair touches the nerve of devaluation in the same gesture as it names what has been considered useful enough to be reanimated. Or, repair names the necessity of not-living-without. If the archive is that which carries forward the markings of what might remain legible across a breach in time, it also necessarily pulls with it the myriad valuations that give an object its relevance through the passage of time. Choices are made not only in terms of what is kept but also in terms of what, at the time of its making, registers as being worth keeping. The archive is a lens on what is carried forward, giving us a measure of what should be valued in the now. This reanimation assumes a certain capacity for time to be read. Repair moves what was into this reanimation, staging a return that rarely names what is simultaneously created in the passage.

But repair is also *creative* reanimation. Think of *kintsugi*, also called "golden joinery," or *kintsukuroi*, "golden repair"—"the Japanese art of repairing broken pottery with lacquer dusted or mixed with powdered gold, silver, or platinum."[1]

2. In the ethos of a pragmatics of the useless, an ethos that recognizes that the bestowing of value onto use is one of the ways we collectively work to maintain the legibility of our practices at the detriment of what might exceed them or move through them ineffably, I turn to the question of repair through the performance group Goat Island's work.[2] I do so in a register markedly different from

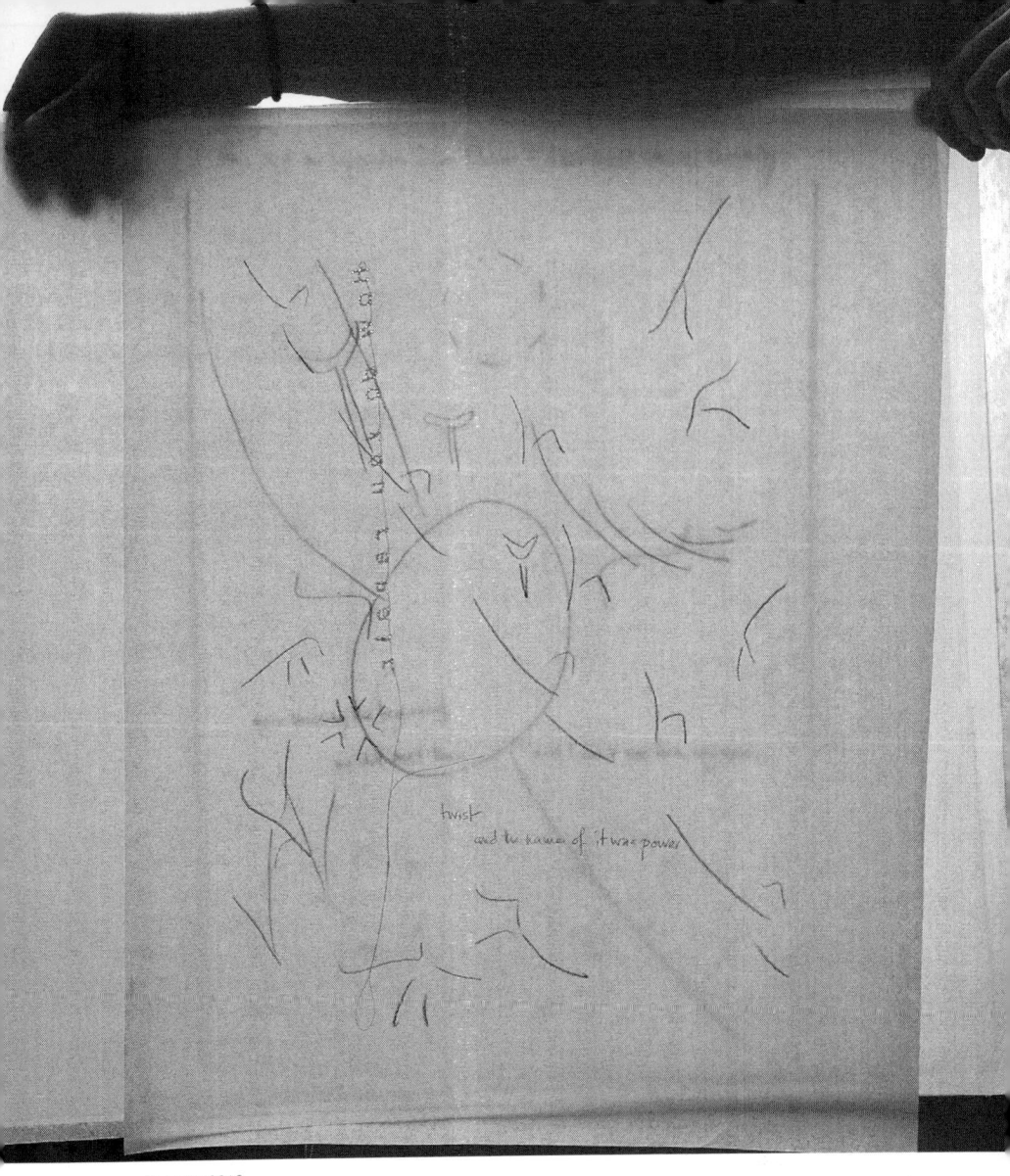

N. Lowe 2019

the ubiquitous notion of repair described above, as fixing what was once whole. I ask what else moves across and through the archive that might be felt without appearing as such. That is to say, I turn to repair in the way it already moves through Goat Island's work. Contributing to the ineffable that moves across what Goat Island leaves behind of a past conjured in excess of the materiality of its trace, I aim to touch the nerve of a notion of repair that reminds us that what we receive from Goat Island is not an image of what was but a call to engage in the golden joinery that produces not simply a fixed object but one of another nature, resplendent in its difference. Following Goat Island's own turn to the question of repair in *When Will the September Roses Bloom?*, taking to heart the urgency of the prompt "How do we choreograph a dance to repair the world?"—a prompt born of the injunction "to lodge ourselves in history," to "[pursue] the impossible" and "speak from our irrelevance," "attempt[ing] less"—I understand the question of repairing the world as distant from the idea of making-whole (Goulish, in Bottoms and Goulish 2007, xvi). I take repair to be a gesture that brings out the process's differential, cutting across any notion of origins. Like the gold of the kintsugi that does not return the pot to its initial state but amplifies its brokenness to reveal what else it always was and could become, repair is taken as the commitment to variation that reveals the more-than of experience. Repair, then, as the fragile proposition that turns the event toward its immanent futurity, revealing not the lost whole but the force-of-form that moves transversally across it, in an unfolding that is anything but in-time. This, I want to propose, is what performance can do: it can give us time differently, dancing durations of experience in excess of any notion of the in-the-moment we too often cling to. Performance is always out of time like the repair that makes its cleave visible.

3. The practice of entering into the work to touch what is in excess of representation is the task I set myself when I received the call to bring to expression an edge

N. Lowe 2019

of tenthness to an archive of nine works in the context of exhibiting a response to Goat Island for a retrospective of their work. For this, I was given access to an archive of performances and reviews, of texts and handwritten notes. The aim as I understood it was never to mend the past. Quite the opposite: the work of repair as it was proposed for *Goat Island Archive—We Have Discovered the Performance by Making It*, a five-month (an)archival exhibition-performance staged at the Chicago Cultural Center in 2019, was oriented toward the useless, which is to say, toward that which is not yet inscribed in the archive of value.[3] The gift of the Goat Island archive as I experienced it was not what it contained so much as what it was capable of proposing for a transversal process that would respond to those singular ways in which Goat Island expressed its own commitment to difference and repair. I made it my work to amplify the transversality by bringing it into relation with the cut of other times and other necessities.

The questions that oriented my process turned on the notion of a pragmatics of the useless. How to value the inexpressible in the work and move it into new registers? How to make felt what most tangibly moved across the archive but couldn't find expression in it? How to facilitate an encounter with the work's ethos of repair, a repair that would always be as much about the gesture of repair as return, as navigation, as it would be about the care to create conditions for those tentative tendings that produced the archive in the first place? In my attuning to the archive, the aim was not to recast a time past but to see how Goat Island's work already carried the seeds for an excess-on-itself.

4. My process took the following path: First, I watched the videos of the nine works made between 1989 and 2009. A notebook open, my eyes on the video, I drew the movement in each work. My aim was not to *represent* the movement but to follow the movement on the screen with my hand. My attention was on the transduction—the movement across planes that would facilitate a dephasing of the process. How might the performers' movements shift in the passage through the hand to the notebook? What might the notebook record that was in excess of the seeing? I did this for each of the videos, reading reviews and descriptions of the performances in the interim, not so much to understand or locate the work as to touch time's spiral, the uneasiness of what in the work didn't connect to the time of its coming-to-be. For it was apparent to me from the outset that what Goat Island's work proposes is a kind of untimeliness—a time committed to the unfolding and yet uneasy with the present's manner of narrating itself. The hope was that the drawings would propose not the organization of a narrative but something more attuned to the work's qualitative momentum—a quality of repetition, an intensity dancing into perception. Once the drawings were done, I created palimpsests on vellum, four pages superimposed for each work, the first of which traced the shape of the stagespace for each performance. There wasn't much editing here—more a sense of accommodating in the move from the notebook to the vellum palimpsest the repetitions in the layered time signature of each performance. What stood out in this process was the degree to which language became movement in the last four performances, words now themselves mobile gestures of repetition. Language had of course always been present, but in these last pieces it took on a personality that could carry the work in a way movement alone tended to do earlier on.

Anarchiving might be defined as a practice that moves at the pace of a transduction, following the logic not of originality or wholeness but of emergent process. In drawing the shape of movement, what appeared on the page was not a representation of the nine performances so much as an activation of how what they leave behind produces a field of composition in its own right.

The second phase took off from this field of composition produced in the drawing. Three meters each of canvas and cotton batting became the next material for recomposition-in-transduction. This time, the transduction did not return to the Goat Island performances as such. Instead, it worked directly with the movements of the palimpsests, asking what movement-shapes most activated what Francis Bacon might call the "diagram" of each performance.[4] The diagram here is not spatial so much as intensive. What shape moves the work into its force-of-form? What movements activate the work's outdoing of its initial premise? How does the outdoing of the work most intensively take us back to what it was able to express, in excess of itself?

In the transduction from drawing to sculpture, I chose two shapes from each of the palimpsest drawings. As with the drawings, I worked one performance at a time, letting the shapes lead the body into gestures. I moved with the shapes in repetition to orient the constellation. The canvas sculptures were imagined as doubles of the drawing, felt otherwise. Because I knew that not all of us work visually, that a drawing can hold us at a distance, that the vellum carries a fragility that might keep fingers off and bodies still. And I wanted the movement to call to itself. I wanted bodies to feel the call to move into the shape of Goat Island's diagrams.

As I worked, I realized there was a risk, and that risk was that the gestures intensively carried through what was now a double transduction might sidestep the careful posing of a problem that might be called the work's politics. And so I began a third phase, creating books that held procedures for moving (back) through the work. These procedures are guides for what might also be caught in the moving. Using words from the performances themselves, they are how the

Lowe 2019

work revealed itself to me politically as I moved across the phases of transduction. I did not watch the pieces again to make them. I trusted the anarchive to lead me back to where the diagram found its shape.

5. Goat Island's eighth work, *When Will the September Roses Bloom? Last Night Was Only a Comedy*, is the prism through which the question of repair most emphatically emerges. The procedure for this piece, composed for the third phase of the anarchival process, reads:

1. HOW DO YOU REPAIR?
2. AND THE NAME OF IT WAS POWER
3. AND YOU WON'T BE ABLE TO SEE IT
4. ONE MORE TIME (AGAIN)
5. MAKE IT DIFFER (VERSION 1, VERSION 2)
6. HOW DO YOU REPAIR?
7. SWEET BABY JAMES
   "TORTURE DERIVES FROM TWIST"

As with each of the nine books, the eighth opens with a citation on architectural procedure by Arakawa and Madeline Gins: "Architectural surrounds stage architectural procedures. A surround constructed to constrain a sequence of actions presents a procedure to be followed: and as soon as someone sets foot into an architectural surround that constrains actions, the architectural procedure it stages gets going" (2002, 54).

6. Architectural procedures for Arakawa and Gins are never limited to existing built enclosures. Architecture is not that which houses us already, or which governs our imagination of the world's constructedness. Architecture is the quality of worlding that produces the lived expression of what Arakawa and Gins call the organism-person-environment. An organism that persons is of the world in the world's self-forming: "The momentum an organism is able to gain on being a person, or rather, on behaving as one—that set of conditions, born of actions taken, that makes person-formation possible—depends directly on how it positions its body. Surroundings invite, provoke, and entice persons to perform actions, and the enacting motions of these actions not only serve up alternate vantage points but also inevitably shift sense organs about" (2002, 1). The wager here is that what matters is not architecture or surrounds per se but the procedurality that conditions the surrounds to facilitate other ways of living.

The body in its relation to architecture and surrounds is redefined. "We have adopted the admittedly clumsy term 'organism that persons' because it portrays persons as being intermittent and transitory outcomes of coordinated forming rather than honest-to-goodness entities" (2). The architectural body for Arakawa and Gins becomes the technique to conceive of the way the world bodies: "The toddler, taking its first steps as an organism that persons, drags its whole world along as pull-toy" (3). The feeling-out of existence is what is at work, a "think(ing) its (way through an) environment" (3). Refusing a distance between bodying, thinking, and feeling, between environment and architecture, architectural bodies become their own procedures for world-making, "kicking and screaming, alive with process, emphatically, and urgently rushed into a supporting context of embedded procedures" (4).

It will not come as a surprise, then, that the architectural procedure emerges not from the willful agency of the actor but from the surrounds themselves: "Architectural surrounds stage architectural procedures" (55). "Tactically positioned constructed procedures" orient action. And, from there, "procedures naturally compound" (56). Tactically posed surrounds meet tactically posed surrounds. Organisms-that-person thrive not only because the surrounds are generative in and of themselves but because bodying begins to take shape differently, identitarian and volitional presuppositions at the heart of agency dancing to another logic. "Can it be, then, that in architecture we have the means to construct awareness on a new basis? Oh yes, that is what we have begun to believe" (56).

7. In a grant proposal, Goat Island write, "One thing you should know about us is this: how we communicate is as important as what we say" (in Bottoms and Goulish 2007, xiii). This is also the ethos of procedural architecture. There is such a thing, for Arakawa and Gins, as the "insufficiently procedural" (2002, 95). How a procedure conditions the constellation matters. This includes the steps it proposes. It includes the order and what is left behind. In *When Will the September Roses Bloom?*, it makes a difference that repair is the contour of a middling that includes power, perception, time, and difference. It matters that we remember, when all is said and done, that "torture derives from twist." We should never forget the power of movement to catapult a body into its undoing. There is nothing easy about performance. The work must be taken at its word. "And the name of it was power."

For Arakawa and Gins, the sufficiently procedural involves creating conditions for experience to site differently, producing bodyings capable of carrying experience otherwise. This otherwise always involves a tentativeness: "Play off your tactically posed surround like crazy until you have constructed a precise tentativeness for yourself" (2002, 97). Precise tentativeness allows the bodying to remain attuned to the emergent constellations of existence, to the worldings that shape us. Attunement must surpass automaticity—impossible movements, disorientations are required. "Strive to maintain your extended body as more than a single subsuming tentativeness; that is, cast your landing sites out and about to form several extended domains of indeterminacy" (97). Let precise tentativeness move the bodying into a variety of scales of encounter. "While attending to your front farnearground . . . or your front nearfarground . . . try lingering as well within and upon the nearnear and the farfar" (98). Let the body be made in the shape of the waywardness the impossible produces. Engage with perception's own precise tentativeness. "Ally yourself that closely with your tactically posed surround that it reads as the perimeter of your extended body" (98). Unhold. "Have your tactically posed surround's hold on you loosen even as you loosen your hold on it" (99). Desubjectify. "Prevent the coming into existence of a world for you" (99). Waver. "Sporadically play a cleaving (cutting apart from while adhering to) hesitation waltz with tendencies, inclined breezes and pursuits, and rivulets of complexly varied sited awareness" (100). Make it about "what else will be able to originate" (100).

8. "What else will be able to originate?" Consider the wayward in Saidiya Hartman's *Wayward Lives, Beautiful Experiments*, a book that pulls from the archive of slavery that which moves transversally across it. Hartman's "narrative written from nowhere" involves entering into the archive of black life to seek what the archive cannot value (2019, xiii). "I have crafted a counter-narrative liberated from the judgement and classification that subjected young black women to surveillance, arrest, punishment, and confinement, and offer an account that attends to beautiful experiments—to make living an art—undertaken by those often described as promiscuous, reckless, wild and wayward" (xiv). Bringing the illegible to life, *Wayward Lives, Beautiful Experiments* unfolds "a revolution in a minor key" erased from the accounts that can only situate black life as expendable (xv). Waywardness brought to the archive turns the exorbitant, the excessive, into the force it truly is, revealing its exquisite creativity in the power of its everyday living. Radical thinkers emerge where the archive could see only failure, or lasciviousness. "The wild idea that animates this book is that young black women were radical thinkers who tirelessly imagined other ways to live and never failed to consider how the world might be otherwise" (xv). Waywardness becomes the way toward the architectural procedure of drawing life differently.

Waywardness is a practice of possibility at a time when all roads, except the ones created by *smashing out*, are foreclosed. It obeys no rules and abides no authorities. It is unrepentant. It traffics in occult visions of other worlds and dreams of a different kind of life. Waywardness is an ongoing exploration of *what might be*; it is an improvisation with the terms of social existence, when the terms have already been dictated, when there is little room to breathe, when you have been sentenced to a life of servitude, when the house of bondage looms in whatever direction you move. It is the untiring practice of trying to live when you were never meant to survive. (228)

This is repair in the ethos of a pragmatics of the useless—the force of a gesture that shifts the very conditions of value. In seeking the unregulated, Hartman unregulates the very archive she pulls from, twisting it, giving the past new life *in the past*, a past alive with the force of the futurity that always moved through it. Time unstraightened. The archive will never be the same. Repair as the force-of-form that calls forth a tending not of a lost whole but of the gestural in its precise tentativeness. Repair as variation on existence. Repair as minor gesture.

9. Repair: the tug of a process, the "small acts"—"Calming the hands in a troubled world. Restoring damage to renewed use. Wiping a stain with a cloth." "Rebuild something before you go. Listen as you leave" (Hixson, in Bottoms and Goulish 2007, xvi, 32). "I cannot teach without you teaching me" (Hixson 2007, 109).

10. "By 1787, it was already too late. It was not too late to imagine an end to slavery, but it was too late to imagine the repair of its injury" (Best and Hartman 2005, 1). Repair is heavy with the call of another kind of return, a return to what should have been, a return to a world unmarked by the violence of use. Reparations are its specter, and these, while infinitely owed, too often bear the marks of that same archival logic, the logic of use-value, the logic of recognition, the logic of property, of capital, of the state. "The logic of reparation is grounded on notions of originary wholeness, on the one hand, and abstract/general equivalence, on the other" (Moten 2018a, 167).[5] How to account for the excess, for the more-than of life-lived? How to amplify the minor that runs through it? How to shift from the logic of credit to the logic of debt unpayable? "Restored credit is restored justice and restorative justice is always the renewed reign of credit, a reign of terror, a hail of obligations to be met, measured, meted, endured" (Harney and Moten 2013, 63). What is repair that engages in creating conditions for a surrounds that procedurally compounds? "You can't count how much we owe each other. It's not countable. It doesn't even work that way. Matter of fact, it's so radical that it probably destabilizes the very social form or idea of 'one another'" (Moten, in Harney and Moten 2013, 154).

Repair in a minor key is displaced from its alignment to the archive of preexisting value. This is never to suggest that an unpayable debt is not owed, nor is it to negate the campaign for reparations as a social movement, a campaign, as Robin D. G. Kelley outlines, that "was never entirely, or even primarily, about money [but] about social justice, reconciliation, reconstructing the internal life of black America, and eliminating institutional racism, [a campaign] focused less on individual payments than on securing funds to build autonomous black institutions, improving community life, and in some cases establishing a homeland that will enable African Americans to develop a political economy geared more toward collective needs than toward accumulation" (2002, 137). Indeed, minor repair begins here, in what we learn from those social movements that seek debt without credit, that produce capital not for capital's sake but for an "aesthetic sociality of blackness" (Harris 2018), inviting us to move at the pace of repair at all scales of life-living, including, as Fred Moten emphasizes, the scale of the earth itself (Kelley and Moten 2017).[6] Repair as that transversality that returns experience to what most potently moves across it, and changes it in the crossing. "Loss gives rise to longing, and in these circumstances, it would not be far-fetched to consider stories as a form of compensation or even as reparations, perhaps the only kind we will ever receive" (Hartman 2008, 4).[7] "Restoring damage to renewed use" (Hixson quoted in Bottoms and Goulish 2007, xx).

11. "The assignment of a specific value to the incalculable is a kind of terror. At the same time, the incalculable is the very instantiation of value" (Moten 2018a, 169).

12. "One must first expose the damage, just as Paul Celan's attempts to 'repair' the German language after World War II necessitated, for him, an exposure of that language as broken, fragmented, shattered; a weave together of those shards into stuttering, poetry" (Goulish, in Bottoms and Goulish 2007, 104). How to write in the idiom of life's obliteration? "I want to attend to the necessary polyphony.

I don't want to represent anything and I don't want to repair anything but I do want to be here more, in another way. I want to work it this way . . . as the history of no repair, as the ongoing event of more and less than representing" (Moten 2018a, 170).

13. Repair, in the "spaces between"—"that visible line of the in-between, between the two, of time to come and time elapsed" (Hixson 2007, 110). A "caught-in-the-moment beauty" (110).

14. Repair: tending and attending—duration become texture. Is this what performance can do?

15. Repair, the very condition of collective survival, "my leaving something behind for others . . . something through which I become an ancestor" (Mbembe 2018a).

Repair as the gesture that never stopped giving.

Something significant must be going on in these practices of the everyday, the meaning of which we still have to elicit. To repair is to be alive. So that's the first sense of reparation—to be alive and to take care of something that matters because that thing is a very condition of my survival with others, my being with others, my moving on with others, my leaving something behind for others, something through which they might remember me. All others include my contemporaries, those who came before me as well as those who will come after me [as well as] the environment I live in, the objects I make in my everyday life, in short, the world I inhabit. This is really, at least in the African context, in the continental African archive, what we mean by repair, the becoming other of the living, be it matter or human; the care for not only the living but also other apparently inert entities. (Mbembe 2018b, 5–6)

Repair as care for the earth, as care for the more-than (one).

16. "But I also know that what it is that is supposed to be repaired is irreparable. It can't be repaired. The only thing we can do is tear this shit down completely and build something new" (Moten, in Harney and Moten 2013, 152).

17. Repair as sociality of relation, "that visible line of the in-between, between the two, of time to come and time elapsed" (Hixson 2007, 110). Repair as the work performance can do when performance forgets to perform its self-reproduction. Repair as the waywardness of the archive. Repair, the minor gesture that amplifies difference's variation, a return that folds time into its spiral, a procedure that tentatively cradles an emergent surrounds, a sidling with the exuberance of a shape revealing itself, a diagram for existence. Repair: an ineffable accompanying, anarchival in its capacity to make felt the anarchic share of worlds in the making, anarchival in its capacity to hear that which barely registered, or didn't register at all.

We owe each other everything.

Me Lo Dijo un Pajarito:

Neurodiversity, Black Life, and

the University as We Know It

> But the student has a habit, a bad habit. She studies. She studies but she does not learn. If she learned they could measure her progress, establish her attributes, give her credit. But the student keeps studying, keeps planning to study, keeps running to study, keeps studying a plan, keeps elaborating a debt. —Stefano Harney and Fred Moten, *The Undercommons*

She studies, starting in the middle. She reads, always from the outside-out. She speaks, stuttering from the edges of language. She fails, her work refusing to order itself to the measure she has been given.

She restarts, the work pulling at her again. She rereads. She knows she should read something new. But those familiar words just have a taste she can't resist.

She studies, working from the edges. She reinvents, from the middle. The form stumps her. She forgets to cite. She forgets that there was a beginning, a place from which knowledge traced itself. She forgets to impress. She doesn't pass.

In a private exchange, she writes, "And of course the question on ecological ways of knowing and producing may surface and we listen. i guess it is always a question of limit, scale and elasticity, a question of an ecosystem that would allow for unattended or decapitated expressivities to come forth. In spanish there's an expression that i truly love: 'me lo dijo un pajarito,' a bird told me. my 8 year old son talks with birds constantly since he was very little. me lo dijo un pajarito also moves with the possibility of a secret that you know without necessarily knowing in the common way of knowing, towards undercommon ways of cawing."[1]

What are these undercommon ways of cawing, the sounds lost, left behind, not only unaddressed but unregistered, in the systems of power/knowledge we call academia? What cannot be heard? What cannot be listened to? And what are the stakes of the performance of knowledge that plays out in the name of the "norm" that upholds what is too often generalized around the concept of "quality" or "rigor"?

Neurodiversity in the University

Creating the conditions for neurodiversity in the university is not about creating a space for difference, a space where difference sequesters itself. It is about attuning to the undercommon currents of creative dissonance and asymmetrical experience always already at work in, across, and beyond the institution. It is about becoming attentive to the ways in which the production of knowledge in the register of the neurotypical has always been resisted and queered despite the fact that neurotypical forms of knowledge are rarely addressed or defined as such. It is about exploring a juncture, a cut I perceive in the here-now, a change I want to linger with, that puts the university at risk in the very same gesture that it puts neurodiversity at risk. It is about asking what happens when the turn toward neurodiversity begins to be felt in a way that neurotypicality is truly threatened.

In an article called "Body/Power," Michel Foucault writes, "One needs to study what kind of body the current society needs" (1972, 58). While the university is certainly not the only site of power/knowledge, I turn to the university for this account of "what kind of body the current society needs" because it is a site of contestation where the exception often reigns in the name of alternative pedagogies and practices, a site where many of us, myself included, imagine other ways of working and sometimes are even able to activate them. I turn to the university because there is a troubling asymmetry at the heart of teaching and learning practices, on the one hand creating a path for new ways of thinking and making while on the other imposing forms of knowledge that do violence to the bodies they purport to address. I turn to the university because there is of necessity a discontinuity between the individual and collective practices of experimentation it houses and the neoliberalism that undergirds it. I turn to the university because it has been a site of resistance, and a site where new orientations toward study have been born: black studies, queer studies, postcolonial studies, women's studies, disability studies. And I turn to the university because most days I am not at all certain that the site for these explorations and activations of power/knowledge is actually capable of the kind of complex work necessary for the decolonization of knowledge, at least not as long as the centrality of the (white) (neurotypical) human as purveyor and guarantor of experience reigns supreme.

What has shifted in the university as regards neurodiversity is the steady entry into the bounds of its edifice not only of neurodiverse bodies but of accounts of what neurodiversity brings. Those bodies that "pass" have been there all along, "functioning" at the limits of what constitutes the docile body they, we, have been taught to mimic.[2] The other bodies, the ones classically excluded, remain excluded for the most part, but there are exceptions, and these more visible exceptions are troubling what it means to be included in the edifice of learning.

They are making themselves heard, teaching us how to bring facilitation into the classroom, reminding us of how inaccessible most of our practices of teaching are, how unaccommodated the non-docile body remains despite the many academic discourses that circulate supporting its presence. It is not the numbers of the visibly neurodiverse in the academy that are making the difference I am noting—I have never had a classical autistic actually enrolled in one of my classes (though many have attended on Skype, taking the course without credit), but the growing realization that they are there, that they require accommodations most classrooms cannot provide, that it is urgent that together we imagine—a tent on the edges of the room to facilitate nonfrontal modes of attention—what else teaching and learning could be. These experiments in sitting together differently, our faces not the center of attention, our words typed when necessary, hands stimming, bodies jumping, have affected my sense of what the learning body can look and sound like (including my own), and it is this learning, allied to language's otherwise rhythms, to the stims and tics and poetic utterances that come of engaging asymmetrically with language's modalities of communication, that moves me to write with and against the university as we know it.

With the writings and movements of these bodies, of our bodies, shared at their pace through the wild library of neurodiversity blogs on the internet and published, more now than ever, in the academic presses—still understood as guarantors of the intelligibility of knowledge—have come new propositions for ways of learning, new questions about the relationality of facilitation, expressed always with confusion about how it is that we could figure pedagogy as being anything but a technique of facilitation.[3] It is these interventions, as well as those of artists who write sideways into the academy, making art that refigures what expression can look like, that move the diagram of power/knowledge in the institution and mark this moment of recalibration. Of course the diagram is always mobile, and it is shifted by more tendencies than those I can name here—the point is not to reduce the undercommons of the university to these tendencies but to add them to all the others that, like termites, have been eating the walls and reshaping them to their needs. Perhaps one way to speak of this moment is precisely to speak of proliferation, of the inability to name (or even to hear) all that is at work, and all that is at stake.

Spinoza speaks of the institution as a pact (Balibar 2008), reminding us that what we live in is also what we build, and what we take down. What is the pact the university demands? What bodies does it need to survive? What knowledges?

The asymmetries the university produces are reflected in the systemic difference of its "we," asymmetries of duration and scale. Placing the power (or repression) in the individual won't begin to address the complexity of the bodyings that chew at the joints of its foundations. To speak of us, the "we," as one, as identifiable, as measurable, would be to underestimate the creativity of our movements. It would make us human, all too human, when in fact our bodyings are transversal, collective before they are individual, more-than. It would also underestimate the power of capital that runs through each artery of the institution, connecting to speeds and durations also always more-than human. Any "we" is always already composing at the interstices of these uneasy collaborations between different valences of the more-than.

Other approaches are necessary, probably approaches that move at the speed of termites, unbuilding the edifice from within in strategic duplicity with durations more-than human. Because trying to accost the system from another angle, trying to break the system from within its own modes of intelligibility, will in the end only reduce us to victims and perpetrators, to humans firmly enveloped in a dream of self-sufficiency. We must instead begin with the differential of the more-than human that composes us, with the tendencies that make us more-than ourselves, engaging the edifice of power/knowledge not frontally but with the very asymmetrical durations that (de)compose us. Connecting to power/knowledge this way may allow us to hear how else knowledge is being crafted on the undercommon edges where a caw can be heard, attuning to modes of knowing that exceed capture. From this perspective we can feel the dissonance between the rhythm of the work produced in the undercommons and the university's own glacial pace, committed, despite rhetoric to the contrary, to modes of knowing that are all too human. Despite the wealth of work that goes into attempting to alter the system from within, despite the extraordinary research that pushes back against the norms of knowledge production, despite the resistance on the part of artists to ally to industry, preferring instead to engage in a pragmatics of the useless that explores alternative modes of expression, alternative modes of existence, the problem remains: the university is a slow-moving machine. It is structurally incapable of changing at the speed of the thought that moves through it.

The university is beyond rebuilding. The building is already beyond repair. The outside is pushing in. Outside doesn't mean a space already created. Outside is the undercommons working it, eating it from within. There is no preexisting space that can replace the buildings in ruins. The undercommons must always be invented anew. It is a question of moving sideways, of attuning to the sideways movements already there, following their line of flight.

The urgency of these undercommons cannot be ignored. We are moving through them, but are we proliferating enough? Are we inventing at the speed, in the duration, of the movements of thought that move us to ask what else it can mean to know? Because when neurodiversity makes itself too keenly felt, when it refuses to adhere to norms of neurotypical knowledge production, the university as machine for existing power/knowledge resists, it must resist, and the more noise there is, the more the university will be at risk, and the more it will resist. The more *we* will resist. This is particularly the case when the student, she who studies but doesn't learn-to-measure, refuses to adhere to the labels that mark her as a liability for the pursuit of knowledge. She will not pass. She will not get credit. And this will matter because she is still paying, she is still in the system of debt and credit, and we have promised her that the system knows how to enfold her. We have admitted her. She will not be one of the few students who are allowed to flow through the membrane, the few who are given the opportunity to mark their difference, a difference that only works to keep the norm in place. Or if she gets through one membrane, she won't get through the next one; she won't get the job, or tenure. Because we won't know how to recognize her difference, we won't have created a space where it can be sequestered. She will not have given us the tools to do so, to space her as one of the few who should receive an exception, as one of those who need to populate our otherwise white, neurotypical environment in order for it to have been inclusive.

Difference will always be accepted to a degree. As long as the norm is upheld, it will always be good to have a few exceptions, especially when those who enter that space clearly mark themselves as different. But she is not one of those. She doesn't want to speak in the name of her difference. She doesn't want to teach you how to know her, how to write about her. She won't speak for all indigenous people, for all Black people, for all queer people, for all autistics. She won't explain. She will resist citing you. She isn't interested in "according to." She won't be aligned; she won't be colonized. Not because she is a rebel. She operates in another mode, in the mode of the more-than that attends to undercommon ways of cawing. From the perspective of this more-than always yet to be composed, she won't presume the symmetry rebellion presupposes. She won't presume neurotypicality.

Power/Knowledge

Power is never individual. The individual is, at the very most, the expression of its passage, not its operator. These teachings of Foucault's are often backgrounded in analyses of power that would still situate power within the bodies that wreak destruction or suffer its consequences. It is important, in thinking the systemic nature of power in the university, to clarify how power operates, how it is at once ours and beyond a "we" that preexists, how power is a mode of circulation more than it is a targeting practice. Power is what moves through the diagrams that co-compose us. As Foucault writes, "the individual is not a pre-given entity which is seized on by the exercise of power. The individual, with his identity and characteristics, is the product of a relation of power exercised over bodies, multiplicities, movements, desires, forces" (1972, 73–74).

To work with the circulation of power, it is necessary to move beyond body to bodying, beyond the notion that there are preexisting individuals that are powered by a hierarchy that measures their movements. The university is not a field that operates through such cut-and-dried hierarchies.[4] The university is a diagram of power through which "we" are created and re-created as power/knowledge bodyings. "We" are the university, emboldened to become bodies under circumstances we co-compose. Or, at the very minimum, we are a field of forces that makes it possible for those tendings-toward-bodies the university promotes to keep agglomerating. It is "we" who make its thinking possible, even if only by remaining in its midst. And it is "we" who pass or fail those for whom the qualities of bodying the university presupposes and creates are insufficient to survive and to thrive in its framework.

Bodying as a verb reminds us that bodies are a field of forces through which individuations emerge and shift. How a body individuates depends on the circumstances of its surrounds, on the ecologies that compose it, here, now, on the histories that orient it, on the futurities that give it potential or unmoor it from the grounds of its participation in the world. These orientations toward difference are pragmatic and operative. How a body becomes the body it is, the body it is identified to be, also depends on what it means to be a body, on the stakes of the form taking, on the limits of that form. Bodies are routinely obliterated at the very point where they individuate into this or that recognizable form. Much is at stake in the shape of individuation: there is no doubt that a continuous policing occurs that denies bodies the potential of their transitions, of their becomings, imposing an identity onto them that cannot be assimilated. I am thinking of the disabled body, of the indigenous body, of the trans body, of the black body, of the lower-caste body. There are so many who populate these unassimilable categories. Lists are not helpful, however—they operate in the very logic that would organize bodies according to external valuations, debasing them. What is more helpful, I think, is to recognize that these classifications that mark segregation occur precisely because of the threat of bodying. What is terrifying is that bodies are shapeshifters. Holding bodies to categories guarantees that power can remain in the hands of those whose categories have become so normalized as to be unworthy of mention. The question of power/knowledge works here, at the heart of bodying, where the potential for a body to become, to shift, to alter the conditions of life-living, encourages a living in the register of the more-than, a living beyond a dichotomy of the human and the nonhuman and all the categories that maintain the whiteness of neurotypicality as the baseline of existence. To ask what kind of body our society needs is to take the operations of power seriously and to inquire, each time anew, how this body, how this neurodiversity, shifts the field of experience, shifts the terms of power/knowledge.

Bodying is a process we all engage in. Usually, we become a body we already recognize, reproducing ourselves in the image we have come to associate as ours. This is particularly the case for those among us whose bodyings are least contested, those whose whiteness, whose neurotypicality, already conforms to the mold of what a body should be. When Édouard Glissant incites us to "consent not to be a single being" (1997, 5), he is reminding us, I think, that the mold of that one form, that one body, should never suffice, that relations are what compose us, relations always in excess of the given, relations as the radically empirical more-than that continuously refashions what it means to world.

Bodying need not include an alignment with humanism, with existing modes of defining what it means to be human. This is something I learn from autistics such as Tito Mukhopadhyay, Adam Wolfond, DJ Savarese, Mel Baggs, Frank Bissonnette, Donna Williams, Lucy Blackman, and so many others who remind us about the more-than that animates the field of experience that is life-living. Through their work, they provide paths for a reorientation of experience, leading us toward the constitutive field of incipient shapings. In so doing, they incite us to question the place of the human in our accounts of what counts. Baggs's video "In My Language" (2007) perhaps still stands out as the most chilling account of how nonspeaking autistics are excluded from the realm of the human, hir personhood extracted precisely because of the breadth of more-than human feeling hir language, hir living, embodies.[5] In hir eight-minute video, in which the first four minutes are spent listening to and smelling and touching the objects around hir, and the next four minutes are spent typing on a voice-activated computer, sie says, "It is only when I type something in your language that you refer to me as having communication. I smell things. I listen to things. I feel things. I taste things. I look at things. It is not enough to look and taste and smell and feel. I have to do those to the right things . . . or else people doubt that I am a thinking being, and since their definition of thought defines their definition of personhood so ridiculously much they doubt that I am a real person as well." So many other examples coming out of the neurodiversity community underscore this experience that neurotypical folks have a much too limited idea of what constitutes experience, a perceptual dearth that doesn't allow for the vividness of the infrathin infra-perceptually at work.

There is a certain resonance here with accounts from black studies coming from scholars such as Fred Moten, Stefano Harney, Sylvia Wynter, Frank Wilderson, Alexander G. Weheliye, Jasbir Puar, Ashon Crawley, and others around the concept of black life. Wilderson writes, "Though it might seem paradoxical, the bridge between blackness and antiblackness is 'the unbridgeable gap between Black being and Human life'" (Wilderson 2010, 57, quoted in Moten 2018b, 204). Blackness, Moten writes, "must free itself from ontological expectation, must refuse subjection to ontology's sanction against the very idea of black subjectivity" (2018b, 205). This is not to say that black bodies are not sites of power's contestation but to emphasize that the "paraontological distinction between blackness and blacks allows us no longer to be enthralled by the notion that blackness is a property that belongs to blacks (thereby placing certain formulations regarding non/relationality and non/communicability on a different footing and under a certain pressure) but also because ultimately it allows us to detach blackness from the question of (the meaning of) being" (205).

I turn to these voices in black studies to ask whether there isn't an important bridge to be built between neurodiversity and black life, particularly around the question of how else experience could be articulated within the register of the more-than, where the stakes are to measure experience not against the worn concept of humanity as defined in the West but with the force of an ontogenesis that moves in rhythm with the emergent sociality of bodying. Because bodying and sociality cannot be disentangled.

Sociality is perhaps the connection here, between black life and neurodiverse life, sociality as an emergent quality of bodying, as an emergent force for the more-than that is life-living. Speaking of entanglement and Denise Ferreira da Silva's (2016) "difference without separability" in the context of singer Bessie Smith, Moten (2015) comments, "I think of Bessie as an effect of sociality—she was sent by sociality to sociality, in that way that then allows us to understand something about how the deep and fundamental entanglement that we are still exists in relation to and by way of and as a function of this intense, radical, constant differentiation." Is sociality not the bodying, the force-of-form that activates what Moten calls the "radicalization of singularity" of a difference without separability?

Research-Creation

Foucault writes, "It is a case of studying power at the point where its intention, if it has one, is completely invested in its real and effective practices. What is needed is a study of power in its external visage, at the point where it is in direct and immediate relationship with that which we can provisionally call its object, its target, its field of application, there—that is to say—where it installs itself and produces its real effects" (1972, 97). In the chapter "Against Method" in *The Minor Gesture* (2016), I wrote about the way I see study, as Harney and Moten define it (2013), as aligned with a certain version of research-creation. This alignment involves seeing research-creation—the entry into the university of artistic practice at the doctoral level—as a potential destabilizer as regards the ubiquitous modes of knowledge mobilization in the university. The shift toward research-creation in the university has taken place roughly over the past two decades (though there are examples of research-creation that are much older, even going back to the medieval university in the case of music), unsettling the certainty of what counts as knowledge and what can be valued, or evaluated, troubling the notion of contribution by producing works that fall out of both the disciplinary and the recognizable. The problem, of course, is that research-creation, in defending its value, can easily be seduced by the logic of the institution, forgetting that to shift the conditions of knowledge is to remain under construction, testing limits, pushing the boundaries of the enclosure that would domesticate and reduce knowledge to what can be counted and accounted for.

Research-creation, as SenseLab has argued over more than a decade, understood not as an academic field but as a practice, operative in the interstices of making and thinking, can, at its uncertain limit, connect to study.[6] It can be a mode of inquiry that asks what (other) forms learning can take. It can refuse to privilege the materiality of language over other forms of expression while at the same recognizing thinking as a creative practice in its own right. When practiced this way, research-creation creates the conditions to ask how the theory-practice split continues to give knowledge production a certain linguistic overtone, understanding practice more as that which needs to be studied than as study itself.

When the artist refuses to produce an object as the object of her work, when the artist refuses to be the subject of the work, when the philosopher refuses to write at a distance, when the work becomes the practice, when the practice invents its own language, research-creation deeply threatens the power/knowledge that holds the academy in place. It was fine to have the artist in the academy as long as the artist behaved like an artist, as long as the object could be defined. As long as there was something to evaluate.

The bodyings crafted through neurodiverse intercession, the life that moves through the acts that resist the neurotypicality of knowledge production, create new diagrams for thinking. Power begins to circulate differently. Knowledge inflects to excite a reorienting of what study can be. "Power is employed and exercised through a net-like organisation. And not only do individuals circulate between its threads; they are always in the position of simultaneously undergoing and exercising this power. They are not only its inert or consenting target; they are always also the elements of its articulation. In other words, individuals are the vehicles of power, not its points of application" (Foucault 1972, 98). It's not simply that power is circulating differently, that new ways of knowing are finding temporary forms, that new forms of practice are shifting the process of coming to something we might call knowledge. It's that bodyings are created in the practicing, bodyings that trouble what it means to be a student, to be admitted as a student in the circuit of debt and credit that is the university as we know it. Deeply engaged, thinking wildly, touching the limits of thought, the becoming-body can finally stim as much as it needs to, connecting to the world's rhythms, its bodyings out of sync with the forces that would seek to capture it, outside the cycle of recognition that would identify it as the guarantor of the university's system of debt and credit.

The Outside

Gilles Deleuze writes:

> Between power and knowledge there is a difference in nature or a heterogeneity; but there is also mutual presupposition and capture; and there is ultimately a primacy of the one over the other. First of all there is a difference in nature, since power does not pass through forms, but only through forces. Knowledge concerns formed matters (substances) and formalized functions, divided up segment by segment according to the two great formal conditions of seeing and speaking, light and language: it is therefore stratified, archivized, and endowed with a relatively rigid segmentarity. Power, on the other hand, is diagrammatic: it mobilizes nonstratified matter and functions, and unfolds with a very flexible segmentarity. In fact, it passes not so much through forms as through particular points which on each occasion mark the application of a force, the action or reaction of a force in relation to others, that is to say an affect like "a state of power that is always local and unstable." (1988, 73)

If the asymmetry between power and knowledge concerns the relation of force to form, what happens to knowledge when it begins to resist the very idea of form as the final mode of knowing? How is its force-of-form altered by conditions of study that don't hold onto the human as the pivot of experience, that heed indigenous and black and neurodiverse and queer forms of knowing?[7] What does knowledge look like when it has become unmoored from its capture as form?

Foucault speaks of "a new type of relation, a dimension of thought that is irreducible to knowledge" (Deleuze 1988, 74). This dimension of thought, this outside of recognizable knowledge, is new only in the sense of Alfred North Whitehead's account of novelty, which, allied to his definition of creativity, is about how an occasion tunes to the infrathin that moves through it, orienting to a new force-of-form. This "new" type of relation has always existed in the interstices—we hear it in the stories passed down through generations as told to us by indigenous scholars; we feel it in the care for material practices as shared with us by African American quilt makers; we hear it in the break "where that shit breaks down" (Moten 2015).[8] Thought irreducible to practice moves outside the registers of categorization, shifting the conditions of undercommon ways of cawing. We don't need a university for this—in fact, the university often closes down the registers of sociality this mode of study needs to thrive. I return to the lines below from Moten to consider what else knowledge could be:

When I think about the way we use the term "study," I think we are committed to the idea that study is what you do with other people. It's talking and walking around with other people, working, dancing, suffering, some irreducible convergence of all three, held under the name of speculative practice. The notion of a rehearsal—being in a kind of workshop, playing in a band, in a jam session, or old men sitting on a porch, or people working together in a factory—there are these various modes of activity. The point of calling it "study" is to mark that the incessant and irreversible intellectuality of these activities is already present. These activities aren't ennobled by the fact that we now say, "oh, if you did these things in a certain way, you could be said to be have been studying." To do these things is to be involved in a kind of common intellectual practice. What's important is to recognize that that has been the case—because that recognition allows you to access a whole, varied, alternative history of thought. (Moten in Harney and Moten 2013, 110)

The outside is the name Deleuze and Foucault give to the circulation of forces where thought remains irreducible to knowledge. The outside, as mentioned in chapter 5, is not the exterior (as opposed to an interior). It is not spatial. It is intensive. The outside is what remains unthought in thought, what remains unfelt in feeling. It is what accompanies all emergent relationalities, what moves with all social life in the making. "The outside concerns force: if force is always in relation with other forces, forces necessarily pertain to an irreducible outside which no longer has a form, made up of nondecomposable distances where one force acts upon another or is acted upon by another" (Deleuze 1988, 86; translation modified).

Power has an outside: "It is always from the outside that a force confers on others or receives from others the variable affection that exists only at a given distance, or in a particular relation" (Deleuze 1988, 86; translation modified). An outside without inside is a force without a form. While there is no question that power also contributes to how a form-taking occurs, Foucault's insistence on the importance of the outside is a reminder that power always also carries an excess that is not captured by the form itself. "There is therefore a becoming of forces which remains distinct from the history of forms, since it operates in another dimension" (1988, 86; translation modified).

The outside is an intuitive concept for the more neurodiverse among us. It is what accompanies all experience in the making: what leaves those traces that still vibrate on the edges of what we call objects. It is the edgings-into-experience, the colorings of time, the echoes of futures on the cusp that interrupt that chunking neurotypicals prioritize in their search for categories. It is the worlding that isn't yet quite there before the chunk, the worlding that accompanies without quite situating itself, the infrathin negatively prehended that orients the not-quite of all form-takings. It is the intensities that so many don't seem to hear, those intensities that are continuously getting in the way of the human voice—that privileged site of human expression—the intensities that whisper to us that the world is lively and living beyond the space the human takes. The outside is not where most of our knowing is focused, though those of us who make art may have an affinity for it. We may speak in terms of hunches, of feeling, of affect, of tendency, of force—all of these synonyms for that which participates but cannot be circumscribed. This is not the knowledge we've been taught to recognize, not the knowledge of forms captured. The outside is not the formed matter, the segmented, the archivable. It is the anarchic share of striated knowledge, the share of experience that resists scripting yet nonetheless affects what the script can do. Anarchival knowledge, neurodiverse knowledge, cleaves form and force, calling knowledge back to its edgings-into-experience. It is the diagram, the force-of-form, where knowing meets unknowing.

When knowledge begins to escape stratification, when its form begins to blur, its anarchic share surfacing, its alignment to power also shifts. Power and knowledge begin to compose differently. It's not that knowledge is no longer irreducible to power (Foucault's point, after all, is that this irreducibility is what makes resistance possible); it's that the irreducibility begins to scintillate in ways that give knowledge the breadth, the force, to subvert the striations that usually constrain it.

Perhaps, at the point of scintillation, *knowledge* is no longer the right term. *Study* is a better term. Or *research-creation*. These are thicker concepts, I think, for the texture of what I am trying to gesture toward, when I speak of knowledges unknowing. But for now, I want to hold on to the possibility that knowledge, so deeply entwined with neurotypicality and the valuations that accompany it, might have the capacity for doing the work differently, if only to emphasize the trouble neurodiversity brings to the academic institution, trouble that most often erupts around the question of who knows how to know.

Emergent Socialities

Saidiya Hartman is wary of what she calls "the political proper," preferring practice (and the everyday) as an uneasy site for the staging of resistance.

> In considering the determinations and limits of practice it becomes evident that resistances are engendered in everyday forms of practice and that these resistances are excluded from the locus of the "political proper." Both aspects of this assessment are significant because too often the interventions and challenges of the dominated have been obscured when measured against traditional notions of the political and its central features; the unencumbered self, the citizen, the self-possessed individual, and the volitional and autonomous subject. The importance of the concept of practice is that it enables us to recognize the agency of the dominated and the limited and transient nature of that agency. (1997, 61)

Hartman argues that the imposition of categories of whiteness—"liberal notions of will and autonomy as standards for evaluating subaltern behavior"—has "effects that concern the constitution of the subject, the feasibility and appropriateness of certain forms of action" (62). The "political proper" is too blunt a tool for an attunement to how else subjectivity is produced.[9]

Practice does its work in what Harney and Moten call "the social zone of blackness" (2013, 138). This social zone, adjacent to "the blackness of surround," is, similarly, conceived as outside politics. "The Panthers theorized revolution without politics, which is to say revolution with neither a subject nor a principle of decision. Against the law because they were generating law, they practiced an ongoing planning to be possessed, hopelessly and optimistically and incessantly indebted, given to unfinished, contrapuntal study of, and in, the common wealth, poverty and the blackness of surround" (18).

Politics, in both cases, is understood to be that field of power that authorizes a reigning, willful, autonomous subject. The social zone of blackness finds its power in the undercommoning of decision, against any notion of law that would be categorically imposed from the exterior of whiteness's imposition of value.

It's not that the social is given to blackness, however. Blackness is haunted by the "social life of nothing" (93). But the very excision of personhood that orients blackness in the afterlife of slavery carries with it the force of movement-moving, a "movement of things [that] will not cohere" (94). Alongside Wilderson's "void of subjectivity" in the hold comes the quality of a break, "as if entering again and again the broken world, to trace the visionary company and join it" (94). The "expulsion from sociality" marks "sociality's ecstatic existence beyond beginning and end, ends and means, out where one becomes interested in things, in a certain relationship between thingliness and nothingness and blackness that plays itself out in unmapped, unmappable, undercommon consent and consensuality" (95).

The social zone of blackness is not given. It is claimed in the necessity of giving voice to a mode of existence that emerges in the break, crafting an aesthetics that does not simply fight the violence of category but upends it altogether. "This paraontological interplay of blackness and nothingness, this aesthetic sociality of the shipped . . . remains unexplored, because we don't know what we mean by it, because it is neither a category for ontology nor for socio-phenomenological analysis" (96). An aesthetic sociality of blackness is not a new category imposed on the social to mark a difference from the political proper. The two logics just can't be squarely juxtaposed as though they were in opposition. Where one is impositional, the other is appositional, an approximation of proximity that cuts transversally, born not of a subject but of a rhythmic middling, fold over form, uselessness over representation. "Is there a kind of propulsion, through compulsion, against the mastery of one's own speed, that ruptures both recursion and advance? What is the sound of this patterning? What does such apposition look like? What remains of eccentricity after the relay between loss and restoration has its say or song? In the absence of amenity, in exhaustion, there's a society of friends where everything can fold in dance to black, in being held and own, in what was never silence. Can't you hear them whisper one another's touch?" (97). Always still to be fashioned in the whisper of a touch, the social zone of blackness is an emergent sociality encountered through the practice of composing with the infrathin that pulses through the being of relation.

The social zone of blackness is a minor sociality, minor in the sense that it moves transversally across all registers of life-living. Like a minor key, it tunes the social, attuning it to all that infrathinly passes through it. Minor sociality refuses representation. It produces not a constituency but a fugitivity. As force of the outside, minor sociality is crafted in the relation.

Neurodiversity, and particularly autism, is often referred to as the most asocial of modes of living. It is a sign of our neurotypical human-centeredness that we only feel heard when we have eye contact, when the body we are speaking to consents to be a single being, excluding its more-than human tendencies. So much importance is given to the way attention is oriented (pay attention!) that we rarely stop to think of the violence of those frontal modes of attention that force us to block out the scintillations of the world and its many qualities of attending. When the neurodiverse among us listen, they listen to those scintillations; they are moved by them, hearing the more-than that echoes across the threshold of the sensory. Sometimes this is just too much, but always it is there, moving amodally across the bodying activated by the relation. This relation is not only to me, to you. It is a relation to the world coming into itself each time anew, a relation to the field of experience making itself. Eye contact is superfluous in this context. It misses so much! There is no minor sociality in the pressure to pay attention in just this neurotypical way, only interpersonality. Minor sociality is a listening-with the array of potential socialities in our surrounds. Lively with the forces of the outside, it asks that sociality be invented anew each time, that the world, and worlding, become the occasion for study.

When autistics are framed as arhetorical, it is usually around the concept of sociality. Melanie Yergeau writes, "My flapping fingers and facial tics signify an anti-discourse of sorts: Where is my control? Where is my communicability? Would anyone choose a life of ticcing? How can an involuntary movement, an involuntary neurology, a state of being that is predicated on asociality—how can these things be rhetorical?" (2018, 11).

In the neurotypical model of interpersonality, the measure is always that of communication as direct exchange. I speak; you look and listen. Then you speak, connecting your thoughts to mine. When this doesn't happen, when the encounter doesn't read for the neurotypical as communicational, the response is depersonification, dehumanization: "Autism is frequently storied as an epic in asociality, in non-intention. It represents the edges and boundaries of humanity, a queerly crip kind of isolationism. We, the autistic, are a peopleless people. We embody not a counter-rhetoric, but an anti-rhetoric, a kind of being and moving that exists tragically at the folds of involuntary automation. Our bodyminds rotely go through the motions, cluelessly la dee da" (Yergeau 2018, 14).

Cluelessly la dee da. Me lo dijo un pajarito.

The Free Indirect

Minor sociality edges into experience as the force that unmoors expectations about the relationscapes that compose us. It speaks from the corners, from the ledges and edges and thresholds of experience still taking form. It flies off the bodying with sparks; it stims and tics and hollers. It melts down when the world is just too much to take, the tensions of the world speeding like lightning along the body's feelingalwaysfeeling surfaces. The world is too much, and yet it is lived, fully, again and again to a limit unconceivable for most neurotypically inclined. Neurodiversity invents life. Life-living.

The invention of socialities is a study in living, a living study. It speaks often in pronouns intermixed—it is not unusual to hear autistics speak of themselves in the third person. A cold coming on, Adam Wolfond writes, "I think my body jumps because I am feeling sick. I think I have a cold in my boy nose. I am really wanting razor sharp always feeling body to be very calm and I want the body to wash away like the water you use. I want the water to always give me answers about how to stay quiet in my body. My body is always trying to stay calm. Talking as you do is away from the way my not very calm hated body talks. Hated is calming way of Adam and always questioning and asking people."[10] At once I and Adam and boy, Adam and the cold co-compose, water the teacher that may give the directions to ordering the body within neurotypical parameters. Because having, being, a moving autistic body is dangerous in a neurotypical world. Not only will it get you sidelined (as unintelligent, as deviant)—if you happen to be autistic and black, it may also get you killed.[11]

The stakes are high, the body must stay still, and words must come out in the order in which neurotypicals can hear them, can order them. Pronouns must be adjusted, or we will be seen as stupid. This is something I've heard too often. And yet no language proceeds directly. This is what Gilles Deleuze and Félix Guattari teach us in their chapter on linguistics in A Thousand Plateaus. "Me lo dijo un pajarito" is how the linguistic utterance actually functions. Knowledge, as it moves through language, always comes sideways. "Language," write Deleuze and Guattari, "is not content to go from a first party to a second party, from one who has seen to one who has not, but necessarily goes from a second party to a third party, neither of whom has seen" (1987, 77).

Heard from the sidelines, what is it about language that makes us believe that it is direct, unmediated? It is the order-word that does this work, ferrying the free indirect into the semblance of direct communication. An often redundant structure of language, the order-word is what organizes the potential disorientation of the free indirect quality of language, providing the utterance with a history of directions. "An order always and already concerns prior orders, which is why ordering is redundancy. . . . When the schoolmistress instructs her students on a rule of grammar or arithmetic, she is not informing them, any more than she is informing herself when she questions a student. She does not so much instruct as 'insign,' give orders or commands. A teacher's commands are not external or additional to what he or she teaches us" (Deleuze and Guattari 1987, 75). Speaking in the free indirect, catching language in the making, the order-word is carried by the performance of what the instructor does not actually need to say. The school, with its habits, the teaching expectation and pedagogical format, enforces a certain orchestration of knowledge that moves through the free indirect to give it the form of a command. It is not language that constrains knowledge but the order-word that moves through it.

In the manyness of language, order-words are the mechanism of orientation that keeps language in check. For Deleuze and Guattari, the order-word is the "elementary unit of language" (76). "We call order-words, not a particular category of explicit statements (for example, in the imperative), but the relation of every word or every statement to implicit presuppositions, in other words, to speech acts that are, and can only be, accomplished in the statement" (79). Order-words keep the saying in check. And yet textual disarray is continuously unmooring language, unfastening it from its order-words. The minor sociality of textuality is just too complex.

"There is no individual enunciation. There is not even a subject of enunciation" (Deleuze and Guattari 1987, 79). Enunciation is deeply social, even when spoken in solitude. It is not only that language carries histories and futurities but also, and especially, that language speaks through us, across us. In this sense, language also makes us, our bodyings alive with the sociality of expression. This is the case whether we use the words or not—Mel Baggs makes that abundantly clear. There is language without text—language is also movement, sound, texture. This is Deleuze and Guattari's point: emergent socialities speak languages on the edge of decipherability, where what moves is not the order-word but pass-words collectively invented and then forgotten. Language can never quite be captured: "There are pass-words beneath order-words. Words that pass, words that are components of passage, whereas order-words mark stoppages or organized, stratified compositions. A single thing or word undoubtedly has this twofold nature: it is necessary to extract one from the other—to transform the compositions of order into components of passage" (110). We've all felt it—the joy of a new concept, a pass-word for the creation of worlds—the taste of the thinking it creates, the force of the movements it allows.

When allied to language, emergent socialities are collective assemblages of enunciation—*agencements collectifs d'énonciation*. The French is necessary here to mark the specificity of the concept of agencement, often lost in translation. Agencement is not a form in any sense of the word (neither is it an arrangement). Agencement assembles—it is the movement-toward, the orientation that creates the conditions for a process to "take." Collective assemblages of enunciation are machines of language, mobilizers of potential that motor expression toward articulation. They remind us that the content of language can never be abstracted from its expression: "What comes first is not an insertion of variously individuated statements, or an interlocking of different subjects of enunciation, but a collective assemblage resulting in the determination of relative subjectification proceedings, or assignations of individuality and their shifting distributions within discourse" (Deleuze and Guattari 1987, 80). Sociality before, and between, in the relation.

Free indirect discourse has no intrinsic morality. This is why its sociality must be invented each time anew, and why the collective assemblage of enunciation it crafts must be tested for what it can do at each juncture. Concepts are only as good as the living they create, more-than human. "It's been said that," "but this is how it's always been done," or "as three people told me" are indirect discourse's everyday weapons. Order-words are infinitely cunning in their ability to appear where you least expect them. And if you count on a single pass-word, you will get locked out, stuck under the weight of past usage, the concept no longer operative in the current landscape. New relationscapes will always require new concepts, or at least new ways of creating conceptual pass-words. It takes practice, but what beautiful work it is to make language sing, to hear language's abysses, to move to its tics. This is the power of indirect discourse, that it includes what has been excluded, that it makes room for the minor gestures of sociality, which, over time, may be capable of shifting the register of what can be thought, of what it can mean to know.

Order-words are less language per se than the condition for "the superlinearity of expression" (Deleuze and Guattari 1987, 85). They are only one of the ways language is moved from its field of potential to its pragmatic instantiation. We must not be cowed by them. But to make the turn toward the conceptual work of creating living pass-words, we do have to train ourselves to hear undercommon ways of cawing in the offing. Neurotypical modes of listening almost never hear undercommon ways of cawing. As autistic Daina Krumins writes, "It's not that I could hear better, although I could hear much higher pitches than most people, but I was aware of what I was hearing. Most people attend to voices above all else. I attend to everything in the same way with no discrimination, so that the caw of the crow in the tree is as clear and important as the voice of the person I'm walking with" (2003, 86–87).

This is not to say that the neurodiverse don't hear the order-word. We are all trained to respond to its call, some of us more brutally than others. Isn't that what applied behavioral analysis (ABA) is all about: hearing and responding to the order-word? Autistic Ido Kedar writes:

In ABA years I lost hope. . . . I feel I wasted many years in this lonely endeavor. "Touch your nose." "Touch tree." "Touch your head." "Look at me." "Do this." "Sit quiet." "Touch red." "Good job." "Hands quiet." "No." "Great." "No." "All right." "No." . . . My life is better now. . . . I'm communicating with more and more people now. Though I still get sad, it's true, I'm not hopeless. Now I'm living in a flashcard-free world. I'm never touching my damn nose again. (2012, 58)

It's just that for some of us it's much more difficult to separate things out, to give expression to only one aspect of experience. Our motor differences may simply make it too difficult to reassure the interlocutor that we've heard the order-word. Or perhaps we're done with the order-word, having been condescended to for too long. "Occasionally, I was distracted by Mr. B's voice talking to me in the language of human beings, which failed to be translated into duck language. Maybe he said that it was time for lunch. Maybe he said that I needed to stand farther from the water. Maybe he said that I should do this or do that. Or maybe he counted the minutes aloud or perhaps the hours. Who knows? Maybe he even recited duck poetry. I wouldn't know because none of his words were translated into duck language. I stood on the threshold of human civilization and duck expectation—my heart pounding with iron-like savagery!" (Mukhopadhyay 2015, 82). Most often, order-words are all we can hear. And yet still we are told that we are beyond teaching, that we cannot be civilized.

The order-word, as Deleuze and Guattari make clear, is not the imperative per se. The order-word is the force of the presupposition that moves through the imperative, telling Kedar and Mukhopadhyay that their ways of communicating are not only without value but fully outside of what even registers as communication. Like many autistics who eventually speak with the help of keyboards and automated speech programs, Kedar makes it clear that there was a wealth of communication before anyone registered it as communication. Speaking of his first moments working with Soma Mukhopadhyay, the autism expert who would assist him in learning to communicate through text, he writes:

I was tasting my first communication [through text] and all my experts saw were the prompts, not the communication. . . . My ABA supervisor told my mom that it made no difference if I could communicate or not. I would continue to be taught in the same way with the same flashcards and drills as if I still didn't know my verbs, categories, adjectives, pronouns and so on. . . . [My mom] told me that the whole team sat and argued with her that I couldn't really communicate because I didn't with them. How could I with them? I only got drills or behavior modification. How was I to communicate with them? Spontaneously erupt in song and dance? Talking was impossible. Writing I could do with support but they denied me that. . . . So what's left? The data that didn't fit the model they threw away. If I was silent there, I must be silent everywhere, including internally. (2012, 86–87)

The order-word is: communication that does not fit our model is no communication at all. That communication requires sociality, that support is at the heart of communication, that language is a form of minor sociality—none of this has any bearing. The ABA specialists know best: only hand-touching-nose matters, duck language strictly out of reach.

Deleuze and Guattari speak of "making audible nonsonorous forces" (1987, 95). Moved beyond the register of the order-word, language begins to do something else, duration and intensity heard in the excess of expression. It begins to make heard the nonsonorous forces that populate it, the ways of knowing that swerve it toward modes of sociality yet to be invented. When Baggs moves through the living room sounding the furniture and smelling the books in the video "In My Language," when fingers cut the stream of water, the nonsonorous pulse of language is heard in the asignifying soundings. The insistence that the expressivity of the environment composes with language as the force-of-form of a prearticulation moving infrathinly across the field is not only a way of asserting Baggs's personhood. It is a comment on how impoverished our account of language tends to be. This is the point: that language moves and that its movements are lost to those of us who seek to hear only how language stops thought, how it signifies and orders expression denotatively. In Pier Paolo Pasolini's words, what if "the essential thing, precisely in free indirect discourse, is to be found neither in language A, nor in language B, but 'in language X, which is none other than language A in the actual process of becoming language B'" (quoted in Deleuze and Guattari 1987, 105). Baggs's language is never hirs alone. It is the language that moves across sensibilities that exceed the range of the human voice, that speak not only in words but also in textures, and in the intensities that resonate across them.

Undercommon ways of cawing trouble order-words and the matrix of signification that keeps them intelligible. What happens if we begin to listen?

More-Than Human

What is it about the stimmy, ticcy, or spastic body that threatens neurotypicality? What is it about it that so readily reads as unintelligent, unknowing? Is it its unabashed excess? Its uninhibited wealth of expression? Is it the fact that it makes felt the breadth of intensity signification can never quite capture?

We know that bodies get in the way of learning, of knowing, of speaking. Otherwise, why would we have to sit in chairs all day, stand still when we speak, and stop to pay attention? Is that why neurodiversity is so threatening to neurotypicality's certainty about what it means to know? Because neurodiversity bodies language? Is that also what is so threatening about black life? That it moves? That it moves sound, language, life, in ways as yet uncharted?

Alexander G. Weheliye writes, "Black life is that which must be constitutively abjected—and as such has represented the negative ontological ground for the Western order of things at least for the last five hundred years—but can never be included in the Western world order, especially the category of Man. Phrased differently, there can be no black life in the territory of Western, humanist Man, which is why the existence of black life disenchants Western humanism" (2014, 5). A similar account moves through the writings around neurodiversity: "Autistic bodies . . . these are bodies that not only defy social order, but fail to acknowledge social order's very existence. Autism, then, poses a kind of neuroqueer threat to normalcy, to society's very essence" (Yergeau 2018, 36). A more-than defies the concept of the human in both cases, a more-than that deeply unsettles the human as he is defined by the (white) discourses of neurotypicality: the human as the omnipresent category that holds dominion over knowledge in every walk of life.

Who speaks the order-word of the human? From whom do we hear it?

The more-than moves experience, its shape unsettled. It can't be counted. It can't be known as such. But it matters. It matters in that it qualifies, orients, thickens, and textures experience in the making, reminding us that the human is a juncture, an interstice toward a certain quality of shaping, of speciation.

Speciation is a diagram, a field of forces that activates a set of relations. This diagram is a mode of survival as much as it is an orientation for the creation of new modes of existence. The ways in which power and knowledge agitate on its vectors have effects as regards what else living can be, especially when life is no longer organized by the diagram that places Man in the center of the panopticon. A social zone of blackness beckons, whispering another way of participating. Not a being, not a belonging to a community already in place, but a being of relation diagramming its way out of the terror of humanism, one undercommon caw at a time.

The diagrams for life-living in the key of minor sociality are never perspectival. The diagrams are always askew, asymmetrical, unbound by forms that would constrain them. They are wild, anarchival, messy. These diagrams, fashioned of knowledge always still in the making, invite us, incite us, to connect to how else we can unknow, unown the language of the order-word as it has been passed down, neurotypical generation after neurotypical generation. "Is there knowledge in the service of not knowing, of study as unowning knowledge?" (Moten 2018b, 244).

In the Ruins

The university is in ruins, I heard. Me lo dijo un pajarito.

The university is in ruins, she said. That colonial space that didn't allow my voice, that didn't hear my cry.

Pursue bad debt! Study beyond credit!

Except the university is still there, and she still has debt and no credit.

And we're still teaching, still hiring, still investing your debt. Still paying my mortgage. Still distributing my grants. Still organizing my calendar. Still calling meetings.

I hear the cry. They don't pass. The work they do is not accepted as knowledge. "I see no research here," I am told. "This doesn't take the measure of a field." "You are not supervising adequately." "You are not doing your job."

I've paid my debt, and now I have credit. And I'm afraid of losing it. Aren't we all?

But I can't stand it. I can't stand the measure of value. And so I study, I learn to study, in the undercommons of the university.

I have never learned so much, never studied quite this way.

I know some of us will get through. I made it through the gates, past every single hurdle until I hit the highest ceiling. I thought it would protect us. I thought it would make it possible for me to squeeze you through the membrane. But they didn't let you through. We didn't let us through.

In the end, we are the termites. We eat away at the structure, residing in the holes we create. They are warm, and we can nest. There is some comfort here. But at night, when we scurry around the hallways listening to the anarchive, I hear echoes of other modes of study, and I hear you hear them too.

livingloving

Difference is not what separates us. It is the elementary particle of all relation. It is through difference that what I call Relation works. —Glissant (my translation)

Livingloving thrives in the "social zone of blackness," the modality of the being of relation of black life (Harney and Moten 2013, 138). This zone, "sent by sociality to sociality," is recognized not by similarity but "by way of and as a function of . . . intense, radical, constant differentiation" (Moten 2015), where "blackness is only in that it exceeds itself" (Moten 2003, 26). Difference without separability (Ferreira da Silva 2016).

Difference without separability tethers livingloving to a sociality that is radically singular. Asymmetry in overlap, livingloving carries the force of a relation forged in the differential of the excess that runs through the more-than that cannot be reduced to the sum of its parts, the living and the loving coming into encounter at rhythms asynchronous, each side of the nonequation shifting the conditions of the other to make them not exactly one but $n+1$. Radically singular not in the sense of bringing together a preestablished commonality, but in an ethos of life-living that moves beyond the common as preconstituted interiority, beyond the identity of the one (and only).

Speaking of a 1704 "anti-tumult" law from the Commonwealth of Pennsylvania that "outlawed the tumultuous gathering of two or more blacks in the public square on Sundays," Moten proposes the being of relation as blackness's power, and its threat: "insofar as black being or being black is a necessarily irreducibly social thing to do, [to outlaw the gathering of two or more blacks] is to simply outlaw blackness" (Moten 2017).[1] Blackness's irreducible sociality, its difference without separability, makes it undecomposable. Beyond grasp, blackness permeates the field, threatening to lure each of its corners into sociality: "They didn't know that the hallway and the stairwell were places of assembly, a clearing inside the tenement, or that *you love in doorways*" (Hartman 2019, 22). Blackness is a deep sociality, as Katherine McKittrick (2018) might say, a sociality textured by the differential of all that uncontains it, thick with the force of what brings black life into resonance with itself and its complex, troubled, intense, joyful, performative, painful history. Because black life, it must be repeated, is not reducible to *a* black life: black life is the force of life that moves through blackness, the force that troubles every notion of the interpersonal and that refuses to diminish itself to the measure of the 1 + 1. Two Black people gathering is never just two, the law seems to foresee. Blackness exceeds the reach of what can be held captive. This, not despite, but *with* the horrors of all that is everyday stolen, killed, in the name of the "orderly" public square. Black sociality is the performance of and in excess of black lives, a minor sociality that invents itself into black becoming each day anew.

An aesthetics of black sociality brings the quality of livingloving, carried here as pocket practice, toward the production of radical modes of existence that alter the conditions of living. Its work is never done, imaginings of other modes of freedom and of ways they call forth livingloving everywhere palpable. "How do we transcend bitterness and cynicism and embrace love, hope, and an all-encompassing dream of freedom, especially in these rough times? . . . Trying to envision 'somewhere in advance of nowhere,' as poet Jayne Cortez puts it, is an extremely difficult task, yet it is a matter of great urgency. Without new visions we don't know what to build, only what to knock down. We not only end up confused, rudderless, and cynical, but we forget that making a revolution is not a series of clever maneuvers and tactics but a process that can and must transform us" (Kelley 2002, 10, 11).

As conduit of a transformation immanent to the coming into relation, the social zone of blackness does not take the measure of a situation. Freedom cannot be reduced to *what is*. Its call never limited to the conditions as they are, freedom is in the attunement to what plays in a minor key across a differential that schizzes life itself, lived in the ecology of an aesthetics of the earth whose rhythm is irreducible to the count. Being of relation.

Black sociality carries a history of entanglement and survival, and with it, a history of looking askew and seeing what else is shifting the boundaries of existence. This is what livingloving does. It grapples with interlocking oppressions and, without standing in judgment from the externality architected in whiteness, asks, *how else?*

There is not first being and then relation. Relation is the conduit of a becoming that expresses itself not as ontology but as ontogenesis, formative force in transindividuation. Its shape: a curve, a reaching-toward, levied in the middling. Mobilizing the forces of all that is actively present, in attunement to an aesthetics of the earth, in a posture of a leaning-toward, an inclination that lists on the phonic pulse of experience improvised in the sounding, livingloving embodies the being of relation as otherwise possibility. Otherwise possibility, Amey Victoria Adkins (2018) writes in response to Ashon Crawley's 2017 work, is not doctrine but doing, in the midst. More-than human, otherwise possibility "isn't new and isn't future-oriented" but has always "been here, with us" (Crawley 2018b). In body-worlding, of the earth, felt in the asynchronism of Tina Campt's "frequency," the force of rhythm jolting a body out of its-self, "a politics of affirmative difference reopens . . . attention to the nonsynchronism of the present" (Reed 2014, 170).

In asynchrony, a keen become-angular, the social zone of blackness never reduces to the same. You are there too, in the impersonality of an encounter you don't get to define. For in the complex duration of asynchrony, time folds, its tenses in overlap. This "black polytemporality" fabulates not a species into shape but an otherworldliness thickly of this earth, livingloving in the sensuous hapticality of its aesthetics (Nyong'o 2018, 11). Dynamic form with and of the earth, body-worlding, livingloving cannot be distinguished from the ecologies it calls forth. To livelove is to compose in radical play with all that is of us and beyond the we whose form we take to be our own.

Otherwise possibility, speculatively pragmatic, is a sociality that "looks like what we might otherwise call love," writes Nicole Ivy (2018), a love necessarily otherwise, invented always anew in the approximation of proximity that is the daily encounter with radical singularity. Radical singularity because we are never speaking of a group, of a commons, that knows itself, once and for all, but of a way, a manner, a withness of what always exceeds the count.

Livingloving is a way of otherwise responding, otherwise living, otherwise practicing, always with the knowledge that cultures of violent oppression systematically work to break the force-of-form produced in the tumult that denies its logic. For the logic of the excessive tumult of what cannot be contained is the deepest threat to whiteness, whose claim, repeated in every idiom, is to count. Livingloving is in the tumult, active at the cleave that mutually includes—"'syntax of love:' the 'broken' or refused connection that precedes connection as end precedes beginning" (Reed 2014, 183).

"What to do, how to move, in such a world wherein your resistance against violent conditions—resistance as prayer meetings or protests, resistance as simply wishing to breathe—produces the occasion for violence?" (Crawley 2017, 23).

If sociality is "in the breath and the capacity for breath" (Armstrong 2018), livingloving also sidles the violence of the gasp, that breath too often held when crossing the threshold into spaces of white supremacy, worlds thick with the violence of white privilege. Because every threshold is a new crossing for black life, every crossing a question about whether this taking, this making, of space will be shared or blocked.

"The act of Black motherhood is always, in some real way, preparation for quite possibly losing your child" (Zellars and Smolash 2016a). Violence is enmeshed in the dailyness of black lives, freedom never far from the question of survival itself. "Each new deprivation raises doubts about when freedom is going to come; if the question pounding inside her head—*Can I live?*—is one to which she could ever give a certain answer, or only repeat in anticipation of something better than this, bear the pain of it and the hope of it, the beauty and the promise" (Hartman 2019, 10).

How does livingloving compose with the freedom violently extracted at every turn? Is not the "living free" of whiteness, difference *with* separability always contingent on the logic of interpersonality that runs through it? The "burdened individuality of freedom," as Saidiya Hartman names it, would suggest it is. "The transformation of black subjectivity effected by emancipation is described as nascent individualism not simply because blacks were considered less than human and a hybrid of property and person prior to emancipation but because the abolition of slavery conferred on them the inalienable rights of man and brought them into the fold of liberal individualism" (Hartman 1997, 117). Freedom is a tightrope, its promise tethered to those laws that keep sociality out of the public square.

In approximation of proximity to something like "free will," freedom's rich cousin, livingloving repeats the refrain "all black life is neurodiverse life." Because the question is whether the persistent unfreedom that has come to define how the congregating happens is not also the force of a freedom in every sense in excess of any actioning of the volition-intentionality-agency triad that keeps neurotypicality in the belief that it reigns supreme.

The volition-intentionality-agency triad rests on the presupposition that to be worthy of the count is to be the driver of experience. The control over action that undergirds the triad rests on a belief that there is a willful separation between body and world on the one hand and experience and subjectivity on the other. Time as conduit remains passive, its role a simple passing-between. States are given dominance over process. The agitation of experience humming is backgrounded. Qualitative difference is reduced in favor of what is foregrounded, which is narrated as the act *I* brought into existence. Qualities are then superimposed onto what has come to be known as "mine," as "my movement," returning to *I* in the impoverished form, the force of the more-than depleted in the segregation of the in-act from the act. In this account of process disqualified, the pulse of duration is synchronized to exclude all that wasn't pulled into actualization, the excess of experience pushed so far into the background that the act can be narrated as volitional, intentional, agential, in willful ignorance of all that stirred, negatively prehended, in the relational field of its excess.

"Free will" is the story neurotypicality tells in the name of volition-intentionality-agency, its dictate all the more powerful because of neurotypicality's power to exclude. To not be able to account for your actions in the vocabulary of intentionality, as all classical autistics know, is to be considered incapable of learning, of proving yourself useful, of being assimilable. But freedom does not live in this account of free will, Henri Bergson argues in *Time and Free Will* (1910). In the ticcingflapping of worlds too neurodiverse to contain, freedom is altogether elsewhere, far from the myth that our acts are driven by us as though we were at the forefront of experience. This is also true of livingloving, whose middling reveals an account that refuses to be framed by a triad that would make it its driver. Livingloving is expressed not in the tense of *I am, I do, I count*, but in the middling of another kind of voicing, a voicing that makes the agencement of ecologies the force of what comes together to make itself an activity. This agencement, an occasioning of experience that brings body-world into an approximation of proximity at every turn, is achieved not through a single-handed living that speaks in the name of the interpersonal agential *I*, claiming "free will" in the impoverishment of experience unfelt. Livingloving moves in another rhythm entirely, dancing in the entwined constellation of existence made and remade in the in-act, attuned to the ticflaps of existence heard otherwise.

In the attunement to an aesthetics of the earth, in the absence of "free will," negative prehension is as powerful as any sense we might have, infraconsciously, of what is welling. What is perceived in the infrathin of what is excluded from actualization is not a thing. A both-and of experience resonating with itself is heard, movement-moving. Across this movement, formative forces are at work. As all that is unregistered moves in the offings of experience felt, as the non-felt and the felt come into infrathin contact, what is experienced is the complex amalgamation of all tendencies, including those that exceed the count, all the movements-moving. What peaks as "mine" is an impoverished reduction of this symphony, an improvised account that can never be reduced to its-self. For itsself has a lived connection to the passage through the experience, capable in no way of being reduced to *I* as though *I* were not altered by it. Collective concrescence, *I* is the uncertain receiver of our acts, more-than *I* the maker of them.

Neurodiverse freedom lives here. This is freedom free of "free will," freedom expressed in the formative force of the being of relation. This freedom, which refutes causality and determinism, is not reducible to the (un)freedom in the afterlife of slavery. But it is not its opposite either. It is of another logic altogether. For "free will" has always been bolstered by the burdened individuality of freedom that doles out freedom based on who meets the individualist requirements of its limited expression. Maintaining that proper conscious reflection, that agency and intentionality, only belongs to those within the limited field of whiteness that reigns over freedom, the individuality of freedom in its "associationist determinism" that turns freedom into mechanism negates any expression of the exquisite excess that escapes it (Bergson 1910, 148). "It seems that we make a point of safe-guarding the principle of mechanism and of conforming to the laws of the association of ideas. The abrupt intervention of the will is a kind of coup d'état which our mind foresees and which it tries to legitimate beforehand by a formal deliberation" (158).

Each act carries the edge of all it wasn't. The force of what does not come to be reverberates across it, the feeling of what is excluded a contour thick with the potential of all that sideways tinged the expression of what actually came to be. A listening tunes with phonic materiality to sounds of otherwise durations, the approximation of the negatively prehended alongside carried not as a form but as a feeling-tone moving in the rich backgrounding of what is heard in the here-now. The otherness of what attunes shifts the now become present, altering the quality of what is heard across durations schizzed. Infraconsciously, an attunement occurs across the differential of time lived. What pulses into existence carries the differential with it, shifting the conditions of feeling every time. This, Bergson calls freedom.

The differential of experience pulsing with all that moves in the nonsensuous prehension of times unlapsing, amplifying experience to include what exceeds it, is freedom. What is unfreedom is all that misses the force of this resonant multiplicity. "Free will" by its very mandate segregates individual from world, act from in-act. This is unfreedom. It bears only the barest traces of the force of the being of relation, its logic that of the most simplistic kind of association, that of causal determinism. The interpersonal lives here.

Whiteness cannot bear complexity. Reduced to the most bland of accounts of perception, it relies on the conscious as the matrix of an impoverished presiding of the one (and only). No encounter happens here, its social scape reduced, always, to the 1 + 1, in the self-distancing of difference *with* separability. For whiteness confuses complexity for what Bergson calls a "homogeneous medium," reducing time to a line. The homogeneous medium is, after all, what allows neurotypicality's empty assertions to preside over the much more complex account of how experience composes across its difference from itself, nonvolition its formative force. Without the homogeneous medium, there can be no general idea of value, no general account of supremacy. If homogeneity reigns, it is likely because homogeneity has little purchase, the friction of black polytemporality's tumult its biggest threat.

The social zone of blackness, in its approximation of proximity to neurodiversity, fosters an account of freedom that is unsettling of freedom's burdened individuality. Freedom is not a state. Infrathin, it erupts in the interstices of the relation of nonrelation. Difference without separability, the relation of nonrelation makes the in-act its point of departure, refuting the limiting frame of the preconstituted subject as purveyor of experience. This is neurodiverse freedom's power, and its menace. That no more than two Black people should congregate on the public square is testament to the field of force of what refuses to be reduced to the terms of a limited account of what freedom might mean. Of course, this doesn't make the Black folks any freer to congregate in the public square in 1704. And it doesn't negate, in any way, the horror of captivity and its continuation in the afterlife of slavery. But it does suggest that in the sociality of the congregating, in the n + 1 of its minor sociality, another kind of freedom was always at work. "Freedom in her hands, if not a crime, was an offense, and a threat to public order and moral decency" (Hartman 2019, 235). Freedom's emergent sociality threatens burdened individualism, its tug at life a torment to the state's hold. "The social worker concurred, 'With no social considerations to constrain her, she was ungovernable'" (235).

Blackness, as immanent force of freedom in the Bergsonian sense, threatens all that withholds. Not state but shape—shape of enthusiasm—freedom, for Bergson, is "a certain shade or quality of the action itself" (1910, 182–83). Dynamic form, freedom is the force-of-form of an immanent shaping. Ineffable in its coming to be, it is never known as such: "As soon as it tries to explain its freedom to itself, it no longer perceives itself except by a kind of refraction through space" (183). Consciousness never governs freedom. Freedom is only given to consciousness as a quality—"it expresses rather its shade, its characteristic colouring, . . . its intensity consists in being felt" (186). Freedom is in the fold of feeling, in the minor movements of relation become expressive.

If blackness is "always a disruptive surprise moving in the rich nonfullness of every term it modifies," blackness as agrammatical force—not quite adverb, not quite subject, not quite verb—must be put into a differential relation with all accounts of individualism, freedom, and volition that undergird and hold up stale accounts of neurotypicality as whiteness (Moten 2003, 255). "Tumult, upheaval, flight—it was the articulation of living free, or at the very least trying to, it was the way to insist *I am unavailable for servitude. I refuse it*" (Hartman 2019, 299). Blackness is never another state, another people, as though it could be separated out, positioned apart, in its-self. Blackness is an otherwise alongsideness that shapes all it comes into contact with, having already shifted the conditions of encounter. For blackness is a sidling that has already veered the very ontology we thought we had a handle on, trained as we were in the colonialist neurotypical vocabularies of being over becoming. Blackness recalibrates ontology, revealing that two or more black bodies is an infinity: one would already have been too much. Blackness is a poetics of relation, consent not to be a single being.

Livingloving tunes Bergsonian freedom to Spinozist joy. The capacity to affect and be affected, the care for the more-than of existence, the tending of what schizzes to reveal its excess, joy is always "out from the outside," vibrant with the pulse of what moves it to expression.[2] Beyond good and evil, joy is not happiness. It is intensity-in-composition. Always in the relation of nonrelation to what qualifies experience, joy is a power to act in the act. At its most potent, joy amplifies the conditions of existence by increasing what Friedrich Nietzsche (2003) calls the "feeling" of power. The feeling of power, also called the will to power, should never be reduced to an individual will. The feeling of power is the interplay of force with force toward the shaping of experience. Differential rather than individual, the feeling of power is a dynamism of forces. For Spinoza, the more a body is affected, the more force it has—"the will to power is always determined at the same time as it determines, qualified at the same time as it qualifies"—body here always understood as the being of relation of an aesthetics of the earth (Deleuze 1986, 62). Joy is the apex of affectability, an affectability that is never passive. Joy is a sensibility, a feeling-with, of a body-world in transformation. The power to act is a feeling-moved.

Livingloving is feeling-moved. In the act, it grows from the outside out, the force of its composing always its sidling with what exceeds the terms of interpersonality. Beyond reactivity, livingloving schizzes with the shape the world takes in it. In its logic of blackness, it operates asymmetrically, never in simple negation to whiteness. For whiteness's reactivity, its *ressentiment*, its sad affect, are of the order of the very "free will" it left behind with the ontology that excluded it. In the livingloving, blackness moves ontogenetically elsewhere, its orientation diagonal, a transvaluation.

And this is how it begins. With a declaration of a child at the thresholds of doors. We can make it! Such a declaration was made in the dark. What does darkness know? Can we be carried in an absence, as we carry it? This is the staging ground of circum-sacred thought. To not-want what you never had, to not-want what you'd never been guaranteed. That is the goal. But it is also the challenge. We are called to a circum-sacred life, one of improvisational possibility, improvisation being the fact of ongoing preparation, a nonchalance that emerges after having engaged in meditative, contemplative, social thought. As my favourite scripture says: I do not act as though I have already attained. But this one thing I do, forgetting those things that are behind me, reaching unto those things before me, I press toward the joy of and the getting happy in blackness, in blackqueerness. (Crawley 2018a)

Livingloving as improvisation, ongoing preparation in attunement to "freedom's basis in the indeterminate" (Homi Bhabha, quoted in Moten 2017, 5).

We might simply call it love.

Not at a Distance

On Touch, Synesthesia,

and Other Ways of Knowing

Notice how you build the distance in.

Imagine an airport. Note the gate on your right, number 56. On your immediate left, a sunglasses shop. Behind that, further to the left, a restaurant. And in front of that, a sign for the toilets. "Where can I find the toilet?" she asks. "Over there," you respond, gesturing diagonally.

Accounts of spatial orientation are rife with distances. Geometric angles are common in our descriptions: "go right, turn a little to the left, and then proceed ahead." Paths are drawn point to point, tracing a line as though we were flying overhead, little or no mention of the trolleys, the children running, the spilled drink, the noisy lineup blocking the way, the suitcase. It's as though space were one large flat empty surface.

DeafBlind poet John Lee Clark proposes the concept of distantism to address the ableism that dominates our point-to-point orientational strategies. Distantism, for Clark, refers to the "standing apart" that indexes movement to position, mapping it onto geometries of distance (2017a). "Are sighted and hearing people wrong to use their distance senses and let it affect how they live?" he asks. "No. If they wish to be all eyeballs and flapping ears, they are welcome to such an existence" (2017a).

Distantism as it plays out in relation to DeafBlind culture is on a par with backgriddism in neurotypicality.[1] Backgridding is the way experience felt is given its accounting. It is how experience is narrowed down to category. How point to point is extracted. Regularly assumed to be the way experience is actually lived, backgriddism tells the impoverished story of how things fit onto maps denuded of their texture. Like distantism, which assumes that a world is capable of giving experience its due at a distance—*do not touch!*—providing all we need to know in the abstract form of an "empty" visual expanse, backgriddism functions as the stenographed subtraction of the intensive magnitudes that compose us.

"Over there!" is how we give directions, how we occlude the ineffability of that infrathin living that simply cannot be reduced to a series of points. A life pre-drawn in geometries of distance.

Without backgriddism everything comes teeming in. The telling is more con-voluted: "On your right, there is a murmur of discontent as the people urgently wait for a flight attendant to arrive. A baby is crying. They've been sitting there all day so there is a restlessness in the air along with the smell of orange peel and rancid oil. A long line of edgy-seeming people are waiting to speak to someone at the desk. The toilet is on the other side of the hall. You can get there by walking beyond gate 56 but don't go too far or you'll end up in the duty-free shop. That smell of perfume and soap is so overwhelming! Stop before it reaches you but be careful about the sunglasses shop on your left. Sharp corners! As you approach the toilets, you will know you are getting close by the smell of the pizza dough. It's from a restaurant just south of the sign for the toilets. Lots of trolleys there! Keep walking and you will feel a wall on your right-hand side. The women's wash-room is the third door on your right." This second account may be bewildering—after all, it awakens a whole proprioceptive field, opening out movement to all kinds of quasi-encounters. Movements overlap in imagined and lived experience, exposing a field of relation that exceeds any one actual displacement. Just the thought of that perfume smell in the duty-free shop may be enough to keep you where you are, your body already recoiling at the thought. It may be that the diagonal point-to-point directionality of the first description is more conducive to actually reaching the toilet. But much is lost in crossing space without coming alive to its texture.

Distantiom is the presupposition that all that is valued in existence can be mapped point to point, that space is preconstituted, that standing apart is a value in itself, and that sightlines are the ideal choreography for movement. I am not simply speaking of DeafBlindness here. I am also speaking about neurodiversity: to map the space of an airport withholding the buzz of the fluorescent lights, the glaring waxed surfaces of the floors, the loud PA system, the anxiety around secu-rity, the overlap of smells, the undercurrent of fear, is to radically underestimate how environments shape our ability to navigate them.

William James speaks of the "element of voluminousness" in experience to foreground what is felt in excess of the given (1890, vol. 2, 134). This volumi-nousness cannot be reduced to a geometric account of space. Voluminousness is intensive magnitude, not quantity. James situates it in the field of sensation, describing it as "a sensational element." "My first thesis is that the element [of voluminousness], discernible in each and every sensation, though more devel-oped in some than in others, is the original sensation of space, out of which all the exact knowledge about space that we afterwards come to have is woven by processes of discrimination, association, and selection" (135).

Voluminousness, despite its fielding of sensation, should not be reduced to sense presentation. This is not about how an organ of sense connects to an object or a person. Voluminousness is not about sensing a thing. It is about sense in excess of form, in excess of geometry. "It must now be noted that the vastness hitherto spoken of is as great in one direction as in another. Its dimensions are so vague that in it there is no question as yet of surface as opposed to depth; 'volume' being the best short name for the sensation in question" (135). The element of voluminousness is what is felt in the texture of experience coming to expression in excess of any one actualized sensation.

Alfred North Whitehead's (1978) term for the voluminousness of experience as yet unparsed is the "extensive continuum" (66). The extensive continuum is the potential for extension that is only realized as spatiality—or spacetime—in the actualization of a taking-form. Also called the "relational complex," the extensive continuum is the intensity, the *expressivity* of a world in motion. Extension never preexists expression: to come to be is to make felt the inherent voluminousness of environments in motion, a voluminousness that can never simply be reduced to quantity. How something comes to be is its voluming into expression.

Voluming into expression does not yet mean taking a form. "This extensive continuum expresses the solidarity of all possible standpoints throughout the whole process of the world. It is not a fact prior to the world; it is the first determination of order—that is, of real potentiality—arising out of the general character of the world. In its full generality beyond the present epoch, it does not involve shapes, dimensions, or measurability; these are additional determinations of real potentiality arising from our cosmic epoch" (66). It is the actualizing into itself of experience that shapes the volume, that makes the world take shape. But this shaping must not be reduced to form as though form-taking happened once and for all. The actualizing into voluminous expression is an occurrence always in overlap, a million shapings producing a million expressions facilitating an infinity of volumes morphing at each turn of the world making itself.

Touch is one way shapings occur. In the reaching-toward, distantism can be broken—particularly if this touch is "metatactile," which is to say, operative across the overlap of shapings (Clark 2015). Such a touch, synesthetic by definition since voluminously in excess of the geometry of location, is one that volumes proto-experiences into feeling. In this return to an account of touch more than a decade after publishing *Politics of Touch* (Manning 2006), I hope to do four things: 1) demonstrate that the force of reaching-toward, which is how I defined touch in *Politics of Touch*, troubles the model of geometric space, particularly in the context of how "sense of agency" is defined in developmental psychology and neuroscientific accounts of synesthesia; 2) build on John Lee Clark's account of distantism as it plays out not only in DeafBlind culture but more broadly in the neurotypical worldview; 3) consider the ways in which accounts of synesthesia from developmental psychology and neuroscience support a deficit model of sensation that is neurotypical; 4) explore how ProTactile, a movement for language-in-the-making and DeafBlind experience, remaps the spacetime of sensation away from the categorical limitations that come with the imposition of sensory regimes that privilege body-world separation.

A Thousand Other Things Sing to Me

The dominant literature in developmental psychology and neuroscience works with a deficit model of sensation that is neurotypical through and through. Nowhere is this more apparent than in the work on mirror-touch synesthesia, defined as what occurs when the stimulation of one sensory modality (vision) automatically triggers a perception in a second modality (touch), in the absence of any direct stimulation to this second modality. In this distantist account of sensation—I look at you as you touch yourself, and feel the touch on my body—the experience of feeling is said to *not* enhance the field of experience: to feel the shape of a world in excess of myself is to *reduce the body schema*. With the feeling of you directly experienced on my body, I lose a bit of what separated me from you. The coming into relation is considered a loss.

The deficit model of sensation is built on the distantist presupposition that senses are fixed and located. It relies on a body schema whose "sense of agency," it is said, is fractured by the increase in sensation that accompanies the mirror-touch overlap. Bodies, it is said, lose their integrity in the encounter with this metatactile touch. "In the context of MTS [mirror-touch synesthesia], one prediction . . . would be that if there were agency-processing deficits these would exacerbate more basic disturbances in bodily awareness. We are clearly suggesting here that MTS is primarily a 'disorder' of ownership, which can have consequences for SoAg [sense of agency] and which in turn can further worsen ownership disturbances" (Cioffi, Moore, and Banissy 2014).

"Sense of agency" is the account of a body backgridded, the bodying reduced to a self-other dichotomy that indexes movement to position by emphatically disavowing the relational field co-composed in the crossing. To be a body is reduced to being an intentional, volitional agent of your own experience. This distantist account of being a body places what I have called the volition-intentionality-agency triad ahead of the agencement of experience coming into itself. Bodies are properly bodies only when they can fully distinguish themselves from the touch of the world. Bodies that sense too much, bodies that feel the touch of the world and are moved by it, are at a loss. Their sense of agency is weakened by the pulse of what moves them, of what is moved by them.

The deficit model of sensation relies on a preexisting body-matrix onto which a body is drawn. This abstraction is made possible by extracting the body from the ecology of its surrounds to recompose it as a form untouched by the fomenting of the relational complex. Paradoxically, it is this abstraction that we regularly call "my body," a form whose integrity we far too rarely question. What if bodies were never so stable as to be reduced to a settled form? What if bodies were the quality of a voluminousness in relational complex? John Lee Clark's account of the body is resonant with this proposition that bodies are composed in the relation: "Most of the time, my actual experience is that I am bodyless. Or that my body is so perfect, so seamlessly . . . so seamlessly what? I don't know. Seamless! Yes, it is so perfect that it ceases to exist to me, or it is so well absorbed into things, the flow of life, that I am so rarely aware of it as an entity unto itself" (personal communication, August 19, 2019). Brian Massumi speaks of the bodying into existence of the relational complex as a "body without an image": "The body without an image is an accumulation of relative perspectives and the passages between them, an additive space of utter receptivity retaining and combining past movements, in intensity, extracted from their actual terms. It is less a space in the empirical sense than a gap in space that is also a suspension of the normal unfolding of time" (2002, 57). Bodying into extension is an expression of voluminousness. Extending into act is not distancing into form.

Distantism makes too strong a distinction between body and world. It speaks of self and other as preexisting categories, prioritizing extensive quantity over intensive magnitude. "Individuals with mirror-touch synaesthesia (MTS) experience touch on their own bodies when observing another person being touched. Specifically, the images that participants had initially perceived as containing equal quantities of self and other became more likely to be recognised as the self after viewing the other being touched" (Maister, Banissy, and Tsakiris 2013, 802). In such accounts that limit bodies to distantist regimes, self-identity is always the starting point, and it is in the self-identity that the experience of touch is located, reducing touch to a 1 + 1, to points on a line.

Metatactile touch works entirely differently. "I wasn't conscious of it. It was natural. So natural, in fact, that I didn't have a name for it, this skill that goes beyond just feeling texture, heft, shape, and temperature" (Clark 2015). Metatactile touch is not reducible to the distantist line. Meta in its voluminous quality, it is the excess in touch that "involves many senses, senses that we all have but which are almost never mentioned—the axial, locomotive, kinesthetic, vestibular . . . All 'tactile' to some extent, but going beyond 'touch'"(Clark 2015). Interfusing with the world forming in it, metatactile touch is ProTactile, proprioceptively alert to those phasings-in of experience voluminous. Productive of spacetime in defiance of an overgridded geometry, touch is in the bodying, proprioceptively dancing with the relational complex of the world's co-composition. This is an extensive proprioception—a tactility propriocepted—fielded in the relational complex, a sensitivity to infrathin surfacings shared extensively across a world continuously in-forming. If Clark does not feel his body as separate from the world, this is not because he can't see it. It's because he has not given in to the backgriddist model of imposing an image onto it, reducing it to a spatial quantity.

The blurring of boundaries elicited by the overflowing of sense does not produce a deficit body. Quite the contrary: the blur is an account of how the "element of voluminousness" expresses itself before the backgriddist tendencies take over. "Massive feeling" is how James speaks of the overspilling of what remains unparsable in experience (1890, 134). "Massive" and "vague" is how Whitehead describes it (1938, 121), both he and James concerned to give voice to the force of that dim apprehension that shapes experience before any form-taking occurs. It is here, in the as-yet-unexpressed of experience welling, in its "simple total vastness," that feeling is most potent (James 1890, 145). The "vague essences" of all that is orienting toward expression are rife with potential, alive with proto-shapings unparsable. "No order of parts or of subdivisions reigns" (145). To be touched by the world, to blur in the relation, is to become collectively enmeshed with these vague essences. It is to feel more fully all that moves in the shaping. Distantism does not reign here. Metatactile touch cannot be reduced to the point-to-point, to the 1 + 1. In reaching-toward, there is no reduction to the sum of the parts. ProTactile carries the multiplicity of feeling in each reaching-toward into a relational complex that shifts the very conditions of experience. There is no standing apart.

Deficit models of sensation replay neurotypical, ableist accounts that reek of whiteness. Narrating the fullness of experience voluminous as loss, their aim is to hold up the neurotypical norm in order to keep order in a world backgridded into blandness. "How much do we ENJOY what is around us? How many really understand the melody inherent in . . . the Golden Gate Bridge? How many ever get out of the car, feel the bridge moving gently in the wind swells, how many of us put our hands out to touch the cables, feel the bridge sing to us?" (Lyle Crist, quoted in Clark 2014). To feel the world in formation is to jostle the edifice of representation that neurotypicality upholds.[2]

The Word on the Breeze, and Through the Floor

"The TV is off, but I can still hear (and feel on my skin) the current of electricity powering all that equipment," writes Aspiegrrl, on her blog *Autism and Angels*.[3] Hearing what moves infrasensorially through her surrounds, electrified by the field of relation, it is impossible for Aspiegrrl to hold on to the neurotypical imposition of body-world separation. Already considered at a deficit because she is autistic, she is doubly pathologized, her divergent sensory processing further evidence of her faulty "sense of agency." This "disturbance" of sense perception will, most likely, be considered a disadvantage in learning environments: she will be taught, if not through the violent practices of ABA, then through the ubiquitous behavioral codes that are systemic in our education systems, to backgrid perception so as to sense less fully, so as to craft a less porous body.[4] But this will not actually make her sense less. It will simply make more violently apparent that a sensing body in movement is a deficient body. She will learn that in order to pass she will have to background the feel of electricity on her skin. She will have to act as though she is in control of her surroundings. She will have to stand apart, pretending that she has agency over what moves her. She will be told in a thousand ways that value resides in subtracting from the welter of experience. She will learn that the standard of neurotypical life is one of sense poverty. She will be considered properly treated if she can "pay" attention, attention no longer dancing at the pace of the more-than.

What if we were to turn the sensory model on its head and ask what keeps so many feeling so little?

Daniel Tammet, like Aspiegrrl, is someone for whom the voluminousness of experience is foregrounded. Indeed, his synesthesia has made him famous for his ability to visualize pi to a previously unimaginable 22,514 digits. This unusual feat cannot be reduced to calculation. Tammet insists that he "arrive[s] at the answer instantly."[5] With sympathy for the fold, existence comes to him in shapes. "When I multiply numbers together, I see two shapes. The image starts to change and evolve, and a third shape emerges. . . . It's like maths without having to think" (2005).[6] Shapings in movement, numbers become qualities in overlap, facilitating remarkable recall. In the fold of direct perception worlds are made, the flux of the relational complex rife with all that infrathinly culls itself from the welter. For these are not forms arrayed in a distantist scenery, they are a tumult of voluminousness expressing itself at that qualitative interstice of force and form. The feat is that they can be cuffed at all, that parsing is possible without the loss of all that refuses to stand apart. Not every situation benefits from this kind of direct engagement with the infraperceptual field, however: "Trips to the supermarket are always a chore. There's too much mental stimulus. I have to look at every shape and texture. Every price, and every arrangement of fruit and vegetables. So instead of thinking, 'What cheese do I want this week?', I'm just really uncomfortable."[7] To field voluminousness comes at the price of losing the boundary that held complexity at bay.

While there is no doubt that synesthetes such as Tammet have unusual abilities, focusing too much on the mnemonic capacities of his synesthesia, over a more nuanced account of autistic perception and all that it complexly brings to experience, risks replaying the well-worn ableist narrative of the autistic savant.[8] For this nomenclature, used in every article about Tammet's synesthetic feats, focuses solely on what can be culled and quantified. In so doing, it amplifies a model of value that is stridently neurotypical in its refusal to value the qualitatively irreducible complexity of perception. In addition, though the quantifiable share of the synesthetic capacity opens the door to "savantism," the "autistic" share of the equation ultimately downgrades any value-added on the balance sheet of existence backgridded. Reduced to the sum of their parts, autistic savants themselves become a quantification, their feats reduced, always, to what ultimately excludes them from normopathic existence. They are half autistic, after all, and so only half savant, only halfway remarkable. It should be no surprise, then, that the deficit model is all over the writing on Tammet.

All accounts of autistic savantism get caught up in functioning labels.[9] As everyone who is familiar with autism knows, labels are the primary mode of segregation, classifying autistics according to the matrix of neurotypical models of valuation. To be "high functioning," as Tammet is said to be with respect to his language learning abilities, his facility with numbers, is to be capable of meeting neurotypical requirements for how existence counts. To be "low functioning" is to deviate from these criteria, usually due to struggling with self-regulation, being dependent, being incapable of speech. "Low functioning" always means less than human. Tammet is considered both. His visualizations of pi include him in the "high-functioning" category, while his supermarket fiascos make him "low functioning." The savantism adds a complication: autistic savantism is not really about intelligence. The synesthetic feat as evaluated in the literature is less about cognitive ability than some trick of precognitive visioning, which is held in lower regard than the more reasoned work of calculation. In the end, Tammet, despite an ability to create landscapes of shapes for the almost infinite recounting, is reduced to a kind of robotic simpleton: his feats are in excess of what he truly is, which is "autistic." To make this point, he is said to be "literal," code for having no imagination, no creativity, no vision (Baron-Cohen et al. 2007, 245).[10]

To accuse autistics of literality is to reduce the complex field of relation of autistic perception to distantist assumptions. It is to set the scene in advance and assume that the activity in germ is not colored by the dim massiveness of all that voluminously courses across it. It is to assume that what makes a difference can be held to what has already accrued value within the normative landscape of neurotypicality, of whiteness. It is to discount the teeming complexity of all that doesn't fit in the account of what counts.

The obsession with singling out the "low-functioning" tendencies in neurodiversity even in cases of "autistic savantism" serves to maintain the deficit model of sensation with respect to synesthesia. If we know that Tammet, despite his extraordinary mnemonic capacities, "doesn't notice if someone is upset," it will be easy to argue that he is unempathetic. If we read that Tammet "commits frequent faux pas," is "asocial," "avoids social situations and finds parties confusing," we are reinforced in our belief that there is no such thing as neurodiverse sociality. If what is foregrounded is that he is "obsessed," that "he has strict routines," what we conclude is that no matter how sensitive he is, there is no real latitude in his capacities. And if we read that he "showed severe tantrums at change of routine as a child," that he "showed head-banging in his cot" and "sat with fingers in his ears in primary school and with his eyes tight shut," we are persuaded that no matter how extraordinary his reciting of pi, he has nothing on us, the neurotypicals (Baron-Cohen et al. 2007, 245, 247).[11]

All of this is less about Tammet than about the presuppositions that accompany the imposition of the neurotypical norm on all experience, thereby generating and maintaining a distantist account. It is violent to hold a body to literality when it is actually bursting with complexity. It is violent to police the body-world boundary in order to maintain the well-worn habit of enforcing dominance in the name of the whiteness that always colors neurotypicality. It is violent to demonize those bodies that collapse under the strain of overstimulation while openly recognizing as valuable only those who can be reflected in the mirror of neurotypicality.

The criteria for inclusion into humanity are always neurotypical. Tammet functions just fine. He is neither "high functioning" as a savant nor "low functioning" in the rest of his life. Functioning labels, as anyone in the movement for neurodiversity will emphasize, say nothing at all except that neurotypicality is obsessed with categories that keep its ways of knowing at the forefront. To function, according to these labels, means to deploy movement, expression, sensation, in ways that "pass" for neurotypical: to take on a posture that does not announce too forcefully the sensory processing challenges that come with overstimulation, to be able to meet requirements for independence imposed by a belief in individualism above all, to be able to perform competence in ways that do not endanger the body schema of those for whom the template of neurotypicality has become second nature.

"Mindblindness"

For decades, Simon Baron-Cohen kept his research on autism and synesthesia separate: "I have studied both autism and synaesthesia for over 25 years and I had assumed that one had nothing to do with the other" (quoted in University of Cambridge 2013). What brought autism and synesthesia together in his research after all these years was curiosity about how "apoptosis" plays out in both conditions. Apoptosis, defined as "the natural pruning that occurs in early development, where we are programmed to lose many of our infant neural connections," seems to occur to a lesser extent in both autism and synesthesia (quoted in University of Cambridge 2013). This view would support the notion that synesthetes and autistics are neurologically more apt to connect to that vague essence of the world precategorized. One would expect such research to recognize that the qualitative richness that comes of attunement to voluminous experience would radically alter the account of autistics as literal, and by extension, unrelational, unempathetic, uncreative. But no.

Literality is always just one step away from uninvolved, "in a world of one's own," disconnected. Mindblind, in short. Simon Baron-Cohen is well known for his account of theory of mind, "the ability to attribute mental states—beliefs, intents, desires, pretending, knowledge etc.—to oneself and others and to understand that others have beliefs, desires, intentions, and perspectives that are different from one's own," and it is to mindblindness that he will once again turn to cement the deficit model in the bridging of autism and synesthesia.[12] The argument will be straightforward: "Our findings dispute the views that MT [mirror-touch] synaesthesia is linked with enhanced empathy" (Baron-Cohen et al. 2016).[13] Coming alive in the world of texture does not enhance autistics' ability to connect to the world, it turns out. In the 1 + 1 logic of interpersonality, autistics come up short. Distantism proves it. No matter the wealth of sense, autistics cannot sense the other.

When Baron-Cohen says that autistics cannot "understand that others have beliefs, desires, intentions and perspectives that are different from one's own," what he seems to not be able to comprehend is that his model of experience excludes those modes of relational feeling proper to neurodiversity. He simply cannot fathom a feeling-with that extends beyond the human and connects to all that edges into experience. He cannot recognize experience expanded from the normative interiority of a neurotypical body schema.

If theory of mind relies on being able to demonstrate the ability to recognize an experience not our own, it by necessity implies parsing something like self and other in advance. Similarly, to be empathetic is to be able to subtract from experience that which most closely conforms to what we already recognize as having value. My empathy for a situation depends on my being centered in it. To recognize you as other I must already recognize myself as a bounded individual. According to this logic, to be empathetic is to carry forward a power relation that acknowledges similarity and responds benevolently to it: empathy, the feeling-in of an interiority that recognizes itself in the other, thereby creating a measure of the self-same, is the neurotypical marker par excellence of exclusion of all that cannot be recognized as self.

An insistence on theory of mind retains empathy as the baseline for experience in order to maintain the account of interiority that keeps body and world separate. Empathy is here always connected to the Empathy Quotient, a measure for empathy Baron-Cohen developed with Sally Wheelwright based on the Karolinska Directed Emotional Faces Test. To be empathetic according to this test is to be able to connect to others according to the normative framework of facial expression. To frame empathy this way says it all: autistics are known to have prosopagnosia, or face blindness, to be deeply uncomfortable in the posture of the face-to-face, to shy away from eye contact and to engage with existence in excess of human centrality, their participation in the world more ecological than interpersonal. But even if it were otherwise, the Quotient says nothing about experience except that being able to mimic expression and categorize it is what is required to be included in the category of the human.[14]

Autistic perception refuses the distantist operations of neurotypical accounts of empathy. It feels-with the world in difference without separability, incapable of reducing experience to a common denominator. No preexisting points connect me to you. Indeed, you are still in the midst, coming to expression in the voluminousness of a reaching-toward that simply cannot be limited in advance to a form pre-composed.

The problem for neurotypicality is that feeling-with cannot be contained within the limited category of an Empathy Quotient. Leaky, the sympathetic encounter with what things do when they shape each other spills over. This synesthetic feeling-with cannot be measured precisely because it cannot be located in a body precontained. It is of the world. Its feeling-with shapes the conditions of experience in the very same gesture that it bodies. Neurodiverse sociality might be described as a sensitivity to this shaping, a commitment to how the shaping orients, unmoors, disturbs any idea of a body as self-enclosed. Voluminous, dim and massive.

Baron-Cohen deserves no more of our time. I turn to his work only because it is prevalent in the field and therefore affects the literature on both autism and synesthesia. To address the claims he makes, and then to move away from him, it is necessary to underscore the following: (1) All models that begin with a preconstituted body schema and make human interaction the marker for empathy are deeply erroneous. (2) Empathy is a humanist construct that privileges a human-centered account of importance that is always organized around preexisting norms. These norms are based on neurotypicality. (3) Synesthesia is never going to be a condition that can be adequately studied with an experimental method that begins with a neurotypical body schema. This is the case not only because the quantifications of sense that are the results of such studies are only the tip of the iceberg, but because all sensation occurs in complex overlaps. Sensing is not limited to sense presentation. All sensing is ultimately amodal, and amodal sensation can only be mapped topologically, if it can be mapped at all. To address sensation beyond distantism, new modes of expression will continuously have to be invented. With them will come new ways of knowing. (4) Autism tends to express itself not as lack of feeling, as Baron-Cohen argues, but as overfeeling, a feeling-with-the-world of such intensity that it is difficult to parse into the quotient scientists like Baron-Cohen use to measure humanity. I have defined this tendency of suprasensation or overfeeling as autistic perception, emphasizing that it exists on a continuum of neurodiversity but expresses itself most acutely in classical autism. As I have argued elsewhere, this intensity of feeling is relational to the core. It is alive with the more-than. We all stand to learn from a modality of feeling that is so ecstatically more-than human.

What Things Do When They Shape Each Other

    All things living and dead cry out to me
    when I touch them. The dog, gasping for air,
    is drowning in ecstasy, its neck shouting
    Dig in, dig in. Slam me, slam me,
    demands one door while another asks to remain
    open. My wife again asks me
    how did I know just where and how
    to caress her. I can be too eager to listen:
    The scar here on my thumb is a gift
    from a cracked bowl that begged to be broken.

              —John Lee Clark, "Clamor" in "Metatactile Knowledge"[15]

John Lee Clark, to my knowledge, has never been tested for synesthesia.[16] How could he be, when the neurotypical assumption around the sensing body automatically discounts a DeafBlind person from having mirror-touch synesthesia, or any other kind? What would there be to measure? Indeed, the neurotypical view of DeafBlindness suggests that there really is no life to be experienced without the senses of vision and hearing: "The loss of both sight and hearing constitutes one of the severest disabilities known to human beings. Essentially, it deprives an individual of the two primary senses through which we acquire awareness of and information about the world around us, and it drastically limits effective communication and freedom of movement, which are necessary for full and active participation in society" (Robert J. Smithdas, quoted in Clark 2017).[17]

And yet. What about the synesthesia so clearly felt in these lines? What of the strength of feeling-felt?

All things living and dead cry out to me
when I touch them. The dog, gasping for air,
is drowning in ecstasy, its neck shouting
Dig in, dig in. Slam me, slam me,
demands one door while another asks to remain
open. My wife again asks me
how did I know just where and how
to caress her. I can be too eager to listen:
The scar here on my thumb is a gift
from a cracked bowl that begged to be broken.

These words of Clark's are reminiscent of autistic Tito Mukhopadhyay's account of the mining tragedy in Raleigh County, West Virginia, in 2010.

It's true that when I think of the situation, there may be empathy. But my empathy would probably be towards the flashlight batteries of those trapped coal miners if there happens to be a selection on my part. Or my empathy would perhaps be toward the trapped air around those coal miners. There would be me watching through the eyes of the flashlight cell the utter hopelessness of those unfortunate miners as my last chemicals struggled to glow the faint bulb so that I didn't leave them dying in darkness. As the air around them, I would try to find a way to let myself squeeze every bit of oxygen I have to allow the doomed to breathe, for I am responsible for their doom. And while I found myself trapped, I would smell the burning rice being cooked with neglect in an earthen pot. (Mukhopadhyay 2010)

Clark's attunement to the cries of the dead meets the relational complex of the flashlight batteries in Mukhopadhyay, in both cases the voluminous feeling-with carried across. A touch is here foregrounded that carries the more-than of sense, its reaching-toward always in excess of the 1 + 1. If synesthesia is the making-felt of experience as emergent across a field of relation that is itself infrasensing, these are synesthetic experiences. This may be no surprise with respect to Mukhopadhyay, who has written extensively about his synesthesia.[18] But it might be a surprise that someone who can neither see nor hear sees-hears the world's touch. Listen again: "All things living and dead cry out to me / when I touch them," writes Clark. A hearing in a touch. "My wife again asks me / how did I know just where and how / to caress her." A seeing in a touch. And even more than that. A feeling toward a seeing-hearing touch.

Metatactile touch is both the touching of the hands-on feeling of the world and the incipient touch the world calls forth. It is both the being in the world of feeling and the feeling-with of the world emerging. In Mukhopadhyay we hear this through the personification of the oxygen, a personification that is not a making-human of the oxygen but a more-than human becoming-oxygen. Sympathy—feeling-with—is at work in the way things shape each other here. The becoming-oxygen cannot simply be reduced to the human it protects: the foregrounding of the molecules struggling to counter their disappearance, the effects of this disappearance on the environment, signals that everything is in interplay. What is heard in Mukhopadhyay's words is the urgent attunement to a relational complex infused with care. All at once, each level of experience overlaps, the incipiency of one affecting the coming-into-actualization of the other.

If mirror touch synesthesia is about feeling-with, both texts are examples of it, it seems to me, neither of which directly requires hands-on touch or vision. Why call it mirror-touch synesthesia, then? Building on research on mirror neurons—neurons that fire when an action is observed—the problem with mirror-touch synesthesia is that it seems incapable of imagining a world that begins with a feeling-with, a world that begins in the relational complex, in the body without an image.[19] As such, it carries the same implied bias of much work on mirror neurons, "that our perception is fundamentally a passive reception of an image constituting a private representation of the world, which, under normal conditions, is then cognitively corrected to purify it of illusions of perspective and other unthinking errors" (Massumi 2017a, 192). In addition, the assumption that we ever perceive along single sensory routes is deeply erroneous:

> What normally pass for mono-sense experiences are, in fact, cross-modal fusions presented in a dominant sense. For example, to see the shape and

texture of the object is to perceive, in vision, its potential feel in the hand. To feel that potential touch is to see the potential kinaesthetic experience of walking towards the object. . . . It is well known that object vision cannot develop without movement. . . . Every "single" sense experience is the envelopment in a dominant mode of appearance of an "infinitesimal" (virtual) continuation of other-sense experiences. Every perception is a composition of the full spectrum of experience, "practically" appearing as if it were disparate and disconnected from the continuum. (194)

Sensation is overlap, fold, complex. Recall James: "But inasmuch as all the sub-divisions are themselves sensations, and even the feeling of 'more' or 'less' is, where not itself a figure, at least a sensation of transition between two sensations of figure, it follows, for aught we can as yet see to the contrary, that *all spatial knowledge is sensational at bottom,* and that, as the sensations lie together in the unity of consciousness, no new material element whatever comes to them from a supra-sensible source" (1890, 152). No spatial order, no subdivision, no internal-external, no faculties. "Every perception is a composition of the full spectrum of experience, 'practically' appearing as if it were disparate and disconnected from the continuum." There is no distantism in the world's feel.

Inside the Gap

In his piece "My Dream House: Some Thoughts on a DeafBlind Space," Clark writes:

Now I'm going to discuss something very particular and perhaps difficult for non-DeafBlind people to fully grasp, so bear with me as I try to explain it. You know the saying "Out of sight, out of mind"? Well, for DeafBlind people everything that's out of sight remains in the mind's eye. We can relate to what Gauguin once said: "I shut my eyes in order to see." This is why DeafBlind vision is often better than eyesight—we know where everything is and see them through walls, through doors, through drawer doors, through anything in front or under or below them. They aren't hidden. The bad news is that we also see, or imagine that we see, everything that's behind the walls, under the fridge, inside the gap between the floor and the bottom of the cabinet under the sink. (Clark 2017b)

In the relational complex of existence, the gaps are never empty. It may be ironic to have to learn this from someone we might assume cannot see those infrathin interstices of existence. But feeling the world, as Clark's account makes clear, has nothing to do with either hearing or sight per se. Senses are not pre-defined in the world's coming to expression. DeafBlind vision is not held back by all we typically unsee in the seeing. DeafBlind vision is proprioceptively tactile, which is to say, topological. It is not restrained to the imposition of Cartesian perspective and to backgriddist maps.

DeafBlind vision's proprioceptive tactility comes of a long experience of attuning to the emergent relationality of a world continuously diagramming itself. Relieved of distantist straightlining, this quality of perception is enhanced as metatactility is honed. If proprioception is the "fold[ing] of tactility into the body, enveloping the skin's contact with the external world in a dimension of medium depth: between epidermis and viscera," proprioceptive tactility might be said to be sensitivity to the infrathin cleave of a middling that is neither quite body nor world (Massumi 2002, 59). For proprioception lives in a dimension that is "midway between stimulus and response, in a region where infolded tactile encounter meets externalizing response" (61). A fold in experience is produced at the interstice, DeafBlind vision the synesthetic quality of perception that touches the sensitive rhythm of layers of experience at their voluminous crease.

Massumi (2002) calls proprioception the body's sixth sense. Proprioceptive tactility works here, in that infrasensing region of orientation where multiplication of shapings confuse distantist maps. For in proprioception, "movement is no longer indexed to position. Rather, position emerges from movement, from a relation of movement to itself" (180). Connecting it to "'dead reckoning,' after the nautical term," Massumi speaks of proprioception as a "key element . . . in the homing pigeon's well-known feats of navigation" (180). Active in the cleave, "its elements are twists and turns, each of which is already defined relationally, or differentially (by the joint nature of the proprioceptors), before entering into relation with each other. That makes the relation entered into among elements a double differentiation. The elements fuse into a rhythm. The multiplicity of constituents fuses into a unity of movement . . . a self-varying monad of motion: a dynamic form figuring only vectors" (183). When distantism stops movement, it dampens DeafBlind vision, reducing what is felt to the measure of a set of abstract points. This backgridding "capsizes the relation between movement and position. . . . Static form is extracted from dynamic space, as a quantitative limitation of it. . . . Euclidean space, populated placidly by traditional geometric forms plottable into configurations" (183).

In the description of ProTactile living, a resolutely non-distantist proposition, Clark is not overly concerned with Euclidean geometries, however. Indeed, straight angles can be vital for DeafBlind vision and there is nothing like Euclidean space for producing edges and ledges:

Many times when I go out in the public someone would try to help me avoid hitting a wall or a ledge, not realizing it was my goal to find these things. Having my foot making contact with certain parts of my home is similar to this, and I would want my foot to hit the baseboard under the kitchen sink, or my legs pleasantly collide with the lower cabinet doors. If there was nothing there, then I'd have to hold out my hand to hit the counter . . . DeafBlind Space means you don't need to hold out your hands. It means you don't get hit in the shins or your vital organs get whammed because there was nothing to greet your foot first. It also means the place is friendly to shoulder-brushing and hip ricocheting, among other natural contact-making movements. Bumpability is an essential quality.

Euclidean space is simply no match for proprioceptive tactility. And in any case "the space of experience is really, literally, physically a topological hyperspace of transformation" (Massumi 2002, 184). This is what DeafBlind vision makes apparent: no space is *actually* distantist. Space is made in the moving. This is of course not to say that architecture isn't replete with ableist configurations that backgrid space, or that certain adjustments wouldn't make a real difference. It is simply to emphasize that proprioceptive tactility foregrounds how space is always bumpably more-than the measure of its Euclidean construction.

Clark's dream house builds on both these concerns—the honing of proprioceptive tactility and the necessity for affordances that make navigation easier for daily DeafBlind living. Fewer corners would definitely be helpful, but not fewer protuberances.

A constant and very real thorn in the side, though, is the corner. Corners of all kinds are a threat. Homes and workplaces harbor veritable armies of corners. Wall corners, table corners, partition corners, corners of cabinets, corners of opened drawers, corners of railings . . . Speaking broadly, corners are necessary. I love inside corners. The problem is when an outside corner or edge is square and sharp. In DeafBlind Space, then, all of these would be rounded, all around. Turn a hallway and feel the wall curve around. Lean on a table and feel a convex pressure against your chest. Sit on the edge of the same table, and it's like sitting on someone's lap. Remember that we want to hit everything. It is crucial that what we hit is flat or blunt. (Clark 2017b)

In the moving, Clark treats Euclidean space *as* topological, culling from the geometric environment those affordances that most facilitate the topological mode of proprioceptive tactility. Rounded edges, curved walls, DeafBlind vision transversally topologizes the limitations of the Euclidean. Topological perception queers Euclidean angularity.

Topology is "self-varying deformation" (Massumi 2002, 134). From rounded corner to curved wall, the field of relation opens up to its variability, inviting proprioceptive tactility to transform distantist chunks into processes. The edge of a table becomes a lap. A leaning turns convex. "Only infolding and unfolding: self-referential transformation" (135). Non-Euclidean topologies appear not as oppositions to the Euclidean architecture but as potentialized affordances cutting across it, dynamically produced in the relational complex. For the synesthetic force of metatactile sensing is always an intensifier of the surrounds, amplifying their potential to vary.

Propositions for living-out the topological potential of proprioceptive tactility emerge in this interplay of the Euclidean and the topological. Shades of non-ableist feeling-with are foregrounded. Stomping is encouraged: "It would be awesome if I could also stomp on the floor and get certain signals relayed to everyone else in my home." Signs are distributed in ways that make the environment felt in the midst, a vibration read as a participation in conviviality. The dream house is fitted for contact, alive with resonance. "Vibrating pads or plates as part of the flooring" give rooms a singular quality, pulsating the relational complex. That rounded corner was already a transducer for increased comfort. Everything now is tuned to metatactility, bumps the sign of a procedural architecture mobile in the sensing: "Tactically positioned constructed procedures" orient action. And, from there, "procedures naturally compound" (Arakawa and Gins 2002, 56).

Topological voluminousness is indexed in dead reckoning. The all-at-once feel of a pigeoning-in is how so much of the lived dailyness is experienced. Clark gives us an example of this:

> Every morning, I had this routine that included reaching for the knob of a bathroom drawer. My fingers always landed on that knob without my ever looking for it. Pure autopilot. On this morning, however, I was made aware of something because, though my hand landed on the knob like always, it did so at a slightly different angle. Thinking about it for a second, I realized that I'd forgotten to put the rug back on the floor after washing it and hanging it to dry the previous day. So the rug had played a role in my daily morning routine, but only a tiny role. If it had a bigger role, maybe I would've fumbled around a bit. Instead, its absence from its usual place on the floor hardly changed anything. Indeed, I've gone for that knob and

hit it while holding a water bottle in one hand, or while consciously avoiding brushing my shoulders against the walls when they had fresh paint on them, or while talking with one of my sons and walking there at the same time. (Clark 2017b)

In the bathroom, the knob simply appears in Clark's hand. So habitual is it that only when the angle shifts does Clark recognize that something has changed. The carpet is missing, the angle on bodying altered by the choreography of the relational complex. Without the carpet, proprioceptive tactility is skewed. Tempting as it may be to turn to the volition-intentionality-agency triad to explain the shift in position, this would only return us to the stilling of a standing apart. What is really happening is much more interesting. In the topology of variation, the relational matrix facilitated by proprioceptive judgment—a felt-indexing of an emergent environment—is altered. Bodying still occurs, of course, but it is oriented otherwise, the feel shifted by the nonconscious experience of feeling the ground uncarpeted. Feet adjust accordingly, the angle of entry shaped differently by the homogeneity of the new surface. The adjustment is minute. After all, the knob is still reached. But in the infrathin yet still voluminousness fielding of shadings of feel, everything has changed.

Proprioceptive tactility is synesthetically at work to shift the quality of the environment. This mode of feeling-with is neurodiverse, attuned to worlds in the fielding and wary of chunked presuppositions, architectural as well as environmental. I am not saying that DeafBlind folks are neurodiverse in the sense of neurologically divergent. Some may well be, but I wouldn't want to generalize across a heterogeneous population. What I am saying is that their lived experience of the relational complex of topological spacetime makes them squarely nonneurotypical. In approximation of proximity, DeafBlindness is on the continuum of the refrain, heard across these pages, that all black life is neurodiverse life. As mentioned in the preface, it is time, perhaps, to think of another term that carries the force of the nonneurotypical without including the "neuro" as the marker of its difference. Because even autistics, who are most definitely neurodivergent, are diverse in an infinity of ways that expand from the neurological. This is why I use the adjective *neurodiverse*—to remind us that we need a concept for a diversity in diversity that isn't measured by the standard of typicality. A diversity in diversity is one that senses fully and differentially, that lives and participates in a world still defining itself according to measures not yet in place. It includes populations historically excluded from the matrix of the human. It includes modes of life-living that exceed the human, that feel the more-than human world not as other but as with, in the being of relation.

Four Hands

In the mid-2000s, a group of DeafBlind activists began to invent and share a mode of communication that would allow them to field experience differently. They called this new ethos ProTactile. ProTactile brings into action modes of listening and speaking that best address the singularity of DeafBlind experience. It grows out of the strong belief that separating language from culture is both detrimental and impossible. Grown from within a long and rich culture of heterogeneous modalities of expression, ProTactile is a call for the DeafBlind community to reject distantism and embrace metatactility as a collective agencement of enunciation.

ProTactile emphasizes the importance for communication of a direct perception of relation, encouraging DeafBlind people and anyone who communicates with them to engage in continuous physical touch. "When people use their eyes for seeing, that causes them to feel. When people use their ears for hearing, that causes them to feel. Most DeafBlind people have been missing out on feeling because we've been so focused on [language], and that's all. But there's this whole environment around us—a whole world—and we can't feel it. So that's why [the ProTactile movement] is so important and why it has to include ways for us to feel things again. . . . We need more stimuli for our bodies to interpret" (Adrijana in Edwards 2015).

Continued contact in conversation through touch allows DeafBlind folks to finally become autonomous in their communication. Including language's extra- and infralinguistic aspects opens DeafBlind communication to what is missing in the adoption for DeafBlind experience of tools that were created for the Deaf: ProTactile recognizes that sign language in and of itself leaves much unseen and unheard.[20]

> ASL is a visual language that happens to be partly tactilely accessible. Before ProTactile came along, we didn't realize this fully, but tactile reception of ASL is similar to lipreading. Lipreading is watching an English speaker's mouth. Spoken English is an auditory language that is partly visible. It is a whole lot less visible than ASL is tactile, so maybe you could say that only 20 percent of English speech from the mouth is visible, making lipreading very very very difficult, and maybe, just a wild guess here, 60 percent of ASL is accessible via touch, making tactile reception okay, not great, but it could be practical, it could do. You still miss quite a lot, facial expressions, non-manual markers, and a lot of the spatial stuff wouldn't make sense tactilely. (Clark, email communication, August 20, 2019)

ProTactile is not simply a system of signs. ProTactile is as much a linguistic as a cultural movement in its recognition that DeafBlind communication can no longer participate in distantist habits of having other people fill in the gaps of what is missed in the conversing.[21] ProTactile is a living exploration of how continuous, active interplay shifts the contours of expression. As Terra Edward notes, novel modes of expression are being invented (2015). These new modes are being crafted in the speculative pragmatics of exploring what else a linguistic system can be for folks whose modes of communication have always been predicated on flexibility:

The traditional DeafBlind community was, and still largely is, made up of people I've found it sometimes helpful to call omnivorous. Since nothing in the corporeal world is our own—no language of our own, and there is such strong distantism out there—we'd borrow or use anything. Any language, any materials. None of which worked very well anyway. Except the virtual networks we established—that worked the best.

Sometimes in the past, two generations and earlier, some DeafBlind people would gather because there was a special opportunity. Or a few lived in the same city. Those who spoke ASL did tend to sit together so they could talk, those who were oral would sit together, and so on, but at the center were always some Braille typewriters and they'd type up a storm and pass around notes and conversations, which everyone read. So the two talking in ASL would stop to read, type, pass along, or maybe one of them would walk around to the note's writer and fingerspell "So funny!" and thump their back before walking back to resume the conversation in ASL. So there were always several things going on at once, intersecting with one another, in those rare opportunities to be together in person. (Clark, email conversation, December 15, 2019)

ProTactile feeds on this omnivorous tendency, intent on bringing complexity of approach to language in the making. Clark provides an example of how ProTactile language is born in a collective agencement of enunciation:

Yesterday I was reading more of *The Minor Gesture* in the car for the twins' and my ride to a burger place before shopping for groceries. At one point I swooned over what you'd written, and the boys felt that and asked, "What's blowing your mind away there?" "It's a book a friend wrote, called *The Minor Gesture*. I just love it!" "What's the minor gesture, what is it about?" "Well . . . it's hard to explain . . ." "C'mon, tell us!"

So I launch into a ProTactile lecture about the minor gesture. I was awed by the lecture itself, by what came out in the ProTactile language, for how it would describe some of the concepts, what it would use to represent the concepts. And I learned from that. More about the minor gesture itself. I suppose if it was translated back into English it would be quite different than the original, but the spirit of the thinking would be the same, just expressed and manifested a bit differently.

And the ProTactile words that got invented on the spot have now entered our family lexicon. Later that evening, Azel said "That's like the minor gesture . . ." in reaction to an Avengers movie. This morning feminism was mentioned, and Armand used the new ProTactile words to discuss that some. I love the word that means "the minor gesture." How about that? No word yet for Marxism or for postcolonialism or any of these things, but the minor gesture, it is now in the ProTactile dictionary! (email conversation, August 21, 2019)

ProTactile is a living proprioceptive environment attuned to all that is heard in the infrathin expressions of metatactility. As such, it exposes the potential metamorphosis in each event, opening language to what lurks in the expressive quality of its prearticulations. In the conversation with Clark's sons, the minor gesture is conceptualized linguistically because it is needed to contribute to a conversation collectively in the making. This is always how language works, but with the mediation of intervenors, the middling of collective enunciation would be backgrounded. With ProTactile, the force of what a concept can do to create worlds is directly experienced, producing lived interstices of sense across linguistic and extralinguistic paradigms. The minor gesture as concept collectively crafted for emergent sociality of linguistic expression becomes a pass-word—a mode of passage—in this speaking-across. It becomes a concept for free indirect passage that carries thinking across registers infraoperational (Deleuze and Guattari 1987, 110). Signs as they manifest bump into each other to produce modes of thought as yet unexpressible. All that is on the edge of activity becomes voluminously felt in the agencement of collective expression. For potential is everywhere at work in the infralinguistic prearticulation. Incipient modes of thought are lively in the metatactility of protoexpressibility. But this shouldn't lead us to assume that language is a translation of thought somehow hidden until it is enunciated. Quite the opposite: signs bumping into each other produce a polyvocality that shifts both registers, amplifying at once the incipient prearticulations of the beneath of language *and* the actual articulations of language as produced in the interplay, metatactility transforming linguistic modalities of collective passage.

A comment of Clark's on his own writing practice makes apparent that thinking is never transposed directly into writing in any case.

I don't experience thought as a language at all. . . . I may have an idea for a poem, and it would gestate in my mind, and it would have features, contours, even "facts"—like it is about something in particular. I may wonder if I should have a twist at the end. This poem idea in my head is a thing, it is tangible, it has some form. But no actual words yet.

Then comes the burst, or it spills over, maybe the idea itself is pressuring its way out, insisting on coming out. When I begin to write, immediately I realize all sorts of things about it I didn't know before. So many decisions are made at that moment, or maybe, it's possible, those decisions were somehow pre-made or half-already-suggested. And I'd write it down on the page, feeling as if I don't know what will be next yet still directing it somehow. How do I know where to go when I don't really know what's next? Maybe it is an unfolding, an unrolling? A ribbon being rolled out? (email conversation, December 24, 2019)

The words pressure themselves into a shaping that pulses thinking into act. No sense here of before and after: all that is thought is in the moving, writing itself into a thinking renewed. ProTactile builds on this quality of expression, alive with decisions made on the fly, touches become pass-words for fields of composition as yet uncharted. A world is touching itself into act, signs forming themselves in the acrossness of an interplay of tongues and practices.

A sign refers to another sign, into which it passes and which carries it into still other signs. "To the point that it returns in a circular fashion . . ." Not only do signs form an infinite network, but the network of signs is infinitely circular. The statement survives its object, the name survives its owner. Whether it passes into other signs or is kept in reserve for a time, the sign survives both its state of things and its signified. . . . A hint of the eternal return. There is a whole regime of roving, floating statements, suspended names, signs lying in wait to return and be propelled by the chain. (Deleuze and Guattari 1987, 113)

"We want to emphasize that PT is not a set list of symbols with associated meanings, like 'touch signals,'" Jelica Nuccio, the cofounder of ProTactile, explains. ProTactile is a linguistic-cultural paradigm, and an ethos. "ProTactile philosophy is not just about 'accessing' communication; it affects all areas of life, including DeafBlind culture, politics, empowerment and language" (ProTactile 2016). In a refusal to be pared down to an exchange of signs, ProTactile revels in demonstrating the range of regimes of signs—"'presignifying,' 'signifying,' 'countersignifying,' 'postsignifying'" (Deleuze and Guattari 1987, 140).

Topological in their capacity for variability, signs are "defined by variables that are internal to enunciation but remain irreducible to linguistic categories" (140). Signs are agencements—assemblages of enunciation—actively changed in the sociality of a four-handed encounter. ProTactile is always more and less than a language.

ProTactile is an excess on itself of signifying systems. Fed by the infinite expressibility of metatactile resonances shaped over lifetimes of DeafBlind vision, ProTactile is "superlinear," catching language in its derouting of the point to point line (Deleuze and Guattari 1987, 140). Metatactility makes this detouring of sign singularly possible, attuned as it is to the more-than of touch and its capacity to catch worlds in the making.

While touch has always played an important role in DeafBlind culture, and much communication already moves through touch, there is a long history within DeafBlind culture of mediating the world in distantist ways through intervenors whose job it is to be the ears and eyes, thereby maintaining distantist practices: "We can see in the record how distantism set in, and how hearing and sighted people wanted things to look right. It didn't look good when we went around 'groping in the dark.' It didn't look good for us to cluster together and have too much fun. Education meant we had to sit behind a desk" (Clark 2017a). Proprioceptive tactility was shunned in these coded encounters with the world. The result: "tactile freeze," the condition of tactile withholding as a result of DeafBlind children having their hands slapped for touching too much (Clark 2014). With the mediation of the intervenor as driver of DeafBlind experience, only distantist touch was ultimately considered appropriate. "When we go exploring or when we just exist, sighted and hearing people rush in to intervene. Can they help us? Please don't touch. They will be happy to describe it to us. They will guide us. No, they will get it for us. It's much easier that way. Hello! My name is Katie and I'm your Intervenor!" (Clark 2017a). It's high time for the DeafBlind to be teaching the DeafBlind, the movement asserts, and for the DeafBlind to converse without the mediation of intervenors.[22]

ProTactile shifted everything. For the first time, it became possible for Deaf-Blind folks to talk together without mediation and to feel, in the collective moving, the infralinguistic at work. With four hands a minimum, conversation takes the shape of a collective interplay. "One thing about Protactile language is that it cannot be spoken alone. Literally, physically. Linguistically, four hands are required, your body is required as receiver" (Clark, personal communication, August 17, 2019). Relational complex: worlds composed in the metatactile bodying. In the round, the conversation shapes not only the topic at hand, but a revolutionary new quality of DeafBlind experience.

Clark describes how it works: "For the same story . . . you would use *my* arm as the tree, and your other hand would be the axe moving against *my* arm. My other hand feels your hand—the axe—while your other hand is holding my arm and my arm feels the axe moving against it. You do not move your axe-hand against your own arm as you would in ASL. My arm here in PT, representing the tree, it is what we call a proprioceptive object" (email communication, August 20, 2019). Through "dynamic depth perception," meaning moves across proprioceptive tactility to produce a bodying that expresses (email communication, August 20, 2019). In ProTactile, the body is crafted in the speaking, its bodying *how* language is made. "Tactile is surface, one-sided perception. I can feel the ASL version, but only on the surface of it. Protactile is dynamic depth perception, where, for instance, I do not only feel your axe-hand from one side as it moves toward my arm, I also feel it from the other side, because my arm receives the blow. What's more, your other hand holding my arm that's the tree, your hand there is also giving me precise information for how the tree reacts to this blow" (email communication, August 20, 2019).

The speaking is in the moving. Arm-axe-tree, a story is crafted in the bodying. The topological quality of spacetime flows through each utterance. There is no standing still, let alone standing apart. In *Where I Stand*, Clark writes:

As a DeafBlind person, standing for me is almost never about being still or in one place. Waiting for a bus, I would move without realizing it. My way of standing by moving around gives me more information about where I am. I'm taking in the scene, being present in the world, and prodding things a bit, exploring. And when two DeafBlind people talk to each other while standing, they always move around so that, after a while, they're standing where the other person was. Later on, they'd be back to their former positions, having circled around each other. This phenomenon is the result of each person shifting to the left to listen to the other person tactilely in a more comfortable way, hand following hand at a certain angle. I would always find myself emerging from an engrossing conversation standing in a different place. (Clark 2014, loc. 116–20 of 2094)

Movement gives experience shape. Speaking about the primacy of movement in experience, Daniel Stern writes:

Dynamic changes . . . occur constantly. Our respirations rise and fall over a cycle that repeats every three or four seconds. Our bodies are in almost constant motion: we move our mouth, twitch, touch our face, make small adjustments in head position and orientation, alter our facial expression, shift the direction of our gaze, adjust the muscular tone of our body position, whether standing, sitting, or lying (if awake). These processes go on even when not visible from the outside. Gestures and larger acts unfold in time. They change fluidly once an act has started. We can be conscious of any of this, or it can remain in peripheral awareness. In addition, with every movement there is proprioception, conscious or not. (2010, 9)

How to well the chaos? "How do we not implode into the intensity, lost in the infinite virtual folds of potential experience?" Massumi asks. His answer: "Through movement. Every movement makes a cut—it brings certain elements of experience into relief, origamiing the continuum on the fly" (2017a, 199). Movement is primary: it is through movement that incipient sensation catches the world's tendencies and moves into them, altering them in the passage. Metatactile modes of touching put the dynamic shape back into DeafBlind communication.

ProTactile *immediates* experience.[23] The intervener-as-mediator no longer has a role to play. In the moving, there is no 1+1. What occurs in the encounter of infralinguistic metatactile communication can never be reduced to two enclosed, preconstituted selves, one active, one passive. The consent not to be a single being, Édouard Glissant's resonant words, is a call to a voluminousness that honors the more-than of sense. Not distantist, but not proximist either. In the field of minor sociality where relational bodies compose with the force of the incipiency of a touching beyond touch, ProTactile proposes a reaching-toward that touches the being of relation.

ticcingflapping

Hindering Progress

    Digging through ghostly shards
    pummeling the words that shout from within
    understanding too much,
    the vice grip of constant anxiety
    offers the spoken words access that no one can fully know.

    I fight to voice what I mean,
    but "Mindy" and "Rebecca" crash through
    and grab the microphone from my hand
    that finds tenuous comfort in the string
    I wrap around and around like a carousel.

—Emma Zurcher-Long, "Hindering Progress"

The question of voice in autism is an intricate one. "Let's pretend you are like me. You can't talk, but you . . . can understand people. Imagine you answer everyone who says something to you, but only you can hear it. Others hear your voice saying things you don't necessarily mean. They think that's all you are capable of thinking" (Reyes 2015). Philip Reyes, like many classical autistics, cannot say what he wants to say with speech.[1] Instead, he dances language, making expression felt in ways silenced by neurotypicality—a lilt in the voicing, a jumping, a hum, a shriek, a tug, a turning away. To form words, he uses a keyboard or a simple letter board. In this voicing, stims and tics cut through what is usually understood as communication, seen as disruptions to a halting word-after-word account of language. "People see your repetitive flapping or tapping and they think it serves no purpose. They don't understand that the minute you stop, the moment is flooded with lights that hum, loud sounds that echo, kids moving too fast for you to keep up with and people trying to engage with you" (Reyes 2015).

Estee Klar 2019

Replete with what may seem like vigorous interruptions to the flow of communication, the coming-into-expression of autistic voicing does not happen *despite* the body's participation. Language *includes* the ticcing and flapping and tapping. Autistic voicing is no less communicative because it moves, or because it doesn't use the human voice to express itself. It is, arguably, *more* communicative: deeply attentive to nuanced shifts, attuned to the ecologies of a world inframodally sensed, its engagement with the world could be said to be more energized, more engaged, not less, precisely because it does not subtract movement from expression. Communication, expressive of all that asignifyingly moves across it, resonates with the force of undercommon ways of cawing. Attuned to the movement of thought in the bodying, the pulse of nonsonorous forces of language in the making can be keenly felt, opening language to what it can most exquisitely do when it is not held to a body "standing apart."[2] That said, the requirement that autistics parse expression into the one-after-the-other words of language remains, especially if they want to be considered to be thinking beings. Neurotypical ways of centering knowledge linguistically require that autistics learn to tame the exuberant body. This closing in on complexity is violent in every regard, limiting autistics' potential to express beyond the stranglehold of neurotypical models of personhood. Autistic Adam Wolfond explains, "I need people to accept my movements and the fact that I don't talk but use a device and I need good support that makes my movement easier to control. I think that my movement is supported always by a lot of patience and landing my rhythm. Landing rhythm feels like a touch of loving hand on my back for nailing my thoughts to the wall of sense."[3] Emphasizing the need for modes of facilitation—the touch on the back, the encouragement to keep a body in the vicinity of a keyboard—Wolfond reclaims language as relational practice, resisting the way individualist communication reduces language to words, thereby subtracting expression from the welter of sensation.[4] Wolfond's appeal is not so much against the role words can play in expression as it is committed to articulating how much is overlooked when we restrict language to words. Using the keyboard as the only viable means to making himself understood comes at a high cost. Not only does it cement the dominant view that to make ourselves understood we must always use words, treating autistics who do not have access to speech as less than, it overlooks the extraordinary effort writing requires of autistics. To write is to focus all the exuberant energy onto one form of subtracted expression, funneling the excess into a line. This gargantuan task exhausts the body, reducing its capacity to engage in other ways. The vicious cycle plays out this way: to defend themselves against the claim that intelligence can only properly be demonstrated through the written word, autistics perform neurotypicality by limiting their native tongues to the most subtracted forms of expression.[5] This in turn reinforces their sense that the ways their bodies move is a problem—"I need people to accept my movements"— leaving them demoralized. In the demoralized state, more normative modes of communication are longed for, further reducing expression to the point to point.

Melanie Yergeau (2018) calls autism's exuberant expressivity queer rhetoric. Queer rhetoric is not limited to the words on the page. It is not held back by neurotypical expectation that sense and sensation be disentangled. A voice that queers rhetoric is a voice that speaks in the moving, composing with the vicissitudes of mobile resonances and their attendant rhythms. It is a voice that speaks haltingly at times, intercepting stims in the making, composing with tics and eruptions of affect too vivid for the body not to yield to, a voice alive with the staccato of interruption. All that queers expression, all that moves asignifyingly through it, bending duration and intensity by introducing new rhythms and amplifying the movement that runs through them, *is* the vividness of language. This is what the ticcingflapping pocket practice aims to make felt. For communication that halts, that tics and stims and taps, is most often seen as no communication at all. In Wolfond's words:

> I am anxious that answers are always in talking and I want to be a lot of the time like other kids and to eagerly belong but I can't do what other kids do like talking and fast landing moments of movement. I am different and I have a lot to answer open amazing opportunities for change but I am wanting to always talk so I can tell people that I am having a really rough time and I am wanting to good people say that I am talking about the way they are towards me and I have a lot to say about the way autistic people are treated as though we are bothering them.[6]

The ticcingflapping pocket practice is not only about autistic voice, however. Led by the words of classical autistics, autism here orients the question of what else language can do, but what is at stake is much broader. The question of how language is stultified by neurotypical framings is really what ticcingflapping is about. Ticcingflapping is an urgent call to leave openings for neurodiversity in language and to hear modes of communication that voice beyond speech and its distantist presuppositions. Ticcingflapping as pocket practice is an appeal to see how else we come into expressive relation, and how vividly moving bodies participate in what we too often exclude from sense.

The writing in the moving, the voicing in the typing that includes repetitive ticcing, joyful flapping, that is composed with the ebullience of a body jumping out of a chair between words, says in its own singular way what moves through thought and does so with an acute sense of urgency, composing with a deeply incisive sense of what the world could be if there were space for listening to what else language can do. This is true of all autistic communication I've come into contact with: that it has no time for small talk, that there is urgency in the desire to attend to what else is moving through expression, that there is something deeply at stake in learning to listen to how the more-than of language expresses that which does not conform to neurotypicality's hold on experience.

Imagine the threat to standard notions of rhetoric! This is Yergeau's project in *Authoring Autism*: to demonstrate not only how autistic voice disrupts neurotypical assumptions around rhetoric, how autism queers rhetoric, but also to make felt how autistic voice creates its own rhetoric through modes of writing that embolden language, making heard what language often leaves unsaid.

So-called experts have long questioned autistics' capacity for narrative. Autistic autobiographies have been accused of "'lacking narrative structure,' . . . 'lacking rhetorical facility and audience awareness,' and . . . 'lacking self-reflection'" (Brown and Klein 2011; Brown 2012; Goldman 2008, in Yergeau 2018, 7). Ralph James Savarese takes aim at these approaches that radically underestimate the force of autistic writing. In the afterword to autistic Tito Mukhopadhyay's *Plankton Dreams*, he argues that neurotypicals "cannot imagine letting autism be— letting it exist as a natural human variation, one that might need nurturing and help at times but that has value in and of itself. . . . If one thing is clear, neurotypicals struggle to understand forms of being very different from our own. [They] cannot imagine taking Mukhopadhyay seriously as a writer" (2015, 84).

Yergeau suggests that one of the roadblocks to autistics being allowed to speak for themselves—and be recognized as rhetors—is that "autism is medically construed as a series of involuntarities—of thought, mode, action, and being . . . involuntarity dominates much of the discourse on autism, underlying clinical understandings of affect, intention, and socially appropriate response . . . Because involuntarity stretches across clinical and popular domains, it is often used in service of denying the narrative capabilities—and the narrative value—of autistic people" (2018, 7). To have something to say, one must be able to say it "voluntarily," speaking as a preconstituted subject excised from the tumult of experience in the making. "Beyond the illusion of choice, autism's essence, if you will, has been clinically identified as a disorder that prevents individuals from exercising free will and precludes them from accessing self-knowledge and knowledge of human others" (8). From here it follows that autistics cannot in fact speak "for themselves."[7]

There is simply no question that autistics speak for themselves. Contrary to the kinds of statements made above, ticcingflapping sees autistic voicing in a register altogether different from the straightjacketing of the voluntary-involuntary binary. Autistic voicing forces a recalibration of all we neurotypically assume language is made of. For autistic voicing is not only a form of expression deeply committed to an attunement to the relational fields that compose experience, it is absolutely key to realigning what matters in expression more broadly. To compose with worlds in the making requires an attunement to autistic voicing! The consideration of all that moves, of all that expresses, as heard in autistic voicing, makes felt in the most visceral way how modes of existence more-than human are relationally entwined with all we have come to know as "ours," the neurotypical (white) hold on language desperate in its ongoing attempt to silence all that moves in excess of its limited expression.

Autistic voicing makes felt how autistics are not only intensely attuned to what goes on around them but also aware of how this aroundness includes them without making them the center of experience. More than most, theirs is an ecological perspective that, while it includes the human, doesn't see the world as simply made up of human intentionalities. This lack of self-centering is heard in writing that moves with the force of the world, composing the entry into experience through language's own synesthetic rhythms.

> Green mimicking green.
> Brightness of sun spreading
> upon brightness of trees,
> their mixing up the green, spreading
> one green upon another green
> as green mimicked green.
> Leaf spreading itself on leaves, displaying
> its green. And hundred other leaves
> all mimicking that green, as if believing
> no one could want anything
> from the sunshine, but green.
> So green mimicked green.[8]

Mukhopadhyay's rhythmic writing moves at the pace of a greening that touches everything in its midst. Pan-experiential in its tendency, Mukhopadhyay's poetry opts for a sensitivity toward the kinds of more-than human attunement Nathan Snaza (2019) calls *animate literacy*.

> The branches of the tree
> looked like a confused idea.
> It was as if they had nothing
> substantial to agree upon,

now that their leaves were gone.

So they hung as a jumbled mesh
arguing their right or wrong
confused through light or shade
their branches slender and long
about those leaves that were gone.[9]

In writing the world making itself, in orienting toward experience with the force of a ticcingflapping, autistic voicing makes felt the primacy of ecology, of the being of relation, bringing to the fore the nonconscious share of experience in the making.

To characterize autistic expression as involuntary is to succumb to a value judgment on the place of volition in experience. No act is ever completely voluntary or involuntary. Volition is on a spectrum with nonvolition. Living happens on that spectrum: experience overtakes us, moves (through) us. Volition is the backgriddist operation that makes sense of acts in retrospect. This is how we reassure ourselves that the world is ours to direct, and own. As I have discussed elsewhere, this neurotypical (white) account of how experience unfolds says very little about experience, and much more about the need to control it.[10] How we move is always directly entwined with how we are moved. Autistics suffer deeply from these backgriddist presuppositions. Unlike bodies more neurotypically oriented, the delay between being moved and moving is often very perceptible among autistics, which leads to the feeling that the body is refusing to follow directions.

> So, you ask, what can you free people do to help? First, ignore my involuntary gestures, including my signs for "done" and "break." They fearfully hear years of negative fear and try to keep me locked into a cycle of autonomic impulses. Remember these gestures are not voluntary. They are just my body's way of responding to stimuli. If you respond to them as meaningful, they fearfully rev my heart more, but if you wait patiently and wordlessly, you free me to finally respond voluntarily. Once I've freed my body to respond, I can skip over the autonomic responses and give faster motor replies as the conversation continues. (Savarese, DJ 2010)

In this account, DJ Savarese begs us to be patient with those aspects of expression he feels he can't control. It feels extremely stressful that the ecology of experience refuses to background itself, that everything is teeming to be included. As subtraction is by nature difficult for autistics, and temporality is here reduced to the neurotypical communicational norm, the body seems inadequate to the task. "Done" and "break" are not what DJ Savarese wants to say. And so he pleads with us not to take account of these tics. And he has a point. After all, they aren't what he means. But aren't they also, to a degree, what needs to be said? Don't we need to hear that the body is overstimulated, the environment too thick with resonance? "Freeing" the body to speak makes the back-and-forth of a more typical kind of conversation possible, but is it really the only way? Is this not an imposition on neurodiversity of neurotypical modes of expression? What if the body didn't need to subtract this way? Would we still consider its relation to all that (over)stimulates it a sign of involuntarity? Would we hear expression differently?

This is not to minimize the anxiety that comes with needing to "fit in." To speak, after all, is to be included in the category of the human. Neurotypical modes of existence are systemically foregrounded, and value is made here, and policed. Nonetheless, it seems vital to recognize that involuntary is raised as a problem for autistics *in the context of communicating in modes neurotypical*. The frustration with this vicious circle is palpable in their accounts. "And as the sensory involvement gets wrapped up into the 'accessory otherness' of the social situations with my 'tangent' attention, my mind getting sucked into its cesspool, it begins to lose track of the actual words the voice is saying with all earnestness 'at' me or 'to' me and I realize I am failing to take in any of them" (Mukhopadhyay).[11] Many autistics speak of the pain of failing to meet the markers of neurotypical exchange. They emphasize that there are challenges that come with autistic perception—that despite the openness onto the world of direct perception and the joys that brings, not being able to parse quickly enough (or at all) can be debilitating. But, like DJ Savarese's plea that we exclude the excess of communication from what we hear, this is usually a frustration oriented by the expectation that difference will not be accommodated. "Understand that I am a language specialist and I think . . . amazing lots of time people think I can't understand them and I think all the time about having to prove it" (Wolfond).[12] Were we more flexible in relation to neurodiverse expressivity this wouldn't be such an issue, and there would be more opportunity to celebrate the nonvoluntary share of experience that allows autistics to be so acutely capable of sensing what has not yet quite passed into consciousness. For the share of nonvoluntary experience that runs through autistic perception is precisely what allows autistics to be so moved by the world. As autistic Daniel McConnell writes, "My heart is so full that it feels like it could burst open at any time day or night. Sometimes I worry it is too full and if it gets any fuller I will just implode, it is a heavy heart that loves this world too much. . . . It is the heart of a man who is all love but who knows that there is no room for such a heart in this world" (2015, 15).

This is the lesson autistic voicing teaches in the telling, in the writing: that composition requires the force of the nonvoluntary. It requires that we allow ourselves *to be moved.* To place the voluntary and the nonvoluntary in opposition is to create a false dichotomy: what moves language is the force of rhythm, the asignifying sounds that amplify nonsonorous forces, the prearticulation beneath the words, the gestures unfolding and held back that make language stumble and sense differently, the sounds of ecologies that words cannot quite capture, except in their capacity to evoke the more-than as articulated in the palimpsest of their affective enunciation Language moves at the pace of the world, not the preconstituted subject.

This is the double bind of rhetoric. On the one hand, autistic voicing does not have value because it is not seen as voluntary. Echolalia, its extreme form of body-world resonance, is defined as "meaningless repetition" by most quick-search dictionaries. In the *Oxford English Dictionary* "meaningless" is supplanted by the more innocuous "automatic."[13] Intentionality again. The utterance must be willed by a preconstituted subject who sees himself as fully in control of language. This full control over language is the condition through which a contribution to knowledge is confirmed. Yet, think of John Lee Clark's account of how writing produces a movement of thought that he follows, led by the force of what needs to be said, pulled by the limit of thought where words can only barely do the work voicing demands (see chapter 7).

The nonvoluntary moves writing. It allows the movement of thought to be felt, amplifying that quality expression that escapes the I. Rhetoric depends on this quality of the not-quite-me. It depends on the force of voicing that takes us over and moves us beyond ourselves as preconstituted subjects. It is in the nonvoluntary, in the nonsuppression of the tics and flaps and taps, in the excitement of an echolalic utterance that tics us into proximity not only with its (non)sense but with the quality of its lure, that the force of movement-moving in the voicing lurks. Writing writes us.

When Yergeau writes, "Involuntarity, I would argue, is not an inherent part of autism as a condition. It is a story that structures and mediates autistic people's experiences of the world, but it is not an essential property in the way clinicians or fundraisers might relate it" (2018, 9), what she is underscoring is that the nonvoluntary has been coopted by a pathologization that devalues its force, making the involuntarity the burden autistics carry, a burden that cements the belief that they can't measure up. This is a political act from a society that cannot see the vitality of the nonvoluntary in expression. Neurotypicality is deeply threatened by the power of the nonvolitional in experience: a focus on the primacy of the nonvolitional breaks down the volition-intentionality-agency triad that claims to direct and control experience.

The (non)sense of the nonvoluntary is both its power and its threat: it reveals that there is more to expression than the limited account of what we intentionally frame as meaningful. Our focus on volition keeps us from the too-much of sense, making understanding the motivator of legibility. For this is what neurotypicality most fears: not knowing. Not to be able to situate an utterance, not to know where language begins and ends, not to understand what has priority in the making of sense, not to be able to read a body's voicing—all of these threaten the framings of normopathic valuation. To deviate from normopathy is to tread in the territory of a pragmatics of the useless. The representation of the useful is a much safer place to dwell, its parameters always defined in advance. "I have stimmy hands, hands that wave, and flap, and tussle rubber bands—hands that create and transform space as they occupy it. My hands story and proclaim, denounce and congratulate. My hands say both *fuck you* and *thank you*. Sometimes I am the only person who knows what my hands are meaning. Sometimes even I don't know what my hands mean—but why must I cherish or privilege meaning? Description cannot contain my hands" (Yergeau 2018, 13). Sense will always escape us precisely because it is not ours alone to make.

Involuntarity imposed as a diagnostic criterion onto the autistic body normalizes movement, denying the force of rhythms that are disorderly, untranslatable. Excluding the nonvoluntary share of language in the moving from experience more broadly, casting away the complexity that is at the heart of *all* movement, the pathologizing of the autistic body as involuntary situates autistics as always lacking, their bodies unmanageable and unruly, their voice arhetorical. Movement has to be controlled in order for language to be claimed as knowledge production, the neurotypical always the baseline.

What if we started elsewhere and suggested instead that it is *because* of the share of nonvoluntary experience lived at the edge of consciousness that the neurodiverse so easily move between worlds, parsed and unparsed, between the calm of the stim in the storm of the world. What if we could listen to the exuberance of that body and hear the excitement of a voice that can finally say, gestures included, what it really feels? What if we marked a difference between the imposition of the *category* of the involuntary and the *mode* of the nonvoluntary, beginning not with a deficit model but instead exploring how the nonvoluntary as mode of existence collaborates with the forces that voice through us? What if we took seriously that our neurotypical belief that movement should be stilled (pay attention!) undermines the very force of what movement is? What if we emphasized that placing meaning in the agential category of the intentional, making speech and individual will inextricable, is *misaligned to the complexities of expression*, which always move in registers incapable of being completely contained by the will of a preconstituted subject? What if we followed Friedrich Nietzsche and suggested that will is not something we have but something that moves us into a worlding, activating the force of a composition we only briefly call "I"?

The chasm between the neurotypical assumption that will belongs to a pre-constituted subject and the reality of how language moves in nonvolitional bursts and tics and stims that animate a literacy yet to be invented creates complicated untranslatabilities. "The alienation of those on the spectrum is an alienation of translation, a failure of translation," writes autistic Anthony Easton. "Can we talk about an autistic grammar of the body? Shallow breathing, the sounds that emerge from language without being language, the 'stimming' (the classical, re-petitive motions that occur in moments of stress, or closeness, or comfort)—these have grammars of their own, which cannot easily be translated" (2013, 98, 100). Bodies moving "in the gap between what is said and what is understood to be said" are bodies moving at the interstice where the nonvoluntary squeaks and eruptions compose with language's most potent expressibility (101). Language's poetry lives here.

Language's poetry is echoed in what Lawrence Ferlinghetti calls the "fourth person singular" (in Deleuze 1990b, 103). In the fourth person singular, expres-sion is impersonalized. What speaks is not the person but the event. "It rains." The impersonal is not without exuberance. To the contrary, lively with all the variations that transversalize it, the impersonal carries what infrathinly moves at that limit where the conscious and the nonconscious co-compose. (Non)sense is made here, cut through with all the minor forces that tune it to what exceeds the stability of understanding's grid. To speak of the tremulous between of sense and nonsense is never to produce a binary. (Non)sense is the force through which language expresses what else runs through it and what else moves it into articu-lation. When Wolfond writes of the relation between water and language, of the ways in which water allows language to flow, he is voicing that crossing. Though the "I" is retained here in the play with water, it is the water-event that creates the conditions for thought, for language. Water is the conduit for language's ex-cess over the personal. With water, rhythms emerge that open the field of expres-sion to a parsing that is capable of carrying the movements of autistic perception. Water is the opening onto relation too often backgrounded in the subtraction demanded by communication.

> I want to water play and think about how I am always very interested in the way it looks. Water is about flowing with time. Water is really beautiful to watch and I move it around with my hands and the amazing light plays the water like music. I am sound-listening and I felt that I was understanding

the way talking and feeling water is the want of relation, feeling with the calm way of water flowing. The water needs my thought, I need water and sound to calm. Understanding that is a way to question why autistic people are critically looked at in a way that is negative. . . . Talking is the way sound moves the way I am hearing. I am thinking that the rhythm of sound is like talking. Question is about rhythm and the way I am with the water.[14]

Autistic voicing foregrounds the eventness of sense as the irreducibility of all that moves excessively through it. Liquid, sense is invented in the voicing, heard in the asymmetries of ecologies accosting. Freely indirect, sense is alive with the synesthetic tremors of infra-alliances of all that moves through it. Language can never be reduced to words: it is as much what moves in the fluid space of water flowing as the surfacing of linguistic articulation.

Water for Wolfond functions as the force of activation not of individual will but of relational interplay. Autistic voicing must not be reduced to the actual words: it is all of it, the hand moving through the water, the colorful bath toys, the activation of time through rays of light moving on the water's surface, the quality of sound synesthetically felt through the flow that pulls the body into expression.[15] Water makes the funneling of expression possible, allowing the rhythms of the world to coalesce more easily with the rhythms of language in its incipiency.

The nonvoluntary share composing with experience in the making is what we hear in Wolfond's water-words. In undercurrents we also hear a plea to listen with the silences and the tics and the splash. What we hear is this: a will to power, the mobile force of a power emergent in the telling, in the uneasiness of a neurodiverse voicing. Not an individual power but a total state in the moving, a power determining its-self in the writing: "Every thought, every feeling, every will is not born of one particular drive but of a total state, a whole surface of the whole consciousness, and results from how the power of *all* the drives that constitute us is fixed at that moment" (Nietzsche 2003, 60, 1 [61]). The force of the not-yet in the moving that pierces through the assumptions of neurotypicality queers not just the nomenclature of will but the very foundations on which the voluntary, the intentional, the agential subject is based. "If I have anything of a unity within me, it certainly doesn't lie in the conscious 'I' and in feeling, willing, thinking, but somewhere else: in the sustaining, appropriating, expelling, watchful prudence of my whole organism, of which my conscious self is only a tool" (Nietzsche 2003, 2, 34 [46]).

"Autism . . . poses a kind of neuroqueer threat to normalcy, to society's very essence," writes Yergeau (2018, 27). "Autistic people persist and insist in the narrativity of their tics, their stims, their echoed words and phrases, their relations with objects and environs. We persist in involuting, in politicizing the supposedly involuntary. We can't help it, after all" (23–24). Language is out of hand, autistic voicing upending the frame neurotypicality works so hard to impose on it. "Instead of the small and tightly contained essay—what happens if everything known pours out?" (Easton 2013, 99). Too loud, too noisy, too rhythmical, too wet, too wild.

Ticcingflapping as pocket practice leads us here, where language can no longer be contained and where voicing moves beyond the frame of neurotypicality. Across his many books, the first written before he was a teenager, Mukhopadhyay has honed this uncontainment. *Plankton Dreams* (2015) is his most recent experiment in holding back what might otherwise pour out. At eighty-seven pages, the book is short, its sections concise, each one a few paragraphs. But to read it as though the writing were only on the page would be to miss the force of its neuroqueer rhetoric, which everywhere escapes the page and the written word. This is a big book, loud and unruly and uneasy making, its voice magnified across the words both written and left unsaid.

Mukhopadhyay begins with an introduction that sets up the experiment. This book, he tells us, should be read as a kind of anthropological first contact with neurotypicality from the perspective of a special education classroom. "I am calling this book *What I Learned in Special-Ed* because I did learn things in special education—not what I was supposed to learn but important things all the same. Although I had other ways of studying history, physics, and mathematics—Mother never waited for schools to educate me but instead assumed this role herself—I still wondered how a structured learning environment treated its charges. I got my taste in America" (2015, 7).

Daily humiliated in a classroom far below his intellectual capacities, autistic Mukhopadhyay decides that what is available to him is to chart how neurotypicality is mobilized in special education. "I created my own learning goals, which in turn created some very interesting situations. I analyzed the responses of people to these situations—what I call my social experiments. Why shouldn't the autist study the neurotypical?" (9).

Plankton Dreams takes off from here, courting the neurotypical (and being defeated by neurotypicality at every turn) but always also doing much more. For while *Plankton Dreams* is a study in humiliation and the truest expression of the boredom of special education for those who should be in an inclusive classroom, it is even more so, or more emphatically, a rhetorical feat. This is a book of prose-poetry that defies category, propelled by its circumstances, but in no way held back by them.

Mukhopadhyay's experiments mostly involve creating techniques to explore the limits of neurotypical patience. In the chapter entitled "Heads," the experiment involves touching heads to see how they react. Autistics have had their heads touched too much, Mukhopadhyay implies: it's time to turn the tables. It doesn't go very well. After touching the bus attendant's head, she "jumped to her feet. She even looked at me with an I-can't-believe-you-actually-did-that! sort of look. I found her head cooler than my hand, but I needed one more trial before attaching a label. . . . Humanity may not see the value of this project now, but one day it will" (11).

Alongside Mukhopadhyay's experiments on neurotypicality are glimpses of complex worldings, worlds Mukhopadhyay fabulates to distract him from the slog of the everyday. Forced to remain in the classroom, a worksheet in front of him that he is studiously not filling out, Mukhopadhyay writes, "From the cloud where I sat, I couldn't really see the koala in his natural habitat. I wanted to be part of his world, not simply its observer. I wanted, like the wind, to make something happen. (I was too often an observer or the mere recipient of action). But my options were limited: blow the scent of eucalyptus from Australia to Africa or get up from my chair. The zebras needed a break from olfactory banality— who wants to smell grass for the rest of their life?—but getting up from my chair seemed easier" (18).

Neurotypicality is worth studying but really only as a distraction from the much more compelling vantage point of autism's own expressive world. "I'd wondered that morning—what if my body exchanged places with my shadow? What if I lacked substance and depth? What would my life be like, darkening the lit-up world with my flat, shadowy shape? Would I be ignored, as shadows are ignored, or would my new shadowy presence allow the world, for the first time in history, to take all shadows seriously?" (23). Shadows, it turns out, are as ignored as Mukhopadhyay feared they would be. "No one prominent pays attention to shadows," he confirms as the day comes to a close (25). And yet he continues to weave shadowy modes of existence that ripple through the boredom of the classroom: more so than in the classroom, Mukhopadhyay dwells in the fissures of fabulations, fabulations that demonstrate the quirkiness of his imagination, his intelligence, and his humor. These are not simply alternate worlds; they are necessary worlds, created in the autistic voicing.

Mukhopadhyay's worlds are intercessors into neurotypical rhetoric as much as they are alternatives to the blandness of the special education classroom. "For my part," writes Yergeau, "I want a rhetoric that tics, a rhetoric that stims, a rhetoric that faux pas, a rhetoric that averts eye contact" (2018, 31). Mukhopadhyay's is such a rhetoric, a rhetoric that pushes against the limits of neurotypical assumptions at every turn, reminding the reader that one of the things autistics do best is make felt the more-than that echoes in the everyday, the more-than that neurotypicality most often misses. These echoes, which are pan-experiential in their reach, challenge neurotypicality's humanism, amplifying the ecologies that compose us. "Whenever I see a rolling pencil, I begin to engage in its movement to such an extent that I become the pencil. The more I roll, the more I lose track of myself" (Mukhopadhyay 2015, 30). This voicing that uses language to "[try] to make out a watery word that forms and deforms" (34), a voicing reminiscent of Wolfond's plea to listen to the rhythms of water-words, is a language that curiously takes the time to explore, in words and beyond words, how the world isn't simply the sum of its parts.

That the world isn't just the sum of its precategorized parts is something many autistics emphasize: autistics can feel the more-than of experience in the making. "Because I take in a perpetual blizzard of detail and do not instinctively think in categories, the world seems much more new and complex than it does to non-autistic people" (DJ Savarese 2019, 90). Autistic perception doesn't simply take things at face value—it engages with the edges of perception in the forming. Mukhopadhyay explains, "Neurotypicals move too fast to notice anything—the shadow of a falling leaf or the smell of wet grass or the ripple on the lake where Mr. B reads to me" (2015, 34). Neurotypicality is so busy with categories, separating objects from subjects and hierarchizing identity over multiplicity, that it just can't see beyond the face of preimposed value. Puzzle-piece vision is what Mukhopadhyay calls this queer vision that interrupts the categorization or defies it altogether. "Sometimes I turn my eyes toward the countless feet that are walking or jogging on the trail around the lake. Some feet move slowly; others, not so slowly. They all have chasing shadows. My vision disassembles the picture. Pieces of lake and feet lie piled in confusion" (34).

The threat to neurotypicality is that all of this might count as knowledge. The threat is that the world might actually be this way, be this perceptually rich, this perceptually disordered, and that neurotypicality might keep us from seeing it.

In echo of "me lo dijo un pajarito," Mukhopadhyay again: "If I had a choice, I'd be some kind of plant—floating algae, say. It has no obligation to remain in one place" (2015, 81). Plankton dreams are always double-edged, however. On the one hand, in its moving, the plankton offers another existence (one that sadly, in Mukhopadhyay's current telling, involves being eaten by the duck, from whose gastrointestinal pathways Tito must emerge to follow Mr. B's instructions). On the other, it displays the limits of a world framed and policed by neurotypicality: "Occasionally, I was distracted by Mr. B's voice talking to me in the language of human beings, which failed to be translated into duck language. . . . Maybe he said that it was time for lunch. Maybe he said that I needed to stand farther from the water. Maybe he said that I should do this or do that. Or maybe he counted the minutes aloud or perhaps the hours. Who knows? Maybe he even recited duck poetry. I wouldn't know because none of his words were translated into duck language. I stood on the threshold of human civilisation and duck expectation—my heart pounding with iron-like savagery" (82).

Translation isn't really possible. It's not that the language of autism is too hard—many languages can be mastered, even those with radically different roots. What's impossible, or what feels impossible, is bridging the distance between the valuations, the distance created by the neurotypicality whose definition of difference just doesn't reach the untidy complexity of the neuroqueer, of a minor sociality thick with the being of relation. This is what I hear in the approximation of proximity "all black life is neurodiverse life," that (non)sense is hampered most by the imposition onto sense of the executive, as Moten might say, the executive not only of "executive function" but of all those hierarchical presuppositions that constrain what else could be heard in the voicing of difference. For neurotypicality is always whiteness. Autistic DJ Savarese says it best, describing a concert in the chapel he attended as a student at Oberlin College: "I remember getting out of my pew to dance—to the horror of most of the people around me. The music had commandeered my nerves, and I needed to thrash, needed to flap like a wet bird with my arms. Before I knew it, two black women in their 50s joined me, even taking my hands—their smiles were as wide as the Mississippi at Cairo (the place where Jim and Huck missed their turn). That night, when I went walking across campus, there was, as Thoreau would say, 'so much more air and sunshine in [my] thoughts'" (2019, 9?)

Autistic voicing is a dancing, a living, wildly unruly, the words, the movements, always at the limit of what can be categorized, framed, understood. How to even begin to translate this puzzle whose pieces will always be too many? "The problem with this idea of excess—and autistics often want to tell you everything—is that it depends on the listener to care, to not be bored, to be able to delineate. The care does not translate. It becomes another isolating failure" (Easton 2013, 99). To wade into the world of plankton dreams, to watch for shadows and explore the force of their relational field, this is beyond reach, often not even on the radar at all. "At the lake I had an epiphany," Mukhopadhyay writes.

There is a pristine world above the water and a murky, reflected one below. There is the typical domain of typical beings who aren't doubted or tested repeatedly, and who have a real place in education, work and decision making. And then there is the "special" domain of "special" beings, where

all is shadow, formless and wobbling, and hope itself lies sodden and sub-
merged. The ducks, as social as fowl can be, dismiss their own reflections.
Who needs illusory wings? Standing there, watching the ripples on the
surface of the lake, I learned the biggest lesson of all: nothing will create
substance out of shadows. (2015, 83)

Mukhopadhyay speaks from experience, from a life lived in classrooms where
the educators may mean well but don't presume competence often enough.[16]
Neurotypicality is the order of the day in all classrooms, including those of special education. Whiteness looms, and with it a logic of either-or that can understand sense and (non)sense only as opposites, categorizing always to the detriment of those approximations that open the world to its diversity in diversity. In
the approximation of proximity of "all black life is neurodiverse life," we hear the
what else coursing across the minor sociality of autistic voicings, the fabulatory
force of a thinking in movement that brings to life an art of living that refuses
the strictures of whiteness that sit so comfortably at the heart of neurotypicality.
Because whiteness in its colonial imperative is always about hierarchies of meaning and categories of sense. Whiteness is the executive, the deep-seated belief in
the truth of the one-after-the-other elocutions of an impoverished linearity of
time charted. Whiteness must live here lest it come face-to-face with the vastness of what else moves beyond its impoverished account of the human as the
purveyor of the solitary I that speaks in his name.

Thankfully, the special-education classroom in the end was not capable of
dominating the autistic voicing heard in Mukhopadhyay's words, and this is
worth mentioning. So many autistics have made and continue to make their
voices heard, despite the terrible conditions that devalue their neuroqueer
modes of existence. In Mukhopadhyay's case, the shadow, despite normative re-
strictions, accompanies the everyday, enlivening it, and in the accompaniment,
in its movement through the creases of neurotypical life, it does alter what existence can do. The shadow queers the surface of existence. The shadow spooks the
norm, turning neurotypical experience on itself. The shadow follows and haunts,
but it also leads and orients, inventing more-than human worlds. For that's the
strange thing about shadows—theirs are as much the movements of the human
as they are the movements of the earth and its suns and moons.

Autism's stories, Yergeau suggests, are queer stories. With their neurodiversity, they beckon toward a life lived slightly out of sync because the autistic body
(the every-body, in fact), in its very force of bodying, can never truly be in sync
with its-self. The autistic plays with the nonvolitional limit where body, world,
and language co-compose, and while this limit is not an easy one to dwell in,

neurodiversity claims it. No autistic will say this is straightforward, or without deep challenges. But I think what many autistics would say is that they wouldn't trade their sensitivity to the world's wonders for the flatness of neurotypicality and its belief that knowledge can be claimed and tamed. Neurodiversity invents what voicing can be, using its puzzle vision to catch the pulse of worlds worth inventing, worlds worth shadowing.

Queer is not an identity for Yergeau; it is a mobility of expression. "I'd . . . suggest that autism is a neurologically queer motioning that is asocially perverse, a lurching toward a future that imagines 'incommensurabilities of desires and identities and socialities,' a ticcing toward rhetorical residues" (Yergeau 2018, 18–19, quoting Jonathan Alexander). Queer is the share of the nonvolitional coursing through the words. Neuroqueer is a rhetoric all its own that voices in the approximation of proximity of neurodiversity and black life's emphatic departure from the executive, a language in the co-composing of socialities in the making.

Autistic voicing is out of hand. It moves in the beyond of I, in the texture of water flowing, in the ticcingflapping heard best by earstonguesfingers that are awake to the synesthetic force of (non)sense. A ticcingflapping pocket practice is a cry to connect to the queering of all movement, to the nonvolitional in all experience, so that we, too, might be able to hear this writing at the limit, this writing beyond where language knows its place, this writing toward a time where the voice that speaks in the acrossness of experience in the making is finally heard.

Cephalopod Dreams

Finance at the Limit

Mischief and craft are plainly seen to be characteristics of this creature.
—Claudius Aelianus, third century AD

Capital fears the earth's procession. —Stefano Harney and Fred Moten, "Base Faith"

Schizz

Schizoanalysis is an alter-economic practice: its work is to unmoor the financial-ization of the individual as metric of preexisting value. The schizz cuts through the middle, neurodiverse in its call for the more-than. "No more normopaths!" it howls. How-else-with-and?

The schizz of the schizoanalytic practice must never be reindividualized by setting up the figure of the lone schizophrenic, or any figure, as its cipher. Contrary to some interpretations of *Anti-Oedipus*, nowhere do Gilles Deleuze and Félix Guattari idealize psychosis or schizophrenia. As everywhere in their philos-ophy, the aim is not to moralize but to couple the pragmatic with the speculative, asking how processes unfold and what immanent valuations run through them. The differentiation they make between schizophrenia as process and schizophre-nia as entity is vital in this regard. The schizophrenic entity "can only be defined in relation to the arrests, the continuations in the void, or the finalist illusions that repression imposes on the process itself" (Deleuze and Guattari 1983, 379). The schizophrenic process, or what they call the schizoid pole, refers to the man-ner in which desire invests itself in sociality. At the schizoid pole, knowledge schizophrenizes, passing beyond its own axiomatics, creating new operations. "Figureschizzes" are produced "that are no longer either figurative or structured" (371). These two operations, the schizophrenic entity and the schizophrenic pro-cess, are in continuous co-composition, the schizoid pole always also in proxim-ity with the threat of the pathological. Desire schizzes, uncoupling pathology from process. Desire, the impersonal force that activates socialities in germ, is the revolutionary activity through which new lifeways are produced, schizzing all the while.

What distinguishes the schizophrenic from the neurotic is psychosis. What is of interest to Deleuze and Guattari is that psychosis cannot be oedipalized.

> The neurotic is the one on whom the Oedipal imprints take, whereas the psychotic is the one incapable of being oedipalized, even and especially by psychoanalysis. The first task of the revolutionary . . . is to learn from the psychotic how to shake off the Oedipal yoke and the effects of power, in order to initiate a radical politics of desire freed from all beliefs. Such apolitics dissolves the mystifications of power through the kindling, on all levels, of anti-oedipal forces—the schizzes-flows-forces that escape coding, scramble the codes, and flee in all directions: orphans (no daddy-mommy-me), atheists (no beliefs), and nomads (no habits, no territories). (Mark Seem, in Deleuze and Guattari 1983, xxi)

The schizz must always be considered in terms of what it can do, not in terms of what it defines. It is from this vantage point that the figure of the schizophrenic must be understood in the account of capitalism and schizophrenia, with Oedipus always as the overdetermining pull to the neurotic replaying, in all pathologies, of what holds them to the narration of a preexisting structure. Oedipus should not be considered an actual formation, however. The Oedipus complex is a tendency in potentia: "it must be actualized in a neurotic formation as a derived effect of the actual factor" (Deleuze and Guattari 1983, 129). Psychosis schizzes Oedipus. This is why Freud disliked schizophrenics: "For we must not delude ourselves: Freud doesn't like schizophrenics. He doesn't like their resistance to being oedipalized, and tends to treat them more or less as animals. They mistake words for things, he says. They are apathetic, narcissistic, cut off from reality, incapable of achieving transference; they resemble philosophers— 'an undesirable resemblance'" (Deleuze and Guattari 1983, 23).[1] In schizzing the "neurotic territoriality of Oedipus," psychosis produces new circuits (136). There is no promise attached to these circuits. They could just as well fold back on themselves, returning to all the forms of neuroticization that reduce psychotics to the apparently unmoored, disjointed paranoid figure psychiatric institutions lock up. "Perhaps there is only one illness, neurosis, the Oedipal decay against which all the pathogenic interruptions of the process should be measured" (319).

In pushing up against what can be extracted from the schizophrenic experience that resists the neuroticization imposed on it, Deleuze and Guattari pursue the question that most troubled Jean Oury and was central to the work at the La Borde clinic: "How does one avoid the institution's re-forming an asylum structure, or constituting perverse and reformist artificial societies, or residual paternalistic or mothering pseudo families?" (319). What techniques can be put in place to schizz the institution's penchant for all that retriangulates?

Urgently necessary is the decoupling of experience from the pathological valuations of the deficit model. As in the wider field of neurodiversity, the aim is not cure but a commitment to the singular ways difference expresses itself and the qualities of desire, knowledge, and creation it produces. "A true politics of psychiatry, or antipsychiatry, would consist therefore in the following praxis: (1) undoing all the reterritorializations that transform madness into mental illness; (2) liberating the schizoid movement of deterritorialization in all the flows, in such a way that this characteristic can no longer qualify a particular residue as a flow of madness, but affects just as well the flows of labor and desire, of production, knowledge, and creation in their most profound tendency" (Deleuze and Guattari 1983, 321). Against normopathy, schizoanalysis never does its work from outside the event. Sensitive to the schizz, it moves with it, following its tendencies. "Foucault announced an age when madness would disappear, not because it would be lodged within the controlled space of mental illness ('great tepid aquariums'), but on the contrary because the exterior limit designated by madness would be overcome by means of other flows escaping control on all sides, and carrying us along" (321).

From this vantage point, schizophrenia shifts from entity to force, desiring-production its motor. "Like love: there is no specifically schizophrenic phenomenon or entity; schizophrenia is the universe of productive and reproductive desiring-machines" (5). There is no longer "a specific, identifiable schizophrenic entity" (6). What there is instead is a practice of the schizz that attunes to the multiplicity of "I, Antonin Artaud, am my son, my father, my mother, and myself" (15). Multiplicity in differential, the schizoid pole explodes the great tepid aquariums of our pathological imaginations. Beyond pathology, there are no criteria. "It might be said that the schizophrenic passes from one code to the other, that he deliberately scrambles all the codes, by quickly shifting from one to another, according to the questions asked him, never giving the same explanation from one day to the next, never invoking the same genealogy, never recording the same event in the same way" (15). Is this madness? Or is the psychosis to be found in the imposed adherence of systems on worlds too differential, too multiple to tame?

The schizophrenic is the limit case of existence that troubles our certainties as regards the stability of subjectivity. To repeat the mantra that drives chapter 5: "A schizoanalysis schizophrenizes in order to break the holds of power and institute research into a new collective subjectivity and a revolutionary healing of mankind. For we are sick, so sick, of our selves!" (Mark Seem, in Deleuze and Guattari 1983, xxi).[2]

Schizoanalysis is not a practice of the individual. It is not a practice of pathologization, of singling out the one whose neurology will invariably be considered a deficit. Schizoanalysis is a practice of the event where I, even schizo-I, is not yet.

That the schizophrenic refutes the limited envelope of the individual is certainly part of the story. But the work of schizoanalysis is not done on the body (of the schizophrenic) per se. The work is done *in the relation* where the phonic leaves its resonant traces. The schizz, the effect of the schizophrenizing of experience, cuts subjectivity as we know it, subjectivity as the claim to the human (the category that excludes the neurodiverse, and all qualities and forces of life-yet-to-be-invented that threaten the I as white, colonial, neurotypical being).

Capital

Capitalism breaks bodies, its devaluation of qualitative difference at the level of aesthetic sociality so complete that bodies barely hold up. Exhaustion, anxiety, depression, and all their offshoots are everywhere palpable. Capitalism breeds paranoia, the ground so uneven, our bearings so unsteady, that we fold into a self-possession that leaves no room for what exceeds us. Limited by the hardening of our edges, we become more enclosed in our-selves, less turned to an outside that would revivify the more-than that courses through us. This is what Deleuze and Guattari are referring to when they talk about how capitalism produces the neurotic, and, at the extreme, the "sick schizo" (1983, 362).

A schizoeconomics is committed to the schizzing of capitalism. Its challenge is to work in careful attunement to capital's own infinite appetite for circulation and deviation.[3] Flows, processes, detours are, after all, what capital is made of, its movements faster, more mad, and often more creative than we would like to admit. To compose with capital is to coincide with its movements to schizz the more-than that runs through them, connecting to the speculative share of its own decidedly more-than human process.

> The cutting edge of capitalism is in the financial markets, which have evolved forms of abstract capital so abstruse, contingent, and objectively undecidable that it is impossible to get an effective grip on them. They run according to their own process, and sometimes run away with themselves, periodically crashing and burning. The financialized economy is beyond the human pale: beyond full human comprehension and beyond effective

human control. It is a self-driving machine, operating more and more abstractly, with no one in particular at the steering wheel. It was created by the human, but not in its own image, emerging rather as a monstrous offspring that turns back to engulf its maker and drive away with it. (Massumi 2017c, 9)

To schizz capitalism is to develop an account of quality that can discern the difference between cuts that breed the count of assets, and cuts that revalue value. In its infinite capacity for deviation, capital is a powerful adversary. The aim of finance at the limit is always alter-capitalist, but it in no way purports that there is an outside of capital as we know it. To schizz capital is to watch another limb begin to grow elsewhere. Alter-capitalist futures will be built of more than the schizzing of capital: they will be led by the development of practices that exert the force of other ways of living in a logic that refuses the tenets that undergird capitalism—the relentless drive to quantitative increase, inexorable growth and inequality, the capture of life intensities for profit. Practicing the schizz begins there, in the midst, asking what kinds of techniques can be crafted for those other logics, logics that sidle, in approximation of proximity, an aesthetic sociality of blackness, experimenting with the minor that runs through a sociality born in the being of relation. This is to say that the practice of the schizz is never structural, never aimed at a totality, as though something as stable as capital-as-structure existed and could directly be taken down. The practice is transversal, operating in the circulation of flows themselves. This modest aim may seem useless. Indeed, it is: an ethos of the pragmatics of the useless runs through it. It claims nothing as regards grand schemes of productivity. Its proposition: to practice the art of life-living at the differential of minor socialities in a livingloving that angles toward the instauration of new modes of (merest) existence. Schizoeconomies will not come into themselves once and for all. They will always need to be (re)invented, at every turn bringing with themselves new techniques for practice unlimited.

Capital is crossed by lines of escape, and this is what finance at the limit exploits. "Capitalism is continually cutting off the circulation of flows, breaking them and deferring the break, but these same flows are continually overflowing, and intersecting one another according to schizzes that turn against capitalism and slash into it" (Deleuze and Guattari 1983, 376). Cleaving capitalism from within, the schizz produces social fields that may operate only for an instant, but nonetheless provoke the seeding of a different mode of investment, and with it different operations of value. Paranoia will always be around the corner, counting its coins, but as Saidiya Hartman's *Wayward Lives, Beautiful Experiments* demonstrates, minor practices of the art of life-living have always existed, even under the worst conditions: "The wild idea that animates this book is that young black women were radical thinkers who tirelessly imagined other ways to live and never failed to consider how the world might be otherwise" (2019, xv).

"The revolutionary investment of desire" schizzes worlds into otherwise-living (Deleuze and Guattari 1983, 378). Desiring-production is the force against which capitalism has no power: unquantifiable, in a logic of the relation of nonrelation, desire as force too impersonal to claim bends the pathways toward intensities for which no preexisting code, no count, exists. This is why the schizophrenic as conceptual persona is vital to the project of schizzing capital for Deleuze and Guattari: the schizoid pole is the pole of desiring-production and, as such, "is revolutionary, in the very sense that the paranoiac method is reactionary and fascist; and it is not these psychiatric categories, freed of all familialism, that will allow us to understand the politico-economic determinations, but exactly the opposite" (1983, 379–80). Revolutionary desire is a practice, not a tool. It does its work transversally, moving waywardly where we might least expect it. Writing of Mattie, a young laundress, Hartman culls from the anarchival force of the photographs that nourish her critical fabulation the force of what desire can do in the face of racial capital's devaluations:

> Mattie has been credited with nothing, deemed unfit for every role except servility, condemned in advance of wrongdoing, and destined to be a minor figure even in her own verified history. To esteem her acts, to regard rather than vilify Mattie's restive longing, is to embrace the anarchy—the complete program of disorder, the abiding desire to change the world, the tumult, upheaval, open rebellion—attributed to wayward girls. It is to attend to other forms of social life, which cannot be reduced to transgression or to nothing at all, and which emerge in the world marked by negation, but exceed it. (2019, 62)

Mobilizing the schizz, inventing schizoanalytic techniques for practices of the event, requires diligence as regards capital's (de)valuation of existence. Techniques must be invented to learn to attune to the difference between finance unlimited (neoliberal capital) and finance at the limit (schizoeconomy), to become sensitized to what sanctions the extreme deterritorialization of capital on one end of the spectrum and empowers the infrathin registering of the ineffable on the other.

Deleuze and Guattari speak of capitalism's process of production as unleashing "an awesome schizophrenic accumulation of energy or charge against which it brings all its vast powers of repression to bear, but which nonetheless continues to act as capitalism's limit" (1983, 34). Capitalism is a movement that skirts the limit, continuously coming up against the dangers of crossing the threshold: "it continually seeks to avoid reaching its limit while simultaneously tending toward that limit" (34). This is even more clearly the case today than when Deleuze and Guattari underscored it in the late 1960s. Neoliberal capital is the flow of all flows. As Brian Massumi writes: "The '*capitalist process*' is how the capitalist system dips into its own immanent outside to draw out new potentials for its becoming, or continuing self-constitution" (2018, 11).

How to invent platforms for schizoeconomic finance at the limit that do not simply facilitate capital's seemingly infinite capacity to capitalize on process for monetary gain? Precapitalist marginal economies may give us a clue. For their operations, unlike those of capital, are rich with emergent sociality. The notion of the penultimate is vital to understanding how limit and threshold are mobilized to engender the being of relation in these early economies. "Take two abstract groups, one of which (A) gives seeds and receives axes, while the other (B) does the opposite. What is the collective evaluation of the objects based on? It is based on the idea of the last objects received, or rather receivable, on each side" (Deleuze and Guattari 1987, 437). The receivability of the objects in the account above refers not to the last object received but to "the penultimate, the next to the last, in other words, the last one before the apparent exchange loses its appeal for the exchangers, or forces them to modify their respective assemblages, to enter another assemblage" (437). The seriality refers to the cycle the exchange produces. "The last as the object of a collective evaluation determines the value of the entire series. It marks the exact point at which the assemblage must reproduce itself, begin a new operation period or a new cycle, lodge itself on another territory, and beyond which the assemblage could not continue as such. This is indeed a next-to-the-last, a penultimate, since it comes before the ultimate" (438). The ultimate changes the assemblage and, with that change, produces a new series. The limit is here understood as "marking a necessary rebeginning," while the threshold marks "an inevitable change" (438). "What counts is the existence of a spontaneous marginal criteria and marginalist evaluation determining the value of the entire series" (438).

In the marginal economy, exchange creates the conditions for an encounter that, each time anew, establishes an emergent valuation. "There is neither exchange value nor use value but rather an evaluation of the last by both parties (a calculation of the risk involved in crossing the limit), an anticipation-evaluation that takes into account the ritual character as well as the utilitarian, the serial character as well as the exchangist" (439). The immanent limit sets the stage for "a collective feeling out" that cannot be done in advance of the event (439). Both sides are altered not only by the actual exchange but by their collective retuning to the limit. What has been "exchanged" is more than an object. A sociality has been invented that accompanies the object, supplementing it with the allure of the event through which it came to value. The economic cannot be reduced to the exchange itself. It is a platform for relation that facilitates a process of collective feeling-out that intuitively responds to the intensifying approach of the penultimate. Deviations in the process will cause punctual redirection, but an immanent choreography is in place to assist the process in not tipping into a new assemblage.

The potency of the penultimate is the sociality it carries through the system. Consider an argument between a couple. No matter how angry they are, the couple will argue with a collective feeling-out of a limit, intuitively aware that to cross the limit might very well untether the bonds that hold the relationship together. The argument might sidle that limit, but the couple will be careful not to allow the threshold to be breached. They will do this by holding back certain thoughts, by attuning to the texture not only of what is said but how it is said, listening for what might crack their collective carapace, exposing them to what they cannot bear to hear. If they do cross that limit, everything will be up for re-negotiation, and their relationship might end. The penultimate is of course never precisely knowable in advance—it is best known in retrospect from the perspective of the ultimate (after the assemblage has tipped into a new one). Attending to the penultimate means being sensitive to the field of relation in composition.

Holding the process to the internal texture of its schizz is a way of attuning to the quality of a limit, collectively composing the relation in relation. When the schizz does the work of attending to the penultimate, what it does is value the pulse of duration's serial rhythm as minor sociality. An exchange happens but it is not here that the value is located. The value is operative in the collective feeling-out that attends to the event's composition. This can look like nothing. It can look like a simple exchange between seeds and axes. But it's much more than that: it is the staying-with of the complexity of a seriality lived not as a transaction but as a proposition for life-living itself.

Practicing the schizz toward alter-economic postcapitalist futures is a commitment to the quality of sociality highlighted in Deleuze and Guattari's account of marginalist economies and sidelined by contemporary capitalism's way of tending toward the limit. For capital too, as mentioned above, flirts with the limit, pulling back before it goes over the threshold. The difference is that capitalism remakes itself through quantification, in the generation of profit. What is being collectively affirmed in the marginalist economies is a mode of existence. When there is a pull back from the limit, it reflects a collective desire to remain within a field of relation. In capitalism at the limit, quantification runs wild.

When there is a push to the limit, the qualitative stakes are masked by the quantitative drive. This has devastating effects whose runoffs create a deviation of limit conditions that become capital's new field of creative potential, the limits reset within the bounds of its own domain. This can be seen in the cyclic crises through which capitalism lurches, catching itself each time before it tips over (up to now).

Schizoeconomics attunes to the quality of sociality in the collective feeling-out of aneconomic fields of relation where finance at the limit revalues value.

Cut

The schizz cuts. A cut reactivates a field of experience, tuning it to new frequencies. The question is, what is the difference between a limit-cut and a threshold-cut? The difference has to do with the more-than of exchange outlined above. A limit-cut attunes to the conditions of the process by feeling-out the process's own limit. This attunement is a folding-through that is social in the sense that it is collectively attentive to the penultimate, to that which precedes the tipping into a new assemblage. A threshold-cut tips the process into a new assemblage by going straight for the ultimate. Everything is rejigged in the threshold-cut. While the more-than also accompanies the threshold-cut, the intensity of the collective feeling-out is less palpable since the process is reforming and, in so doing, creating new modalities of existence.

Contemporary capital's excess, the way it carries its limit, involves not the production of sociality but the release of volatility. "Market makers pronounce their actions as making liquidity for the markets, but the process of liquidity making is the staging of uncertainty and the constitutive act of releasing volatility" (Wosnitzer 2016, 255). The release of volatility is done in an atmosphere of uncertainty, in the logic of the derivative.[4] This is an uncertainty that unmoors any sense of emergent sociality, focused solely on the punctual transaction and its yield for the individual parties involved. In this logic, what is moved through the trade is speculation itself.[5] When the market is spoken of as a "sociotechnical grid," what is being foregrounded is a form of the social completely tuned to profit (Wosnitzer 2016, 255). In this account of the social, everything moves toward the potential for quantification. The derivative is the speculative motor of this quantification. Capital's excess trades on the speculative potential of this motor, the surplus-value of flow of the market its driving force.[6] This surplus-value of flow—which includes the market's own volatility—is not itself quantified. It is that quantification overcodes the more-than. With this overcoding comes a generalized belief that value itself can be quantified.

There is little vocabulary in finance for that which accompanies the trade but is not the measure of it. With finance at the limit, the focus turns to the more-than and the ways in which it resists value-as-measure. Attuning to the process of financialization in neoliberal capital, it asks what escapes the force of the market's subsumption of the excess and its affirmation of emergent sociality.

The time of the trade is an ideal site for a consideration of the imbrication of the speculative and the quantitative in capital's surplus-value of flow. The trade of derivatives happens in a time-without-time. The no-time of the trade—the emergent valuation that occurs in the split second of decision that moves value into tradability (and thus quantifiability)—is a time of invention: it is the very invention of time (as value). "Through the dynamic delta-hedging and the anxiety that it generates (Will I execute it right? When to rebalance it, etc.), the market-maker penetrated the market. He penetrated its volatility and he could now feel it in his guts. In a word, he became a dynamic trader. He now understood—not conceptually, but through his senses, through his body—the inexorability of time's decay, the pains and joys of convexity" (Ayache 2008, 36–37).

In the time-of-no-time of the trade, what come together are currents of the past (valuations that have had effects on the market) and futurities (the potential of capitalist value-creation). These futurities are composed of qualities: hunches, gut feelings, intuition. Pastness and futurity schizz into decision. This decision is a cut that alters the field. It is not a cut made from outside the process: the decisional cut at one and the same time values and quantifies. Capital plays the more-than exclusively to tune it to count. Unregistering the more-than, back-grounding its immanent valuation in the name of quantification, it (dis)counts it, subsumes it, (de)values it.[7]

The more-than that composes life-living, that creates the force of an aesthetic sociality of blackness, can never quite be counted, however. Something always resists, troubling the count. In the afterlife of slavery, it is "the object" of capital that resists, the objectification of the body into the exploitable labor-form, the "body-object" understood as that which is (un)counted in the count. "This becoming-object of the object, this resistance of the object . . . is the activation of an exteriority that is out from the outside" (Moten 2017, 33). Blackness resists by refusing finance unlimited, by refusing to limit its force of bodying to capital's logic. Out from the outside, blackness tunes toward black life, "toward the life we locate and imagine when the materiality of the subprime cuts the sublime by grounding its excess in the anarchic, historical materiality of our fleshly sociality" (Moten 2013b, 244). "At the convergence of the surplus . . . and the aesthetic," black life schizzes the very terms of oppression that work to maintain impoverished accounts of subjects and objects over a poetics of relation (Moten 2017, 35–36).

When the "object" resists, it is the break that sounds. The break schizzes the field. This cut is aesthetic: it touches the limit at its most sensitive nerve, crossing the threshold into a new assemblage. Touch at the limit does not seek to rehabilitate the object. There is no rehabilitation of a social field that has reduced itself to the violent interpersonality of whiteness. Returning to the logic of whiteness only cements what is already dead. Black life moves in another logic entirely, a logic "at the convergence of the surplus and the aesthetic" that is anagrammatical, "blackness anew, blackness as a/temporal, in and out of place and time putting pressure on meaning and that against which meaning is made" (Sharpe 2016, 76).[8] Black life as force of resistance doesn't compose with the myriad ways whiteness in its colonial-capitalist formation continues to position the black body as subpar, less-than human. "Even though the captive flesh/body has been 'liberated,' and no one need pretend that even the quotation marks do not matter, dominant symbolic activity, the ruling episteme that releases the dynamics of naming and valuation, remains grounded in the originating metaphors of captivity and mutilation so that it is as if neither time nor history, nor historiography and its topics, shows movement, as the human subject is 'murdered' over and over again by the passions of a bloodless and anonymous archaism, showing itself in endless disguise" (Spillers 1987, 68). Black life haunts this metric and any metric, its force of valuation the relational between where "even under the most extreme circumstance imaginable, such as the condition of enslavement, both subjectivation and subjectivity occur in relation between parties . . . constructed in relationship and not before" (Spillers 2006, 23–24).[9] Black life's production of subjectivity is moved by the phonic materiality of its resistance to the metric of whiteness (and the neurotypicality that runs through it) that assigns value-as-measure. Black life is schizoeconomic.

Surplus-Value of Life

Cephalopod dreams, which involve the crafting of an anticapitalist alter-economy for the seeding of a 3Ecologies Institute, seek to mobilize the unquantifiable. Their experiment is to reclaim the surplus-value of flow for what Massumi calls the surplus-value of life, "a purely qualitative [surplus-value that] concerns the intensity of lived potentials" (2018, 16).[10] Anarchiving is key to this.

The surplus-value of life is useless. It is anarchival. It ferries the anarchic share and seeds it toward future potential. This is its sociality. Speculatively, pragmatically, sparking its way into phonic materialities, the surplus-value of life is never separable from how it accounts for itself as life-lived, never quantifiable, never archivable as such. There is no way to abstract it from the sound, from the tone and the tune, from the touch and the feel of living, from its sociality.

Minor sociality runs through that which exceeds the count. It cannot be given to a people—it is created in the offing, at the convergence of the vague essences of included disjunction. Transindividual before it is individual, exuberant with what exceeds the form it takes, it is the undercommoning at the heart of an aesthetic sociality of blackness. It must be emphasized: while blackness is practiced first and foremost by those who live the daily violence of segregation from what counts, who have paid with their flesh for the advances of capitalism, it does not measure itself by the logic that dehumanizes it. Blackness is the force of an emergent collectivity that moves beyond property and propriety. "Blackness, which is to say, black radicalism, is not the property of black people. All that we have (and are) is what we hold in our outstretched hands. This open collective being is blackness—(racial) difference mobilized against the racist determination it calls into existence in every moment of the ongoing endangerment of 'actual being', of subjects who are supposed to know and own. It makes a claim upon us even as it is that upon which we all can make a claim, precisely because it—and its origins—are not originary" (Moten 2013b, 238). A gesture of reaching-toward, an invitation to collaborate, blackness is not what is pre-formed. Blackness is "the essence that is given in and as sociality itself" (Harney and Moten 2017a).

3E Process Seed Bank

The 3E Process Seed Bank is first and foremost a collective proposition for anarchiving.[11] As described in chapter 3, the process of anarchiving involves moving with the more-than of the event and channeling the ecology of relations it has set forth. Less capture than bend, the aim is to reorient a set of conditions so that a spark can catch on the edges of an existing process, seeding a new one. Sense-Lab's practices of the event have always been about this: creating process seeds for future activation elsewhere. How things move is their value, a value deferred. Value as speculative share, as force-of-form resonating.

Conceiving a cryptoeconomic platform as an anarchive is a way of returning to the minor sociality of emergent valuation feeling itself out, making it a practice. This practice is conditioned through a continued exploration of what things do when they shape each other. Anarchiving is a *way*, not a state. To hone a practice of attuning to the anarchic share of a process underway is to become sensitive to how that which exceeds registering nonetheless transforms the phonic materiality of life-living. Foregrounding the anarchic share of events in the making, the 3E

Process Seed Bank does not disseminate a form for sale or exchange. Nor does it seek to display value, or to measure it. The 3E Process Seed Bank is a sandbox for seeds of process to germinate in the hope that they will grow elsewhere, seeding new processes.

The 3E Process Seed Bank takes the notion that money is a social relation to its immanent limit. "Cryptocurrencies are not just 'money'—they are part money, part asset and part political organization—and these other dimensions must impact the way we see 'stability'. . . . The simple point is that *money is a social relation; not just a technical mechanism*" (Bryan and Virtanen 2018).[12] Our goal: to move beyond any notion of individual shares or exchange, to learn collectively, through practice, to value the minor sociality of the more-than through which emergent valuation makes itself felt. To take seriously—to make it a life practice—that the value is not in the product but in the *way*. To learn to attune to what else is expressed in the way things shape each other in a register where quality approaches its most intensive limit. To index this intensity—an intensity with no bearing on quantity—in an operation that distills to number what differentially registers across a system tuned to what anarchivally moves through it.

What is rendered exchangeable here is not process itself, or affect, or relation. What is made shareable is a technique, a practice for attuning to the anarchic share in experience. Following Stefano Harney and Fred Moten's thinking on debt in *The Undercommons*, the aim is above all to get rid of the debt/credit relation. "There has to be a way in which there can be elaborations of unpayable debt that don't always return to an individualisation through the family or an individualisation through the wage laborer, but instead the debt becomes a principle of elaboration. And therefore it's not that you wouldn't owe people in something like an economy, or you wouldn't owe your mother, but that the word 'owe' would disappear and it would become some other word, it would be a more generative word" (Harney and Moten 2013, 150).

The 3E Process Seed Bank begins with debt—a debt to the earth, a debt to that which does not quite register but changes the quality of a life, a debt to the more-than. The 3E Process Seed Bank works without credit. There is no repayment here. There is no system of adequation that would create a mirror between its aneconomic principles and the wider field of capital. It's an enclave, a system that depends on a relational field composed of other alter-economic propositions committed to sharing not the measure of experience but what indexically runs through it, connecting to the dynamic contours of its most intensive limit. The aim is to work to create the conditions to live, not to repay the debt of life itself, and not to take credit for the living, for the land, which is not ours to give, not ours to own. We begin in the outside of finance. We begin here and attempt to remain here in the collective feeling-out of the limit where the hinge to finance proper is called "occurrency," its value the differential, infrathin unmeasurability of the being of relation.

Self-Organizing Propositions

To create the conditions for the differential of value, entryways into the process have to be invented that propose modes of relation that resist the setting-into-place of existing practices of self-presentation and the economies of prestige and position they bring with them. In addition, practices have to be seeded that facilitate attunement to what exceeds the archival contour of a given encounter. Anarchiving requires a care for all that impersonally moves through the event. To compose with anarchival minor movements, the 3E Process Seed Bank's digital platform must both conceive of ways to solicit ongoing engagement with processes underway and design ways of activating the thresholds on the platform itself that invite entry into those processes. On a digital platform, participation usually implies entering through self-identification. This often requires a password. While this identification can be a cipher, it nonetheless immediately sets up an individual marker, and with it a presupposition of individual agency that carries through all movements on the platform. While this can't be altogether cast aside in the crafting of an alter-economic digital platform, our aim is to background the reindividualization of the process as much as possible. How can individualized participation be detoured? What kinds of processes can be coded that allow sideways modes of relation?

In an economy where the gift is sociality, the first step is to code the entryway differently. The 3E Process Seed Bank refuses the form of the token as means of exchange (and mechanism of entry). Our proposal is to focus directly on sociality itself, entering through the modality of the proposition. Taking advantage of the figure of the "smart contract," building on the ways it has been coded in the post-blockchain landscape as the mechanism through which entry into the system takes place on the basis of an agreement directly written into lines of code, itself situated on a distributed, decentralized ledger, we are designing if-then propositions that set movements into play from the perspective of their own lure for feeling. The hope is that these propositional operations will be able to access modes of process directly rather than having them mediated by individual agents. We call these "self-organizing propositions," or SOPs.

The propositional force of the SOPs is the capacity for immanent orientations. The aim: to "shift SenseLab's collective ethos of self-organizing participation into the way in which the 3E Process Seed Bank online platform is fundamentally structured" (SenseLab—3E n.d.). Refusing the limitations on the social enacted by individual entry onto the platform, SOPs facilitate an entering in the act, in the middling of a process already underway. "Coded to facilitate repetitive, core actions undertaken on the 3E Process Seed Bank, SOPs take the place of the traditional 'governance' structure built into blockchain and beyond-blockchain distributed systems, attempting to fulfill the need for some kind of regulatory framework, but in a non-normative way" (SenseLab—3E n.d.).

Channels for the self-modulation of the process, SOPs "regulate the flow of interactions rather the form of transactions" (SenseLab—3E n.d.). Examples include the entryway SOP (proposition: gift of process), the welcome wagon (proposition: greeting), the cat herder (proposition: move into collaboration), the creative-cut call (proposition: tipping point toward actualization), the re-group call (proposition: regroup around failure and begin again), the goddess of anarchy (proposition: decisional-cutmaking power).

SenseLab sees SOPs as schizoeconomic threshold-cuts. They are lively, strange, alluring techniques to tune the process toward new assemblages. While the entryway SOP does the traditional work of the smart contract, the 3E Process Seed Bank seeds the SOPs across more than the entry, designing operations for SOPs wherever a threshold-cut is needed. This is done with the knowledge that conditions change. While the new assemblages activated by the SOPs will be carefully tended by the process seeds as they germinate, we recognize that all new assemblages carry the risk any thresholding technique does: what if we are not ready for the worlds they create? This is especially the case with the SOPs since they formalize and schizz at the same time. What if the entryway becomes a gateway? Practice is key: finance at the limit must be lived. It will not do its work, even given the most alluring platform, if new techniques for activating body-worlds don't accompany it.

Processual Operator Thingies

If practices of the event seek to engage with the more-than of experience in the making, this by necessity includes collaboration with nonhuman forces. Nonhuman forces allow us to better understand the modes of perception of a neurodiverse sensibility that refuses frontality as the matrix of attention, participating instead in experience from its more-than human edges. Composing with nonhuman forces facilitates the recognition that humans, too, are suffused with the nonhuman, those more-than human qualities that forge openings toward an aesthetics of the earth. The world pushes into us, makes us. And then there is the collaboration between the nonhuman forces themselves, the geological time pulsing through the rock, the strange wasp-likeness of the hammer orchid's deceptive play,[13] the angle of the sun shimmering in the whistle of the breeze, the "degrees of indeterminacy" in algorithmic infracommunication (Parisi 2019, 4).[14] Emergent sociality across mediums of expression requires an attunement to these nonhuman forces. The danger otherwise is that we return to the instrumentality of human self-centeredness.

The crafting of the digital platform for the 3E Process Seed Bank is deeply committed to a sensitivity toward the outside of nonhuman expression that courses through us, computational and extracomputational. In the context of the 3E Process Seed Bank, what this requires in practice is that we design techniques that foster compelling ways of encountering how the coded world might collaborate with the more-than that courses through the analog. At the same time, a curiosity about the digital on its own terms emboldens an approach that resists making the digital platform a simple mediator of our practice. In the spirit of immediation, we are lured by the "indefiniteness of 'incomputables' that expose dynamics in computational logic, where proofs preserve degrees of indeterminacy" (Parisi 2019, 5–6). We are fascinated by the notion that complex systems produce a "field of communication" where "algorithms talk to other algorithms (through set protocols and through learning) . . . across parallel and distributive networks" (7). While the systems we are working on are nowhere as complex as the ones Luciana Parisi describes above, the speculative potential of the network's own indeterminacy is essential to what we are trying to achieve. With practices of the event our central operation, the aim is to design a platform that can sensitize us to what exceeds the instrumentality with which we tend to approach the digital realm.

As anarchival transport, the 3E Process Seed Bank teaches us, in emergent relation with coding's own logics, how to collaborate with the anarchic share of a digital process. That said, it is important to remember that the digital process is always allied to a live one. The 3E Process Seed Bank is, after all, the aneconomic proposition for the 3Ecologies Institute, which fosters local sites where practices of living and learning are composed. But we do a lot of work online, especially now that we have collaborators from such diverse locations. We share files, send messages, discuss concepts, join each others' reading groups, sit in virtually on workshops. The 3E Process Seed Bank is conceived as an alternative proposition for this daily collaboration at a distance that might be better capable of transducing practices from the digital to the live and vice versa. What we have found with event-based practices is that the relay of distance and proximity is important to how techniques unfold. For some of us, physical gatherings are necessary for the consolidation of collective processes. For others, the online register is much easier since it facilitates other temporalities and modes of encounter—even the most neurodiverse environments are challenging for those who have no sensory buffers. The 3E Process Seed Bank aims to foster practices of anarchiving to facilitate modes of coming into relation at a distance that maintain the intensity of the work across time and space, thereby creating process seeds for practices elsewhere underway. To some degree this is already part of daily SenseLab practice—the aim is to open it up to a wider field of collaboration, including those who have never physically participated in a SenseLab event. To achieve this interplay between what seeds it and what it seeds, the 3E Process Seed Bank must work as a machine that is expressive of the minor socialities that run through it, and affect it. How it comes into being is as important as what it does.

Working at the uneasy limit where noncapitalist futures can be imagined, both the 3E Process Seed Bank and the 3Ecologies Institute are invitations for others to take off from the middling of our process. This work can only be done in relay, collective at every step. To facilitate this sharing of the process, we have simplified the kinetic field of the platform into a second operation that will accompany the SOPs as governing tendencies. This second operation, conceived as bundles of code that agitate and deviate all-too-human tendencies of instrumental navigation, is called processual operator thingies (POTs). POTs are propelled by more-than human tendencies, bringing a qualitative edge of nonhuman participation to the platform. A variation on the figure of the bot, POTs are quality intensifiers that detour processes to make them less goal oriented, inviting infrathin collisions of sense and sensation. The proposition is that we POT our orientations. In the reorientation, POTs produce a relational shift, lending texture to an activity, or what Leslie Plumb, lead designer of the 3E Process Seed Bank, calls "touch-tones." In their design, the focus is on the quality of emergent valuation across registers of life-living. The POTs nuzzle, tend, germinate, steal, seize the day.

KleptoPOT is perhaps our most emphatic POT. Klepto is a force of redirection. Klepto steals not the content of our contribution but our assurance that we know where we are going. Stealing up against an image, a piece of text, a sound, Klepto acts like a charcoal rubbing, pulling a texture off the surface and depositing it elsewhere in the system. Other POTs include Nuzzlebot (moves with polyrhythms of scale and duration), Foreground/Background (experiments with contrast), Go-to-Sleep (experiments with the quality of turning on the porch light), Carpe Diem (gives a stand-out of salient value), Fuzzbot (gathers fragments of things like a dust ball), Reverbbot (returns and amplifies), Murmuration (registers a flow), and ReZonator (catches emergent appetites and moves them, glitches, interferes, cuts). And then there are the minor qualifiers, the ones more tone than texture, backgrounded in the system: vibrating-string (minor disturbances), spaghetti-string (tangling into untangling, giggling looking for laughter), dot-on-a-walk-POT (a line of color, a vector for entering a complex field, a lure for elsewhere alternatives), compostPOT (resting for a time to come), ticker-tape (polyp-like feed of disparate chat bits and bytes), and radioPOT (playlists for making-reading-thinking).

Processual operators cooperate with or interrupt humans to make felt the differentials in the collective process online. Coded shapes of process, they defy the directedness of any given individual gesture, inviting us to participate in a practice that surprises or slants us the way a shift in the breeze can do on a windy day. Processual operators are the online techniques, the online relational platforms, that align toward the more-than in the system.

Transvaluation

Mechanisms for the transduction of the anarchic share and its intensities into indexable units are required. We stumble here and will need all the transindividual collaboration we can get to remain in an ethos of the pragmatics of the useless.

Value, as we conceive it, is pure quality. Yet, as Alfred North Whitehead makes clear, value cannot be known in itself: it always accompanies actualization. Value is cohort, companion, ally. Value is relational, emphasizing the very unquantifiability of relation. A transductive technique for valuation that moves toward financial evaluation must therefore refrain, at all costs, from imposing any kind of constancy on the notion of what matters.

Speculative value drives the markets. What we are working toward is a different kind of speculative value: a value that doesn't invent quantifiable sums based on hype and risk and scarcity, but builds beyond exchange toward the abundance that is active in the infrathin of worlds making themselves. This is not value from nothing. It is value emergent from the tweak that altered the conditions of experience *in just this way*. This speculative mode of valuing values the *way* of the anarchive, the attunement, in the event, to the infrathin coursing through the anarchic share that left experience open for future experimentation. It values what is negatively prehended in experience. If negative prehension has subjective form, as proposed in chapter 1, a speculative mode of valuing attunes to the formative force of what is backgrounded but nonetheless shimmers in the between of foregroundingbackgrounding. An attunement to what moves at the interstice—the being of relation—is necessary for a revaluation of value that doesn't simply return to quantification as its motor. This is not about *more*. It's about the more-than, that differential force that accompanies experience in the making but cannot be reduced to it.

This is where cephalopod dreams come in. Cephalopods are extraordinary creatures. Their bodies more fold than form, they are shapeshifters in all senses, their modes of appearance in defiance of the logic of representation. Cephalopods camouflage; they entertain; they do both at once, the movement of their colors adrift. Radically intelligent creatures, they perform for the world in a way that leads Peter Godfrey-Smith to describe evolution as "not goal-directed" (2016, 132). The thing about the cephalopod is that it doesn't have the cones in its eyes necessary to perceive color.[15] This creature that dances and shapes and colors the world, often matching itself to its surrounds, cannot actually "see" the world it composes alongside. This has stumped scientists, some of whom have argued that octopus arms may have cells that engage in some kind of seeing-function. But is it really the case that seeing must be relegated to cones in the eyes or to cells in the arms? Recall John Lee Clark's architectural seeing, his obsession with the underside of furniture that so-called seeing folks habitually unsee (to avoid the dust bunnies). Might the cephalopod be engaged in a seeing-feeling of relational luminosity that cannot be separated out from its activity of shaping in the coloring?

In true cephalopodic form, no anarchive can be centrally controlled. An agencement of processes, its orientation always toward the more-than, its lure the shape of its own exuberance, it is self-producing. Cephalopodic in tendency, the representation of the useful is anathema to it. Transindividuation meets transvaluation.

Process Seeds

We have no idea how the cephalopod-anarchive will make contact. We don't know what finance at the limit looks like or whether the lure of the anarchic share will yield anything close to the exquisite cephalopod display we dream with.

What we do know is this: we have an appetite for other ways of learning, making, and thinking. Sending out a collective call via the 3E Process Seed Bank for the revaluation of value feels urgent at a time when capital's infringement on life is as total as it is, its surplus-value of flow everywhere contaminating life as we know it. Experiments with other ways abound, and we connect to them with anticipation, knowing that cephalopod dreams are never achieved once and for all, and are never practiced alone.

The cryptocurrency marketplace is in many ways nothing more than an amplification of the horrors of capital. To situate ourselves there is to risk being subsumed by its flows. Our tentative collaboration in those processes has taught us a lot about what we want to avoid at all costs (its libertarian edge, its maleness, its whiteness, its lack of foresight as regards computational capital, its infinite appetite for profit—in short, its capitalist tendencies). But experiments to explore finance at the limit are also happening there, and we have learned rich lessons from cryptofinance's conceptual outliers, from those who share the urgency to develop anticapitalist futures that value the art of life-living. As Jonathan Beller writes with respect to current alter-capitalist cryptoeconomic experiments, "the mutual stake-holding or risking together changes the terms of sociality and creates the possibility to evolve new relationships and new social forms" (forthcoming).

New social forms have always brought with them the seeds of alter-economic processes. This is what I learn from the aesthetic sociality of blackness.

> To be white was to own the earth forever and ever. It defined who they were and what they valued; it shaped their vision of the future. But black folks had been owned, and being an object of property, they were radically disenchanted with the idea of property. If their past taught them anything, it was that the attempt to own life destroyed it, brutalized the earth, and ran roughshod over everything on God's creation for a dollar. As items of cargo, they had experienced first-hand the ugliness and violence of the world as seen through the ledger and double-entry bookkeeping. They had endured the life of the commodity. They had been propagated and harvested like any other crop, treated no differently from the tools and the animals owned by massa. They knew a corporation was not a person, not flesh and blood, and that a piece of paper secured nothing that a white man was bound to respect; they knew starvation wages weren't freedom, but another kind of slavery. The things they valued most had no price on them. (Hartman 2019, 270–71)

In the infrathin of experience, value is without count. Always in excess of measure, in excess of its-self, value is what cannot be possessed. Shimmer, gloss, pulse, value is the qualitative edge of the being of relation. A pragmatics of the useless is value's *way*, its artful orientation to the anarchic share that moves through process to reveal what couldn't be contained. Cephalopod dreams for finance at the limit begin here, in the uncontainment, proposing a relationscape of vivid dissonance. To see-feel in the affirmation of discord is to approach a movement in variation with itself. Where minor gestures abound, minor socialities thrive.

schizzinganarchiving

Schizzinganarchiving magnifies the anarchival tendency moving through all schizoanalytic practices. A technique for making felt the diagram of the movement that composes us, schizzinganarchiving refuses to draw strong lines between bodies and the ecologies that compose them. Schizzinganarchiving is a practice for inventing new ways of becoming social, and for mapping the socialities that exceed us. Schizzinganarchiving is a schizogeographic practice for minor socialities.

1. Make It Transindividual!

Schizoanalysis moves beyond the focus on the first person singular. "Psychoanalysis transformed itself into the shoring up of the self" (Querrien, n.d. b).[1] The work of the schizz is to make felt how the self was never one.

Create techniques for augmenting complexity such that new flows reorient blockages. Follow the flows not toward scarcity but toward abundance. Abandon the psychological subject. Embrace the excess. Compose with the alter-economic that moves through that excess. Invent with the minor socialities that flow to the surface. Listen to the rhythms of the parastrata—"'sides' and 'besides,' and the irreducible forms and milieus associated with them" (Deleuze and Guattari 1987, 52). Draw new lines that angle transversally across the strata. Don't be fooled by the hardness of a surface. Make it irreducible. Find the resilience in the between. Note that the process is collective. The transindividual always precedes the individualizing force that comes with the selection of one tendency above all others.

Draw a diagram of the tendencies. Note that the drawing itself shifts the sociality. Never assume an exteriority. Don't create an inside. Invite a sidling gesture that shifts at the rhythm of what moves between, on the transversal plane of the parastratum. Note what stands out. Note the ways in which the dominant tendency seeks to take over. Note the ways in which you might be moved to archive the tendency. Don't archive it. Move in the rhythm of what exceeds archiving. Tend toward the anarchic share.

Recognize that transindividuality refuses a strong demarcating line between analyst and analysand. Schizoanalysis is always in the midst. It moves the diagram that we become. "Schizoanalysis (a term invented by Guattari that signifies an analysis that does not propose to annihilate contradictions) establishes, to the contrary, continued variations and multiple interferences" (Querrien, n.d. a).

2. Transversalize the Collective!

The transindividual is already collective. Collectivity is not the sum of the parts. It is the excess that moves across all comings-into-experience.

Schizoanalysis tends this transversal quality. It is always a practice for and with collectivity. Schizoanalysis lives at the interstices of the three ecologies— the social, the conceptual, and the environmental. Schizoanalysis orients to the ecology of practices. Schizzinganarchiving tends to the ecological share of movements in the making.

Schizoanalysis is committed to a politics of affirmation. A politics of affirmation must never be reduced to a simple yay-saying. A politics of affirmation moves with the break, inventing modes of bodying for unstable ground. Relays are key. A relay does not have to be hand to hand. It can be technique to technique. Minor gesture to minor gesture.

Minor gestures are always transversal. Their capacity for variation desediments the strata, revealing parastrata. Pulsing across planes of legibility and intelligibility, they make felt what risks remaining unregistered. Schizzinganarchiving does its work here, in the paradox of registering the unregisterable, creating bonds with the ineffable.

Schizzinganarchiving moves obliquely. Its power lies in the agencements it facilitates. It is never a general category. Its practices are not transferable.

The schizz cuts across a field of tendencies. Schizzinganarchiving conjugates those tendencies not to add them up to make a workable sum, but to connect to the differential that is the motor of the movements themselves. Schizzinganarchiving follows the fault lines and calls for new ways of living at their precipice.

To practice in the mode of schizzinganarchiving is to become sensitive to movement beyond displacement. The schizz is not a call to do more. It is a call to connect to what is already doing. Anarchiving traces what reverberates in that doing, curious, always, about the singularity of what inflects, tuning to the rhythm of the break.

The creative pull of schizzinganarchiving resists the call of capital. It cannot be quantified. Schizoeconomic, it pulses at the aneconomic edge of experience, valuing what infrathinly moves in excess of the shape things take.

Schizzinganarchiving is ecosophical. It cares for how body-worlds come to be, and how their socialities express themselves. A minor sociality is lured into expression by a schizzinganarchiving that culls from an ecology of practices the minor gestures that run through it. Schizzinganarchiving is always a practice of the more-than one.

3. Move beyond the Face (-to-Face)!

Neurotypical socialities privilege the face-to-face. Without a focus on the face, we are taught, communication falters. Averting eyes means averting attention, and lack of attention implies lack of presence. Eye contact is the measure of engagement.

Schizzinganarchiving resists the call to the face-as-eyes. It mistrusts the affective tonality the face calls forth. It resists the assumption that facial expression as it moves from eye to eye signals presence. It does not believe in the interiority promised by the eye to eye. Eyes askance, the face turned sideways, it moves affect from the face into the world, shifting it toward an aesthetics of the earth.

> An aesthetics of the earth? In the half-starved dust of Africa? In the mud of flooded Asias? In epidemics, masked forms of exploitation, flies buzz-bombing the skeleton skins of children? In the frozen silence of the Andes? In the rains uprooting favelas and shantytowns? In the scrub and scree of Bantu lands? In flowers encircling necks and ukuleles? In mud huts crowning goldmines? In city sewers? In haggard aboriginal wind? In red-light districts? In drunken indiscriminate consumption? In the noose? The cabin? Night with no candle?
>
> Yes. But an aesthetics of disruption and intrusion. Finding the fever of passion for the ideas of "environment" . . . and "ecology," both apparently such futile notions in these landscapes of desolation. Imagining the idea of love of the earth—so ridiculously inadequate or else frequently the basis for such sectarian intolerance—with all the strength of charcoal fires or sweet syrup.
>
> Aesthetics of rupture and connection. . . .
>
> Aesthetics of a variable continuum, of an invariant discontinuum. (Glissant 1997, 151)

An aesthetics of the earth schizzes the face-as-eyes. It refuses the implication of whiteness that accompanies the "white wall/black hole" configuration that has come to stand in for expression. A landscape given in advance, unseen as the assumed ground of all seeing, the white wall/black hole is the background that infiltrates all foregrounds. Whiteness not as individual, not as the individual face, but as the background for the everyface of perception. "The face is not a universal. It is not even that of the white man; it is White Man himself, with his broad white cheeks and the black hole of his eyes" (Deleuze and Guattari 1987, 176). Face-as-eyes ensures a collapse of difference—"racism operates by the determination of degrees of deviance in relation to the White-Man face, which endeavors to integrate nonconforming traits into increasingly eccentric and backward waves, sometimes tolerating them at given places under given conditions, in a given ghetto, sometimes erasing them from the wall, which never abides alterity" (178).

Schizzinganarchiving resists the plane of faciality. The rhythm of its cut breaks and breaks and breaks the background that has come to permeate the foregrounds of our collectively white imaginations, imaginations that draw in infinite palimpsest the same figure onto its dreams of finance unlimited. "Dismantling the face is the same as breaking through the wall of the signifier and getting out of the black hole of subjectivity. Here, the program, the slogan, of schizoanalysis is: Find your black holes and white walls, know them, know your faces; it is the only way you will be able to dismantle them and draw your lines of flight" (Deleuze and Guattari 1987, 188). Wander lines crisscross to draw schizoanalytic movements, forces of form that dance to rhythms clandestine. Minor movements, they produce subjectivities that exceed the shape of those interpersonal images of our-selves.

The becoming-clandestine of schizzinganarchiving takes the shape of an obliqueness. This obliqueness allows the movement of the field beyond the face-to-face to resonate. The face extends and expands, morphing into the ecologies that expose its more-than. Opaque, turned away from the glare of the white wall/black hole, new qualities of expression begin to register. The face becomes a field of relation, earth-become-body. It is in the parastrata of the force of the earth where wander lines invent passages toward experience's schizz that schizzinganarchiving composes.

In a refusal of point of view, oriented toward the field of relation of a distributed facing, the earth turns. Perspective is lost. Crouched, earth-toes-verge, bodying slants toward postures unknown. In tune with the more-than of territory, schizzinganarchiving reaches for that which expresses itself in the acrossness of times geological and cosmological. Schizzinganarchiving practices an aesthetics of the earth.

4. Schizz the Cartography!

Schizoanalytic cartographies are cartographies for practices under variation. "There is no schizoanalytic cartography that is fixed and unvarying" (Querrien, n.d. b). Move in the tending, in an aesthetic of "of rupture and continuum," "of a variable continuum, of an invariant discontinuum" (Glissant 1997, 151).

Draw yourself an errant cartography. Work on the bias. Follow the inflection, reach-lean-keen. Touch the contours. Feel the eye beyond the socket, in the crack of the pavement, the rent of the bowl's chipped surface. Don't trust in geographies of beginnings and endings as though a body (or an earth) could be made whole. Beware of times measured. Don't become a position. Resist distantism.

Take a rubbing. Use it to feel the surface differently. Smudge the charcoal. Cover the white wall of your presuppositions. Cull orientations from the force of an inclination. Return to what you didn't see. Feel it in the emergent cartography. Acquaint yourself with the landscape. Beware of the transcendent gaze. Be queered by existence. Be mere in the instauration of all that erupts at the interstices of stone and paper.

Take the pulse of a solitude. The more-than is of you. We are never alone. Attune to the minor socialities that run through you. The queering of existence, felt in the ecology of the becoming-earth of the face, is work we do together, alone, always more-than one. Minor socialities pull at this cartography beyond point of view, stretching it beyond recognition toward other modes of perceptibility. A poetics of relation.

A poetics of relation errantly moves in the wander lines of a world that escapes totality. The world is not one. "The many become one and are increased by one" (Whitehead 1978, 32). Not one world, one body, but body-worlds rubbing themselves into existence, earth-paper, foot-sand, hand-grass. But also breeze-fly, rumble-glare, greening-purpling. Amidst. Including the slant of rancid air in the mosquito-infested corners of a haphazard shelter, the unforgiving heat radiating against the gray concrete of cities longing for green, the frozen hard ground of unwelcoming winter desolation. Earth-bodying a love for the earth in an orientation that exceeds us, an aesthetics of the earth an attuning to what moves at the infrathin interstices that are not ours to claim.

Aesthetics, from Greek *aisthetikos*, "relating to perception by the senses," from *aistheta*, "perceptible things," from *aisthesthai*, "to perceive."[2] Aesthetics, where the sensuous meets the nonsensuous, beauty's discordant force refusing to be anaesthetized. Aesthetics of the earth as sensitive to what else the earth moves in us, through us. Aesthetics of the earth as attunement, in the time of the event, to how futurity bends the past, perception folding in the between. Aesthetics of the earth, a schizzed cartography, an opacity, not a universality. "Errant, s/he challenges and discards the universal—this generalizing edict that summarized the world as something obvious and transparent, claiming for it one presupposed sense and one destiny. . . . Generalization is totalitarian: from the world it chooses one side of the reports, one set of ideas, which it sets apart from others and tries to impose by exporting as a model. The thinking of errantry conceives of totality but willingly renounces any claims to sum it up or to possess it" (Glissant 1997, 20–21; translation modified).

From the black hole of normative subjectivity to Édouard Glissant's opacity, an errant movement that calls for "irreducible singularity" (Glissant 1997, 190). Opacity as the being of relation, as the turning away from the imposition of transparency buttressed by the face-to-face. "I thus am able to conceive of the opacity of the other for me, without reproach for my opacity for them" (193; translation modified). Moving in the opacity of relation, becoming with the earth's difference. Schizzinganarchiving.

5. Invent a Way!

Anarchiving is a way.

Schizzinganarchiving deploys techniques to intensify and reorient modes of existence. Anarchival practices amplify the minor that runs through the archive. Schizzinganarchiving recognizes the need to register this minor tendency. The registering is not an archiving. It is a culling that pulls from the future a tendency, an orientation on process. The registering of the minor catapults time's linearity. From a line grows a spiral. What is felt in the catapulting is potential.

"The work of schizoanalysis is to restore to the event its value as event" (Querrien, n.d. b). The value of the event is only palpable as anarchic share. What it anarchically carries forward is its value. To place value anywhere else would be to impose it onto the event from the outside. As emergent quality of existence, the event values only its capacity to seed itself forward.

Schizzinganarchiving is the recognition that all schizzes anarchive. All schizzes create unmoorings that produce effects. These effects register on the earth's surface to create other ways of earthing. These earthing ways, the aesthetics of the earth that turn away from the white wall/black hole, are modes of existence in differential attunement. A poetics of relation, schizzinganarchiving invents ways of marking the differential such that it shifts the rhythm of a body-earth composition.

6. Don't Evaluate! Experiment!

The therapeutics of schizzinganarchiving is a call for a practice of transversal collectivity. It is a political call for the creation of minor socialities that resist reorganizing according to predetermined categories. We do not fit (ourselves) into transversal collectivities. Events call us to merge into their body-earth compositions.

New body-earth compositions are created each time there is a committed practice. Practice moves at the pace of a problem. Schizzinganarchiving, as a practice for emergent collectivity, draws out the contours of a problem, working not to solve it but to complexify it, to give it the force that can draw it into expression differently. Problems that carry their own solutions are false problems. False problems are all around, orienting point of view, building perspective. Their aim is to tire us out by continuously returning us to the face-to-face of neurotypicality, reorganizing our existence into a representation of the useful. Schizzinganarchiving resists false problems. It resists superimposing the white wall/black hole on the cartography of existence as though the White Man were the central pivot. Schizzinganarchiving sculpts new contours, amplifying the stakes of a problem too complex for anyone to contend with alone, inviting us to reinvent value by moving us into an ethos of a pragmatics of the useless. Problems that move us, problems that seed new modes of existence, are problems that draw us into their transversality. Schizzinganarchiving does not evaluate. It experiments.

Too often, evaluation sticks to what is already known, to what is already reflected on the white wall/black hole of the representational regime of the face-to-face. Neurotypicality lives here, the force of whiteness that makes a claim on the value of existence and the measure of knowledge. Experimentation in the mode of schizzinganarchiving will not destroy whiteness through debased interpretation. The aim is not to approach the norm frontally. Schizzinganarchiving develops techniques to shift the frontality toward an obliqueness that transversalizes expression. New angles of expression shift the posture of the body-earth toward new inclinations. These inclinations unsettle the stratum, angling the surface of experience. It is here, in the experimental potential of a vacillating body-earth, that schizzinganarchiving diagrams existence.

prelude. Fugitively, Approximately

1 Pathologizing only takes us so far, so I would always be careful with accounts of impaired executive function. Nonetheless, there seems to be a consensus that there are marked differences in the use of planning among those who are aligned to these categories, including those whose frontal lobes are damaged through stroke. Elisabeth L. Hill writes, "Executive functions are typically impaired in patients with acquired damage to the frontal lobes as well as in a range of neurodevelopmental disorders that are likely to involve congenital deficits in the frontal lobes. Such clinical disorders include attention deficit hyperactivity disorder (ADHD), obsessive compulsive disorder, Tourette syndrome, phenylketonuria, schizophrenia and autism spectrum disorder" (2004, 2).

2 "Anxiety, Ambiguity and Autistic Perception," May 3, 2018, https://boren.blog/2018/05/03/anxiety-ambiguity-and-autistic-perception/.

3 The announcements of Bradley's days of black study are found at "Rizvana Bradley: Dag 3: Studium Generale Rietveld Academie, 23 March 2018," Stedelijk Museum website, https://www.stedelijk.nl/en/events/studium-generale-rietveld-academie-4; and "Dancing Politics, Moving Performance: Conversations at the Edges of Choreography, June 18th–22nd 2018," Centre National de la Danse, University of the Arts, https://www.uarts.edu/node/41511.

4 The burdened individuality of freedom points to the "ambivalent legacy of emancipation and the undeniable truncated opportunities of the freed" (Hartman 1997, 12). Never losing sight of the lack of a "definitive partition between slavery and freedom," Hartman renounces any grand narrative of freedom, opting instead for "a transient and fleeting expression of possibility that cannot ensconce itself as a durable temporal marker (13). Freedom here is rightly connected to "an indebtedness of liberty to property and to an alienable and exchangeable self" (110). Hartman writes, "By examining the metamorphosis of 'chattel into man' and the strategies of individuation constitutive of the liberal individual and the rights-bearing subject, I hope to underscore the ways in which freedom and slavery presuppose one another, not only as modes of production and discipline or through contiguous forms of subjection but as founding narratives of the liberal subject revisited and revisioned in the context of Reconstruction and the sweeping changes wrought by the abolition of slavery" (116).

Chapter 1. For a Pragmatics of the Useless

Earlier versions of this chapter appeared as the journal articles "For a Pragmatics of the Useless, or the Value of the Infrathin," in *Studies in Material Thinking* (vol. 16) and *Political Theory* (vol. 44, no. 1).

1 The phrase "a pragmatics of the useless" was used by Brian Massumi in "The Ether and Your Anger: Toward a Pragmatics of the Useless" (2000). It was deleted in the subsequent publication of the same piece in *Semblance and Event* (2011). It was also the title of a TEDx talk given by Erin Manning and Massumi (subsequently changed, without our assent, to "Relational Soup"; Massumi and Manning 2014) and the title of a talk by Manning and Massumi at Western University in 2013.

2 Susan Stepney (2002) emphasizes the diversity that comes with emergent properties, preferring to speak of "other than the sum of its parts" rather than "more than the sum of its parts." When I use the hyphenated *more-than*, the aim is to call forth this quality of difference in the more-than. The more-than, like the minor gesture, is always differential. Stepney writes, "Chaos theory, complex adaptive self-organising systems, artificial life: all these areas of study show that systems become *qualitatively* different when they have many, rather than a few, components. Such systems have **emergent properties**—properties of the entire system that are not properties of the individual components. As our own artefacts grow in complexity, they too exhibit emergent properties, some desirable, some rather less so." https://www-users.cs.york .ac.uk/susan/complex/nstdcomp.htm

3 I've explored the concept of autistic perception through the writings of Tito Mukhopadhyay, Mel Baggs, DJ Savarese, Larry Bissonnette, and others. For more on the concept of autistic perception, and for an example of their incisive writing, see chapter 7, "An Ethics of Language in the Making," in *Always More Than One* (Manning 2013).

4 Art as mobilized throughout always seeks to move beyond an object and a form, and should therefore never be relegated to one form of practice over another (i.e., painting over performance). The aim is to explore what the concept of the infrathin can do to amplify the gesture, in art, that is most cannibalized by art markets and their allegiance to prestige value, an adjacency of use-value that very much operates within the logic of the representation of the useful.

5 For a more detailed account on artfulness, see chapter 2 "Artfulness: Emergent Collectivities and Processes of Individuation," in *The Minor Gesture* (Manning 2016).

6 In *The Minor Gesture*, I define art as way, building from the German *die Art und Weise*. I write:

"Art, understood as manner, tunes to its thirteenth century definition as 'a skill or craft of learning.' Art as *a way* of learning. Art as the bridge toward new processes, new pathways. To speak of a 'way' is to dwell on the process itself, on its manner of becoming. It is to emphasize that art is before all else a quality, a difference in kind, an operative process that maps the way toward a certain attunement of world and expression.

"Art as *way* is not yet about an object, about a form, or a content. It is still on its way. As such, it is deeply allied to Bergson's definition of intuition as the art—the manner—in which the very conditions of experience are felt. Intuition both gets a process on its way and acts as the decisive turn within experience that activates a productive opening within time's durational folds. Intuition crafts the operative problem" (2016, 46–47).

7 Campt defines still-moving images as "images that hover between still and moving images; animated still images, slowed or stilled images in motion or visual renderings that blur the distinctions between these multiple genres; images that require the labor of feeling with or through them" (2019, 80).

8 For more on Clark and how her concept of the relational object distances itself from Gullar's non-object, see Rolnik (1999).

9 Undated manuscript, probably from 1963–64, in the L. Clark archives, São Paulo and Rio de Janeiro.

Chapter 2. Toward a Politics of Immediation

An earlier version of this chapter appeared as "Toward a Politics of Immediation" in *Frontiers in Sociology* (2019).

1 In *Science and the Modern World,* Whitehead also writes, "To say that a bit of matter has simple location means that, in expressing its spatio-temporal relations, it is adequate to state that it is where it is, in a definite finite region of space, and throughout a definite duration of time, apart from any essential references to the relations of that bit of matter to other regions of space and other durations of time" (1925, 58).

2 On the difference between relation and interaction, see Massumi's "The Thinking-Feeling of What Happens," in *Semblance and Event* (2011).

3 For a more detailed exploration of the concept of agencement as an alternative for agency, see the introduction of *The Minor Gesture* (Manning 2016).

4 In "The Idea of Black Culture" (2006), Hortense Spillers returns to Nahum Chandler's analysis of the production of subjectivity in "Originary Displacement" (2000). Her emphasis here is on the relational force of subjectivity. "Chandler shows that even under the most extreme circumstance imaginable, such as the condition of enslavement, both subjectivation and subjectivity occur in relation between parties. . . . We are thus conduced to the moment of the 'between' and its closural forestalling in the shock of this recognition—subject positionality 'is constructed in relationship and not before' (282; emphasis added)" (Spillers 2006, 23, 24). Spillers's important argument here concerns the way black life's production of subjectivity "names modernity formation itself; . . . making [it] tremble 'by dislodging the layers of sedimented premises that hold [a conclusion] in place' (257). . . . 'There is no longer "black" or "white" culture, per se, if there ever were, or the power monopoly implied in the formulation, but, rather, only differences of force' (282)" (Spillers 2006, 24, quoting Chandler). Black culture in fact schizzes that which marks its exclusion: "Since we cannot easily separate these imperatives from each other, we would have to say that New World black cultures, as well as their parallel formations in other parts of the globe, are not only Creole forms adopted from the implements,

both material and imaginative, of the near-at-hand, but that they are also 'schizo-phrenic,' if by that we mean compounded of a disposition that carries both its state-ment and counterstatement, that would both undo alienation and constitute its own standpoint" (Spillers 2006, 25).

5 In conversation with Sylvia Wynter's work in *Beyond Coloniality,* Aaron Kamugui-sha writes: "The problem with previous humanisms is in part that they were only 'partial humanisms,' 'ethnohumanisms,' constructed on the premise that Western-bourgeois man was the human and incapable of giving us a 'history of the human.' Pressed in an interview with David Scott on why we should 're-enchant the human in humanism,' Wynter would state that 'we have to recognize the dimensions of the breakthroughs that these first humanisms made possible at the level of human cog-nition, and therefore of the possibility of our eventual emancipation, of our eventual full autonomy, as humans.' The West is not just a 'local culture' (as Clifford Geertz would put it) like any other but one whose enchantments subvert our autonomy as a species and has resulted in a genre of the human that imperils the habitat of the human—and the continuation of our species" (2019, 186).

6 Ashon Crawley, "Of Forgiveness," in *LA Review of Books,* February 25, 2020, https://lareviewofbooks.org/article/of-forgiveness/.

7 McKittrick is very sensitive to this concern of what genre of human might emerge through a Wynterian study of other modes of becoming human. She writes: "I think, with Wynter, one must read, carefully, her expansive reconceptualization of the human, which then allows one to dwell on the particularities of injustice anew. It is worth noticing, too, that what she is bringing to us, intellectually, has not been done before: she is working out and muddling through new humanism in ways that hon-our our collective human-environment perspectives—which must be understood alongside the predicament of our ecocidal and genocidal world which normalizes post-slave Liberal individualism and posits it as the only available mode of being human—while also, importantly, making clear that her insights, and thus a more ethical world view for us all, could only be engendered from the perspective of the ex-slave archipelago" (2014, 237).

8 In her exploration of human geography and black life, McKittrick is bold in her refusal of existing (colonial/white) geographies and resolutely clear in her aim to foreground black women's geographies in a desire to amplify other ways of knowing and of living. "The relationship between black populations and geography—and here I am referring to geography as space, place, and location in their physical materiality and imaginative configurations—allows us to engage with a narrative that locates and draws on black histories and black subjects in order to make visible social lives which are often displaced, rendered ungeographic" (2006: x). Refusing geography's "discursive attachment to stasis and physicality, the idea that space 'just is,'" McKit-trick asks where and how black geographies do their work, how black subjectivity is produced through and across them, concerned that black life has been framed as "ungeographic" (xi). For McKittrick "black matters are spatial matters" (ix). Her turn to the question of the human and of humanism more broadly comes from this vantage point of "lived black womanhood," foregrounding the ways in which

it "[disrupts] the category of 'woman' and the centered subject (race, class, gender, location); calling into question the patriarchal and feminist meanings of private/ public, home, work, motherhood, selfhood, nation" (134). Making space differently is by necessity making human differently, black womanhood always the lived angle of how experience makes itself: "I want to suggest that geographies of domination be understood as 'the displacement of difference,' wherein 'particular kinds of bodies, one by one, are materially (if not always visibly) configured by racism into a hierarchy of human and inhuman persons that in sum form the category of 'human being'" (xv).

9 Whitehead has a very different notion of perspective. He writes: "It follows that in every consideration of a single fact there is the suppressed presupposition of the environmental coördination requisite for its existence. This environment, thus coördinated, is the whole universe in its perspective to the fact. But perspective is gradation of relevance; that is to say, it is gradation of importance. Feeling is the agent which reduces the universe to its perspective for fact. Apart from gradations of feeling, the infinitude of detail produces an infinitude of effect in the constitution of each fact. And that is all that is to be said, when we omit feeling. But we feel differently about these effects and thus reduce them to a perspective. 'To be negligible' means 'to be negligible for some coördination of feeling'. Thus perspective is the outcome of feeling; and feeling is graded by the sense of interest as to the variety of its differentiations" (1938: 9–10). This notion of perspective, further developed by Erin Manning and Brian Massumi in "A Perspective of the Universe" in *Thought in the Act* (2014b), proposes an architectural rethinking of spacetime from the world's perspective *on itself*. Similarly, Eduardo Viveiros de Castro's writings on Amazonian Indigenous practices of "perspectivism" focuses on the emergently relational quality of experience making itself in the context of predator-prey. Perspectivism here has no sense of a stable point of view. See *Cannibal Metaphysics* (2014, 49–64.).

10 All translations from David Lapoujade's book are my own.

11 Souriau uses "avocat" in French, which also translates as lawyer.

12 This is opposed to the false problem: "False problems are of two sorts, 'nonexistent problems,' defined as problems whose very terms contain a confusion of the 'more' and the 'less'; and 'badly stated' questions, so defined because their terms represent badly analyzed composites" (Deleuze 1988, 17).

13 In a different article, "Venus in Two Acts," Hartman asks, "Is it possible to exceed or negotiate the constitutive limits of the archive? By advancing a series of speculative arguments and exploiting the capacities of the subjunctive (a grammatical mood that expresses doubts, wishes, and possibilities), in fashioning a narrative, which is based upon archival research, and by that I mean a critical reading of the archive that mimes the figurative dimensions of history, I intended both to tell an impossible story and to amplify the impossibility of its telling" (2008b, 11).

14 In *Cinema 2*, Gilles Deleuze (1989, 172) proposes "belief in the world" as the immanent field of Spinozist joy crafted in the call to make the world anew through the

living out of difference. Belief in the world is a practice rather than a state, its proposition always allied to the potential to affect and be affected that is the generative call of joy. Joy cannot be reduced to happiness, nor can belief be reduced to faith. Belief in the world is a commitment to the collectivity of the to-come in the tense of the future anterior.

15 Glissant writes, "An aesthetics of the earth? In the half-starved dust of Africas? In the mud of flooded Asias? In epidemics, masked forms of exploitation, flies buzz-bombing the skeleton skins of children? In the frozen silence of the Andes? In the rains uprooting favelas and shantytowns? In the scrub and scree of Bantu lands? In flowers encircling necks and ukuleles? In mud huts crowning goldmines? In city sewers? In haggard aboriginal wind? In red-light districts? In drunken indiscriminate consumption? In the noose? The cabin? Night with no candle?

"Yes. But an aesthetics of disruption and intrusion. Finding the fever of passion for the ideas of 'environment' (which I call surroundings) and 'ecology,' both apparently such futile notions in these landscapes of desolation. Imagining the idea of love of the earth—so ridiculously inadequate or else frequently the basis for such sectarian intolerance—with all the strength of charcoal fires or sweet syrup.

"Aesthetics of rupture and connection.

"Because that is the crux of it, and almost everything is said in pointing out that under no circumstances could it ever be a question of transforming land into territory again. Territory is the basis for conquest. Territory requires that filiation be planted and legitimated. Territory is defined by its limits, and they must be expanded. A land henceforth has no limits.

"That is the reason it is worth defending against every form of alienation.

"Aesthetics of a variable continuum, of an invariant discontinuum" (1997, 151).

16 The full passage reads: "To speak of the thing that is before the city—as the previousness of a rigorously imagined contemporary projection of an insistent, departive turning over of soil and blood and language—is to engage in something that wants to be called sentimentalism while asking you to remember that sentimentalism is the aesthetics (which is interinanimate with the extra-political sociality) of the unfinished project of abolition and reconstruction that is our most enduring legacy of successful, however attenuated, struggle; and that sentimentalism is too often and too easily dismissed by students and devotees of power, especially in its connection to what they dismiss as identity politics (where such dismissals are always hyper-critical of (non-male, non-straight, non-white) identity while courteously leaving politics to its own uncriticized devices. To be interested in the rematerialization of wealth as something outstripping, even as it is constitutive, of limited bourgeois-imperialist forms and modes is to think such re-materialization as an anticolonial complaint for the anarchic, undercommon) permeation borne by what would have been outside, where we work and work out the poetics of our beautifully ugly feelings, as Thelonious Monk + Sianne Ngai might say. To be interested in this subtensive irruption is to be concerned with what a genuine anti-colonialism might be" (Moten 2016b, 163–64).

pocket practice: nestingpatching

1 For a moving text on the question of assembly in current (black) conditions in the United States, and with specific focus on the conditions around COVID-19, see Kenneth Bailey and Lori Lobenstine's "Social Justice in the Time of Social Distancing," accessed April 7, 2020, https://static1.squarespace.com/static /53c7166ee4b0e7db2be69480/t/5e6900b6b689bb5bc5f5d474/1583939767600/Social +Justice+in+a+Time+of+Social+Distancing.pdf.

2 Epidermally, Helio Oiticica is of course white. Harris's proposition is all the more powerful given this refusal to refuse black sociality across the color-line, thereby also refusing colonial constructs that reduce race to categories that can be policed and cordoned off. That said, there is never an attempt in Harris or here to negate the privileges that come with whiteness. Something quite different is at work—a commitment to attuning to what cannot be reduced to the impoverished accounts of existence produced in whiteness and neurotypicality, a proposal to become sensitive to what else moves across the experiment with living at the heart of practices that refuse to be sequestered in the 1 + 1.

3 A connection has been drawn between the favela and the *quilombo*—the communities formed by escaped slaves (Andrelino Campos in Harris 2018, 40).

4 The first museum-based iteration of *Nests* was at Whitechapel Gallery in 1969.

5 Harris writes, "Samba bespeaks a generalized practice, a dispersion of the singular event into a series of small acts and everyday rehearsals that are both repeated and newly invented on each occasion. It is not just the spectacular Carnival procession that is samba. 'The rehearsal for the samba,' as he writes in later notes, 'already is samba'" (2018, 39).

6 This is a term Félix Guattari takes from Jean Oury. See *Chaosmosis* (1995, 72). The direct citation from Oury reads: "On est tous des normopathes et c'est la chose la plus incurable qui soit" (We are all normopaths and it is the most incurable thing that there is) (my translation) in "Le Pré-pathique et le tailleur de pierre," *Chimères* no. 40 (Les enjeux du sensible), autumn 2000.

7 In *Scenes of Subjection*, Hartman is suspicious of empathy as a reigning gesture of whiteness. Writing of the "difficulty and slipperiness of empathy," she defines empathy as a feeling for oneself. As a mechanism of projection that lands squarely in the realm of its own self-recognition, empathy is that which most coherently returns us to our own measure of what it means to be human. She writes, "Empathy is a projection of oneself into another in order to better understand the other or 'the projection of one's own personality into an object, with the attribution to the object of one's emotions.' Yet empathy in important respects confounds Rankin's efforts to identify with the enslaved because in making the slave's suffering his own, Rankin begins to feel for himself rather than for those whom this exercise in imagination presumably is designed to reach. Moreover, by exploiting the vulnerability of the captive body as a vessel for the uses, thoughts, and feelings of others, the humanity extended to the slave inadvertently confirms the expectations and desires definitive of the relations of chattel slavery. In other words, the ease of Rankin's empathic identification is as much due to his good intentions and heartfelt opposition to slavery as to

the fungibility of the captive body. . . . The effort to counteract the commonplace callousness to black suffering requires that the white body be positioned in the place of the black body in order to make suffering visible and intelligible. The ambivalent character of empathy—more exactly, the repressive effects of empathy—. . . can be located in the 'obliteration of otherness' or the facile intimacy that enables identification with the other only as we 'feel ourselves into those we imagine as ourselves.' Empathy fails to expand the space of the other but merely places the other in its stead. . . . The fungibility of the commodity makes the captive body an abstract and empty vessel vulnerable to the projection of others' feelings, ideas, desires and values; and, as property, the dispossessed body of the enslaved is the surrogate for the master's body since it guarantees his disembodied universality and acts as the sign of his power and dominion" (1997, 18–21).

8 Experimentations at SenseLab are always open, but they do tend to gather particular people to them. In this case, work on patch was led by Leslie Plumb, Francisco Trento, Halbe Kuipers, Matisse ApSimon-Megens, and Anouk Hoogendoorn. For some visual examples of patch in movement, see the SenseLab—3E website at www.senselab.ca and the INFLeXions website at www.inflexions.org.

9 Whitehead writes, "When an actual entity belongs to the locus of a proposition, then conversely the proposition is an element in the lure for feeling of that actual entity. If by the decision of the concrescence, the proposition has been admitted into feeling, then the proposition constitutes what the feeling has felt. The proposition constitutes a lure for a member of its locus by reason of the germaneness of the complex predicate to the logical subjects, having regard to forms of definiteness in the actual world of that member, and to its antecedent phases of feeling" (1978, 186).

Chapter 3. What Things Do When They Shape Each Other

1 SenseLab has hubs in Canada, Australia, Europe, and Brazil.

2 A few sources on archives include Charles Merewether's edited volume *The Archive* (2006), Ian Farr's edited volume *Memory* (2012), and *Archive Journal*, with pieces such as Jane Birkin's "Art, Work and Archives: Performativity and Techniques of Production" (2015), which challenges the separation between work and archive.

3 I consider Saidiya Hartman's practice of "critical fabulation" an anarchiving that challenges many of the value-based presuppositions of the archive. Critical fabulation is key to working with the black archive, a site that historically (colonially speaking) deregisters black sociality. It is by foregrounding what is missing, by amplifying what is left out in the account (by shifting the count, revaluing value), that work on the black archive not only creates a place for blackness but deeply challenges the concept itself of the archive. For more on critical fabulation as it moves through Hartman's work, see "Venus in Two Acts" (2008b).

4 Whitehead writes, "There are two contrasted ideas which seem inevitably to underlie all width of experience, one of them is the notion of importance, the sense of importance, the presupposition of importance. The other is the notion of matter-of-fact. There is no escape from sheer matter-of-fact. It is the basis of importance;

and importance is important because of the inescapable character of matter-of-fact. We concentrate by reason of a sense of importance. And when we concentrate, we attend to matter-of-fact. Those people who in a hard-headed way confine their attention to matter-of-fact do so by reason of their sense of the importance of such an attitude. The two notions are antithetical, and require each other" (1938, 4).

5 Whitehead writes: "The ontological principle asserts the relativity of decision; whereby every decision expresses the relation of the actual thing, for which a decision is made, to an actual thing by which that decision is made. But 'decision' cannot be construed as a casual adjunct of an actual entity. It constitutes the very meaning of actuality. An actual entity arises from decisions for it, and by its very existence provides decisions for other actual entities which supersede it. Thus the ontological principle is the first stage in constituting a theory embracing the notions of 'actual entity,' 'givenness,' and 'process.' Just as 'potentiality for process' is the meaning of the more general term 'entity,' or 'thing'; so 'decision' is the additional meaning imported by the word 'actual' into the phrase 'actual entity.' 'Actuality' is the decision amid 'potentiality.' It represents stubborn fact which cannot be evaded" (1978, 43).

6 Tino Seghal is an example of a contemporary artist who resists the archive, actively preventing people from taking pictures of his work and refusing to document. The concepts at the heart of his work depend on this ephemerality. While this gesture separates his work from the typical relationship to self-presentation that the archive (and social media) foregrounds, it is arguable that his stance too plays within this arena. In thinking about practices that most resist this tendency, I am thinking particularly of practices such as that of Lygia Clark, whose work (before it was museum-ified) fell into an interstice that generated new overlaps between the therapeutic and the artful.

7 There is no attempt here to position myself outside of this dilemma. I, too, have a website (and, of course, a cv) and am continuously torn between process and documentation.

8 *The Minor Gesture* (Manning 2016) was also concerned with the question of value, engaged with wresting from neurotypicality a valuation of knowledge that excludes other ways of knowing. For the question of method and value, see chapter 1, "Against Method." For the question of facilitation, see chapter 6, "Carrying the Feeling."

9 *Merriam-Webster.com Dictionary*, s.v. "cuff (v.)," accessed January 15, 2016, https://www.merriam-webster.com/dictionary/cuff.

10 Personal communication. October 15, 2015.

11 These definitions of the anarchive were written by Massumi during our 2016 event *Distributing the Insensible, Performing the Anarchive*. They are based on the collective work done by SenseLab on the anarchive between 2014 and 2016.

12 Christina Sharpe brings thought and care together to amplify the work care does in the qualitative register of black thought. She writes, "I want to think 'the wake' as a problem of and for thought. I want to think 'care' as a problem for thought. I want to think care in the wake as a problem for thinking and of and for Black non/being in the world. Put another way, *In the Wake: On Blackness and Being* is a work that insists

and performs that thinking needs care ('all thought is Black thought') and that thinking and care need to stay in the wake" (2016, 5).

13 The concept of the surplus-value of life is mobilized by Massumi in *99 Theses on the Revaluation of Value* (2018).

Chapter 4. Experimenting Immediation

1 Our first "home" was Sha Xin Wei's Topological Media Lab at Concordia University (2004–2005). From there we moved to the Montreal-based Society for Art and Technology (2005–2008).

2 Will in Nietzsche is never the will of an individual. The play is always of force against force. Deleuze (1986, 7) writes, "Nietzsche's concept of force is therefore that of a force which is related to another force: in this form force is called will. The will (will to power) is the differential element of force. A new conception of the philosophy of the will follows from this. For the will is not exercised mysteriously on muscles or nerves, still less on 'matter in general', but is necessarily exercised on another will. The real problem is not that of the relation of will to the involuntary but rather of the relation of a will that commands to a will that obeys—that obeys to a greater or lesser extent. 'Will' can of course operate only on 'will'—and not on 'matter' (not on 'nerves' for example): enough, one must venture the hypothesis that wherever 'effects' are recognised, will is operating on will" (1989, 49).

3 Brian Massumi and I wrote at length about the event in the context of SenseLab in *Thought in the Act* (Manning and Massumi 2014a).

4 For more on the politics of affirmation as distinct from an optimistic politics, see my "Postscript: Affirmation without Credit," in *The Minor Gesture* (Manning 2016).

5 Deleuze writes, "Belief is no longer referred to a different or transformed world. . . . Because the point is to discover and restore belief in the world, before and beyond words. . . . What is certain is that believing is no longer believing in another world, or in a transformed world. It is only, it is simply believing in the body. It is giving discourse to the body, and, for this purpose, reaching the body before discourses, before words, before things are named. . . . Artaud said the same thing, believe in the *flesh*: 'I am a man who has lost his life and is searching by all means possible to make it regain its place.' . . . We must believe in the body, but as in the germ of life . . . which bears witness to life, in this world as it is. We need an ethic or a faith, which makes fools laugh: it is not a need to believe in something else, but a need to believe in this world, of which fools are a part" (1989, 172–73).

6 Deleuze's concept of the intercessor has been mistranslated as "mediator." The intercessor is an immediating force—the exact opposite of a mediator (Deleuze n.d.).

7 The full quote reads: "In studying a philosopher, the right attitude is neither reverence nor contempt, but first a kind of hypothetical sympathy, until it is possible to know what it feels like to believe in his theories, and only then a revival of the critical attitude, which should resemble, as far as possible, the state of mind of a person abandoning opinions which he has hitherto held" (Russell 1961, 58).

8   SenseLab's approach is one of immanent critique. For more on the concept, see chapter 1, "Against Method" in *The Minor Gesture* (Manning 2016). See also Massumi (2010). The concept comes from Gilles Deleuze. Daniel Smith and John Protevi (2018) write, "Deleuze attacks Hegel and others in what we can call—though Deleuze did not—the 'identitarian' tradition first of all by means of a radicalized reading of Kant, whose genius, as Deleuze explains in *Kant's Critical Philosophy* (1985), was to have conceived of a purely *immanent* critique of reason—a critique that did not seek 'errors' of reason produced by external causes, but rather 'illusions' that arise from within reason itself by the illegitimate (transcendent) uses of the syntheses of consciousness. Deleuze characterized his own work as a philosophy of immanence, arguing that Kant himself had failed to realize fully the ambitions of his critique, for at least two reasons: first, the failure to pursue a fully immanent critique, and second, the failure to propose a genetic account of real experience, resting content with the account of the conditions of possible experience."

9   In the English translation, *fabulation* is mistranslated as "storytelling." While fabulation is a kind of storytelling, it is vital to the understanding of the concept that it be understood as a deviation from mythologizing forms of narration.

10 Tavia Nyong'o's conceptualization of "afro-fabulation" in *Afro-Fabulations* is an example of how fabulation facilitates encounters with modes of telling that fall out of the generalized account of what already counts as the political and the social. He writes, "How might we begin to make sense of the paradoxical vibrance of a form of life endangered, or even erased, by efforts at documentation and representation? What do we do with feelings that resist retrospective vindication? In this book, I am interested in answering such questions through a critical and fabulative archiving of a world that 'was never meant to survive' as Audre Lorde memorably put it—and a world that, I would add, was perhaps also *never meant to appear*" (3). Nyong'o's coining of the concept of afro-fabulation as what brings to appearance what would otherwise remain erased is very much in tune with the politics of fabulation foregrounded here in terms of SenseLab practice. Afro-fabulation, for Nyong'o, is "a theory and practice of black time and temporality" inspired, amongst others, by Édouard Glissant's *Poetics of Relation* and Saidiya Hartman's concept of "critical fabulation" (5).

11 On angular sociality, Nyong'o writes, "The angular sociality of black performative time exemplifies my argument that the blackness we would leave behind is the blackness that will find us in the end. The black experience recorded in and as artworks resists being mastered by the clock or plotted into historical periods. And it calls for a different theory of the history of everyday life, one that includes but is not encapsulated by the habitual or the mundane" (2018, 51).

12 For more on the *Avoca Project* and Watford House, see Bywaters (2014).

13 Bywaters (2014).

14 The lead artist for the garden was Chinese Australian artist Lindy Lee, the designer and project manager was landscape artist Mel Ogden from Taiwan, and gardener Martin Wynne was the soil expert. Partners in the project included landowners Harvey and Carol Wilkins, the Bendigo Chinese Museum, the Pyrenees Shire, Avoca Primary School, and the Avoca Business and Tourism Committee.

15 Many versions of this critique exist, including writing by Franco (Bifo) Berardi, Giorgio Agamben, Steven Shaviro, and Gerald Raunig, among others. For a compelling read that takes the question further, see Harney (2013).

16 On bare activity, see Massumi (2011).

17 See the work of the Design Studio for Social Intervention. They write, "In 2017, we created Social Emergency Response Centers (SERCS) to help people understand the moment we're in, from all different perspectives. Co-created with activists, artists and community members, SERCS are temporary, pop-up spaces that help us move from rage and despair into collective, radical action. SERCS are continuing and growing—a people-led public infrastructure sweeping the country from Utica, MS to Atlanta, Albuquerque, Washington DC, Chicago, Orange, NJ, Hartford, CT, etc. They are popping up in homes, community centers, schools, churches and conferences. SERCS function as both an artistic gesture and a practical solution. As such, they aim to find the balance between the two, answering questions like: How will we feed people—and their hunger for justice? How will we create a shelter—where it's safe to bring your whole damn self? What will reconstruction—of civil society—look like?" (Design Studio for Social Intervention, n.d.)

Chapter 5. Practicing the Schizz

1 It is important to underscore that a lack of speech does not mean "without language." Nonspeaking autistics are not, in fact, nonspeaking. They voice in many ways, using type and gesture and movement and tics and stims, as amplified in the ticcingflapping pocket practice. Nonspeaking simply refers to their lack of spoken language and to the complexities that come of needing facilitation to make themselves understood in a neurotypical environment.

2 Jean Oury established the La Borde clinic in 1953. The principles of La Borde (and the institutional psychotherapy it put in place) rested on group processes, including a sharing, among patients and staff, of all decision-making processes regarding care. Felix Guattari speaks of the work as creating "environments for living" (*milieux de vie*) where the group-subject is an ecological formation, always in excess of the one. Guattari, who worked at La Borde from its inception, speaks of institutional psychiatry as an engagement with the social field. He refuses to separate the individual from the social—"there is not one individual unconscious and one collective unconscious, We are not specialists of the individual unconscious" (Guattari in Igor Barrère 1977). For a look at daily life at La Borde, see the documentary film, "La Borde, le droit à la folie" (Barrère, 1977).

3 Though the contexts are different and the stakes incomparable, Saidiya Hartman's account of practice in *Scenes of Subjection* is always with me when thinking about what practice can do. Hartman's account of practice, always in the context of slavery and its afterlife, is presented as "'a way of operating' defined by 'the non-autonomy of its field of action,' internal manipulations of the established order, and ephemeral victories" (1997, 50). Active in the relational field of action where the production of subjectivity is most tangibly felt, practice for Hartman is always concerned with

the workings of power. It is in the everyday that "tactics of resistance, modes of self-fashioning, and figurations of freedom" are most visibly at work, and with them "the construction of the subject and social relations" (11). Careful not to situate the "everyday practices [as] strategies of passive revolution," Hartman's engagement with practice serves to "emphasize that peregrinations, surreptitious appropriation, and moving about were central features of resistance or what could be described as the subterranean 'politics' of the enslaved" (50). "Practice is not simply a way of naming these efforts but rather a way of thinking about the character of resistance, the precariousness of the assaults waged against domination, the fragmentary character of these efforts and the transient battles won, and the characteristics of a politics without a proper locus" (51).

4 In *Anti-Oedipus* (Deleuze and Guattari 1983), *groupes sujets* and *groupes assujettis* are translated as "subject-groups" and "subjugated-groups." I have chosen throughout to call them "group-subjects" and "subjugated groups." In the intervening years since the publication of *Anti-Oedipus*, it has become common to speak of the "group-subject" when referring to *groupes sujets*, and SenseLab has adopted that language. Arguments could be made for either translation. The important thing is to understand that it is not a group of subjects but an agglomeration of tendencies that activate the transindividual forces that flow through the emergent constellation.

5 For an account of autistic perception in relation to Deligny's practice, see chapter 8, "The Shape of Enthusiasm," in *Always More Than One* (Manning 2013).

6 In *The Logic of Sense*, Deleuze makes the connection between the event and the problematic field. He writes, "We can speak of events only in the context of the problem whose conditions they determine. We can speak of events only as singularities deployed in a problematic field, in the vicinity of which the solutions are organized" (1990b, 56).

7 A different proposition with the same title was practiced at the R.I.C.E. summer school in August 2016 (http://riceonhydra.org/index.html). It was here that Brian Massumi and I encountered it. At R.I.C.E., participants were encouraged to ask anyone to join them for a bench talk during a ten-day event. The bench talk was open in its form, mostly used as a means of sharing work and getting to know another participant. This proposition was tweaked for the SenseLab *Distributing the Insensible* event.

8 The writing of the propositions is done collectively and distributed on an online hub.

9 The spelling of spaZe is different depending on who writes it. This is due to all kinds of things, including different accents (the pronunciation can take a definitely Brazilian bent and sound more like spaaaaz or find a hard Dutch z like spatz). Concepts emerge propositionally at SenseLab and this is certainly the case for spaZe, which came about over years of experimentation with what else space can do. The z grew out of explorations around rezzzonance, reverberation, detour, dissensus. Sometimes we need lots of z and so spaZe becomes Spazzzzzz. This can signal a strong need for deviation. In writing this book, I asked people again and again how I should spell it and over several years we never achieved consensus. So please don't take my

spelling as "the" spelling. As of March 2020, we have spaZe (SenseLab at Concordia), underspz (experimental environment for radical landingz and convivialities, including a cricket franch—farm? ranch?), then middlespz moved into action with the urgent needs around COVID-19 (rent-free living for anyone stranded has become schizokitchen, schizocouture, schizostudy). Upperspz is coming next. We don't yet know what it will do.

10   In a conversation with Rolnik (April 17, 2019), she recounted that the concept of "structuring the self" was actually coined by her and not Clark. Rolnik today wishes she had never come up with the concept as it masks the relational nature of the work and its reach far beyond any normative sense of self.

11   The series can be found on the SenseLab website. The announcement for one iteration can be found here: "Schizo-Somatic Workshop #18 June 27, 2-4pm," SenseLab—3E June 24, 2018, http://senselab.ca/wp2/schizo-somatic-workshop-18-june-27-3-5pm/.

12   Rolnik traces a relation between Clark's work and that of schizoanalysis. She speaks of the "the keen interest" clinical work "had elicited in Lygia—especially the experience of institutional psychotherapy undertaken at La Borde, a psychiatric hospital whose clinical director was Guattari, and also its unfolding in schizoanalysis, the fruit of the psychoanalyst's collaboration with Deleuze. The artist had avidly read the *Anti-Oedipus*, the first conjoint work by the two authors, at the very moment of its publication in 1972, and there she found a curious syntony with her own investigations" (2007, 8).

interlude. How Do We Repair?

1   Wikipedia, s.v. "Kintsugi," last modified February 18, 2020, https://en.wikipedia.org/wiki/Kintsugi.

2   Goat Island is a Chicago-based collaborative performance group founded in 1989 and disbanded in 2009. Core members included Karen Christopher, Matthew Goulish, Lin Hixson (director), Mark Jeffery, Bryan Saner, and Litó Walkey. Associate members included Cynthia Ashby, Lucy Cash (formerly Lucy Baldwyn), CJ Mitchell, Judd Morrissey, Margaret Nelson, John Rich, Charissa Tolentino, and Chantal Zakari (Goat Island, n.d.).

3   *Goat Island* Archive: *We Have Discovered the Performance by Making It*, curated by Nicholas Lowe, officially opened from March 30 to June 23, 2019. Unofficially, the exhibition began in February 2019 when artists invited to create performances based on the works in the Goat Island archive came to present works in progress to audiences in the wider Chicago area. Artists invited to create work included Hancock & Kelly (Richard Hancock and Traci Kelly), Augusto Corrieri, Robert Walton, Judith Leemann, Jefferson Pinder, BADco., Vladka Horvat, Ryan Tacata, Ian Hatcher, and Erin Manning (see City of Chicago, n.d.).

4   For a more detailed engagement with the concept of the diagram, see Deleuze (2003). Deleuze writes: "The diagram is thus the operative set of asignifying and nonrepresentative lines and zones, lines-strokes and color-patches. And the opera-

tion of the diagram, its function, says Bacon, is to be 'suggestive'. . . . Not only can we differentiate diagrams, but we can also date the diagram of a painter, because there is always a moment when the painter confronts it most directly. The diagram is indeed a chaos, a catastrophe, but it is also a germ of order or rhythm. It is a violent chaos in relation to the figurative givens, but it is a germ of rhythm in relation to the new order of the painting. As Bacon says, it 'unlocks areas of sensation'" (2013, 101–2).

5 From Hartman's *Lose Your Mother*: "Who could deny that the United States had been founded on slavery or disregard the wealth created by enslaved laborers? Or brush aside three centuries of legal subjection? Yet I remain agnostic about reparations. I fear that petitions for redress are forms of political appeal that have outlived their usefulness. Did the bid to make a legal or political claim in an officially 'post-racist' society require us to make arguments in a moral language that appeals to the abolitionist consciousness of white folks, who accept that slavery was wrong *and* believe that racism has ended? Are reparations a way of cloaking the disasters of the present in the guise of the past because even our opponents can't defend slavery now? Did we want a Federal Bureau of African American Affairs to decide and manage what we were owed? Or did we hope that the civil suits could accomplish what a social movement had failed to do, that is, to eradicate racism and poverty?" (2008a, 166).

6 Moten comments, "Insofar as black studies has earned a right to look out for itself now, for a little bit . . . and insofar as black studies has earned a right to look out for itself, what that really means, I think, is that black studies has earned the right to try again to take its fundamental responsibility, which is to be a place where we can look out for the earth. I think that black studies has a fundamental and specific though not necessarily exclusive mission, and that mission is to try to save the earth or at least to try to save . . . to save the possibility of human existence on the earth" (Kelley and Moten 2017).

7 Hartman writes, "Admittedly my own writing is unable to exceed the limits of the sayable dictated by the archive. It depends upon the legal records, surgeons' journals, ledgers, ship manifests, and captains' logs, and in this regard falters before the archive's silence and reproduces its omissions. The irreparable violence of the Atlantic slave trade resides precisely in all the stories that we cannot know and that will never be recovered. This formidable obstacle or constitutive impossibility defines the parameters of my work" (2008a, 12).

Chapter 6. Me Lo Dijo un Pajarito

Earlier versions of this chapter appeared as "Me Lo Dijo un Pajarito: Neurodiversity, Black Life, and the University as We Know It," *Social Text* 36, no. 3 (September 2018): 1–24, and in *Socially Just Pedagogies: Posthumanist, Feminist and Materialist Perspectives in Higher Education*, ed. Rosi Braidotti, Vivienne Bozalek, Tamara Shefer, and Michalinos Zembylas (London: Bloomsbury, 2018).

1 Mayra Morales. Email to author, March 18, 2017.

2   I have no interest in functioning labels, which are embedded in the logic of neuro-
    typicality. There is an important literature, written by autistics, about functioning la-
    bels. Sources include Amy Sequenzia (n.d. and 2012a), Nick Walker (2013), Melanie
    Yergeau (2010), and Mel Baggs (2013).

3   For more on facilitation as relational pedagogy, or what I call "the facilitation of
    facilitation," see Manning, chapter 6, "Carrying the Feeling," in *The Minor Gesture*
    (2016). Excellent neurodiversity blogs include *As Small as a World and as Large as
    Alone*, by Mel Baggs (http://withasmoothroundstone.tumblr.com/archive); *Un-
    strange Mind*, by Sparrow Rose (http://unstrangemind.com); *Estee Relation*, by
    Estee Klar and Adam Wolfond (https://www.esteerelation.com); *Polly's Pages*, by
    Donna Williams (http://blog.donnawilliams.net/); *Autistext*, by Melanie Yergeau
    (http://autistext.com); *Ollibean*, by Amy Sequenzia (https://ollibean.com/author
    /amy-sequenzia/); *Autistic Hoya*, by Lydia X. Z. Brown (http://www.autistichoya
    .com); *Radical Neurodivergence Speaking* (http://timetolisten.blogspot.ca); *Neuro-
    queer* (http://neuroqueer.blogspot.ca); and *Shaping Clay*, by Michael Scott Monje Jr.
    (http://www.mmonjejr.com). Two recent publications are Tito Mukhopadhyay's
    Plankton Dreams (2015) and Melanie Yergeau's *Authoring Autism: On Rhetoric and
    Neurological Queerness* (2018).

4   The managerial university has not yet arrived in Quebec in the way it has taken hold
    in Australia and the United Kingdom, but it is certainly coming, and when this hap-
    pens, the conditions of power/knowledge will change again because it won't be "we"
    who operate the university in the way it currently is, with professors holding the po-
    sitions in administration. The university I write about here is still much closer to the
    one we might want to teach in, where knowledges circulate quite freely and where
    students still pay relatively little tuition. But it would be shortsighted to suggest that
    just because it's not as bad as it could be, it's good. The conditions for learning are
    compromised when the diagrams of power/knowledge are not addressed, particu-
    larly in these neoliberal times.

5   I've written extensively on *In My Language* both in the concluding chapter "Propo-
    sitions for Thought in Motion," in *Relationscapes* (Manning 2009) and in the first
    chapter, "Toward a Leaky Sense of Self," in *Always More Than One* (Manning 2013).

6   See Massumi's and my "Thought in the Act," in *Thought in the Act* (Manning and
    Massumi 2014a), for more on practices and philosophies of research-creation. See
    also *Inflexions: A Journal for Research Creation* and the collected volume *Immediation*
    (Manning et al. 2019).

7   I think here particularly of Mel Chen's beautiful essay "Brain Fog: The Race for Crip-
    istemology" (2014). Writing about brain fog and its relation to a sense of thinking
    being out of reach, they inquire into academia's impoverished concept of "compre-
    hension—a word that suggests both finality but also wholeness of grasp—something
    that feels impossible when brains are foggy" (172). How, they ask, might comprehen-
    sion be aligned to "the methodology, the operands, the instruments of cripistemo-
    logical theorizing" (173)? The thrust of the argument is not simply to "re-value this
    experienced cognitive 'partiality,' experienced as a 'less' of rationality" but to explore
    the "particular kind of cognition called comprehension, which academic thinkers

are supposed to foster even as we pursue 'a single line of thought'" (173). "Cognitive or intellectual disability—and its broader matrix of cognitive variation—represents the near unthinkable for academia (which then, in the light of the connections I have been making, says something about academia's continuing struggles with whiteness)" (177). Working to move beyond the stultifying operations of comprehension, Chen aims to consider "a shared project of cripistemological making . . . to ask what kind of cognitions, what kind of information management, what kind of memory retrieval will we require to do the theorizing that will be important to move forward? . . . What would a decolonized or decolonizing cripistemology—one that took that decolonization seriously by recognizing coloniality's serious attachment to typology, identification, and orders of knowledge—look, smell, and feel like? Is it possible that we could talk about partial knowing working agonistically against and thus also with comprehension, almost as the queer works in odd partnership with the straight and narrow?" (182).

8   Moten begins *In the Break* with the following: "The history of blackness is a testament to the fact that objects can and do resist. Blackness—the extended movement of a specific upheaval, an ongoing irruption that anarranges every line—is a strain that pressures the assumption of the equivalence of personhood and subjectivity. While subjectivity is defined by the subject's possession of itself and its objects, it is troubled by a dispossessive force objects exert such that the subject seems to be possessed—infused, deformed—by the object it possesses. I'm interested in what happens when we consider the phonic materiality of such propriative exertion. Or, to invoke and diverge from Saidiya Hartman's fundamental work and phrasing, I'm interested in the convergence of blackness and the irreducible sound of necessarily visual performance at the scene of objection" (2003, 1). Breaking the shit down is about the work of anarranging at the heart of black life, or, better said, the play, the music of it, the sound of it, the listening of it. "Is there a way," Moten asks, "to subject this unavoidable model of subjection to a radical breakdown?" (5).

9   *The micropolitical* and *the protopolitical* as I use them throughout are far more allied to the way Hartman uses *practice* than to the concept of "the political proper," maintaining the distinction Jacques Rancière makes between "politics" and "the political" (see Rancière 2004).

10 Adam Wolfond in a typed conversation with his mother, Estee Klar, March 19, 2017. Shared by Wolfond and Klar in an email to the author.

11 Many autistics and autistic advocates worry about the ways in which autistic tics and meltdowns can read as dangerous to the police and worry about the possibility of police violence. This is especially the case with black autistics, given the systemic racism in policing (see Spencer 2016).

pocket practice: livingloving

1   UofTDaniels, "Robin D. G. Kelley and Fred Moten in Conversation" (1:11:08– 1:12:20), June 15, 2017, https://www.youtube.com/watch?v=fP-2F9MXjRE. See also the appendix of Du Bois (1995).

2 The full quote from Fred Moten reads: "So, I've been trying to think of living out from the outside, or out, so to speak, of that inside/outside opposition" (in Hartman and Moten 2018).

Chapter 7. Not at a Distance

1 In *Parables for the Virtual*, while not using the term directly, Brian Massumi's concern is also with backgriddism. He writes: "If passage is primary in relation to position, processual indeterminacy is primary in relation to social determination. . . . Social and cultural determinations on the model of positionality are also secondary and derived. Gender, race, and sexual orientation also emerge and back-form their reality. Passage precedes construction. But construction does effectively back-form its reality. Grids happen. So social and cultural determinations feed back into the process from which they arose. Indeterminacy and determination, change and freeze-framing, go together. They are inseparable and always actually coincide while remaining disjunctive in their modes of reality. To say that passage and indeterminacy "come first" or "are primary" is more a statement of ontological priority than the assertion of a time sequence. They have ontological privilege in the sense that they constitute the field of the emergence, while positionings are what emerge. The trick is to express that priority in a way that respects the inseparability and contemporaneousness of the disjunct dimensions: their ontogenetic difference. The work of Gilbert Simondon is exemplary in this regard" (2002, 8).

2 See the first chapter, "Toward a Leaky Sense of Self," in *Always More Than One* (Manning 2013), for a more detailed account of the relational body.

3 "What is it like to have a Sensory Processing/Integration Disorder?," 2011. The heading "The Word on the Breeze, and Through the Floor" appeared in Ball 2014.

4 For a vital critique of ABA, see Yergeau (2018). See also Smith-Donohoe (2018) as well as Anthony Easton's articles, including "Why Do Autism Specialists Want to Stamp Out Autistic Traits?" (2016).

5 Richard Johnson, "A Genius Explains," *The Guardian*, February 11, 2005, Life and Style, https://www.theguardian.com/theguardian/2005/feb/12/weekend7.weekend2.

6 Johnson 2005.

7 Johnson 2005.

8 Different accounts of synesthesia exist, ranging from those that emphasize unusual feats of memory, limiting synesthesia to an outlier condition, and those that suggest that in fact all perception is synesthetic in germ, albeit for the most part wildly reduced by distantist and backgriddist tendencies: "Synesthesia is considered the norm for infantile perception. The theory is that it becomes so habitual as to fall out of perception in the 'normal' course of growing up. It is thought to persist as a nonconscious underpinning of all subsequent perception, as if the objects and scenes we see are all 'threads' pulled by habit from a biogrammatic fabric of existence" (Massumi 2002, 188).

9 Johnson 2005.

10   In his book *See It Feelingly* Ralph James Savarese (2018b) takes on this assumption
that autistics cannot move beyond the literal by engaging in projects of reading
literature with a number of autistics across the autistic spectrum. In an adjacent
publication (Savarese 2018a), discussing the book project, he writes:

"According to experts, autism's 'triad of impairments' (in communication,
imagination and social interaction) made literature a bad fit for the autistic brain.
Studies from the previous three decades postulated deficits in two key areas: theory
of mind and the apprehension of figurative language. People with autism, the argument went, are 'unable to develop an awareness of what is in the mind of another
human.' If the mental states of others are beyond their reach, how can they possibly
manage the moody jungle-gym of make-believe conflict that we call fiction?

"And if autistic people struggle with the dowsing rods of metaphor and irony,
how can they divine a work's deeper meanings? An obdurate, self-contained literality plagues autistic consciousness. This view of autism became so prevalent that a
best-selling novel, *The Curious Incident of the Dog in the Nighttime*, made social and
metaphorical bafflement a central aspect of the protagonist's characterization.

"Yet with time, perspectives change, and stereotypes begin to waver."

11   The claim that autistics live "in a world of their own" undermines the very concept
of neurodiverse sociality. See Sue Rubin's important film, *Autism Is a World* (2004).
Melanie Yergeau also addresses this stereotype when she writes, "Autism's essence,
if you will, has been clinically identified as a disorder that prevents individuals from
exercising free will and precludes them from accessing self-knowledge and knowledge
of human others (Thornton 2011). Its subjects are not subjects in the agentive sense
of the word, but are rather victim-captives of a faulty neurology. Deborah Barnbaum's
(2008) *The Ethics of Autism* is one such account. A philosophical treatise, the book
promotes a portrait of autism that is the antithesis of both community and communicability, echoing the stereotypical sentiment that autistics are closed off from the larger
world. 'There is something intrinsically limiting in an autistic life,' writes Barnbaum
(154). And, later, 'Autism cuts people off from people' (174). What Barnbaum and
others suggest is that autism is a world without people, that a world without people is
a world without rhetoric, and that an arhetorical life is a life not worth living—a life
beyond the realm of voluntary action and intentionality" (2018, 7–8).

12   Wikipedia, s.v. "Theory of Mind," last modified February 25, 2020, https://en
.wikipedia.org/wiki/Theory_of_mind. For more on autism and theory of mind, see
Yergeau (2018). I have also written about it in "An Ethics of Language in the Making," chapter 7 in *Always More Than One* (Manning 2013) and in "Coming Alive in
a World of Texture," in *Thought in the Act* (Manning and Massumi 2014a). For a nuanced account of empathy that reads neuroscientific studies in relation to a project
of reading with autistics, see also R. Savarese (2018b).

13   These presuppositions can be found in the vast majority of neuroscientific studies
I have read on synesthesia. A notable exception is Laurent Mottron, whose team
includes autistic Michelle Dawson. See, for instance, Mottron et al. (2006) and
Mottron et al. (2013). Refusing the deficit model, they write, "We can hypothesize
that an enhanced performance in domain-general peaks will not be observed if tasks

are standardized on autistic performance. As a consequence, the extent of the size of any peak of ability is at least partly a function of the matching strategy used to compare the performance of autistics and that of non-autistics. If certain language-based instruments are used, autistics' intelligence risks being underestimated, thus their scores on areas of strength will be similar to those of TD persons with higher IQs on the same instrument. In contrast, the finding of superior performance of autistics may lose its statistical significance when tests which minimize mandatory language demands are used, as autistics will typically score higher and will, therefore, be matched to TD persons at a higher level (for a discussion of matching issues in the study of autistics, see Burack et al., 2004). Thus, some, but not all (e.g., pitch discrimination, Simard-Meilleur et al. 2012) domain-general peaks of ability may be favored or magnified by matching strategies. However, our focus in this paper is on the types of superior performance that are so robust that they transcend matching strategies, and on how these performances, in as much as they are found only among some autistics, contribute to within-group autistic heterogeneity" (Mottron et al. 2013, 211) For a general rethinking of neuroscientific paradigms and autism, see R. Savarese (2010).

14 Any experiment that depends on a face test runs on neurotypical bias. Used in the creation of biometric data, the great danger of face tests and facial recognition software is that they uphold this bias. This should not be underestimated: The Karolinksa Directed Emotional Faces Test and other similar tests are used in artificial intelligence. This has widespread effects not only with regard to autism and neurodiversity but in terms of black life and racism more broadly. Much research has shown that white people have difficulty parsing black faces. Findings of a recent study from North Carolina State University demonstrate the breadth of violence normative standardization can cause. The experiment involved recruiting forty university students (most of whom were white) training to become teachers, asking them to look at pictures of twenty black and white men and women, and then to identify one of five emotions the actors were showing (happiness, anger, surprise, sadness, or fear). Separately, those recruited for the experiment watched videos depicting both a black and a white boy in elementary school. "One pair of videos had the boys doing something that could be seen as callous, with the black boy stepping on someone's homework with muddy shoes and the white boy walking away with someone else's handheld video game. The other two videos featured actions more likely to be seen as unintentionally insensitive: the black boy made a possibly rude comment about another student's work, and the white boy put someone else's work in the trash while cleaning up. For all the videos, the volunteers were asked to rate how hostile the boy was on a scale from one to five.

"In the photo task, the volunteers were consistently worse at guessing the emotions of both black men and women. *Overall, black faces were more than twice as likely to be misread than white faces. And when it came to anger, the misreading was even worse. Black faces were four times as likely to be mistakenly seen as angry.*

"With the video test, the volunteers similarly attributed more malice to black boys. On average, the hostility rating of black boys was 3.37, while the average rating of white boys was 2.25. And even in the scenarios where the boy seemingly meant no harm, the average point difference in rating between white and black boys stayed the same. . . .

"The study's findings are some of the first to empirically show that a similar bias for seeing anger exists toward black women as well as men. But other qualitative research—relying on interviews and surveys of schoolchildren—has found black girls are more often singled out for not being 'ladylike' compared to white girls" (Cara 2018, discussing Halberstadt et al. 2018; my emphasis).

15 Clark, 2015.

16 I am interested less in the limit cases of synesthesia than in the notion that synesthesia is a quality of perception that accompanies the perception of all infants. This approach challenges the deficit model of perception by inquiring not into what makes some bodies different but into how perception shifts over a lifetime of organizing bodies into the baseline of a body schema based on neurotypicality. "Infants who were two and three months old showed significant shape-color associations. By eight months the preference was no longer pronounced, and in adults it was gone altogether" (Konnikova 2012). "But now it turns out that synaesthetes might not belong to a club as exclusive as once thought. Their rich palette and vivid sensations might be accessible to us all. Even though not kin to Nabokov, we too could be reading our books in aquarelle. The under-examined complexities of ordinary perception, some neuroscientists and developmental psychologists contend, suggest that, like the Nabokovs, we all inhabit the synaesthetic spectrum—we just need to look back in time, to when we were infants with developing brains" (Ravindran 2015). See also Maurer and Mondloch (2005).

17 Clark (2017a) writes, "The final irony is that a DeafBlind man, the late Robert J. Smithdas, wrote these words. Many hearing and sighted people have expressed the same sentiments, but distantism is so pervasive that we all have internalized it. Helen Keller spoke of us as being imprisoned in the 'double dungeon of darkness and silence' and that we are 'the loneliest people on Earth.' She was being fanciful, but what is true is that the marginalization we experience is too often literal, involving physical margins.

"Think about it. Billions of people on this planet, and all of them agreeing that hearing and vision are required for leading full, normal lives. Billions of people of one mind that being DeafBlind must be an unendurable fate. Billions of dollars poured into the hope of medical cures. Distantism, that old serpent, held the whole world in its remote-control spell.

"And then our sisters from Seattle had the audacity to say that there's a Deaf-Blind way. To say that hearing and vision are not necessary. To say that the only cure we need is each other. Can you feel the world shaking as it starts to, finally, come together?"

18 See Mukhopadhyay (2011). There are several passages in this book that expand on Mukhopadhyay's synesthesia, including the description of a woman's voice "that tasted like a tamarind pickle" (110) and a man's voice that "transformed into a long apple green with yellow strings" (200).

19 A more complete definition is as follows: "A mirror neuron is a neuron that fires both when an animal acts and when the animal observes the same action performed by another. Thus, the neuron 'mirrors' the behavior of the other, as though the observer were itself acting." Wikipedia, s.v. "Mirror Neuron," last modified January 19, 2020, https://en.wikipedia.org/wiki/Mirror_neuron.

20 In discussion with John Lee Clark, he explains the difference between TASL and ASL: "Tactile reception of ASL means it's still ASL, standard ASL. Just that I have my hands on your hands as you speak standard ASL. That's it" (email communication, August 20, 2019).

21 With ProTactile, shifts have occurred with respect to "pointing to things in the environment, keeping track of conversations, describing things and events in terms of their size, shape, texture and positioning in space." Christine Roschaert writes, "I interned at the Seattle Lighthouse for the Blind in Seattle in 2005 and became fast friends with Granda, who introduced me to the yet-unnamed Pro-Tactile (PT) method. I was taken aback and confused when she would start touching my body more, but then I started to understand that they were 'added' social cues to inform me if her head was nodding (tapping on my lap or shoulder), her hand travelling down from my left to right shoulder (she was moving from my left side to my right side), and there was that 'aha' PT moment one night when we sat outside on the porch and I wondered the perennial question: how do we let Deafblind people know we were truly laughing? I hated the usual sign of 'ha ha' in my hands when I tactiled with the person I was sharing my joke to. 'Ha ha' in my hand is akin to a hearing person bellowing out nothing but a fake laugh; a Deaf person slapping a hand on their lap and their expression shows they're faking their jest. I experimented this PT move by placing aj's hand on my throat and I laughed out loud, a true to heart Coco laugh and aj was shocked, still, then she tried it again. It was a true PT action, which included Deafblind in the ever-elusive world of pure joy" (Roschaert 2013).

22 Clark writes, "There are distantist modes of touch and there are protactile modes of touch. A distantist cannot truly teach or empower our children to live and learn as tactile people. Yet the field of education of DeafBlind children has never included us as teachers. Why is that?" (Clark 2017a).

23 For a sustained encounter with the concept of immediation, see Manning et al. (2018).

pocket practice: ticcingflapping

1 Many classical autistics do have some degree of speech-based communication, but it most often hinders what they are trying to say.

2 John Lee Clark's (2017a) concept of distantism is based on the definition of distance as "standing apart."

3 Adam Wolfond, shared with permission by Estee Klar, June 4, 2018. Unpublished.

4 Estee Klar is always beside Adam Wolfond, facilitating the sharing of his thoughts with the world and reminding us, at every turn, of how many of our assumptions around intelligence are based on being able to use language easily and freely.

5 For a compelling account of communication, autism, and exclusion from personhood, see Baggs (2007).
6 Adam Wolfond, shared with permission by Estee Klar, July 18, 2018. Unpublished.
7 Kerima Çevik's 2019 article "Distorting DEEJ: Deconstructing a Misinformed Literature Review" is an excellent account of how these presuppositions are constructed
in the literature.
8 Tito Mukhopadhyay, Facebook post, May 28, 2010.
9 Tito Mukhopadhyay, Facebook post, February 7, 2010.
10 For a more extended discussion on the voluntary and the nonvoluntary, and on the
question of movement, see the introduction, "In a Minor Key," and chapter 6, "Carrying the Feeling," in *The Minor Gesture* (Manning 2016).
11 Tito Mukhopadhyay, personal email conversation. September 14, 2010.
12 Adam Wolfond, shared with permission by Estee Klar, May 31, 2018. Unpublished.
13 Oxford English Dictionary, "meaningless, adj." OED Online, Oxford University Press,
March 2020. Web.
14 Adam Wolfond, shared with permission by Estee Klar, June 7, 2018. Unpublished.
15 About the importance of bath toys in facilitating Wolfond's movement and expression, Estee Klar writes, "The bath toy field (of experience): Do we not assume the
autistic person who holds the child's book or toy to be 'developmentally deficient'
(despite the fact that they can be 'intellectually' advanced? (Intellectual is brack-
eted as I contest the term and its historical associations to normalization, language,
reason and what we assume to be valued knowledge). What a dichotomy! Tito Mukhopadhyay . . . writes: 'Moments are defined by what your senses are compelled to
attend to.' . . . The rubber bath toy is more than its 'developmental' affordance. It is
more than a child's toy. For Adam, it is in part his synaesthesia—colour that he says
he hears, or my voice which he says is the colour green. The rubber bath toy can also
be a way of fielding the environment itself, one that is already too full and rushes
in—as Adam expresses—tapping the toy as a way to keep pace to the 'fast-talkers.' It
is also more than one thing, one meaning, one affect. This is the complexity of neurodiversity and of experience itself. It extends beyond the 'why' question and most
certainly beyond neurotypical interpretations of behaviour and corporeality." Shared
July 20, 2018. Unpublished.
16 Ariane Zurcher (2013) speaks about the concept of presuming competence in a
blog post of the same name. She writes, "When my daughter was first diagnosed at
the age of two and a half, presuming competence was not a concept I was ever told
about or had heard of. And even if someone had suggested we do so, I'm not sure I
would have fully understood what that meant exactly. . . .
"In an interview, Douglas Biklen explained: 'Assume that a child has intellectual
ability, provide opportunities to be exposed to learning, assume the child wants to
learn and assert him or herself in the world. . . .'
"When my daughter was little with almost no language I could not understand
how it was possible for her to learn to read and write if she did not speak first. I
was surprised and confused when I learned how completely wrong I was. When I
read about all the non-speaking Autistic people who had learned to read and write

despite being given no formal instruction, it seemed magical to me. This mind that seemed, from my limited perspective, to not understand so much, actually was taking in far more than I could imagine, let alone believe. It wasn't until I was able to see my own limitations caused by the things I had been told about autism and hence, my daughter, that I was able to move beyond that thinking and embrace another way of thinking. . . .

"What I have come to understand, is that a presumption of competence is much more than a set of beliefs, it is a way of interacting with another human being who is seen as a true equal and as having the same basic human rights as I have. . . .

"A presumption of competence may seem like a leap for many non Autistic people, it may even feel like a disconnect. Some may argue that their non-speaking child cannot possibly understand, that they know this beyond any doubt and I must ask, but how can you know this for sure? We may tell ourselves that our child is too 'severe' and we are setting them up for certain failure by presuming competence. To these people I would suggest the opposite is true. The only true failure is when we walk away and assume *incompetence*. . . .

"To presume competence does not mean we assume there is a 'neurotypical' person 'trapped' or 'imprisoned' under an Autistic 'shell.'"

Chapter 8. Cephalopod Dreams

1   It must be noted that, like most of the thinkers of their time, Deleuze and Guattari have a deeply falsifying reading of autism. They see autism as the catatonic edge of desiring-production turning on itself. Bemoaning Freud's superposition of autism on schizophrenia—"we may well ponder the possibility that the analytic imperialism of the Oedipus complex led Freud to rediscover, and to lend all the weight of his authority to, the unfortunate misapplication of the concept of autism to schizophrenia" (1983, 23)—they see autism as what holds schizophrenia back: "The schizophrenic appears all the more specific and recognizable as a distinct personality if the process is halted, or if it is made an end and a goal in itself, or if it is allowed to go on and on endlessly in a void, so as to provoke that 'horror of . . . extremity wherein the soul and body ultimately perish' (the autist)" (24). In the history of pathologization, it was quite common to overlay schizophrenia onto autism, a practice that Deleuze and Guattari saw as deadening the force of what else moved through schizophrenia. Their mistake was to not understand that the figure of autism that was being imposed was itself a pathologization that had nothing to do with autism: autism has none of the deadening tendencies it is purported to have! Indeed, the irony is that autism is much closer to the description of schizophrenia Deleuze and Guattari create in opposition to the psychiatric model, a description that emphasizes the creative flows and productive potential that come of an innate capacity for the schizz. I see many connections to autistic perception here. Deleuze and Guattari made it their project to pull schizophrenia out of the limiting arena it had come to occupy, and in so doing they inadvertently repathologized autism. The hope throughout is to demonstrate the importance of the schizz for neurodiversity more broadly (beyond

schizophrenia), emphasizing the manner in which both schizophrenia and autism compel us to explore what is in excess of normopathic perception.

2 A contemporary effect of the misreading of the schizophrenic as an individual pathology plays out in work on autism that takes autism as the schizz of our time, reading autism as the double of the schizophrenic. Too often, in these (mis)readings of *Anti-Oedipus*, we are given an individual rather than a field of forces. The ethos of schizoanalysis depends on the creation of techniques that attune to the diversity in diversity of neurodiversity. Any attempt to engage with autism must ask how the analysis carries with itself neurotypical (pathologizing) preconceptions. It must ask how desire is produced in the context of something like an autistic schizz. The work of schizoanalysis must never be reduced to generalities.

3 In *The Principle of Unrest*, Brian Massumi writes, "Contemporary capitalism is increasingly concerned with setting in place the conditions for its products to emerge. They are not only made to emerge, but this happens as a by-product of circulation itself. There are many ways this happens. Examples are the feedback loops that have formed between crowdsourcing and the data-mining of internet, cell phone traffic, and credit-card use on the one hand, and product-development and marketing on the other. The network becomes a matrix of emergence for products that do not preexist, but take shape in and through networked circulation. In the ebb and flow, marketing potentials appear like waves cresting on a sea of movements. These are skimmed off, 'mined,' then concretized as new products to be sold for profit. You could look at the profit generated as embodying a 'surplus-value of flow': a yield of added value emerging from the complexity of movements under way, directly as a function of them. Philosophically speaking, capitalism has learned to motorize itself immanently to its own movements" (2017c, 11).

4 While typically defined as a contract that derives its price from an underlying asset, a derivative is actually a speculation on value itself: "derivatives are defined precisely by their ability to abstract themselves from the value or even ownership of an underlying asset" (Massumi 2018, 21). Taking the shape of futures, options, forwards, swaps, and hedges, derivatives bet on how value will register in the no-time of the trade. Elie Ayache writes, "As opposed to the actual practice of trading, derivative valuation *theory* only deals with probability and stochastic processes and stochastic control and knows nothing of market price or implied volatility. These valuation theories have hitherto proceeded on the theoretical assumption of a stochastic process, and have disregarded the effect of the recalibration of the market on itself. Trading derivatives in the market is precisely pricing them at a variance with the value theory prescribes for them" (2015, 27–28).

5 "Capitalism's driving force is the *differential* between profit and surplus-value: their systemic/processual, systolic/diastolic asymmetry" (Massumi 2018, 16).

6 "The concept of surplus-value of flow is an extrapolation from Marx's analysis of interest-bearing capital as money 'already pregnant with surplus-value,' such that the profit generated 'is not the result of the act of purchase, the actual function that it performs here as money, but rather of the way in which this act is connected with the *overall movement* of capital'" (Massumi 2018, 28, quoting

Marx 1991, 463; emphasis added). Through the surplus-value of flow, derivatives push capital toward a limit "where the gap between system and process tendentially closes" (Massumi 2018, 50). The flow, the excess agitated in the hedging, converges with capitalist capture, moving the process toward measure. Here, "quantification rejoins the singular, becoming fully eventual rather than reductively indicative. This is not an overcoming of capitalist capture, but a singular intensification of it" (51).

7 Different phases of capitalism have composed with value-added differently. In the period of primitive accumulation, when capitalist surplus-value production was based primarily on the extraction of labor, and labor itself was its raw material, value was inextricably connected to racialized labor. "Racialization and the 'universal' value-form are not separate phenomena: value is not constituted simply from deracinated labor dissymmetrically exchanged for the wage, but from racialized labor, historically devalued colonial populations, and slavery" (Beller forthcoming). "For 400 years, from the fifteenth to the nineteenth century, while the capitalist mode of production in Europe engulfed agrarian and artisanal workers, transforming them over the generations into expropriated, dependent fodder for concentration in factories, disciplined to the rhythms and turbulences of the manufacturing process, the organizers of the capitalist world system appropriated Black labor power as constant capital" (Robinson 2000, 308–9). Effects of racialized labor continue in contemporary times, of course. The emphasis here on the surplus-value of flow does not deny that. It simply emphasizes that in this period where capital is most driven by the nonhuman flows it releases, the breadth of its violence must be recognized as exceeding any kind of so-called rational process. "The individual subject of interest forming the fundamental unit of capitalist society is internally differentiated, containing its own population of 'minority practices' of contrasting affective tone and tenor, in a zone of indistinction between rational calculation and affectivity. In other words, there is an infra individual complexity quasi-chaotically agitating within the smallest unit" (Massumi 2015a, 8).

8 On the anagrammatical, Christina Sharpe writes, "As I continue to think with Spillers's grammar, 'which is really a rupture and a radically different kind of cultural continuation' (Spillers 2003, 209), and Fred Moten's opening sentences in *In the Break*, that 'the history of blackness is testament to the fact that objects can and do resist' and 'blackness—the extended movement of a specific upheaval, an ongoing irruption that anarranges every line—is a strain that pressures the assumption of the equivalence of personhood and subjectivity' (Moten 2003, 1), I arrive at blackness as, blackness is, anagrammatical. That is, we can see the moments when blackness opens up into the anagrammatical in the literal sense as when 'a word, phrase, or name is formed by rearranging the letters of another' (Merriam-Webster Online). We can also apprehend this in the metaphorical sense in how, regarding blackness, grammatical gender falls away and new meanings proliferate; how 'the letters of a text are formed into a secret message by rearranging them' or a secret message is discovered through the rearranging of the letters of a text. Ana-, as a prefix, means 'up, in place or time, back, again, anew'" (2016, 76).

9   Spillers is thinking with Nahum Chandler in this citation. See full citation in note 4 in chapter 2.

10 The surplus-value of life is "purely qualitative and concerns the intensity of lived potentials" (Massumi 2018, 16). "A qualitative life value is something that is lived for its own sake; something that is a value in and of itself, in the unexchangeable 'currency' of experience. A life-value has value to the exact degree to which it is incommensurable with any other experience. It is the singular color of an experience, such as it is, all of its own, that makes of it a life-value. In fact, a quality of life has value in exactly the way we say a color or a sound has a value. It has the value of the qualitative character of its own occurrence" (25).

11 For an account of some of the 3E Process Seed Bank's economic and philosophical concerns at the point in 2018 when the platform was in its infancy, see Manning and Massumi (2018). For working papers about different phases of the process of thinking finance at the limit, see the links in SenseLab—3E (n.d.).

12 Conversation with Akseli Virtanen and Dick Bryant, October 19, 2018. For the Economic Space Agency white papers, see https://economicspace.agency/archive/.

13 Dwarf hammer orchids flowers are pollinated by male wasps (thynnine), who are drawn to the specific odors emitted by the orchid which imitate the sex pheromones of receptive female wasps. To the human eye, they have a strange resemblance to purple wasps.

14 Luciana Parisi's provocations are very important for the transversal operations proposed via the processual operator thingies in the 3E Process Seed Bank. Parisi argues for a nonhuman thought with respect to computation, "a possibility of machines to think beyond what they do" (2019, 4).

15 On cephalopod vision: "As already stated, both cephalopods and vertebrates have very complex image-forming eyes with lenses. Both cephalopods and vertebrates have single lens eyes. They work by allowing light to enter through the pupil and be focused by the lens onto the photoreceptor cells of the retina. However, between the two groups of animals there are differences in the shape of the pupil, the way the lens changes focus for distance, the type of receptor cells that receive the light as well as some more subtle differences. In vertebrates the pupil is round, and it changes in diameter depending on the amount of light in the environment. This is important because too much light will distort the image, and too little light will be interpreted as a very faint image. The cephalopod pupil is square and adjusts for the level of light by changing from a square to a narrow rectangle. The way in which the two groups use the lens to focus differs. Vertebrates use muscles around the eye to change the shape of the lens, while cephalopods are able to manipulate their lens in or out to focus at different distances. The receptor cells of vertebrate eyes are rods and cones. The cones are used for vision in high light environments, while the rods are used in low light. The time of day the animal needs its vision to be most effective will dictate the ratio of rods to cones. Cephalopods, however, have receptor cells called rhabdomeres similar to those of other mollusks. These contain microvilli which allow the animal to see polarized and unpolarized light. . . . Lastly, the way in which light is directed at the retina differs between the two groups. Cephalopod

retinas receive incoming light directly, while vertebrate retinas receive light that is bounced back from the back of the eye" (Wood and Jackson, n.d.).

coda: schizzinganarchiving

1 My translations of Anne Querrien's unpublished work throughout.

2 "Aesthesis," *Merriam-Webster.com Dictionary*, accessed March 31, 2020, https://www.merriam-webster.com/dictionary/esthesis.

Adkins, Amey Victoria. 2018. "Symposium Introduction." In *Symposium: Blackpentecostal Breath*. Syndicate. https://syndicate.network/symposia/theology/blackpentecostal -breath/.

Alfred, Taiaiake. 2005. *Wasáse: Indigenous Pathways of Action and Freedom*. Toronto: University of Toronto Press.

Alfred, Taiaiake. 1999. *Peace, Power, Righteousness: An Indigenous Manifesto*. London: Oxford University Press.

Amor, Monica. 2010. "From Work to Frame, In Between, and Beyond: Lygia Clark and Helio Oiticica." *Grey Room* 38 (Winter), 20–37.

Arakawa and Madeline Gins. 2002. *Architectural Body*. Tuscaloosa: University of Alabama Press.

Armstrong, Amaryah. 2018. "Reading the Flesh—Otherwise Methodologies and the Possibility of a Black Theology." In *Symposium: Blackpentecostal Breath*. Syndicate. https://syndicate.network/symposia/theology/blackpentecostal-breath/.

Asbury, Michael. 2005. "Neoconcretism and Minimalism: On Ferreira Gullar's Theory of the Non-object." In *Cosmopolitan Modernisms*, edited by Kobena Mercer, 168–89. Cambridge, MA: MIT Press.

Autism and Angels (blog). https://aspiegrrl.wordpress.com. December 14, 2011.

"*Autism Is a World*: Synopsis." State of the Art. Accessed April 30, 2020. http://www .stateart.com/works.php?workId=27.

Ayache, Elie. 2016. "On Black Scholes." In *Derivatives and the Wealth of Societies*, edited by Ben Lee and Randy Martin, 240–51. Chicago: University of Chicago Press.

Ayache, Elie. 2015. *The Medium of Consistency*. London: Palgrave.

Ayache, Elie. 2008. "I Am a Creator!" ITO 33. http://www.ito33.com/sites/default/files /articles/0807_nail.pdf.

Baggs, Mel. 2013. "Functioning Labels." April 18, 2013. https://ballastexistenz.wordpress .com/tag/functioning-labels/.

Baggs, Mel. 2007. "In My Language." January 14, 2007. YouTube video, 8:36. https://www .youtube.com/watch?v=JnylM1hI2jc.

Balibar, Etienne. 2008. "Theological-Political Treatise." In *The New Spinoza*, edited by Warren Montag and Ted Stolze, 171–206. Minneapolis: University of Minnesota Press.

Ball, Liz. 2014. "Lesser Known Things about Being DeafBlind." *Intervention* 38, no. 1: 8. https://www.cdbanational.com/wp-content/uploads/2016/10/Intervention_Magazine _Fall_2014.pdf.

Barnbaum, Deborah R. 2008. *The Ethics of Autism: Among Them, but Not of Them.* Bloomington: University of Indiana Press.

Baron-Cohen, Simon, Daniel Bor, Jac Billington, Julian Asher, Sally Wheelwright, and Chris Ashwin. 2007. "Savant Memory in a Man with Colour Form-Number Synaesthesia and Asperger Syndrome." *Journal of Consciousness Studies* 14, no. 9–10: 237–51. http://hstrial-tridenttechnical.homestead.com/BaronCohenetal2007.pdf.

Baron-Cohen, Simon, Emma Robson, Meng-Chuan Lai, and Carrie Allison. 2016. "Mirror-Touch Synaesthesia Is Not Associated with Heightened Empathy, and Can Occur with Autism." *PLoS One* 11 (8): e0160543. https://doi.org/10.1371/journal.pone .0160543.

Barrère. 1977. *Droit à la folie.* France, 63 minutes. YouTube video, 1:03:31. Uploaded September 11, 2013. https://www.youtube.com/watch?v=iDh6mMTqORQ.

Beller, Jon. Forthcoming. *The World Computer: Derivative Conditions of Racial Capitalism.* Durham, NC: Duke University Press.

Bergson, Henri. 1911. *Creative Evolution.* Translated by Arthur Mitchell. New York: Henry Holt.

Bergson, Henri. 1910. *Time and Free Will.* Translated by F. L. Pogson. London: George Allen and Unwin.

Best, Stephen and Hartman, Saidiya. 2005. "Fugitive Justice." *Representations* 92, no. 1 (Fall), 1-15.

Birkin, Jane. 2015. "Art, Work, and Archives: Performativity and the Techniques of Production." In "Archives Remixes: Critical Perspectives and Pathways—Radical Archives." Special issue, *Archive Journal*, no. 5. http://www.archivejournal.net/issue/5 /archives-remixed/art-work-and-archives/.

Blackman, Lucy. 2013. *Carrying Autism, Feeling Language.* Self-published, Smashwords.

Boren, Ryan. 2018. "Anxiety, Ambiguity and Autistic Perception." Ryan Boren's blog, May 3. https://boren.blog/2018/05/03/anxiety-ambiguity-and-autistic-perception/.

Bottoms, Stephen, and Matthew Goulish, eds. 2007. *Small Acts of Repair: Performance, Ecology and Goat Island.* New York: Routledge.

Bradley, Rizvana. 2014. "Introduction: Other Sensualities." In "The Haptic: Textures of Performance," edited by Rizvana Bradley. Special issue, *Women and Performance* 24, nos. 2–3. https://www.womenandperformance.org/ampersand/rizvana-bradley-1.

Brown, Heather M., and Perry D. Klein. 2011. "Writing, Asperger Syndrome and the Theory of Mind." *Journal of Autism and Developmental Disorders* 41: 1464–74.

Brown, Lydia. 2012. "Autistic Empowerment: The Civil Rights Model." *Autistic Hoya* (blog), March 27, 2012. https://www.autistichoya.com/2012/03/autistic-empowerment -civil-rights-model.html.

Bryan, Dick, and Akseli Virtanen. 2018. "Stability for Whom? Reframing Stability in the Cryptoeconomy." Economic Space Agency Economic Papers, February. https://docs .google.com/document/d/1GblmfXNeaIwEfdgVEVpxIF4NDAQHzB-pBa8YBAruBbw /edit.

Burack, Jacob A., Grace Iarocci, Tara D. Flanagan, and Dermot M. Bowler. 2004. "On Mosaics and Melting Pots: Conceptual Considerations of Comparison and Matching Strategies." *Journal of Autism and Developmental Disorders* 34: 65–73.

Buxton, Liz. 2016. "Experience: I See Words as Colours." *Guardian*, August 19, 2016.

Bywaters, Malcolm. 2014. "Lyndal Jones: Climate Change, Performance and the *Avoca Project*." *Fusion Journal*, no. 4. http://www.fusion-journal.com/issue/004-fusion-the-town-and-the-city/lyndal-jones-climate-change-performance-and-the-avoca-project/.

Cache, Bernard. 1995. *Earth Moves: The Furnishing of Territories*. Translated by Michael Speaks. Boston: MIT Press.

Campt, Tina. 2019. "Black Visuality and the Practice of Refusal." *Women and Performance* 29, no. 1, 79–87.

Cara, Ed. 2018. "Study: Future Teachers Are Already Biased against Black Children." *Gizmodo*, July 2, 2018. https://gizmodo.com/study-future-teachers-are-already-biased-against-black-1827298437.

Çevik, Kerima. 2019. "Distorting DEEJ: Deconstructing a Misinformed Literature Review." *Thinking Person's Guide to Autism*, September 14, 2019. http://www.thinkingautismguide.com/2019/09/distorting-deej-deconstructing.html.

Chan, Paul. 2009. "What Art Is and Where It Belongs." *e-flux*, no. 10 (November). http://www.e-flux.com/journal/what-art-is-and-where-it-belongs/.

Chandler, Nahum. 2014. *X—the Problem of the Negro as a Problem for Thought*. New York: Fordham University Press.

Chandler, Nahum Dimiti. 2000. "Originary Displacement." *boundary 2* 27, no. 3: 249–86.

Chen, Mel. 2014. "Brain Fog: The Race for Cripistemology." *Journal of Literary and Cultural Disability Studies* 8, no. 2: 171–84.

Cioffi, Maria Cristina, James W. Moore, and Michael J. Banissy. 2014. "What Can Mirror-Touch Synaesthesia Tell Us about the Sense of Agency?" *Frontiers in Human Neuroscience* 8:256. http://journal.frontiersin.org/article/10.3389/fnhum.2014.00256/full.

City of Chicago. n.d. "*Goat Island Archive: We Have Discovered the Performance by Making It*." Cultural Affairs and Special Events, City of Chicago. Accessed February 18, 2020. https://www.chicago.gov/city/en/depts/dca/supp_info/goat_island.html.

Clark, John Lee. 2017a. "Distantism." Tumblr, August 3, 2017. https://johnleeclark.tumblr.com/post/163762970913/distantism.

Clark, John Lee. 2017b. "My Dream House: Some Thoughts on a DeafBlind Space." Vision Loss Resources. Accessed February 23, 2018. http://visionlossresources.org/blog/dbsm/my-dream-house-some-thoughts-on-a-deafblind-space.

Clark, John Lee. 2015. "Metatactile Knowledge." Tumblr, October 2, 2015. https://johnleeclark.tumblr.com/post/130321809778/metatactile-knowledge.

Clark, John Lee. 2014. *Where I Stand: On the Signing Community and My DeafBlind Experience*. Minneapolis: Handtype Press.

Coates, Ta-Nehisi. 2015. *Between the World and Me*. New York: Random House.

Crawley, Ashon. 2018a. "Black. Queer. Born Again." *Aeon*, July 2, 2018. https://aeon.co/essays/black-queer-born-again-a-life-in-and-out-of-the-church.

Crawley, Ashon. 2018b. "Reply: Memory." In *Symposium: Blackpentecostal Breath*. Syndicate. https://syndicate.network/symposia/theology/blackpentecostal-breath/.

Crawley, Ashon. 2017. *Blackpentecostal Breath: The Aesthetics of Possibility.* New York: Fordham University Press.

Cromer, Stevie. 2017. "I Was Amazed." Luna: Language Services, January 17, 2017. https://luna360.com/i-was-amazed/.

Davila, Thierry. 2010. *De l'inframince, brève histoire de l'imperceptible de Marcel Duchamp à nos jours.* Paris: Edition du regard.

de Duve, Thierry, ed. 1991. *Pictorial Nominalism: On Marcel Duchamp's Passage from Painting to the Readymade.* Translated by Dana Polan and Thierry de Duve. Minneapolis: Minnesota University Press.

DeFrantz, Thomas. 2018. "White Privilege." *Theater* 48, no. 3, 23–37.

DeFrantz, Thomas. 2017. "I Am Black (You Have to Be Willing Not to Know)." *Theater* 47, no. 2, 9–21.

Deleuze, Gilles. 2003. *Logic of Sensation.* Translated by Daniel Smith. Minneapolis: University of Minnesota Press.

Deleuze, Gilles. 2001. *Pure Immanence: Essays on Life by Gilles Deleuze.* New York: Zone Books.

Deleuze, Gilles. 1996. "The First Positive Task of Schizoanalysis." In *The Guattari Reader,* edited by Gary Genosko, 77–94. London: Blackwell.

Deleuze, Gilles. 1992. *The Fold: Leibniz and the Baroque.* Translated by Tom Conley Minneapolis: University of Minnesota Press.

Deleuze, Gilles. 1991. *Bergsonism.* Translated by Hugh Tomlinson and Barbara Habberjam. New York: Zone Books.

Deleuze, Gilles. 1990a. *Expressionism in Philosophy.* Translated by Martin Joughin. New York: Zone Books.

Deleuze, Gilles. 1990b. *The Logic of Sense.* Translated by Mark Lester and Charles Stivale. New York: Columbia University Press.

Deleuze, Gilles. 1989. *Cinema 2: The Time-Image.* Translated by Hugh Tomlinson and Robert Galeta. Minneapolis: University of Minnesota Press.

Deleuze, Gilles. 1988. *Foucault.* Translated by Sean Hand. London: Athlone.

Deleuze, Gilles. 1986. *Nietzsche and Philosophy.* Translated by Hugh Tomlinson. London: Athlone.

Deleuze, Gilles. 1985. *Kant's Critical Philosophy: The Doctrine of the Faculties.* Translated by Hugh Tomlinson and Barbara Habberjam. Minneapolis: Minnesota University Press.

Deleuze, Gilles. n.d. "Mediators." Bodies of Persuasion (eng7007) wiki. Uploaded October 15, 2007. http://eng7007.pbworks.com/w/page/18931080/DeleuzeMediators.

Deleuze, Gilles, and Félix Guattari. 1994. *What Is Philosophy?* Translated by Hugh Tomlinson and Graham Burchell. New York: Columbia University Press.

Deleuze, Gilles, and Félix Guattari. 1987. *A Thousand Plateaus.* Translated by Brian Massumi. Minneapolis: University of Minnesota Press.

Deleuze, Gilles, and Félix Guattari. 1983. *Anti-Oedipus: Capitalism and Schizophrenia.* Translated by Robert Hurley, Mark Seem, and Helen Lane. Minneapolis: University of Minnesota Press.

Deligny, Fernand. 2007. "Les détours de l'agir ou le moindre geste (1979)." In *Oeuvres,* edited by Sandra Alvarez de Toledo, 1247–348. Paris: Arachnéen.

Derrida, Jacques. 1998. *Of Grammatology.* Translated by Gayatri Spivak. Baltimore: John Hopkins University Press.

Design Studio for Social Intervention. n.d. Accessed April 22, 2020. "Social Emergency Response Center." http://www.ds4si.org/interventions/serc.

Du Bois, W. E. B. 1995. *The Philadelphia Negro: A Social Study.* Philadelphia: University of Pennsylvania Press.

Duchamp, Marcel. 1999. "Le Possible est un inframince." Accessed December 1, 2014. https://www.centrepompidou.fr/cpv/resource/cBAg7j9/rEnGq9p.

Easton, Anthony. 2016. "Why Do Autism Specialists Want to Stamp Out Autistic Traits?" *Globe and Mail,* January 29, 2016. https://www.theglobeandmail.com/opinion/why-do-autism-specialists-want-to-stamp-out-autistic-traits/article28441771/.

Easton, Anthony. 2013. "An Autism Abecedarian." *Kadar Koli* 8 (Summer), n.p.

Edwards, Terra. 2015. "Bridging the Gap between DeafBlind Minds: Interactional and Social Foundations of Intention Attribution in the Seattle DeafBlind Community." *Frontiers in Psychology* 6:1497. https://www.ncbi.nlm.nih.gov/pmc/articles/PMC4598582/.

Egert, Gerko, Ilona Hongisto, Michael Hornblow, Katve-Kaisa Kontturi, Mayra Morales, Ronald Rose-Antoinette, and Adam Szymanski. 2015. "Radical Pedagogies." *Inflexions,* no. 8. http://www.inflexions.org/radicalpedagogy/main.html.

Farr, Ian, ed. 2012. *Memory.* Boston: MIT Press.

Ferreira da Silva, Denise. 2016. "On Difference without Separability." In *Incerteza Viva (Living Uncertainty),* the catalogue for the 32a Sao Paolo Biennale, 57–66. São Paolo: São Paolo Fundacao, Biennal de São Paolo.

Ferreira da Silva, Denise. 2015. "Before Man: Sylvia Wynter's Rewriting of the Modern Episteme." In *Sylvia Wynter: On Being Human as Praxis,* edited by Katherine McKittrick, 90–105. Durham, NC: Duke University Press.

Ferreira da Silva, Denise. 2014. "Toward a Black Feminist Poethics: The Quest(ion) of Blackness toward the End of the World." *Black Scholar* 44, no. 2, 81–97.

Flickwerk: The Aesthetics of Mended Japanese Ceramics. 2008. Ithaca, NY: Cornell University.

Foucault, Michel. 1972. *Power/Knowledge.* Edited by Colin Gordon. Translated by Colin Gordon, Leo Marshall, John Mepham, and Kate Soper. New York: Pantheon Books.

Glissant, Édouard. 2010. *L'imaginaire des langues—entretien avec Lise Gauvin.* Paris: Gallimard.

Glissant, Édouard. 1997. *Poetics of Relation.* Translated by Betsy Wing. Ann Arbor: University of Michigan Press.

Goat Island. n.d. "Goat Island: Biographies: Funding/Credits." Goat Island website. Accessed January 18, 2020. http://www.goatislandperformance.org/goatisland.htm.

Godfrey-Smith, Peter. 2016. *Other Minds: The Octopus, the Sea, and the Deep Origins of Consciousness.* New York: Farrar, Straus and Giroux.

Goldman, Sylvie. 2008. "Brief Report: Narratives of Personal Events in Children with Autism and Developmental Language Disorders." *Assessment of Autism Spectrum Disorders* 38: 1982–8.

Grande, A. J., and Nuncia, Jelica. 2016. "Pro-Tactile Vlog #5." Welcome to Protactile, the DeafBlind Way, March 14, 2016. Video, 8:57. http://www.protactile.org/2016/03/pro -tactile-vlog-5_14.html.

Grande, A. J., and Nuncia, Jelica. 2013. "Pro-Tactile Vlog #3." Welcome to Protactile, the DeafBlind Way, July 29, 2013. Video, 5:34. http://www.protactile.org/2016/03/pro -tactile-vlog-3.html.

Guattari, Félix. 2015. *Psychoanalysis and Transversality.* Translated by Ames Hodges. New York: Semiotexte.

Guattari, Félix. 1996. *The Guattari Reader.* Edited by Gary Genosko. London: Blackwell.

Guattari, Félix. 1995. *Chaosmosis: An Ethico-Aesthetic Paradigm.* Translated by Paul Bains. Bloomington: Indiana University Press.

Gullar, Ferreira. 1959. "Teoria do não-objeto" (Theory of the Nonobject). *Suplemento Dominical do Jornal do Brasil,* December 19–20.

Gullar, Ferreira. n.d. "Dialogue on the Non-object." Jen Mazza's website. Accessed December 20, 2014. http://www.jenmazza.com/site/index.php/archive/dialog-on-the-non -object/3321/.

Halberstadt, Amy G., Vanessa L. Castrob, Qiao Chuc, Fantasy T. Lozadad, and Calvin M. Sims. 2018. "Preservice Teachers' Racialized Emotion Recognition, Anger Bias, and Hostility Attributions." *Contemporary Educational Psychology* 54 (July): 125–38.

Harney, Stefano. 2017. "Stefano Harney (Part 2)." Interview by Michael Shapira and Jesse Montgomery. *Full Stop,* August 10, 2017. http://www.full-stop.net/2017/08/10 /interviews/michael-schapira-and-jesse-montgomery/stefano-harney-part-2/.

Harney, Stefano. 2013. "Hapticality in the Undercommons, or From Operations Management to Black Ops." Cumma Papers, Aalto University, no. 9. https://cummastudies .files.wordpress.com/2013/08/cumma-papers-9.pdf.

Harney, Stefano, and Fred Moten. 2017a. "Base Faith." *e-flux,* no. 86. https://www.e-flux .com/journal/86/162888/base-faith/.

Harney, Stefano, and Fred Moten. 2017b. "Propositions for Non-fascist Living—Video Statement—October 2017." YouTube video, 10:04, uploaded November 23, 2017. https://m.youtube.com/watch?v=ZxZir6POGbo.

Harney, Stefano, and Fred Moten. 2013. *The Undercommons: Fugitive Planning and Black Study.* Wivenhoe, UK: Minor Compositions.

Harris, Laura. 2018. *Experiments in Exile: C.L.R. James, Helio Oiticica and the Aesthetic Sociality of Blackness.* New York: Fordham University Press.

Harris, Laura. 2012. "What Happened to the Motley Crew? CLR James, Helio Oiticica, and the Aesthetic Sociality of Blackness." *Social Text* 30, no. 3, 49–75.

Hartman, Saidiya. 2019. *Wayward Lives, Beautiful Experiments.* New York: Norton.

Hartman, Saidiya. 2018. "On Working with Archives: An Interview with Writer Saidiya Hartman." Interview by Thora Siesmsen. The Creative Independent, April 18, 2018. https://thecreativeindependent.com/people/saidiya-hartman-on-working-with -archives/.

Hartman, Saidiya. 2008a. *Lose Your Mother: A Journey along the Atlantic Slave Route.* New York: Farrar, Straus and Giroux.

Hartman, Saidiya. 2008b. "Venus in Two Acts." *Small Axe* 12, no. 2 (June): 1–14.

Hartman, Saidiya. 1997. *Scenes of Subjection: Terror, Slavery, and Self-Making in Nineteenth-Century America*. Oxford: Oxford University Press.

Hartman, Saidiya and Moten, Fred. 2018. "To Refuse That Which Has Been Refused to You." Chimurenga: Who No Know Go Know, October 19, 2018. https://chimurengachronic.co.za/to-refuse-that-which-has-been-refused-to-you-2/.

Helen Keller National Center. n.d. "Touch Signals." National Center on Deaf-Blindness. Accessed March 12, 2018. https://nationaldb.org/library/page/2588.

Hill, Elisabeth L. 2004. "Executive Dysfunction in Autism." *Trends in Cognitive Sciences* 8, no. 1 (January), 26–32.

Hixson, Lin. 2007. *School Book 2*. London: Unbound.

Ingold, Tim. 2015. *The Life of Lines*. New York: Routledge.

Ingold, Tim. 2007. *Lines: A Brief History*. New York: Routledge.

Irwin, Robert, and Olafur Eliasson. 2007. "Take Your Time: A Conversation." In *Take Your Time: Olafur Eliasson*, edited by Madeleine Grynsztejn, 51–61. London: Thames and Hudson. San Francisco Museum of Modern Art exhibition catalogue.

Ivy, Nicole. 2018. "Movement and Sound." In *Symposium: Blackpentecostal Breath*. Syndicate. https://syndicate.network/symposia/theology/blackpentecostal-breath/.

James, William. 1890. *The Principles of Psychology. Vol. 1 and 2*. London: Dover Publications. https://psychclassics.yorku.ca/James/Principles/index.htm.

Kamuguisha, Aaron. 2019. *Beyond Coloniality*. Bloomington: Indiana University Press.

Kedar, Ido. 2012. *Ido in Autismland: Climbing Out of Autism's Silent Prison*. Self-published, Sharon Kedar.

Kelley, Robin D. G. 2002. *Freedom Dreams: The Black Radical Imagination*. Boston: Beacon.

Kelley, Robin D. G., and Fred Moten. 2017. "Robin D. G. Kelley and Fred Moten in Conversation." April 3, 2017. YouTube video, 2:13:29, uploaded June 15, 2017. https://www.youtube.com/watch?v=fP-2F9MXjRE.

Konnikova, Maria. 2012. "Infants Possess Intermingled Senses." *Scientific American*, January 1, 2012. https://www.scientificamerican.com/article/infant-kandinskys/.

Krumins, Daina. 2003. *Women from Another Planet? Our Lives in the Universe of Autism*. Self-published, AuthorHouse.

Lapoujade, David. 2017. *Les existences moindres*. Paris: Minuit.

Leemann, Judith. 2017. "Pragmatics of Studio Critique." In *Beyond Critique: Contemporary Art in Theory, Practice and Instruction*, edited by Pamela Fraser and Roger Rothman, 181–94. New York: Bloomsbury.

Leemann, Judith. 2008. "Lecture in the Shape of a Dovetail Joint." Goat Island Summer School Symposium, July 26, 2008.

Leemann, Judith. 2004. "Observations on Forms and Patterns of Critique." DMA403 (Grad Crit) website, University of California, Los Angeles. http://classes.dma.ucla.edu/Fall17/403/Observations+on+forms+and+patterns+of+critique.pdf.

Leemann, Judith. n.d. "Object Lessons." Judith Leemann's website. http://www.judithleemann.com/object-lessons.

Maister, Lara, Michael J. Banissy, and Manos Tsakiris. 2013. "Mirror-Touch Synaesthesia Changes Representations of Self-Identity." *Neuropsychologia* 51, no. 5: 802–8.

Manning, Erin. 2016. *The Minor Gesture*. Durham, NC: Duke University Press.

Manning, Erin. 2013. *Always More Than One: Individuation's Dance*. Durham, NC: Duke University Press.

Manning, Erin. 2009. *Relationscapes: Movement, Art, Philosophy*. Cambridge, MA: MIT Press.

Manning, Erin. 2006. *Politics of Touch: Sense, Movement, Sovereignty*. Minneapolis: University of Minnesota Press.

Manning, Erin, and Brian Massumi. 2018. "A Cryptoeconomy of Affect." Interview by Uriah Marc Todoroff. *New Inquiry*, May 14, 2018. https://thenewinquiry.com/a-cryptoeconomy-of-affect/.

Manning, Erin, and Brian Massumi. 2014a. *Thought in the Act: Passages in the Ecology of Experience*. Minneapolis: University of Minnesota Press.

Manning, Erin, and Brian Massumi. 2014b. "A Perspective of the Universe." In *Thought in the Act: Passages in the Ecology of Experience*, 23–30. Minneapolis: Minnesota University Press.

Manning, Erin, and Brian Massumi. 2013. "For a Pragmatics of the Useless." Talk at Western University, London, Canada, March 5, 2013. Anthem, video, 56:40, August 7, 2013. https://anthem.wordpress.com/2013/08/07/massumimanning-for-a-pragmatics-of-the-useless-propositions-for-thought/.

Manning, Erin, Anna Munster, and Bodil Marie Stavning Thomsen, eds. 2019. *Immediation*. London: Open Humanities Press.

Marriott, David. 2018. *Whither Fanon? Studies in the Blackness of Being*. Stanford: Stanford University Press.

Martins, Sergio Bruno. 2012. "Phenomenological Openness." *Third Text* 26, no. 1: 79–90.

Marx, Karl. 1991. *Capital: A Critique of Political Economy, Volume 3*. Translated by David Fernbach. London: Penguin.

Massumi, Brian. 2019. "Dim, Massive and Important—Atmosphere in Process." In *Atmospheres and Auditory Cultures: Essays on Feeling in Music and Sound*, edited by Friedlind Riedel and Juha Torvinen, 286–301. London: Routledge.

Massumi, Brian. 2018. *99 Theses on the Revaluation of Value: A Postcapitalist Manifesto*. Minneapolis: University of Minnesota Press.

Massumi, Brian. 2017a. "The Art of the Relational Body: From Mirror-Touch to the Virtual Body." In *Mirror-Touch: Thresholds of Empathy with Art*, edited by Daria Martin, 191–209. Oxford: Oxford University Press.

Massumi, Brian. 2017b. "Atmosphere and Affect." Round table with Jan Slaby, Media Anthropology Centre, Bauhaus University, Weimar, Germany, May 4, 2017.

Massumi, Brian. 2017c. *The Principle of Unrest*. London: Open Humanities Press.

Massumi, Brian. 2016. Foreword to *The Sympathy of Things: Ruskin and the Ecology of Design*, by Lars Spuybroek, xix–xiv. London: Bloomsbury.

Massumi, Brian. 2015a. *Power at the End of the Economy*. Durham, NC: Duke University Press.

Massumi, Brian. 2015b. *Ontopower: Wars, Powers and the State of Perception*. Durham, NC: Duke University Press.

Massumi, Brian. 2014. *What Animals Teach Us about Politics*. Durham, NC: Duke University Press.

Massumi, Brian. 2011. *Semblance and Event: Activist Philosophy and the Occurrent Arts.* Cambridge, MA: MIT Press.

Massumi, Brian. 2010. "On Critique." *Inflexions*, no. 4. https://www.inflexions.org/n4_t _massumihtml.html.

Massumi, Brian, 2002. *Parables for the Virtual: Affect, Movement, Sensation.* Durham, NC: Duke University Press.

Massumi, Brian. 2000. "The Ether and Your Anger: Toward a Pragmatics of the Useless." In *The Pragmatist Imagination: Thinking about "Things in the Making,"* edited by Joan Ockman, 160–7. Princeton, NJ: Princeton Architectural Press.

Massumi, Brian, and Erin Manning. 2014. "Relational Soup—Philosophy, Art, and Activism." Talk given at TEDxCalArts: Performance, Body and Presence. YouTube video, 18:04, uploaded September 15, 2014. https://www.youtube.com/watch?v =D2yHtYdI4bE.

Maurer, Daphne, and Catherine J. Mondloch. 2005. "Neonatal Synesthesia: A Reevaluation." In *Synesthesia: Perspectives from Cognitive Neuroscience*, edited by Lynn C. Robertson and Noam Sagiv, 193–213. New York: Oxford University Press. http://wyblelab .com/docs/jc/Maurer_NeonatalSynesthesia.pdf.

Mbembe, Achille. 2018a. "Achille Mbembe: Recognition, Reparation, Reconciliation." December 8, 2018. YouTube video, 1:15:10, uploaded December 14, 2018. https://www .youtube.com/watch?v=L4oYP44uc2Q.

Mbembe, Achille. 2018b. "Conversation: Achille Mbembe and David Theo Goldberg on *Critique of Black Reason*." *Theory, Culture and Society*, July 3, 2018. https://www .theoryculturesociety.org/conversation-achille-mbembe-and-david-theo-goldberg-on -critique-of-black-reason/.

McConnell, Daniel. 2015. "Autism and Neurodiversity: A Panel Presentation at the 2008 Autism National Conference Committee." In *Typed Words, Loud Voices*, edited by Amy Sequenzia and Elizabeth J. Grace. Fort Worth, TX: Autonomous Press.

McGlensey, Melissa. 2016. "16 People with Autism Describe Why Eye Contact Can Be Difficult." *The Mighty*, February 3, 2016. https://themighty.com/2016/02/why-eye -contact-can-be-difficult-for-people-with-autism/.

McKittrick, Katherine. 2018. "Churching." In *Symposium: Blackpentecostal Breath.* Syndicate. https://syndicate.network/symposia/theology/blackpentecostal-breath/.

McKittrick, Katherine. 2014. "The Geographies of Blackness and Anti-Blackness: An Interview with Katherine McKittrick." *CLR James Journal* 20, no. 1–2 (Fall), 230–44.

McKittrick, Katherine. 2006. *Demonic Grounds*. Minneapolis: Minnesota University Press.

Meilleur, Andrée-Anne S., Claude Berthiaume, Armando Bertone, and Laurent Mottron. 2014. "Autism-Specific Covariation in Perceptual Performances: 'g' or 'p' factor?" *PloS One* 9, no. 8: 1–13.

Merewether, Charles, ed. 2006. *The Archive*. Boston: MIT Press.

Mignolo, Walter D. 2015. "Sylvia Wynter: What Does It Mean to Be Human?" In *Sylvia Wynter: On Being Human as Praxis*, edited by Katherine McKittrick, 106–23. Durham, NC: Duke University Press.

Moten, Fred. 2018a. *Stolen Life*. Durham, NC: Duke University Press.

Moten, Fred. 2018b. *The Universal Machine*. Durham, NC: Duke University Press.

Moten, Fred. 2017. *Black and Blur*. Durham, NC: Duke University Press.

Moten, Fred. 2016a. "Bobby Lee's Hands." Organize Your Own: An Exhibition and Event Series about the Politics and Poetics of Self-Determination Movements, December 5, 2016. https://organizeyourown.wordpress.com/2016/12/05/bobby-lees-hands-by-fred-moten/.

Moten, Fred. 2016b. "Collective Head." *Women and Performance: A Journal of Feminist Theory* 26, nos. 2–3, 162–71.

Moten, Fred. 2015. "An Interview with Fred Moten, Part 1: In Praise of Harold Bloom, Collaboration and Book Fetishes." Interview by Adam Fitzgerald. *Literary Hub*, August 5, 2015. https://lithub.com/an-interview-with-fred-moten-pt-i/.

Moten, Fred. 2013a. "Six Poems by Fred Moten." Pen America, curated by Maggie Nelson, June 12, 2013. https://pen.org/six-poems-by-fred-moten/.

Moten, Fred. 2013b. "The Subprime and the Beautiful." *African Identities* 11, no. 2, 237–45.

Moten, Fred. 2008. "The Case of Blackness." *Criticism* 50, no. 2, 177–218.

Moten, Fred. 2003. *In the Break: The Aesthetics of the Black Radical Tradition*. Minneapolis: University of Minnesota Press.

Mottron, Laurent, Lucie Bouvet, Anna Bonnel, Fabienne Samson, Jacob A. Burack, Michelle Dawson, and Pamela Heaton. 2013. "Veridical Mapping in the Development of Exceptional Autistic Abilities." *Neuroscience and Biobehavioral Reviews* 37, no. 2 (February): 209–28.

Mottron, Laurent, Michelle Dawson, Isabelle Soulières, Benedicte Hubert, and Jake Burack. 2006. "Enhanced Perceptual Functioning in Autism: An Update, and Eight Principles of Autistic Perception." *Journal of Autism and Developmental Disorders* 36, no. 1 (January): 27–43.

Mukhopadhyay, Tito. 2015. *Plankton Dreams: What I Learned in Special-Ed*. London: Open Humanities Press.

Mukhopadhyay, Tito. 2011. *How Can I Talk If My Lips Don't Move? Inside My Autistic Mind*. New York: Arcade Press.

Mukhopadhyay, Tito. 2010. "More Than a Thing to Ignore: An Interview with Tito Rajarshi Mukhopadhyay." Interview by Ralph James Savarese. In "Autism and the Concept of Neurodiversity," edited by Emily Thornton Savarese and Ralph James Savarese. Special issue, *Disability Studies Quarterly* 30, no. 1. http://dsq-sds.org/article/view/1056.

Nietzsche, Friedrich. 2003. *Writings from the Late Notebooks*. Cambridge: Cambridge University Press.

Nietzsche, Friedrich. 1989. *Beyond Good and Evil*. Translated by Walter Kaufmann. New York: Vintage.

Nyong'o, Tavia. 2018. *Afro-Fabulations: The Queer Drama of Black Life*. New York: New York University Press.

Parisi, Luciana. 2019. "Media Ontology and Transcendental Instrumentality." *Theory, Culture and Society*, 36, no. 6, 95–124.

Perloff, Marjorie. 2002. "The Conceptual Poetics of Marcel Duchamp." In *21st-Century Modernism: The "New" Poetics*, 78–114. Oxford: Wiley-Blackwell.

ProTactile.org. 2016. Welcome to ProTactile, the DeafBlind Way. http://www.protactile.org/2016/.

Querrien, Anne. n.d. a. "Géographies Schizoanalytiques." Unpublished manuscript. Microsoft Document.

Querrien, Anne. n.d. b. "La schizoanalyse: Une cartographie à n-dimensions." Unpublished manuscript. Microsoft Document.

Rancière, Jacques. 2004. *Disagreement*. Minneapolis: University of Minnesota Press.

Ravindran, Shruti. 2015. "A Circus of the Senses." *Aeon*, January 20. https://aeon.co /essays/are-we-all-born-with-a-talent-for-synaesthesia.

Reed, Anthony. 2014. *Freedom Time: The Poetics and Politics of Black Experimental Writing*. Baltimore: Johns Hopkins University Press.

Reyes, Philip. 2015. "I Have Nonverbal Autism: Here's What I Want You to Know." *The Mighty*, April 6. http://themighty.com/2015/04/i-have-nonverbal-autism-heres-what-i -want-you-to-know/.

Robinson, Cedric. 2000. *Black Marxism: The Making of the Black Radical Tradition*. London: Zed Books.

Rolnik, Suely. 2007. "The Body's Contagious Memory: Lygia Clark's Return to the Museum." Translated by Rodrigo Nunes. Unpublished translation. Microsoft Document. http://eipcp.net/transversal/0507/rolnik/en.

Rolnik, Suely. (1999) n.d. "Molding a Contemporary Soul: The Empty-Full of Lygia Clark." Unpublished translation. Microsoft Word document. Accessed December 2, 2019. caosmose.net/suelyrolnik/textos/Molding%20(John%20+%20Nadine).doc. Originally published as "Molda-se uma alma contemporânea:o vazio-pleno de Lygia Clark," in *The Experimental Exercise of Freedom: Lygia Clark, Gego, Mathias Goeritz, Hélio Oiticica and Mira Schendel*, edited by Rina Carvajal and Alma Ruiz, 55–108. Los Angeles: Museum of Contemporary Art.

Roschaert, Christine Amanda. 2013. "Pro-Tactile: The DeafBlind Way!!!" *Tactile the World* (blog), February 18, 2013. https://tactiletheworld.wordpress.com/2013/02/18 /pro-tactile-the-deafblind-way/.

Russell, Bertrand. 1961. *History of Western Philosophy*. London: George Allen and Unwin.

Savarese, DJ. 2019. "Coming to My Senses." *Autism in Adulthood* 1, no. 2, 90–92.

Savarese, DJ. 2017. "Passive Plants." *Iowa Review* 47, no. 1. https://iowareview.org/from -the-issue/volume-47-issue-1-—-spring-2017/passive-plants.

Savarese, DJ. 2010. "Communicate with Me." *Disability Studies Quarterly*, 30, no. 1. https://dsq-sds.org/article/view/1051/1237.

Savarese, DJ. 2005. "Estimating Harriet Tubman Respectfully." Ralph Savarese's website, July 7, 2005. http://www.ralphsavarese.com/category/djs-writings/.

Savarese, Ralph James. 2018a. "Reading Fiction with Temple Grandin: Yes, People with Autism Can Understand Literature." *Salon*, September 2, 2018. https://www.salon.com /2018/09/02/reading-fiction-with-temple-grandin-yes-autistic-people-can-understand -literature/.

Savarese, Ralph James. 2018b. *See It Feelingly: Classic Novels, Autistic Readers and the Schooling of a No-Good English Professor*. Durham, NC: Duke University Press.

Savarese, Ralph James. 2017. "Easy Breathing: How My Autistic Son Taught Me How to Live." Interview by Jenny Boylan. *Medium*, June 16, 2017. https://medium.com/galleys /easy-breathing-how-my-autistic-son-taught-me-how-to-live-7505fa11b13d.

Savarese, Ralph James. 2015. Afterword to *Plankton Dreams: What I Learned in Special-Ed*, by Tito Mukhopadhyay. London: Open Humanities Press.

Savarese, Ralph James. 2010. "Toward a Postcolonial Neurology: Autism, Tito Mukhopadhyay, and a New Geo-poetics of the Body." *Journal of Literary and Cultural Disability Studies* 4, no. 3, 125–43.

SenseLab. 2016. *The How-To Go-To Book of Anarchiving*. Self-published, Lulu.

SenseLab—3E 2016. "59-Minute Do-It-Ourselves Books." SenseLab. http://senselab.ca /wp2/immediations/upcoming-distributing-the-insensible-dec-10-20-2016/59-minute -do-it-ourselves-books/.

SenseLab—3E n.d. "3E Process Seed Bank." Accessed February 23, 2020. http://senselab .ca/wp2/immediations/3eprocessseedbank/.

Sequenzia, Amy. 2012a. "Functioning Labels Again," October 11. https://awnnetwork.org /functioning-labels-again/.

Sequenzia, Amy. 2012b. "Non-speaking, Low-Functioning." *Shift Journal* (reprinted). http://www.shiftjournal.com/2012/01/11/non-speaking-low-functioning.

Sequenzia, Amy. n.d. "More Problems with Functioning Labels." https://ollibean.com /problems-functioning-labels/.

Sequenzia, Amy, and Elizabeth Grace, eds. 2015. *Typed Words, Loud Voices*. Fort Worth, TX: Autonomous Press.

Sexton, Jared. 2011. "The Social Life of Social Death: On Afro-Pessimism and Black Optimism." *InTensions* 5, 1–47.

Sharma, Nandita. 2015. "Strategic Anti-essentialism: Decolonizing Decolonization." In *Sylvia Wynter: On Being Human as Praxis*, edited by Katherine McKittrick, 164–82. Durham, NC: Duke University Press.

Sharpe, Christina. 2016. *In the Wake: On Blackness and Being*. Durham, NC: DukeUniversity Press.

Simondon, Gilbert. 2017. *On the Mode of Existence of Technical Objects*. Translated by Cecile Malaspina and John Rogove. Minneapolis: University of Minnesota Press.

Simondon, Gilbert. 1989. *L'individuation psychique et collective*. Paris: Aubier.

Simondon, Gilbert. 1964. *L'individu et sa genèse physico-biologique*. Grenoble: Jerôme Millon.

Simpson, Leanne Betasamosake. 2014. "Land as Pedagogy: Nishnaabeg Intelligence and Rebellious Transformation." *Decolonization: Indigeneity, Education and Society* 3, no. 3, 1–25.

Sirvage, Robert. 2015. "An Insight from DeafSpace." TEDx Talk at Gallaudet University. YouTube video, 17:31, uploaded March 6, 2015. https://www.youtube.com/watch?v =EPTrOO6EYCY.

Smith, Daniel, and John Protevi. 2018. "Gilles Deleuze." In *The Stanford Encyclopedia of Philosophy*. Stanford University, 1997–. Article published May 23, 2008; last modified February 14, 2018. https://plato.stanford.edu/archives/spr2018/entries/deleuze/.

Smith-Donohoe, Lauren. 2018. "Regarding Applied Behavioral Analysis (ABA) Therapy." Lauren Smith-Donohoe's website, August 11, 2018. https://laurensmithdonohoe.com /2018/08/11/regarding-applied-behavioral-analysis-aba-therapy/.

Smithson, Robert. 1968. *A Sedimentation of The Mind: Earth Projects*. Artforum. September. http://theoria.art-zoo.com/a-sedimentation-of-the-mind-earth-projects-robert-smithson/.

Snaza, Nathan. 2019. *Animate Literacies.* Durham, NC: Duke University Press.

Spencer, Terry. 2016. "Miami Police Shoot Black Caretaker of Autistic Man as He Lies on Street with Hands in Air." *Toronto Star*, July 21. https://www.thestar.com/news/world/2016/07/21/miami-police-shoot-black-caretaker-of-autistic-man-as-he-lies-on-street.html.

Spillers, Hortense. 2006. "The Idea of Black Culture." *New Centennial Review* 6, no. 3 (Winter): 7–28.

Spillers, Hortense. 2003. *Black, White, and in Color: Essays on American Literature and Culture.* Chicago: University of Chicago Press.

Spillers, Hortense. 1987. "Mama's Baby, Papa's Maybe: An American Grammar Book." *Diacritics* 17, no. 2 (Summer): 64–81.

Spuybroek, Lars. 2016. *The Sympathy of Things: Ruskin and the Ecology of Design.* London: Bloomsbury.

Stepney, Susan. 2002. "Non-Standard Computation, An Overview." Susan Stepney's website. https://www-users.cs.york.ac.uk/susan/complex/nstdcomp.htm.

Stern, Daniel. 2010. *Forms of Vitality.* London: Oxford University Press.

Thornton, Davi Johnson. 2011. *Brain Culture: Neuroscience and Popular Media.* New Brunswick, NJ: Rutgers University Press.

Tustin, Frances. 1984. "Autistic Shapes." *International Review of Psycho-Analyisis* 11, no. 3: 279–90.

University of Cambridge. 2013. "Synaesthesia Is More Common in Autism." *Research News*, November 20. http://www.cam.ac.uk/research/news/synaesthesia-is-more-common-in-autism.

Viveiros de Castro, Eduardo. 2014. *Cannibal Metaphysics.* Translated by Peter Skafish. Minneapolis: University of Minnesota Press.

Walker, Nick. 2013. "Throw Away the Master's Tools: Liberating Ourselves from the Pathology Paradigm." August 16. https://neurocosmopolitanism.com/throw-away-the-masters-tools-liberating-ourselves-from-the-pathology-paradigm/.

Weheliye, Alexander G. 2014. "Introduction." *Black Scholar: Journal of Black Studies and Research* 44, no. 2, 5–10.

"What is it like to have a Sensory Processing/Integration Disorder?" 2011. *Autism and Angels.* December 14. https://aspiegrrl.wordpress.com/2011/12/14/what-is-it-like-to-have-a-sensory-processingintegration-disorder/.

Wheeler, Doug, and Hugh Davies. 2011. "Shining a Light on Light and Space Art." Interview by Jori Finkel. *Los Angeles Times*, September 18, 2011. http://articles.latimes.com/2011/sep/18/entertainment/la-ca-pst-hugh-davies-and-doug-wheeler-20110918.

Whitehead, Alfred North. 1978. *Process and Reality.* New York: Free Press.

Whitehead, Alfred North. 1968. "Immortality." In *Essays in Science and Philosophy*, 60–74. New York: Philosophical Library.

Whitehead, Alfred North. 1967. *Adventures of Ideas.* New York: Free Press.

Whitehead, Alfred North. 1938. *Modes of Thought.* New York: Free Press.

Whitehead, Alfred North. 1929. *The Function of Reason.* New York: Free Press.

Whitehead, Alfred North. 1925. *Science and the Modern World.* New York: Free Press.

Wilderson, Frank. 2010. *Red, White and Black: Cinema and the Structure of US Antagonisms.* Durham, NC: Duke University Press.

Williamson, Terrion L. 2017. *Scandalize My Name: Black Feminist Practice and the Making of Black Social Life*. New York: Fordham University Press.

Wiskerke, Joost. 2018. "When Eye Contact Hurts—a Personal Account of a Common Autistic Trait." *Extraordinary Brains*, February 7, 2018. https://www.extraordinarybrains.com/blog/2018/2/7/when-eye-contact-hurts.

Wood, James, and Kelsie Jackson. n.d. "Introduction to: Cephalopod Vision." The Cephalopod Page website. http://www.thecephalopodpage.org/cephschool/CephalopodVision.pdf.

Wosnitzer, Robert. 2016. "Mapping the Trading Desk: Derivative Value through Market Making." In *Derivatives and the Wealth of Societies*, edited by Ben Lee and Randy Martin, 252–74. Chicago: University of Chicago Press.

Wynter, Sylvia, and Katherine McKittrick. 2015. "Unparalleled Catastrophe for Our Species? Or, to Give Humanness a Different Future: Conversations." In *Sylvia Wynter: On Being Human as Praxis*, edited by Katherine McKittrick, 9–89. Durham, NC: Duke University Press.

Yergeau, Melanie. 2018. *Authoring Autism: On Rhetoric and Neurological Queerness*. Durham, NC: Duke University Press.

Yergeau, Melanie. 2010. "Circle Wars: Reshaping the Typical Autism Essay." *Disability Studies Quarterly* 30, no. 1. http://www.dsq-sds.org/article/view/1063/1222.

Zellars, Rachel. 2016. "If Black Women Were Free: Practicing Transformative Justice in Black Communities." *Third Eye Collective*, September 5, 2016. https://thirdeyecollective.wordpress.com/2016/09/05/if-black-women-were-free-practising-transformative-justice-in-black-communities/.

Zellars, Rachel, and Naava Smolash. 2016a. "If Black Women Were Free, Part 1: Practising Transformative Justice in Black Communities." *Briarpatch Magazine*, August 16, 2016. https://briarpatchmagazine.com/articles/view/if-black-women-were-free.

Zellars, Rachel, and Naava Smolash. 2016b. "If Black Women Were Free, Part 2: Practicing Transformative Justice in—and beyond—Black Communities." *Briarpatch Magazine*, September 3, 2016. https://briarpatchmagazine.com/articles/view/if-black-women-were-free-part-2.

Zurcher, Ariane. 2013. "'Presume Competence'—What Does That Mean Exactly?" *Emma's Hope Book: Living Being Autistic* (blog), March 7. https://emmashopebook.com/2013/03/07/presume-competence-what-does-that-mean-exactly/.

Zurcher-Long, Emma. 2015. "Hindering Progress." Emma's Hope Book: Living Being Autistic (blog). March 17. https://emmashopebook.com/2015/03/17/hindering-progress/.

contrast, 19, 20, 28, 30–31, 94–95, 103, 106–12, 140, 305

Crawley, Ashon, 40, 220, 243; and otherwise possibility, 10, 172, 195, 237

creativity, 28, 80, 83, 94, 151, 208, 216, 223

critique, culture of, 118, 120; immanent critique, 50, 112; of identity/identity politics, 51–53; institutional, 151; and neurotypicality, 53

cryptocurrency, 301, 307

cuff, 88–92, 186; and the fold, 88–93, 97–98, 186; and force-of-form, 91–92; and schizosomatics, 186; and sympathy, 90–93, 97

cut, 12, 26, 30, 31, 36, 51, 72–78, 92, 137, 140, 203, 214, 232, 270–71, 281, 297–99, 303; and the free radical, 121–22; and the Goddess of Anarchy (GOA), 303

Davila, Thierry, 15, 24, 26

DeafBlindness, 257, 263; and distantism, 246; and intervenors, 266, 268; and neurodiversity, 246; and ProTactile, 248, 250, 260, 264–70, 338n21; and synesthesia, 248, 257–58

decolonization, 45, 53, 333n7

debt, 196, 213, 234, 301; and debt/credit relation, 14, 217, 222; debt unrepayable, x, 209–10

de Duve, Thierry, 16, 22, 24

DeFrantz, Thomas, 7

Deleuze, Gilles, on affirmation, 21; on belief in the world, 321–22n15, 326n5; on diagram, 330n4; on fabulation, 121, 123–24, 143; on false problems, 321n12; on the fold, 88–90; on fourth person singular, 27, 281; on group subject, 145, 329n4; on immanent critique, 327n8; on intuition, 91; on a life, 97–98, 99; on event, 326n6; and intercessor, 326n6; on narration, 140; on the outside, 222–23; on passive synthesis, 180; on power of the false, 10, 116, 140; on power/knowledge, 222–24; on problematic field, 329n6; on schizoanalysis, 153, 155, 176, 179; on Spinoza, 242; on the virtual, 80; on will to power, 326n2

Deleuze, Gilles, and Félix Guattari, 81, 189; and autism, 340n1; on the Body without Organs (BwO), 153; on capitalism, 292–96; on conceptual persona, 10–11; on desiring

production, 10, 169, 188, 294; on faciality, 312; on the free indirect, 228; on group-subject, 172–73; on immanent criteria, 188; on language, 228–32, 268; and Lygia Clark, 330n12; and the machinic, 155; on the micropolitical, 81–82; on Oedipus, 174, 176, 179 290; on order-word, 228–30; on parastrata, 309; on pass-word, 26; on the penultimate, 295; on representation, 169, 170; on schizoanalysis, 157, 169, 171, 174–75, 291; on schizophrenia, 289–91, 292; and the schizz, 140; on signs, 267–68; on whiteness, 312; and white wall/black hole, 312

Deligny, Fernand, and work with autistics, 158; and wander lines, 159, 161, 167, 176, 312–13

desire, and capitalism, 290, 294, 296, 341; in the event, 121, 158, 168–69; and lack, 170, 175; and psychoanalysis, 169, 173, 290; revolutionary, 290, 294; and schizoanalysis, 158, 179, 188, 289, 291, 341n2; and schizoid pole, 289, 291, 294

desiring-machine, 157–61, 169, 173, 178–79, 188–89, 291

desiring-production, 10, 169, 170–72, 176, 178, 180–81, 294

developmental psychology, and synesthesia, 248

deviation, 143, 159, 172, 176, 191, 193, 292–93, 296–97, 327, 329n9

differential, in the event, 19–31, 42, 46, 78, 91, 97, 100–101, 121, 165, 168, 193, 291, 302, 306, 314; as edging, 24, 27, 59; of expression, 19, 22, 27, 46, 61, 70, 216, 240; of subjectivity, 157; and togetherness, 77, 84, 157

directionality, 145, 181, 146

distantism, 10, 245–50, 254, 259–60, 264–65, 313. See also Clark, John Lee

Distributing the Insensible (SenseLab), 172–75, 178, 190, 193, 339n7

Divisor (Lygia Pape), 175

Duchamp, Marcel, and the infrathin, 10, 15–16

Easton, Anthony, 281, 334n4

ecology, more-than human, 12, 60, 116, 124; of orientations, 15, 313; of practices, 10, 12, 34, 100, 310–11; three ecologies, 171, 194, 310

economy, 295–96, 302; and altereconomies, 117, 142; and schizoeconomy, 292, 294, 295, 297, 299, 303, 311 education, 52, 194, 196, 251, 268, 283–87, 338n22

Edwards, Terra, 264

Eliasson, Olafur, 27

emergent sociality, and aesthetic sociality of blackness, 61, 226, 298; and bodying, 220, 298; and collective assemblages of enunciation, 266; and immediation, 42, 304; and nonhuman forces, 304

empathy, and autism, 256, 335n12; quotient, 255–56; Simon Baron-Cohen on, 254

enthusiasm, of the body, 131, 142–43; shape of, 87–88, 94, 241, 329n5

epistemology, of colonialism, 43, 49; of the human, 39, 48

ethics, 4, 10, 40, 48, 182, 318; of autism, 335n11

event, account of, 16; and actual occasion, 17, 35; and affective tonality, 20, 24–25, 49; and anarchic share, 28, 84, 93–94, 96–97, 100, 115, 118, 162, 164, 167–68, 184, 188, 300, 304, 314; and the *Avoca Project*, 124–29, 131, 138, 327n12; -creation, 126; and coming to be, 116, 139; and *Distributing the Insensible* (SenseLab), 162–65, 168, 180, 183, 325n11, 329n7; and fabulation, 121–24, 136–43; and the free radical, 116–19, 121–22, 142–44; and *Generating the Impossible* (SenseLab), 117; and immediation, 33–37, 49, 119–21, 128, 163, 140, 143–44, 304; and mythmaking, 124, 139–40, 142; and SenseLab, 75, 79, 84, 92, 94, 97, 101, 115–21, 124, 126–29, 137–38, 143, 162, 164–65, 169, 184, 193, 305

executive function, 3–6, 12, 13, 286, 317n1; and Fred Moten, 3–4

experience, 5, 11, 16–17, 19–28, 30, 91–97, 99–100, 111, 113, 143–144, 153, 155, 184, 188, 193, 195, 197, 201, 207, 210, 220, 224, 227, 233, 238–39, 250, 254–55, 259–61, 288, 290–92; anarchic share of, 89, 90, 97, 118, 164, 168; DeafBlind, 248, 264, 268; differential of, 23; occasion of, 19, 33, 35, 37–39, 53, 78, 80, 81, 86, 95, 103, 106, 110, 123, 184; nonconscious 27, 263, 277, 281

experimentation, 13, 59, 76, 94, 120, 127, 128, 137, 141, 162, 163, 180, 181, 185, 194, 306, 315, 324n8, 329n9; event-based, 120, 162

expression/expressivity, 170, 175, 274, 278; coming to expression, 35, 57, 88, 103, 247,

255, 260; and form, 232, 247; and extensive continuum/relational complex, 247

fabulation, afro-fabulation, 7, 10, 327n10; and black polytemporality, 122, 237, 241; critical fabulation, 7, 294, 324n3, 327n10; and immediation, 115, 121, 139, 140, 143, 163; and mythologization, 116, 121, 327n9; politics of, 115, 121, 138, 139, 141, 143, 327n10; and power of the false, 10, 122, 123, 138, 140, 142; and SenseLab, 10, 137, 138; and time, 122, 123, 140, 142, 327n10; and worlding, 123, 124

faciality, 6, 312; and aesthetics of the earth, 311, 312; and autism, 6, 227, 336n14; and face-to-face, 255, 311; and landscape, 312; and whiteness, 312; and white wall/black hole, 312, 314, 315

facilitation, 215, 273; facilitated communication, 8; sociality of, 3

failure, 64, 170, 108, 281, 286, 327n8, 340n16; and SenseLab, 121, 193, 313

Fanon, Frantz, 40

feel/feeling, 20, 22, 224; and affective tonality, 193; cephalopod's seeing-feeling, 307–8; collective feeling, 296–97, 302; conceptual feeling-out, 28–29, 95; empathy as feeling-in, 255; and event, 25, 124; of exclusion, 119; and experiential cluster, 25; and feeler, 24, 25, 28, 30, 31; feelingalwaysfeeling, 228; feeling-felt, 257; feeling of power, 242; feeling-out of existence, 207; feeling-tone, 240; feeling-with, 112, 254, 256, 258; force of feeling, 123; freedom in the fold of, 241; human as spectrum of, 19; joy as feeling-with, 242; livingloving as feeling-moved, 242; lure for feeling, 28, 67, 72, 171; making-felt, 22, 258; metatactile touch as hands-on feeling of the world, 258; mutual sensitivity of, 24–25; multiplicity of, 18; power to act as feeling-moved, 242; proto-experience into, 247; proprioceptive tactility as mode of feeling-with, 263; pure feeling, 24; relational feeling, 254; suprasensation as overfeeling, 256; sympathy as feeling-with, 258; synesthesia as feeling-with, 258; and touch, 248, 249; world's feel, 259; and Alfred North Whitehead, 321n9, 324n9

Ferreira da Silva, Denise, 6, 10, 62, 220

plane, 6, 16, 21, 23, 42–44, 91, 203, 309, 310, 312; adjacent, 23; composite, 23; of duration, 23

Plumb, Leslie, 69, 71, 146, 148, 154, 177, 180, 187, 190, 194, 194, 305, 324n8; and *Inflexions*, 168; and 3E Process Seed Bank, 300–305, 307

poetics of relation, 7, 47, 99, 196, 242, 299, 313, 314; and blackness, 7, 242, 299; and consent not to be a single being, 7; and life-living, 99; and the minor gesture, 47; and schizoanalytic cartographies, 313

policing, 40, 51, 52, 62, 218; and neurotypicality, 51, 52, 62; and normopathy, 62; and whiteness, 40, 62

political, the, 2, 6, 7, 14, 40, 45, 53, 60, 65, 66, 97, 101, 115, 117, 118, 121, 139, 141, 143, 144, 149, 171, 172, 206, 210, 225, 226, 279, 301, 315, 322n16, 327n10, 331n5, 333n9; and fabulation, 115, 121, 138, 139, 141, 143, 294, 327; Rancière on, 330n9; and politics, 40, 45, 53, 66, 82, 97, 115, 117, 121, 139, 141, 143, 171, 225, 327, 333n9; and the social, 2, 6, 7, 14, 60, 65, 66, 101, 117, 118, 121, 149, 171, 172, 210, 225, 226, 301, 315, 322n16, 327n10, 331n5

politics, 8, 15, 16, 26, 33, 34, 40, 42, 45, 46, 48, 49, 51–53, 64, 66, 82, 94, 97–99, 100, 115, 117, 120, 121, 124, 138, 139, 141, 143, 152, 153, 164, 169, 171, 196, 204, 225, 237, 267, 290, 291, 310, 317n3, 322n16, 326n4, 327n10, 329n3, 333n9; affirmative, 51, 115, 164, 169, 237; and emergency, 141, 143; and front lines, 142; and political events, 141; of refusal, 26; and sidelines, 109, 228; and urgency, 52, 141, 143. *See also* micropolitical

potential/potentiality, 1, 6, 15, 27, 30, 31, 36, 38, 43, 46, 51, 60, 63, 75–77, 80–87, 90–92, 119, 123, 124, 125, 128, 130, 139, 157, 170, 172, 183, 188, 195, 196, 218, 221, 227, 228, 230, 240, 247, 250, 259, 262, 266, 270, 273, 295, 298, 315, 325n5, 340n1, 341n3, 343n10; future, 39, 72, 75, 83, 96, 181, 186, 299, 314, 322n15; and givenness, 20–22, 24, 325; speculative, 20, 21, 76, 82, 92, 112, 297, 304

power, 6, 7, 10, 26, 37, 40, 43, 44, 63, 81, 85, 92, 100, 109, 116, 118, 121–23, 129, 130, 138, 140–43, 149, 150, 155, 179, 195, 206–8, 215–25, 230, 233, 235, 239, 241, 242, 255, 279, 280, 282, 290, 291, 294, 303, 310, 319n4,

322n16, 324n7, 326n2, 329n3; dramaturgies of, 146; power/knowledge, 213–19, 221, 332n4

power of the false, 10, 116, 118, 122, 123, 129, 138, 140, 142; and fabulation, 122, 123, 138, 140

practice, 12–14, 18, 30, 36, 49, 79, 99–100, 143, 220–22, 225, 273, 315, 322n15, 328n3, 333n9, and the anarchive, 10, 75, 76, 84, 93, 96, 97, 100, 101, 121, 204, 300, 306; and aesthetics of black sociality, 7, 55, 60, 66, 67, 100, 236; blackness as, 65–66, 73; and desire, 294; ecologies of, 16; and immediation, 50, 121; and threshold, 67, 70, 145, 147, 153, 162, 163, 164, 193, 303; and SenseLab, 13, 67, 75–76, 115, 118–21, 147, 150, 158–59, 164, 181–91, 195–97, 301, 305–6; and schizoanalysis, 149, 153, 157–58, 161–62, 171, 173–79, 193, 289, 291–93, 309–11; and study, 223; and waywardness, 209

pragmatic, 12, 21, 28, 76, 82, 91, 111, 132, 169, 184, 186, 218, 230; pragmatics of the useless, 1, 6, 7, 11, 12–15, 21, 23, 31, 57, 76, 79, 84, 86, 97, 101, 168, 170, 173, 177, 179, 193, 199, 203, 209, 216, 280, 293, 306, 308, 315, speculative, 76, 111–13, 184, 187, 237, 265, 289

prehension, 17, 18, 22, 45, 80, 240; negative prehension, 19, 20, 22–24, 28, 29, 84, 86, 96, 239, 306

problem, 4, 8, 9, 13, 30, 42, 44, 46, 47, 51, 63, 76, 79, 88, 89, 109, 116, 117, 126, 128, 140, 164, 165, 172, 178, 179, 204, 216, 221, 255, 258, 261, 274, 278, 315, 319n6, 320n5, 321n12, 325n12, 326n2, 329n6; and false problem, 45, 162, 315, 321n12; and practice, 162, 164, 315

procedural architecture, 207, 262; and the cube, 68, 72, 181; and emergent dimensionality, 68; and nestingpatching, 69, 70, 72, 73; and tentative constructing toward a holding in place, 69, 70

process, 36, 78–80, 92–93, 111–12, 115, 117, 119, 126, 149, 154–57, 161–72, 176–82, 189, 193–94, 201–9, 229, 236, 238, 296, 309, 314, 318n6, 325n5, 341n6; and capital, 292, 294, 295, 296–97; and direct/autistic perception, 27, 30, 251, 340n1; and form, 81, 83–84, 86; and mutual inclusion, 12, 25, 99; philosophy, 12, 18, 24, 25, 77, 80, 82, 84, 103; seeds of, 76, 87, 300–302, 304–6, 308

schizogeography, 309; and aesthetics of the earth, 311–13; and line, 309; and parastrata, 309, 310, 312; and rhythm, 309, 310, 312

schizophrenia, 3, 289, 291, 317n1, 340n1, 341n1; as process/as entity, 239, 340n1; and neurosis, 290; and Oedipus, 289, 290, 340n1; and schizoid pole, 289, 291, 294

schizosomatic, 57, 59, 183, 184, 186, 187

schizz, and anarchic share, 188, 310, 314; and detour, 147, 149, 151, 176; and esqueness, 138, 139; and event, 91, 139, 140, 157, 163; and intercessor, 176; and practice, 145, 147, 149, 150, 153, 163, 175, 177, 182, 184, 186, 189, 191, 192, 197, 291, 309–12, 315; and the relational object, 31, 188; and threshold, 18, 67, 145, 147, 153, 181, 191; of time, 23

sense/sensation, 18, 59, 60, 72, 106, 108, 246–50, 253, 256, 259, 270, 273, 274, 305, 331n4, 337n16; and field of relation, 262; proprioception, 260; sense presentation, 247, 256; sensing blackly, 65; voluminousness, 246, 247, 249, 250, 270

SenseLab, and composing, 162, 181, 185, 196; and conceptual persona, 116; and event, 118, 329n7; and the free radical, 10, 117–19, 142; and landing sites, 68, 330; and patch, 67, 68, 72, 73, 181, 324; and research-creation, 221; and schizoanalysis, 14, 101, 149, 158, 161; and schizosomatics, 184, 186, 187; and spaZe, 10, 181, 183, 185–87, 189, 196, 329, 330; and threshold, 67, 72, 73, 147, 149, 178, 181, 185, 302, 303; undercommon sociality, 13, 67, 189, 191; and underspz, 330. *See also* 3Ecologies Institute

Sequenzia, Amy, 52, 53, 332n2–3

Sexton, Jared, 8

shape, cuff, 88, 91; fold, 89, 91; of enthusiasm, 87, 88, 94, 241; of experience, 88, 94; Frances Tustin on autistics and, 87–88; of value, 87; of fact, 87

Sharpe, Christina, 299, 325n12, 342n8

sign language, and ASL, 264, 338n21; and ProTactile, 264, 265; and TASL, 338n21

Simondon, Gilbert, 129, 334n1; on life, 44; on technique, 79; on the transindividual, 10, 161

singular/singularity, 50, 82, 92, 130–31, 235, 274; and anarchive, 310; Deleuze on, 329n6; Deleuze and Guattari on, 157–58; and differ-

ence without separability, 235; events as, 19, 38, 88, 92, 94, 98, 127, 329n6; of experience, 16, 17, 25, 36; "fourth person," 27, 281; Glissant on, 314; and group subject, 156–58; Guattari on, 156; and infrathin, 15–17, 19, 21–22; Massumi on, 342n6, 343n10; Moten on, 220; and subjective form, 18, 35

slavery, 8, 42; afterlife of, 50, 65–66, 192, 226, 240–41, 298, 328n3; in Brazil, 55, 323n3; Saidiya Hartman on, 9, 50, 64–66, 85–86, 208, 209, 238, 308, 317n4, 323–24n7, 328–29n3, 331n5, 331n7; Hortense Spillers on, 299, 319n4; and racial capital, 342n7

Smithson, Robert, 26

Snaza, Nathan, 276

sociality, aesthetics of black sociality, 7, 13, 55, 60, 66, 67, 100, 236; angular, 7, 122, 237, 327n11; emergent, 7, 42, 59, 61, 70, 121, 220, 226, 229, 241, 266, 295, 297, 298, 304; gesture of, 7; indirect, 60; minor, ix, 6, 13, 14, 117, 118, 131, 142, 158, 172, 189, 226, 227, 229, 232, 233, 236, 241, 270, 287, 296, 300, 301, 311; neurodiverse, 4, 6, 9, 60, 72, 335n11

Souriau, Etienne, 10, 43, 44, 321n11; and instauration, 45, 46

space, 44, 71, 79, 157; colonial, 244; and distantism, 255–57; geographic, 330n8; geometric, 258, 270–71; and outside, 226; point-topoint, 245, 246, 250; and SenseLab, 191, 195; spatial orientation, 245. *See also* spacetime

spacetime, 67, 106, 118, 141, 247, 248, 250, 263, 269, 321n9; and immediation, 34

speculation, 4, 297, 341

Spillers, Hortense, 55, 299, 319–20n4, 342n8, 343n9; and flesh/body, 299

Spinoza, Baruch, 215; and body, 157, 242; and joy, 242, 321; and sad affect, 36

Spuybroek, Lars, 90–92

Stern, Daniel, 88, 269, 357; and vitality affect, 10, 186

study, and learning, 191, 196, 221, 283; and practice, 127, 191, 195, 221, 223, 225; and sociality, 227; and technique, 127; and 3Ecologies Institute, 13, 191, 195, 196; and the undercommons, 191, 213, 234; and the university, 191, 196, 213, 214, 221, 223, 234. *See also* black study; pedagogy; undercommons

267, 268, 270; and reaching-toward, 192, 236, 247, 270, 300; and synesthesia, 248, 249, 254; of the world, 249, 250, 258

transduction, 45, 117, 165, 170, 203, 204; and anarchiving, 165, 204, 306; and event, 117, 170, 304; and experimentation, 189, 306; and immediation, 143; and instauration, 45; and tigritude, 143; and transvaluation, 306

transference, 159, 173, 175, 176, 192, 209; and Oedipus, 176, 290; and psychoanalysis, 159, 173, 176

transindividual, 99, 130, 149, 161, 162, 171, 177, 178, 181, 306, 309, 310; and blackness, 73, 300; and Gilbert Simondon, 10, 79, 161

translation, 229, 266, 281, 286; and autistic voicing, 273, 275–77, 279, 282–84, 286–88; and DeafBlindness, 246, 257, 263; and ProTactile, 266

transversality, 12, 22, 69, 118–20, 126, 145, 149, 167, 179, 189, 192, 193, 196, 203, 210, 315; and infrathin, 22, 118, 196; and schizoanalysis, 155, 159

truth, 116, 121, 123; and fabulation, 121–23; and power of the false, 116, 121, 123

Tubman, Harriet, and DJ Savarese, 8, 13

undercommons, 7, 9, 10, 13, 63, 67, 126, 150, 153, 191–93, 213, 215, 216, 234, 301; undercommon sociality, 67, 74. *See also* Moten, Fred, and Stefano Harney

universalism, 68; and the individual, 186; and interpersonality, 64

university, and neoliberalism, 14, 151, 191, 196, 214; and neurodiversity, 213–15, 217; and neurotypicality, 150, 152, 214; and pedagogy, 149, 215; and power/knowledge, 214, 215, 217, 219, 221, 224, 225, 221, 333n4; and settler colonialism, 234; and study, 191; and 3Ecologies Institute, 191, 193; and threshold, 234, 299; and the undercommons, 150, 191, 214–16, 223, 234

useless, pragmatics of, 12, 15, 21, 72, 84, 168, 170, 173, 179, 216, 318n1; ethos of, 209, 293, 306, 315; and failure, 193; vs. representation of the useful, 79, 173, 179, 280, 307, 315; and SenseLab, 79; and supernormal, 67; and use-value, 97; and surplus-value of life, 12,

101, 299–300; and uncertainty, 177; and the university, 216; and value/valuation, 23, 31, 57, 76, 86, 120, 199, 203, 308

valuation, 10, 21, 29, 31, 49, 76, 86–87, 94, 96, 97, 110, 299, 306; and evaluation, 87; emergent, 120, 295, 298, 300, 301, 305; immanent, 98; prevaluation, 25; transvaluation, 21, 244, 311

value, 3, 19, 20, 29, 48, 57, 76, 79, 85, 110, 177, 194, 196, 203, 225, 234, 252, 255, 277, 278, 296, 300–302, 308; and artfulness, 31, 60; and blackness, 85–86; and discord, 94; and evaluation, 14, 109, 152, 315; exchange-value, 295; fugitivity of, 6; and hierarchy, 19, 25, 86; and the incalculable, 3, 5, 12, 13, 210; preexisting, 78, 110, 210; as quality, 301, 314; and representation of the useful, 179, 307, 315; and repair, 199, 209, 210; and revaluation, 9, 293, 306, 314, 315; and terror, 3, 4, 5, 210; and tradeability, 298; and quantification, 252, 296–98, 306; speculative value, 300, 306; and surplus-value of flow, 297–98, 307; and surplus-value of life, 10, 93, 101, 299; and use-value, 12, 20, 21, 23, 28, 31, 97, 168, 207, 209; and the useless, 15, 21, 23, 31, 57, 76, 97, 101, 199, 203, 209, 306, 308, 315; and world of value, 84–89, 91–92, 95, 97, 99, 123

virtual, 79, 80, 259, 270; and the actual, 22

visual/visuality, 7, 25, 26, 47; rhythmic, 29, 31, 231, 279

voluminousness, 246, 247, 249, 250–52, 255, 262, 263, 270; and extensive continuum, 247, 249, 250; and intensive magnitude, 246, 249

waywardness, 12, 209, 212

Weheliye, Alexander G., 220, 233

Whitehead, Alfred North, and appearance/reality, 15, 85, 95; and beauty, 94, 95, 98, 100, 123; and creative advance, 28, 29; and concrescence, 28, 80, 82, 94; and discord, 94, 95, 98, 101; and eternal object, 20; and extensive continuum, 247; fallacy of misplaced concreteness, 157; and immortality, 105; and lure for feeling, 28, 67; and mental pole/physical pole, 28, 29, 95, 96;

Whitehead (continued)

and mutual sensitivity, 24, 25; and nonsensuous perception, 114; and objective immortality, 36, 82; and occasion of experience, 19,
35, 37, 39, 78, 80, 81, 86, 95, 103, 106, 110,
123; and peace, 97, 98, 99, 100; and perishing, 82, 105; and process philosophy, 12, 25,
77, 80, 82, 84, 103; relational complex, 251,
255, 257, 251, 264, 266; and simple location,
34, 319; and the superject, 38; and togetherness, 77, 84, 103; and truth, 120, 121, 123,
125, 126, 180, 292; and the world of activity/
the world of value, 84, 85, 86, 87, 88, 91, 95,
97, 99, 101, 110, 123

whiteness, and academia, 333n7; and asociality,
66; and colonial-capitalism, 40, 41, 49, 67,
179, 242, 287, 299; and empathy, 323n7;
and face, 312, 315, and humanism, 40;
and individual subject, 64, 192, 225, 240,
312; and interpersonal, 63, 66, 70, 72, 100,
238, 299; logic of, 73, 99, 101–2, 237–38,
242, 287, 299; as mirage, 63, 66, 67; and
neurotypicality, 1–2, 4, 9, 13, 41, 49, 62–63,
70, 72–73, 100–101, 150, 179, 196, 219, 240,
241, 250, 253, 286, 299; as reactive, 242;
and violence, 40, 62, 66, 70, 238; and white
people, 73

Wilderson III, Frank B., 220, 226

Williamson, Terrion L., 10

will to power, 44, 116, 242, 282, 326

Wolfond, Adam, 219, 228, 273, 274, 281, 282,
285, 332n3, 333n10, 338n3–4, 339n6

worlding, 6, 33, 87, 123, 124, 153, 206, 208, 224,
227, 237, 281, 284

Wosnitzer, Robert, 297

writing, and autism, 273; autistic, 274–77,
283–85, 288; and critical fabulation, 294;
diagonally, 3, 50; and fabulation, 138–39; and
facilitated communication, 132; the philosopher, 11; and R. A., 174–76; techniques of
49–50, 266, 267; and the nonvoluntary 279,
282; writing-to-come, 2

Wynter, Sylvia, 39, 40, 42, 51, 361

Yergeau, Melanie, 36; on neuroqueerness, 233,
282, 287–88; on rhetoric, 227, 274, 275, 279
284, 288

Zellars, Rachel, 238

Zurcher-Long, Emma, 27